Child Welfare and Rights

This book focuses on the role and content of the principle of the welfare interests of the child, considers the extent to which the principle has changed following its varied elevation by the introduction of paramountcy and reviews the distinction between welfare interests and rights.

Providing an updated record of developments in the framework of relevant international law, the book assesses the contemporary relevance of established and emerging themes in the flow of cases dealing with the welfare interests and rights of children in England, Wales, Ireland, the U.S., Canada, Australia, New Zealand, France and Germany. By identifying and analysing the functions of the principle in hybrid proceedings (including adoption from state care and commercial surrogacy) the book completes the analysis of the law relating to children in public (care and protection) and in private (divorce, custody, etc.) family law as a whole, revealing characteristic jurisdictional differences and facilitating a comparative assessment of their significance. By examining the international framework of legislation and related caselaw it identifies and assesses unfolding themes in the law relating to children.

In addition to a digest of international cases and legislation that identifies and tracks the role of this principle in civil and criminal law, lawyers, academics and other researchers will find a wealth of information on how it has evolved to reflect corresponding changes in society.

Kerry O'Halloran – lawyer, social worker and academic – formerly Adjunct Professor to the Australian Centre for Philanthropy and Nonprofit Studies at QUT, Brisbane and Assistant Director of the Centre for Voluntary Action, University of Ulster, has served on a social care tribunal and on a HSS trust adoption panel, has advised the Irish government on law reform matters, and served in a consultancy capacity to various bodies. His many books include several on child care and protection, international adoption, human rights and family law.

Children and the Law

The Principle of the Welfare of the Child
A History
Kerry O'Halloran

Children & the Law
Shaping the Modern Welfare Principle in the British Isles
Kerry O'Halloran

Children, the Law and the Welfare Principle
Perspectives from North America
Kerry O'Halloran

Children, the Law and the Welfare Principle
Perspectives from Australia & New Zealand
Kerry O'Halloran

Children, the Law and the Welfare Principle
Civil Law Perspectives from France and Germany
Kerry O'Halloran

Children, the Law and the Welfare Principle
European Judicial Perspectives
Kerry O'Halloran

Child Welfare and Rights
Differences in Common Law and Civil Law Perspectives
Kerry O'Halloran

Child Welfare and Rights
A Contemporary Family Law Analysis
Kerry O'Halloran

For more information about this series, please visit: Children and the Law: From Welfare to Rights – Book Series – Routledge & CRC Press

Child Welfare and Rights

A Contemporary Family Law Analysis

Kerry O'Halloran

Routledge
Taylor & Francis Group
LONDON AND NEW YORK

First published 2025
by Routledge
4 Park Square, Milton Park, Abingdon, Oxon OX14 4RN

and by Routledge
605 Third Avenue, New York, NY 10158

Routledge is an imprint of the Taylor & Francis Group, an informa business

British Library Cataloguing-in-Publication Data
A catalogue record for this book is available from the British Library

ISBN: 978-1-032-82093-4 (hbk)
ISBN: 978-1-032-83639-3 (pbk)
ISBN: 978-1-003-51038-3 (ebk)

DOI: 10.4324/9781003510383

Typeset in Times New Roman
by Apex CoVantage, LLC

This book is dedicated to Elizabeth with love and huge gratitude for her support and for allowing me the time to get it done.

Contents

Acknowledgements

The foundations for this book were laid in my earlier publications including *The Welfare of the Child: the Principle and the Law*,[1] *The Politics of Adoption*,[2] *State Neutrality: the Sacred, the Secular and Equality Law*,[3] *Child Care and Protection: the Law & Practice in Northern Ireland*,[4] and in my earlier contributions to this series. Given the not dissimilar subject matter and related caselaw, focussed on many of the same jurisdictions, there is inevitably some degree of overlap, and I thank the publishers concerned for their understanding.

A sincere debt of gratitude is owed to those who kindly made room in their busy schedules to read and offer comments on draft chapters. In particular I am most grateful to Ursula Kilkelly[5] and to the many others who contributed along the way. Their encouragement, support and advice have meant a lot, and this book and its author would have suffered without them.

I am very thankful to Routledge, especially to Nicola Sharpe,[6] for commissioning the book and continuing the series. It has been a privilege to be given the opportunity to write so fully on this subject and to have the support of Nicola and Diksha Bhugra[7] throughout what has been a long process.

Responsibility for any mistakes, omissions, inconsistencies or other faults, and for all views expressed, must unfortunately rest wholly with me.

1 Aldershot, Arena/Ashgate Publications, 1999.

2 *The Politics of Adoption: International Perspectives on Law, Policy & Practice* (4th ed.), The Netherlands, Springer, 2021.

3 New York, Cambridge University Press, 2021.

4 Dublin, Thomson Round Hall, 2003.

5 Professor of law, University College Cork, Ireland.

6 Commissioning Editor, Routledge Law Research.

7 Editorial Assistant, Routledge Law Research.

Introduction

Sui juris – or lacking legal capacity – was for many centuries a legal status that children shared with the insane, demented and others with severe intellectual impairment.[1] This, the last in a series of eight books, focusing on as many countries[2] – six common law and two civil law – that traced the emergence of the law's concern for children from its initial *sui juris* context, concludes by reflecting on how that concern led from protecting a child's welfare interests to asserting their rights; considers the nature, extent and constraints of that transition; and examines the resulting implications for family law.

All eight countries share a similar Christian cultural heritage, represented by a not dissimilar family law framework structured around an associated web of traditional religious values. Moreover, lying as they all do on varying points of the liberal democracy spectrum, they have evolved to have much the same concerns regarding the balance to be struck between the interests of state, family and child. This traditional cultural context – enabling these countries and many others to have an understanding of how and why their laws governing families and the welfare of children were similarly constructed – has probably undergone greater change in the past few decades than in as many preceding centuries. The change process – ongoing since the secularisation of marriage – is accelerating, due in part to the disruptive effects of globalisation, multiculturalism and the impact of human rights upon settled cultural verities. It has already introduced fundamental conceptual challenges to family law parameters: at the beginning of human life, with controversy regarding the rights of a foetus, the legality of 'harvesting' embryotic material and of genetic editing; in the middle, with legal confusion surrounding the definition of 'parent' in surrogacy arrangements and the contact rights of grandparents; and at the end, with debate continuing over the rights of those in a 'vegetative' state and the legal right to a medically assisted death. Other challenges directed towards the viability of long-established anchor points in family law – including the institution of marriage, proceedings for divorce, adoption and foster care – may well lead to the gradual shedding of much of that framework.

1 See, further, for example, https://dictionary.justia.com/sui-juris

2 The UK, Ireland, the U.S., and Canada, Australia, New Zealand, France, and Germany.

DOI: 10.4324/9781003510383-1

In this concluding book, the underpinning narrative continues to reflect – in the light of the contrasting information derived from the jurisdictional profiles – on how the balance between the interests of state, family and child has changed. Whereas the previous books focussed on profiling the jurisdictions and identifying differences in accordance with indices of welfare interests/rights, this one seeks to benchmark the extent to which the themes threading through the jurisdictional studies comply with the principles of international law as represented primarily by rulings of the European Court of Human Rights as they give effect to the European Convention on Human Rights and the United Nations Convention on the Rights of the Child 1989. The intention is to draw some conclusions regarding the relative importance of the themes and indices established throughout the series and so be in a position to gauge how the law governing the welfare/rights of children might develop in the future.

Like its predecessors, this final book continues to examine the legal functions of the welfare principle. Constructed in three parts, it considers the relative jurisdictional significance of the themes tracked throughout the series.

Part 1 – 'Children's Rights v. Welfare Interests' – begins the book in three chapters and in general terms, by laying the foundations for the following thematic analysis of how the welfare interests and rights of children are interpreted and balanced in the family law of the eight jurisdictions. Chapter 1 – *Welfare Interests and Legal Rights: Complementary or Conflicting?* – provides an introductory overview which considers the law and its relationship with family and child. It asks: what are the legal functions of the welfare principle in contemporary family law, how have they changed, and which have been upgraded from the protection/promotion of a child's welfare interests to an assertion of their rights? Chapter 2 – *Child as a Legal Entity* – considers the transitional role of a child from being the responsibility of parents to self-actualisation, from being the object to becoming the subject of court proceedings. It assesses the extent to which the law has recognised the elevation of children's interests by conferring a right to give or withhold children's consent to certain decisions affecting their welfare. It considers the associated rights of a child in the court: to be heard, to representation, and to a friendly courtroom setting that facilitates their understanding of and participation in proceedings. Chapter 3 – *Family Life and Family Breakdown* – takes this discussion a stage further by examining the significance of the variety of contemporary family forms for child welfare and rights. It then assesses how the welfare interests and rights of the child are given effect at the point of family breakdown, the most critical event for the future well-being of any child.

Part II – 'Hybrid Family Law and Implications for Children's Rights' – in four chapters, examines what are currently the most controversial topics in that grey area of family law where public and private interests overlap. It considers their impact on family law coherence. Chapter 4 – *Commercial Surrogacy and Parental Abduction* – assesses these two aspects of parenting, or prospective parenting, which are experiencing exponential growth and causing international legal difficulties. Chapter 5 – *Adoption from State Care and Intercountry Adoption* – deals first with what is one of the most controversial practices in contemporary child-care law, the non-consensual adoption of children admitted or committed to state care due to a failure of parental care. It then considers the fading significance of inter-country adoption as a means of becoming a parent. Chapter 6 – *Unaccompanied Migrant Minors, Detention and Trafficking* – assesses the legal consequences of a phenomenon that has suddenly become a signature theme of western society in the 21st century: the mass migration of people from the 'global south', intensifying multiculturalism and cultural clashes and increasing the pressure on state child welfare systems. Chapter 7 – *Poverty, Discrimination and Public Services* – focuses on environmental factors that can and often do create family vulnerability and endanger the welfare interests of very many children: the relationship between poverty and the over-representation of those who are socially disadvantaged in the child welfare and criminal justice systems has to be taken into account in any consideration of children's welfare interests and rights.

Part III – 'Coherence in Family Law: Balancing Welfare Interests and Rights' – is the final section and is contained in one chapter. Chapter 8 – *Family Law Coherence: Welfare Interests and Rights* – offers a final review of these two basic constructs – *welfare interests* and *rights* – that underpin so many European Court of Human Rights rulings on state/family/child relationships. It reviews the gradual withdrawal of the state from family matters and the significance of the growing legal weighting attached to children's rights.

Finally, the *Book Conclusion* brings the book and the series to a close by reprising the knock-on effects of changes from welfare to rights for the legal system: the effect of such changes on the interests of other family members and the adjustments that have had to be made to the courts and legal proceedings to accommodate this change. Given all of this, it asks what are now the parameters of contemporary family law; which strands have emerged as most important for the law relating to children; and what probable developments will shape the future of that law? Is the law relating to children becoming, or has it already become, a stand-alone body of law? Are there any meaningful principles that continue to link it with the main body of family law? If it should become wholly separate, where does this leave family law? Do these developments reflect profound changes in 'family life' in contemporary western society?

Part I

Children's rights v. welfare interests

1 Welfare interests and legal rights

Complementary or conflicting?

Introduction

This chapter is concerned with fundamental questions – What are welfare interests? What are rights? How do they differ? – and, in general terms, when and why did one evolve from the other? At what age and on what issues can a child give a valid consent, and when can they be held criminally liable for the consequences of their actions? As will be seen, there are few concrete answers.

Beginning with a brief consideration of whether there is a conceptual clash between 'welfare' and 'rights' and in the process identifying some differentiating indices, the chapter then examines the meaning and content of welfare interests in contemporary family law. This is followed by an explanation of how a focus on child protection and on capacity to give a valid consent enabled the law to transcend its traditional objectification of children and begin to treat them as subjects and eventually as free-standing parties in civil and criminal disputes. In this way the chapter lays the foundation for an analysis in the remainder of the book of how the binary welfare/rights division plays out on a jurisdictional basis in public, private and hybrid family law contexts.

Welfare and rights

It was once argued by a leading jurist that there was "no inconsistency of principle" between a welfare analysis and a rights analysis[1] and such difference as was perceived was "semantic only and lies only in differing ways of giving expression to [a] single common concept". This view was subsequently endorsed by an equally prominent colleague.[2] It is unlikely that such an interpretation would gain much support today; arguably, the point of the United Nations Convention on the Rights of the Child 1989 (UN CROC) was to emphasise the distinction.

1 *Re KD (Access: Principles)* [1988] 2 FLR 139 (HL), per Templeman LJ, at 141.
2 *Re B (Adoption: Natural Parent)* [2001] UKHL 70, [2002] 1 FLR 196, per Nicholls LJ, at [31].

DOI: 10.4324/9781003510383-3

Concepts and context

Having evolved over many centuries in a Judeo-Christian context, from which it has only relatively recently been released, it is unsurprising that family law in the countries studied has had some difficulty in wholly shedding its characteristic religious hallmarks. Primarily these revolved around the model of the Nazarene family anchored on the rights and duties of parents and their children's need for protection, the former being held in law to be vested with the right to represent the welfare interests of the latter. As Christianity faded, so too did the status of the marital family in society, in its significance to Church and State and as regards the traditional roles and relationships of family members (see, further, Chapters 2 and 8).

Most probably it was the influence of human rights law, with its emphasis on equality and non-discrimination, that finally overturned the rigidly structured and collectively reinforcing legal ties that traditionally bound family members. This allowed a disaggregation process to unfold which as well as facilitating recognition of the legal rights of women as contributors to the family home – a first step towards gender equality[3] – with associated financial entitlements, etc., also permitted separate recognition for the *locus standi* of children to emerge from the aggregate of parental rights. The emergence of children as legal entities with a status separate and distinct from that of their parents was, in retrospect, an inevitable outcome of human rights logic, a product of the democratic liberalism prevailing at that time and a crucial milestone in the development of family law.

The journey from children's welfare to rights is interwoven with an increasing emphasis on duties, personal responsibility and accountability. While a child's welfare interests require third-party protection, their rights are accompanied by first-party duties: both are subject to the caveat that in some circumstances and for some purposes a child may be considered to have sufficient capacity in law to take decisions, contest the rights of others and be held responsible for their own actions. In that event, a child would require, and be entitled to, the legal representation necessary to be a party to proceedings which in turn required child-friendly modifications to processes, court staffing and more generally to the court setting in order to reduce the intimidatory atmosphere and facilitate child participation. Once their new legal status was consolidated and prioritised by the introduction of the paramountcy principle, the role of children in proceedings concerning their welfare began to be transformed in what was perhaps the single most important change to have occurred in family law since female emancipation (see, further, Chapter 3). Thereafter, that body of law together with related courts and processes became gradually reconfigured – around protection for the welfare interests of children,

3 A step negatively reinforced in Ireland as a result of the failure of the 39th and 40th amendments to the Constitution to remove the following provisions: in article 41.3.1, 'The State pledges itself to guard with special care the institution of Marriage, on which the Family is founded, and to protect it against attack'; and in article 41.2.1, 'In particular, the State recognises that by her life within the home, woman gives to the State a support without which the common good cannot be achieved'. The proposal in March 2024 to delete and replace these and other provisions was decisively rejected.

accompanied by a steadily increasing recognition of their rights – and progressively less so around those of their parents.

The concept of 'welfare interests'

The law has struggled with the concept of welfare interests, it was probably more readily understood at a time and in a society integrated around a clear set of social values, which was largely true – if to a varying extent – within all the Christian countries surveyed in this series until around the middle of the 20th century.

When the law began to recognise the separate sets of interests of parent and child, it was usually because a parent had died, abused or abandoned their child, or because the latter was judged to be delinquent or had been convicted of criminal activity, in which case the state provided containment rather than concern for welfare interests. Not until the introduction of the UN Declaration of the Rights of the Child 1959 did a clear international focus on the welfare interests of the child emerge as an independent matter of primary importance. Principle 2 of the Declaration stated that

> [t]he child shall enjoy special protection, and shall be given opportunities and facilities, by law and by other means, to enable him to develop physically, mentally, morally, spiritually and socially in a healthy and normal manner and in conditions of freedom and dignity. In the enactment of laws for this purpose, the best interests of the child shall be the paramount consideration.

So, paramountcy emerged in 1959.

By the 1960s, the relative coherence of society and the settled expectations of family life had begun to unravel as the common underpinning of their Judeo-Christianity belief system was gradually eroded by developments that included the rights and means to control human reproduction, the choice of sexual freedom rather than marital monogamy, rights of the individual replacing an ideological focus on the duties of the collective and the greatly increased expectation that individuals should travel and relocate in pursuit of college education and/or employment. Impermanent family structures, serial parenting arrangements, looser extended family networks and the general absence of stable communities would seem likely to result in children with attachment issues, and for some this will manifest in behavioural problems that may well lead them into the public child welfare and criminal justice systems. In 1970, the seminal case of *J v. C*[4] established that "in applying [the welfare principle], the rights and wishes of parents, whether unimpeachable or otherwise, must be assessed and weighed in their bearing on the welfare of the child in conjunction with all other factors relevant to that issue". In thus laying out the basic ground rules for interpreting the welfare

4 [1970] AC 668 (HL), at 715.

principle, this case also clearly stated that the principle had a restricted application: it was to apply only to disputes that were specifically about an aspect of the child's upbringing; a restriction repeated in the Children and Young Persons Act 1989, s 1(1). So, as in *Richards v. Richards*,[5] where the issue was one of domestic abuse, the principle was found to be inapplicable.

This almost reflexive need, when acknowledging the importance of children's welfare interests/rights, to add that their exercise should be limited in some way or be subject to constraints, is interesting. There is a school of thought that from time immemorial society has held to "the automatic assumption of superiority of any adult over any child"[6] and that this corresponds with other forms of outdated prejudices in relation, for example, to race or gender. It might be argued that such a transference of a human rights perspective from a difference built on exploitation to one built on dependency needs does not really work, but many do view children as small adults for whom quiet reasoning and the simplifying of information are all that is needed to overcome prejudice and bring a large measure of equality to the parent/child relationship.

By the turn of the century, migration – shortly to turn into mass migration – brought a greater mix of cultures and social mores to coexist alongside and to challenge the value system of western societies. Social pluralism, accelerated by social media platforms, added further to the fragmentation process. One consequence of the resulting disrupted social coherence has been a switch in focus from standard objective indicators of 'welfare interests' to more nuanced subjective indicators.

Objective interpretation

Initially, in a common law context, the concern of the law for 'welfare interests' was driven by the English Courts of Chancery in their exercise of the wardship jurisdiction in respect of children, generally orphans, whose care had by default been assumed by the state. Judicial interpretation of 'welfare interests' at that time, in respect of 'wards of the court', was probably mainly concerned with safeguarding a ward's property: the inheritance entitlements of boys and the marriage prospects of girls.[7] Then, in the late 19th century, with the general introduction of child protection and juvenile crime legislation, the courts began to focus on objectively verifiable evidence of welfare being harmed by abandonment, neglect, abuse and criminal activity, etc. Welfare interests, however, had a restricted meaning: it was understood as a reference to matters impacting upon the upbringing of a child. This public law approach was reinforced by the criminal law need for tangible evidence, witnesses, due process, etc.

5 [1983] UKHL J0630-1.

6 See, Pierce, C.M. and Allen, G.B., 'Childism', *Psychiatric Annals*, Vol. 5, No. 7, pp 15–24, 2013, https://doi.org/10.3928/0048-5713-19750701-04

7 See, further, O'Halloran, K., *The Principle of the Welfare of the Child: A History*, Routledge, 2022.

Subjective interpretation

Judge Pinto De Albuquerque, in *X v. Latvia*,[8] noting the 'paramountcy of the child's interests' advised that "every child should be viewed as a subject of rights and not merely as an object of rights".

Private family law began to be stimulated by a rapid growth in litigation in the second half of the 20th century – with the introduction of divorce, increases in judicial separation and in adoption – so the law began to develop a more subjective interpretation that looked to evidence drawn from sciences such as developmental psychology to profile the individualised 'welfare interests' of children. This approach took into consideration such intangibles as evidence of quality of parental care and degree of relative attachments, etc., in relation to the age and particular needs of the children concerned.

As the traditional family structures and accompanying social mores crumbled, an unprecedented volume of family law cases began coming before the courts, bringing with it a disparate range of parenting issues requiring judicial assessment aided by the contribution of expert witnesses, including from psychologists and child psychiatrists (see, further, Chapter 8). The involvement of the latter generated a more sophisticated understanding of 'welfare interests': challenging the verities of previous generations regarding matters such as parental rights, gender-stereotyped parenting, etc., and accepting that such interests could only be sensibly ascertained by taking into account each child's particular attributes and/or needs, their individual personalities and character development, attachments and perception of where he or she 'fits' in the family dynamics. This was further complicated by the ever-growing myriad range of opportunities for harm that challenge the physical and mental health of children in contemporary western society. In keeping with the more relaxed legal approach to marital status and divorce, the state responded by beginning a staged withdrawal from intervention in families where child protection was not a presenting issue.

Welfare interests

Principle 2 of the UN Declaration of the Rights of the Child 1959 stated that

> [t]he child shall enjoy special protection, and shall be given opportunities and facilities, by law and by other means, to enable him to develop physically, mentally, morally, spiritually and socially in a healthy and normal manner and in conditions of freedom and dignity.

Articles 5(b) and 16(1)(d) of the Convention on the Elimination of All Forms of Discrimination against Women 1979 required states to modify parental gender stereotypes and take all appropriate measures to eliminate discrimination against

8 Application No. 27853/09, (2013), at para 41.

women as spouses and mothers and to ensure that 'in all cases the interests of the children shall be paramount'.

In 1970, the English landmark case *J. v. C.*[9] asserted the welfare interests principle but also built in the important caveat that "in applying (the welfare principle), the rights and wishes of parents, whether unimpeachable or otherwise, must be assessed and weighed in their bearing on the welfare of the child in conjunction with all other factors relevant to that issue".[10]

Primary consideration

In 1989, Article 3(1) of UN CROC declared that 'in all actions concerning children, whether undertaken by public or private social welfare institutions, courts of law, administrative authorities or legislative bodies, the best interests of the child shall be a primary consideration': thereby conferring on a child the right to have their welfare interests so treated across a range of issues and forums. Additionally, subsequent articles then established the particular rights held to be vested in a child. Shortly afterwards Article 24(2) of the European Social Charter, as revised in 1996, proclaimed that 'in all actions relating to children, whether taken by public authorities or private institutions, the child's best interests must be a primary consideration'. Such public actions were taken by the authorities in *Wallová and Walla v. the Czech Republic*[11] when the European Court of Human Rights (ECtHR) cited the UN Committee on the Rights of the Child (CRC) finding that in the Czech Republic "the principle of primary consideration for the best interests of the child is still not adequately defined and reflected in all legislation, court decisions and policies affecting children".

In 2013 the CRC issued a 'general comment' in which it made a distinction between 'the right of children to have their best interests assessed and taken as a primary consideration or, in some cases, the paramount consideration'.[12] However, the Committee did not elaborate on 'some cases' and later compounded the lack of clarity when in reference to 'best interests' being 'the paramount consideration' in adoption, it added 'indeed, the best interests of the child are to be the determining factor when taking a decision on adoption, but also on other issues'.[13] Which, again, begs the question – which 'other issues'? It considered that[14]

> the concept of the child's best interests is flexible and adaptable. It should be adjusted and defined on an individual basis, according to the specific situation of the child or children concerned, taking into consideration their

9 [1970] AC 668 (HL).
10 Ibid, at 719.
11 Application No. 23848/04, (2006).
12 General Comment No. 14 (2013) on the right of the child to have his or her best interests taken as a primary consideration, at para 12.
13 Ibid, at para 38.
14 Ibid, at para 32.

> personal context, situation and needs. For individual decisions, the child's best interests must be assessed and determined in light of the specific circumstances of the particular child.

This interpretation would seem to be in keeping with the UN CROC requirement that the 'evolving capacities of the child' should be taken into consideration when judging matters relating to children. When both are read together, the impression given is that a child's rights are left very contingent upon adult's assessment of their circumstances and the extent to which they believe the child's capacity has evolved at that point in time.

The CRC then interpreted the phrase 'best interests taken as a primary consideration', explaining that

> the expression "primary consideration" means that the child's best interests may not be considered on the same level as all other considerations. This strong position is justified by the special situation of the child: dependency, maturity, legal status and, often, voicelessness.[15]

Alluding, perhaps, to the research findings generated in the latter half of the 20th century by a handful of prominent child psychologists and psychiatrists, it warned against a simplistic 'one-size-fits-all' view of child welfare and reiterated its earlier advice that states should interpret child development as a 'holistic concept, embracing the child´s physical, mental, spiritual, moral, psychological and social development'.[16] The Committee identified seven factors held to constitute the best interests of the child: the child's views; the child's identity; preservation of the family environment and maintaining relations; care, protection and safety of the child; situation of vulnerability; the child's right to health; and the child's right to education[17] (see, also, Chapter 8). The breadth of the 'best interests' requirement meant 'the right of the child to have his or her best interests assessed and taken as a primary consideration should be explicitly included in all relevant legislation, not only in laws that specifically concern children'.[18] Subsequently, the Council of Europe Strategy for the Rights of the Child listed the best interests of the child as a primary consideration for decision makers.[19]

However, as has often been pointed out, the term 'primary consideration' and associated language used by the CRC and other bodies is somewhat equivocal. It chooses to apply the term to 'best interests', which is open to subjective interpretation. It does not state that the principle is of 'paramount' importance. It does not even assert that it should be 'the' primary consideration. 'Primary' is itself suspect:

15 Ibid, at para 37.
16 CRC, General Comment No. 5, at para 12.
17 Op. cit., at n 12, pp 52–78.
18 Ibid, at para 30(d).
19 Council of Europe Strategy for the Rights of the Child (2012–2015), CM (2011)171 final, February 15, 2012.

other expressions indicating relative significance could have been used, such as 'most important'. So, also, with 'consideration' which is more indicative of a discretionary rather than an affirmative approach to the treatment of 'best interests'. In short, although often lauded as the gold standard that firmly establishes welfare interests as of paramount importance in matters concerning children, it is at least questionable whether it does so, or even whether this was ever intended (see, also, Chapter 8).

The paramountcy principle

In the UK, the introduction of this principle in s 1 of the Children and Young Persons Act 1989 marked a milestone[20] in the development of the law relating to welfare interests which for a time differentiated UK law from that of most other countries and, to some extent, continues to do so. Initiated in the context of wardship and since consolidated in child care and adoption legislation, this principle ended the uncertainty associated with the fine distinctions previously made between different statutory definitions of the welfare test. From being one among many factors to be judicially considered in proceedings under the 1989 Act related to 'upbringing', welfare interests were elevated by the Adoption and Child Care Act 2002, s 1(2), to become the primary objective 'throughout his life' and was rapidly established as the governing benchmark in all such decisions taken in a public family law context, but this did not mean – or was not then intended to mean – that other considerations did not matter, and a persuasive effort was made by British jurists to construe the established British 'welfare interests test' as being equivalent to the ECtHR analysis of welfare rights as governed by Article 8 of the European Convention on Human Rights (ECHR); an alignment that has generated much contentious debate among British academics in recent years.[21] The jurisdictional variation in the extent to which the law has recognised, interpreted and given effect to the paramountcy principle is explored later (see, Chapter 7).

The concept of 'children's rights'

Legal rights provide for assertive action in the courts by individuals or legal entities (see, further, Chapter 3) for alleged breach of specific duties owed to them as established in national legislation and/or in international conventions. Certain rights have gained international recognition as being of greater importance than others. These are embodied in various international treaties, conventions, protocols, etc.,

20 A milestone that owed a good deal to *J. v. C.* [1970] AC 668 (HL).

21 See, for example: Herring, J., 'The Human Rights Act and the Welfare Principle in Family Law: Conflicting or Complementary?', *Child and Family Law Quarterly*, 1999; Choudhry, S. and Fenwick, H., 'Taking the Rights of Parents and Children Seriously: Confronting the Welfare Principle under the Human Rights Act', *Oxford Journal of Legal Studies*, 2005; Eekelaar, J., 'The Role of the Best Interests Principle in Decisions Affecting Children and Decisions About Children', *International Journal of Children's Rights*, 2015.

some of which are directly binding upon signatory states, others have been legislatively incorporated into national law. While providing specific remedies for specific unlawful acts, legal rights also contribute to generally reinforcing the currency of human rights norms and to building human rights compliant practices. On the other hand, it may also be argued that an adversarial pursuit of legal rights as a means of dealing with complex social problems can lead to a strategic failure to 'see the wood for the trees' and generate fractious social divisiveness. Also, it must be borne in mind that any exercise of rights is contingent upon it not unduly infringing the rights of others. This is of particular relevance in the context of balancing the rights of parent and child as UN CROC, Article 5, requires states to respect the parental right to give 'appropriate direction and guidance in the exercise by the child of the rights recognised in the present Convention', and this has found support in some ECtHR rulings.[22] Balancing the rights of family and state is a concern recognised by the ECtHR, particularly in the jurisprudence generated by Article 8, which has painstakingly established that justification for the state's intervention in family affairs rests on 'whether it was in accordance with the law, pursued a legitimate aim and was necessary in a democratic society'.[23]

As previously noted, human rights are vested as fully in each individual child as they are in adults. Consequently, 'children's rights' comprise a blend of rights specific to children (mainly as enumerated in UN CROC) together with all other human rights (mainly as declared in the ECHR) as elucidated over many decades of rulings made mostly by the ECtHR but also by the Electoral Commission of Jamaica (ECJ) and the CRC.[24] The impact of the norms established through the rulings of these various supranational bodies – primarily the ECtHR – on the law relating to children (as in other matters), and now assimilated into domestic legislation, would be difficult to overstate.[25]

Rights specific to children

Since the Geneva Declaration of the Rights of the Child 1924[26] initiated international awareness of the duties of the state to protect the welfare interests and rights of children, many international instruments have made further declarations to that effect. In 2009, for example, the Treaty on European Union, Article 3(3), declared that one of the aims of the Union was the 'protection of the rights of the child'. Currently, the ECHR and UN CROC are the primary governing bodies of law, but these must now be read in conjunction with an increasing number of Council of

22 See, for example, *Scozzari and Giunta v. Italy*, Application Nos. 39221/98 and 41963/98, (2000).

23 See, for example, *Y.C. v. United Kingdom*, Application No. 4547/10, (2012), at para 130.

24 See, O'Halloran, K., *Children, the Law and the Welfare Principle: European Judicial Perspectives*, Routledge, 2024.

25 See, further, European Parliament's Committee on Civil Liberties, Justice and Home Affairs, *EU Framework of Law for Children's Rights,* 2012, www.europarl.europa.eu/RegData/etudes/note/join/2012/462445/IPOL-LIBE_NT(2012)462445_EN.pdf

26 Followed by the UN Declaration of the Rights of the Child 1959.

Europe conventions,[27] guidance,[28] UN directives and specific protocols addressing issues of child labour, trafficking and prostitution.[29]

As of 2024, UN CROC – a milestone in the transition from the functioning of the law as protector of children's welfare interests to champion of their rights – had been signed by nearly 200 countries, with the notable exception of the U.S., and provides the most relevant and well-known international declaration of rights held to be vested in children. It lists 42 substantive rights that comprehensively address the needs of children and requires national courts, regulatory and administrative bodies to ensure that their decisions broadly comply with the general and specific obligations set out in the Convention. It acknowledges its genesis in ECHR principles, and its complementarity to that Convention has from time to time been stressed in ECtHR rulings.[30] As Judge Jebens stated in *Nunez*[31]: "the protection of the children . . . has become clearer in recent years, and may have increased, as a result of the Court's reliance on other international legal instruments, in particular the CRC", even if others have commented that 'the CRC does not appear to have significant direct impact on decisions made by the ECtHR'.[32] But, as its provisions are not accompanied by an enforcement mechanism, they are wholly dependent upon bodies such as the ECtHR and on assimilation within domestic law to be given effect. The CRC does rule on issues with a specific relevance for UN CROC, and it makes recommendations to states, on the basis of reports filed with it under Article 44 (a 'name and shame' approach) for improvements in national law and practice. So, for example, in four sets of Concluding Observations – 1995, 2003, 2012 and 2022 – the CRC reiterated the pressing need for Canada to establish an 'independent, federal, human rights institution to protect, promote and monitor the implementation of children's rights'.[33] In recognition of its contemporary significance as the fundamental international charter of children's rights, this book continues the practice, maintained throughout the series, of identifying jurisdiction-specific characteristics – especially those of a differentiating nature – and benchmarking them against relevant provisions of UN CROC.

In an EU context, the Lisbon Treaty 2007 established the 'protection of the rights of the child' as an aim of the Union (Article 3) and gave effect to the European Charter of Fundamental Rights, Article 24 of which declares that children now 'have the right to such protection and care as is necessary for their well-being'

27 See, for example, *European Convention on the Exercise of Children's Rights*, 1996.

28 See, for example, CoE, *Guidelines on Child Friendly Justice*, 2010.

29 See, the three UN CROC Optional Protocols: Optional Protocol on the sale of children, child prostitution and child pornography; Optional Protocol on the involvement of children in armed conflict; and an Optional Protocol on a communications procedure.

30 See, for example, *X and others v. Bulgaria*, Application No. 22457/16, (2021), at paras 2 & 4.

31 *Nunez v. Norway*, Application No. 55597/09 (ECtHR, 28 June 2011), at para 31.

32 See, Helland, T. and Hollekim, R., 'The Convention on the Rights of the Child's Imprint on Judgments from the European Court of Human Rights: A Negligible Footprint?', *The Nordic Journal of Human Rights*, Vol. 41, No. 2, pp 213–233, 2023, at pp 232–233.

33 Ibid., at p 7. See, also, www.ohchr.org/en/press-releases/2022/05/experts-committee-rights-child-commend-canada-truth-and-reconciliation

and that their best interests must be a primary consideration in 'all actions relating to children, whether taken by public authorities or private institutions'. As has been pointed out 'the rights of the child now constitute an integral part of fundamental rights which the EU and Member States are bound to respect by virtue of European and international law'.[34]

Rights shared with others

A core set of fundamentally important 'personal' human rights – access to justice, and the freedoms of speech, association, assembly and religion, including rights to equality and non-discrimination – apply within both public and private family law and are as applicable to children as to adults, as are rights to an identity, to legal status, to citizenship and those broadly centred on 'family life'. Many of these are incorporated into the ECHR, and their application to children is frequently the focus of ECtHR rulings. Another set of more 'impersonal' rights – to freedom from poverty, access to health care and education to safe and reasonable accommodation – have a particular relevance for children and are addressed through public service provision. Also, rights to employment opportunities, to adequate welfare benefits, to transport and to freedom from environmental stress, etc., by underpinning parental security must, thereby, contribute towards improving the welfare interests of their children.

Welfare interests in contemporary family law

Welfare interests, an indeterminate concept known to both common law and civil law for many centuries, can only be realistically interpreted in accordance with their cultural context at any point in time, in relation to whether being applied in a civil or criminal law context and, most importantly, as regards the needs of a particular child.[35] Welfare interests may be found in domestic legislation – sometimes referenced as 'welfare' or 'best interests' – when taking its meaning from the specific subject matter being addressed whether this be education, health and safety or any one of a wide range of similar statutes. They are also present in much international legislation and are occasionally the specific subject addressed by a treaty, convention or protocol.

Definition

That the spectrum of matters held to endanger welfare interests varies according to cultural context is illustrated, for example, by the school shootings of pupils by pupils in the U.S., while only in Germany have violent videos been construed as warranting legislative regulations. Cultural context influences not just the types of

34 See, *EU Framework of Law for Children's Rights,* 2012, Op. cit., at p 7.
35 See, O'Halloran, K., Routledge, 2022, Op. cit., at chapter 4.

harm but is also a determinant of the threshold for the degree of harm that constitutes a threat to welfare interests. So, for example, in 2011 Manitoba had an admission to care rate ten times that of Western Australia,[36] while the incarceration rate in the U.S. is reported to be roughly nine times that of Germany (693 and 76 per 100,000, respectively).[37]

However, Maidment's description of welfare interests as 'a deliberately indeterminate standard incorporated into the law in order to allow current social and cultural views about the needs of children' to be taken into account by decision makers, has perhaps withstood the test of time better than most.[38]

Welfare content

In all probability, it was the impact of developmental child psychology – largely in the U.S. – which unlocked a more multidimensional understanding of what might constitute the welfare interests of a child. An appreciation of the innate subjectivity of 'welfare' allowed the judiciary in many continents to interpret it with flexibility, as consisting not only of physical well-being and maintenance but extending it to also include religious and moral upbringing and psychological needs such as emotional attachments, enduring relationships and notions of risk and security. For the purposes of contemporary family law, the universally relevant components may be grouped under the headings of physical welfare, moral welfare and psychological welfare (see, also, Chapter 8).

Physical welfare

The composite duty to safeguard a child's welfare by providing appropriate care and maintenance consists of satisfying the child's needs in relation to matters that include physical integrity, health, medical and dental care, accommodation, environment, hygiene, food and sanitation. Statute law has steadily raised the required standards for meeting such needs and has increased the range and sophistication of related duties, but the basic duty owed to children by their parents, or failing them by the state, to provide for their physical needs and safeguard them from any foreseeable harm, has not changed.

Moral welfare

For at least the past century the courts have acknowledged that while nurture needs were fundamental to a child's welfare interests, meeting such needs was in itself insufficient to fully discharge the duty in respect of the welfare principle. The law

36 See, Brownell, M.D. and Jutte, D.P., 'Administrative Data Linkage as a Tool for Child Maltreatment Research', *Child Abuse & Neglect*, Vol. 37, No. 2, 2013, at pp 120–124.

37 See, *The Crime Report*, 2018, https://thecrimereport.org/2018/04/10/in-germany-its-hard-to-find-a-young-adult-in-prison/

38 See, Maidment, S., *Child Custody and Divorce,* Croom Helm, 1985, at p 3.

recognised the moral and religious components of child welfare by enforcing a parental duty to provide education in relation to the former while also acknowledging a parental right to provide religious training. Both came to be addressed, in effect, by the state through mandatory education programmes. Statute law placed a duty on parents to ensure that every child of school age received suitable education whether in state facilities or, as permitted in some countries studied, by way of home schooling.

However, the moral welfare of a child cannot be fully assured solely by statutory provisions relating to education and religious upbringing. A steadily growing raft of national and international legislation is constantly adding to the areas where contemporary social values indicate new areas for protective intervention. Much law is now directed towards prohibiting specific conduct or circumstances considered likely to undermine moral welfare, such as indulgence in or access to alcohol, cigarettes, solvents, vaping, sexting, betting, gaming and pornography.

Psychological welfare

As society has developed a more sophisticated awareness of children's needs and an understanding of the developmental stages of childhood so the law has refined its recognition and protection of welfare interests. Since the mid-1960s, judicial notice has increasingly been taken of the work of leading child psychiatrists and psychologists[39] and decisions grounded on evidence of the child's emotional and psychological welfare as distinct from material welfare. In particular, the growing importance given to preserving a child's bonds of emotional attachment gave rise to the concept of 'psychological parent' which has gained widespread judicial approval (see, further, Chapter 8). As has been said,[40]

> whether any adult becomes the psychological parent of a child is based on day-to-day interaction, companionship, and shared experiences. The role can be filled by a biological parent or by an adoptive parent or by any other caring adult . . . but never by an absent, inactive adult, whatever his biological or legal relationship to the child may be.

Welfare checklists

Some legislatures have sought to constrain the judicial scope for discretionary interpretation of the welfare principle, provided by the principle's inherent subjectivity, and introduce more consistency in decision-making by imposing 'welfare checklists' requiring an objective judicial focus on specified aspects of 'welfare

39 See, for example, Bettelheim, B., *Love is Not Enough*, Free Press, 1950.
40 See, Goldstein, J., Freud, A. and Solnit, A., *Beyond the Best Interests of the Child*, Free Press, 1973, at p 19.

interests'.[41] This blend of subjectivity – allowing judicial discretion to interpret welfare relative to the needs of a particular child – and objectivity – requiring the judiciary to apply a statutory welfare specification to the needs of all children – may offer helpful guidance but cannot prompt any uniformity of judicial approach as welfare interests can only ever be determined in relation to each child's particular set of needs at a particular time.

Whether or not such welfare indicators are assembled in the form of a checklist and regardless of whether their application is mandatory, much the same matters will be considered by the judiciary – and by other decision makers – when determining what action to take that will best safeguard the welfare interests of a child. Those listed in the next sections are drawn from UK legislation and are typical of the matters generally addressed by judiciary in other jurisdictions (see, also, Chapter 7).

Ascertaining the wishes and feelings of the child

This is a minimum requirement in all jurisdictions studied. Whether or not legal representation is provided, and regardless of whether the child wishes to express his or her views directly to the judge, there is invariably a legal requirement to ascertain the child's views on the issues in contention. However obtained, the weighting then given to the child's views will depend entirely on their age and discernment, though in no jurisdiction is there any suggestion that they will be universally determinative. Particular attention will be given to assessing the child's understanding of the issues, the relative merits of the options available and the consequences of their choices.

Taking into account the child's physical, emotional and educational needs

The court will require an assessment of the child's physical, emotional and educational needs including the impact of any trauma to which he or she may have been exposed. This assessment will need to be on a short-term and long-term basis and to be accompanied by a comparative analysis of which parent or other persons might be best able to cope with those needs.

Bearing in mind the likely effect on the child of any change in their circumstances

Where a change in location and/or in parenting arrangements is being proposed, the court will require a particular assessment focussed on how the child is predicted to cope with such change. This may involve an evaluation of the likely effect of

41 See: for England and Wales, the Children Act 1989, s 1(3); for Ireland, the Child Care Act 1991, s 24 (as amended by the Child Care (Amendment) Act 2022); for New Zealand, the Children Act 2004, s 5; for Canada, the Divorce Act 1985, s 16(3);

such changes: in family home; school arrangements; loss of friends; less ease of contact with parent, siblings and/or relatives; together with, perhaps, the challenge of unfamiliar surroundings and possible language complications.

Giving consideration to the age, sex, background and any characteristics of the child which the court considers relevant

The court will require the assessment of the child to take into account his or her particular profile of age-related needs, strengths, character development, personality and of such personal characteristics that are likely to make the child better able, or less able, to cope with foreseeable future challenges.

Weighing any harm which the child has suffered or is at risk of suffering

The threshold of harm or possible harm being always of primary concern, the court will need a risk assessment of the child's home environment and of those who have in the past, or may in the future, present a risk to the child's welfare. Where there has been a record of past domestic violence, the court will need to know how the child has processed any associated trauma and be satisfied that those responsible will not be in a position to cause harm again.

Assessing the capacity of each parent, and of any other relevant person, in meeting the child's needs

Most jurisdictions now statutorily subscribe to the principle that birth parents maintain joint legal responsibility for their children's welfare even after parental divorce or separation. The court, however, will require a differential assessment of parental capacity to undertake that responsibility. In some jurisdictions, this may entail navigating stereotyped gender parenting presumptions such as that babies and very young children are best cared for by their mothers and that older and adolescent boys would benefit more from paternal care.

Determining which of the disposal options available to the court, if any, would be most appropriate for this child in these circumstances

This is an area of considerable jurisdictional disparity. In the civil law countries studied – France and Germany – the lack of a range of functionally distinct statutory orders is perhaps more than compensated for by judicial powers to authorise or direct such form of civic intervention, or package of service provision, as is deemed appropriate and to thereafter review their effectiveness. Of the common law jurisdictions, only the UK had a full menu of orders – each authorising a discrete and restricted form of state intervention in family affairs – applicable across both public and private family law proceedings, supplemented by a judicial power to employ any combination of such orders as considered necessary with or without the agreement of the parties.

The principle that the welfare interests of a child must be the primary consideration in decisions affecting the upbringing of that child was subject to two conditions. First, as stated in *J v. C*,[42] it applied only to the child's upbringing; all other issues affecting the child's life would be resolved by applying less stringent principles. Second, initially and for many years, the principle was reserved for application by legally designated decision makers, either the mother of an illegitimate child, one or both parents of a marital child, the court, or a guardian or person acting in *loco parentis* with authority from one of the aforementioned. The consent of the child was not required, and even their involvement was at the discretion of others. In such circumstances, the child concerned was devoid of rights other than an entitlement to protection (see, further, Chapter 2).

Jurisdictional differences in interpretation of welfare interests/rights

There is no common definition of 'welfare interests'. Among the eight jurisdictions currently being studied, there would appear to be four different sets of interpretations: the paramountcy principle, as embedded in legislation and applied in the UK and to a lesser extent in Australia, New Zealand and Ireland, which tends to isolate and unconditionally prioritise the rights and welfare interests of the child (though in Ireland this is restricted to public family law matters);[43] the Article 8 version as interpreted by the ECtHR and contingent upon considerations of 'family life' and 'privacy' which govern the EU countries, Ireland, France and Germany; the North American variant, most strongly represented in U.S. caselaw, which leans more towards parental responsibility than paramountcy of child welfare; and the more cursory regard with which the law treats the welfare interests of children belonging to marginal groups such as Indigenous communities and illegal migrants.

The 'welfare test' in the UK

As stated in the 1989 Act, s 1(3), and the 2002 Act, s 1(4), the paramountcy weighting given to welfare interests in the UK makes it the most absolute and unconditional variant of the welfare test. Such is the importance attached to the welfare interests of a child, relative to the interests of all others, that when specified in certain contexts – most obviously in public family law and as regards protection from specific harm – they acquire the status of rights. Conceptually, 'welfare interests' implies an holistic package of welfare determinants that will vary in content as required to match the needs of a particular child, with flexible boundaries that could be redrawn to address matters and relationships of importance to that child. When linked with the paramountcy principle, however, this may result in a somewhat isolationist approach towards the child concerned, an exclusiveness regarding their individualised welfare, serving ultimately to separate him or her from context

42 [1970] AC 668.
43 The Child Care Act 1991, s 4 (as amended by the Child Care [Amendment] Act 2022).

considerations as was demonstrated in a 2013 UK Supreme Court case concerning whether a child of two years of age should be permanently removed from her parents and placed for adoption[44] (see, further, Chapter 5). The fact that it is supplemented by a statutory welfare checklist raises the question as to whether the specification of welfare components adds to or subtracts from the intrinsic superiority of the principle and, in either case, whether this results in parity with ECtHR rulings on welfare interests. It is probable that the statutory references to paramountcy in the child-care legislation of Australia and New Zealand places the principle on much the same footing, relative to other factors, as in the UK.

The 'welfare test' in the EU

There are many and varied references to the child's best interests as the test for decision-making in regards to matters that impinge on a child's upbringing, but it is often unclear as to exactly what weight is to be placed on those interests relative to others. Article 24(2) of the Charter of the EU, for example, proclaims the child's best interests to be 'a primary consideration' in all actions relating to children, no matter whether taken by public or private authorities while Article 3(3) of the Treaty of the EU lists the protection of the rights of the child as one of the EU's aims. It has also been referenced many times by the judiciary of the ECtHR, the ECJ and the Committee of the CRC, sometimes as a 'primary consideration' or other such term, and sometimes as the factor of 'paramount importance'. Whether the difference in wording is genuinely intended to indicate a corresponding difference to be attached to the importance of welfare interests in circumstances of varying gravity, or not, is uncertain. The fact that this uncertainty has been a constant feature for the past 50 years, together with the fact that statutory checklists have not been drawn up to differentiate and promote consistency of interpretation between 'primary', 'paramount', etc., would tend to suggest that such clinical distinctions were not intended (see, further, Chapter 8).

There has long been controversy as to whether the developing ECtHR interpretation of the welfare principle – within the privacy and family life parameters of Article 8 – corresponds to the contemporary rulings of the courts in England and Wales on the same issues. The conceptual basis of the former, after all, is rooted in a rights context which implies holding a balance between the interests of different rights holders: so, for example, the welfare interests of a mother and her baby – being mutually interdependent and constituting 'family life' – would be likely to find joint protection under the Article 8 right to privacy but may not where the paramountcy principle places priority on the separate interests of the child. There is certainly potential for divergence: the ECtHR is constrained by the previous parameters, by the need to respect principles such as 'proportionality', 'subsidiarity' and the 'margin of appreciation', and by the requirement to ensure that domestic decision-making procedures

44 *In the matter of B (a child) (FC)* [2013] UKSC 33. See, also, *YC v. United Kingdom*.

have been in accordance with the law, pursued a legitimate aim, and were necessary in a democratic society.

More generally, there is a problem with jurisdictional differences in the interpretation and weighting given to 'welfare interests'. The lack of consistency was alluded to in the CRC 2023 report on France in which it made the following recommendation that could be applied more broadly across the EU[45]:

> on the right of the child to have their best interests taken as a primary consideration, the Committee recommends once again that the State party strengthen its efforts to ensure that this right is appropriately integrated and consistently interpreted and applied in all legislative, administrative and judicial proceedings and decisions as well as in all policies, programmes and projects that are relevant to and have an impact on children.

This fusion of rights and best interests, their elevation to a primary position relative to all other considerations and their strategic integration across the entire network of relevant decision-making and other forums would seem to indicate that welfare interests are becoming, or have become, the new *grundnorm* in family law.

The 'welfare test' in the U.S.

The Constitution, as interpreted by the U.S. Supreme Court, requires a state to show compelling reason for infringing rights of family privacy and for overriding parental autonomy as these fundamental liberties are protected by the Fourteenth Amendment and its guarantee of due process.[46] The main reason why the U.S. has declined to ratify UN CROC, and why the paramountcy principle cannot be said to function in child-care law as it does in most other developed western countries, is because of the constitutional protection singled out for the rights of parents[47] as established by the U.S. Supreme Court in cases such as *Santosky v. Kramer*[48] and emphatically declared by Thomas J in *Troxel*: "parents have a fundamental constitutional right to rear their children, including the right to determine who shall educate and socialize them".[49] These decisions set the direction of public policy regarding state intervention in family matters on child protection grounds until 2019 when the Family First legislation was introduced.

45 CRC/C/FRA/CO/6-7, at para 17.

46 *Meyer v. Nebraska*, 262 U.S. 390 (1923), *Stanley v. Illinois*, 405 U.S. 645 (1972) and *Wisconsin v. Yoder*, 406 U.S. 205 (1972).

47 See, Volokh, E., 'Parent-Child Speech and Child Custody Speech Restrictions', *NYU Law Review*, Vol. 81, p 631, 2006.

48 *Santosky v. Kramer*, Op. cit.

49 *Troxel v. Granville*, 530 U.S. 57 (2000).

The 'welfare test' in relation to Indigenous and migrant children

Essentially, children in these two groups are treated in accordance with regulatory practices that for the most part run in parallel with domestic laws governing the welfare of children, allowing for some overlap regarding access to public services such as education and health. The gross over-representation of Indigenous children in the child welfare and juvenile justice systems of the CANZUS nations (Canada, Australia, New Zealand, United States), together with the 'warehousing' of many migrant children, illustrates just how set apart these groups are and how little recognition is given to their welfare interests and rights relative to those of other children.

Applying the 'welfare test'

The impossibility of applying the welfare principle as a neutral yardstick – ensuring uniformity of treatment, equality of assessment and equity of outcome for all – in relation to decisions affecting the upbringing of children is highlighted by the range of sharply contrasting circumstances which may need to be addressed.

Children with a disability

Protecting and promoting the welfare interests of a 'disabled' child – meaning one defined, for example in England and Wales, as 'blind, deaf or dumb or suffering from mental disorder of any kind or is substantially or permanently handicapped by illness, injury or congenital deformity or such other disability as may be prescribed'[50] – and doing so in an inclusive manner that while addressing their special needs does not discriminate against them relative to other children of the same age can be challenging. Legislating specifically for the difference between 'normal' and children with disabilities, and then between children with disabilities on the basis of disability type, is now seen as stereotyping and constituting a form of discrimination which can be associated with a degree of stigma unacceptable in a modern pluralist culture where equality rights are regarded as highly sensitive. Failure to get that balance right has resulted in many cases being brought before the ECtHR on behalf of children with disabilities alleging adverse discrimination, most often in an educational context.[51]

Criminal children

In this context the welfare interests of a child offender must be weighed against the gravity of the offence and taken into consideration alongside other factors such as

50 The Children Act 1989, s 17(11).

51 See, further, O'Halloran, K., *Children, the Law and the Welfare Principle: Perspectives from Europe; France and Germany*, Routledge, 2023, at chapter 3.

any harm caused to a victim, reparation, accountability and public policy concerns. Usually effect is given to an offender's welfare interests by exercising discretionary diversionary options, utilising family group conferences and/or through the use of non-custodial disposal measures.

The gravity of the offence is always a primary consideration and one which inevitably constrains the scope for attending to an offender's welfare interests. This is particularly true in relation to children who have killed other children. In that context, the U.S. 2024 conviction for manslaughter of the parents whose teenage son shot dead four pupils in his school, illustrates a growing public policy willingness to widen the scope of culpability and also hold accountable those who bear some responsibility for a child and their actions[52] (see, further, Chapter 3).

The correlation between the age of the offender, the circumstances of the crime and the degree of insight and remorse shown will provide guidance as to the potential for rehabilitation which in turn will determine the extent to which sentencing can accommodate provisions to safeguard the offender's welfare interests.

Child victims

While there has always been at least sympathy for the child victims of criminal offences, the need for a more sophisticated response has become obvious as the range of criminal activity has grown increasingly complex.

Child victims are often also the witnesses – sometime the only witnesses – of criminal activity. As is frequently the case with child sexual abuse proceedings, such children need a dual approach: ongoing treatment and counselling for trauma and protection to prevent any attempt to influence their court testimony. A child may not self-identify as a victim; a child may not be suffering from trauma, perhaps their self-perception is quite the reverse. This could be the case for those who have been the subject of online grooming – who believe they are 'special' and have been selected for whatever spurious reason – for whom the coming to terms with the reality of duplicity and of their manipulation can require specialised counselling.[53] At a more extreme remove, there are children who – because of their relative indemnity from prosecution – are hired as couriers for guns and drugs, or as prostitutes or child soldiers, who again may need to be convinced of their victim status and will require skilled assistance if they are to recover from or learn to deal with the memories of the activities they were involved in.

Trans children

The medical and legal confusion surrounding sexual orientation, gender identity (SOGI) and gender transitioning are at least unsettling for many children and their parents and possibly quite damaging for the welfare interests of some of the former.

52 See, Trial of Ethan Crumbley and Parents, https://news.sky.com/story/ethan-crumbley-parents-of-teenager-who-shot-dead-four-classmates-in-the-us-jailed-for-manslaughter-13111488

53 In this context, note the French 'Melanie Rooms' initiative which provides protected spaces for hearing and caring for child victims of abuse.

Moral concerns generated by SOGI issues have been accompanied by the dilemma of whose consent is sufficient to authorise the use of the 'puberty blockers' necessary to commence the physiological process of gender transitioning in respect of necessarily quite young children. The dilemma of at what age the child concerned may give a valid legal consent to commence a process – the lifelong consequences of which he or she may not fully comprehend – is very much a contentious issue in the jurisdictions studied. How to objectively ascertain the welfare interests of each child, what weighting to give to each child's wishes/consent, and whether, and if so how, these matters should be correlated with the age, maturity, physiology and strength of gender self-identification of such a child are difficult issues for all concerned[54] and have been extensively debated in recent UK cases.[55]

In most developed nations, but not all, legislation has now repealed laws that allowed parental consent to authorise procedures for the surgical intervention necessary to 'correct' genital 'abnormalities' in infants and affirm alignment of sexual organs with declared gender identity.

Unaccompanied migrant children

Responding to the welfare interests of unaccompanied migrant minors – obviously complex, interwoven and urgent – includes assisting them with their disorientation and dislocation as a consequence of separation from parents, family, home, language and immersion in a wholly different culture without any certainty as regards accommodation, meals, whom to trust, personal safety, etc. The pressure to process their migrant/refugee status must necessarily make room for pursuing enquiries as to the whereabouts of parents or any next of kin while simultaneously attempting to stabilise the minor's accommodation, provide access to welfare benefits and possible healthcare and age-related educational or other facilities. The CRC, in its 2023 report on France, urged the authorities 'to ensure that unaccompanied children in transit, in particular in Calais, are not subjected to cruel and degrading living conditions, the destruction of their shelters, the use of disproportionate police force and lack of protection measures'.[56]

Indigenous children

It would seem incontrovertible that the Indigenous children of the CANZUS nations endure, disproportionately, much higher levels of poverty, ill health, admission to state care and juvenile justice systems, and general social disadvantage than their non-Indigenous counterparts. Despite the aspirational goals embodied in international instruments such as the UN Declaration on the Rights of Indigenous People

54 See, further, O'Halloran, K., *Sexual Orientation, Gender Identity and International Human Rights Law: Common Law Perspectives*, Routledge, 2020.

55 *Bell v. Tavistock and Portman NHS Foundation Trust* [2020] EWHC 3274 (Admin) and *ABCD v. Tavistock*, EWCA Civ 1363.

56 CRC/C/FRA/CO/6-7, at para 23(b).

2006[57] and the American Declaration on the Rights of Indigenous Peoples 2016,[58] experience to date indicates that relying solely on laws and policies are a wholly inadequate means of changing practice.

Transitioning from welfare interests to rights: general indicators

The UN CROC declaration of children's rights dates from 1989 but, as it is without any designated enforcement mechanism, there remains some uncertainty as to which of its provisions can be construed as having the force of law – let alone having a uniform jurisdictional applicability – in the sense of imposing a binding duty on others to protect or advance the interests of children. There would seem to be broad agreement that the following factors constitute general indicators of when matters might be elevated from welfare interests to rights: age of the child concerned, gravity of the issue and the opportunity to enjoy family life.

Age of the child

At an early stage in the development of the law relating to children, age became established as a crude indicator of legal capacity which in turn opened the door to a process of recognition for an entitlement to exercise certain rights (see, further, Chapter 3).

Jurisdictional variation in age parameters

Age is most usually used to fix the lower threshold for defining who is a child for certain legal purposes, but it may also be employed as the determinant of the higher threshold for such purposes; as, for example, in New Zealand where it is established that a young person, up to twenty years of age, retains the status of 'child'.

A foetus

The Preamble to UN CROC states that 'the child . . . needs . . . appropriate legal protection before as well as after birth', a proposition that sits uneasily alongside the legal right to abortion upheld, to a varying degree, in all eight jurisdictions presently being considered. Indeed, there is little in the way of conclusive guidance from international law on this matter though the European Commission in *H. v. Norway*[59] did tentatively advise that "in certain circumstances" the foe-

57 See, further, www.ohchr.org/en/indigenous-peoples/un-declaration-rights-indigenous-peoples#:~:text=The%20Declaration%20addresses%20both%20individual,all%20matters%20that%20concern%20them

58 See, further, www.oas.org/en/sare/documents/DecAmIND.pdf

59 Application No. 17004/90, (1992). See, further, www.globalhealthrights.org/wp-content/uploads/2016/12/H.-v.-NORWAY.pdf

tus may enjoy "a certain protection under Article 2, first sentence", but in *Vo v. France*[60] the ECtHR considered it was "neither desirable, nor even possible" to specify whether the unborn child should be considered 'a person' as protected under Article 2.

In England and Wales, a 'child' must have been born before he or she can be defined as such, though the courts have established[61] that a pregnant mother owes a duty of care to her foetus. However, in New Zealand, the courts have gone a step further and ruled that a foetus can come within the legal definition of 'child' and as such is entitled to protection.[62] The ECtHR has found that while embryos do not have a right to life, and therefore the authorities are entitled as required by national law to destroy them,[63] it has not gone so far with its rulings on the status of a foetus. However, in *Parrillo v. Italy*,[64] it ruled for the first time that Article 8 was applicable to the relationship between the applicant and her embryos as they contained part of her genetic material.

Age in a civil context

As was stated in the *Gillick* case,[65]

> An underlying principle of the law . . . is that parental right yields to the child's right to make his own decisions when he reaches a sufficient understanding and intelligence to be capable of making up his own mind on the matter requiring decision.

In *YC v. United Kingdom*[66] the ECtHR advised that

> in seeking to identify the best interests of a child and in assessing the necessity of any proposed measure in the context of placement proceedings, the domestic court must demonstrate that it has had regard to, *inter alia*, the age, maturity and ascertained wishes of the child.

Curiously, age has not been a factor in determining the capacity to legally relinquish a child for adoption: a mother of any age may do so. Inevitably, as developments in the law regarding capacity to consent evolved, this gave added weight to the presence of a child in the courtroom: but only relatively recently has that presence changed from being the object of proceedings to becoming, in some circumstances,

60 Application No. 53924/00, (2004).
61 See, *D (A Minor) v. Berkshire County Council* (1987) 1 All ER 33.
62 See, *In the Matter of Baby P (an unborn child)* [1995] NZFLR 577. This is not disimilar to the interpretation in Irish law.
63 *Evans v. the United Kingdom*, Application No. 6339/05, (2007).
64 Application No. 46470/11, (2015).
65 *Gillick v. West Norfolk and Wisbech Area Health Authority and the DHSS*, Op. cit., at p 251B.
66 Application No. 4547/10, (2012).

a full party whose giving or withholding of consent could potentially determine the outcome (see, further, Chapter 3).

Age in a criminal context

The law would seem to have had a long-standing interest in determining the age at which a child or young person, invariably female, could give a valid consent to a sexual relationship (see, further, Chapter 2), due less to a concern for the welfare of the child and more for the criminal liability of the other party, invariably male, involved. Currently, despite the CRC recommendation that no child younger than 14 years of age should be criminally liable,[67] there is considerable jurisdictional disparity regarding this matter: the UK, Australia and New Zealand have set the age of criminal responsibility at ten years, which has long been of concern to the CRC;[68] in Ireland it is 12 years; in Canada, the age of criminal responsibility is federally set at 12 years as it is in Ireland, while it is 13 years in Germany; in some states in the U.S. it is seven years; but in France there is no fixed age threshold.

Maturity/discernment

The *Gillick* ruling is predicated on the assumption that a child aged 16 years or thereabouts will have acquired the maturity necessary to understand certain issues concerning them and be in a position to make a reasoned decision. Much depends on the complexity or gravity of the issue: dental treatment, routine hospital procedures and suchlike are readily understood and amenable to adolescent decision-making in a way that life-or-death issues are not; the implications arising from decisions to forego blood transfusions or to make choices in relation to cancer treatments are of a different order, and not every adolescent has the capacity to cope with the responsibility and sufficiently understand the consequences to make such decisions (see, further, Chapter 8).

Discernment

In France, instead of a fixed age limit as the CRC have recommended (set, preferably at 14 years of age), the *juges des enfants* applies a 'discernment test' to establish whether the child concerned had the maturity and reasoning capacity to understand the particular circumstances of the case. As regards criminal conduct, the *juge* will determine whether the child has attained a sufficient degree of discernment to be held criminally liable for his or her actions (see, further, at Chapter 5).

67 United Nations, Committee on the Rights of the Child, *General Comment No. 24 (2019) on Children's Rights in the Child Justice System*, CRC/C/GC/24, September 18, 2019, section C.

68 See, Concluding Observations on the Sixth Periodic Report of the United Kingdom of Great Britain and Northern Ireland, 2019, at para 58.

Gravity of the issue

Where there is conflict between the interests of parent and child, the balancing exercise carried out by the ECtHR and the courts in the UK and the U.S. would seem to be significantly different.

Child's right to have welfare interests prioritised

In *Johansen v. Norway*[69] the ECtHR drew attention to the role played by the gravity of the issue in relation to the rights of the child: "the court will attach particular importance to the best interests of the child, which, depending on their nature and seriousness, may override those of the parent".[70] This was reiterated in *Ahrens v. Germany*[71]: "consideration of what lies in the best interests of the child concerned is of paramount importance in every case of this kind; depending on their nature and seriousness, the child's best interests may override that of the parents". Seemingly, only when the matter was sufficiently serious and the risks to a child's welfare sufficiently grave would there be a possibility of the court recognising that the child had a right to have their interests prioritised over those of their parents.[72] This interpretation points to the principle having relevance to public rather than private family law issues.[73]

The previous ECtHR caselaw does not correspond to the rulings of the UK judiciary on similar issues, but the Court has demonstrated a good deal of inconsistency. In *Neulinger and Shuruk v. Switzerland*,[74] for example, it noted that "there is currently a broad consensus – including in international law – in support of the idea that in all decisions concerning children, their best interests must be paramount". Interestingly, that case was determined before *Ahrens*, but the Court made a point in *Neulinger* of discounting the nature and degree of seriousness of the threat to welfare interests, the importance of which was to be stressed in the latter case.

If the later ruling in *Ahrens* is to be taken as representing current ECtHR interpretation of welfare interests, it would seem to be some way removed from the effects of the paramountcy principle as applied by the UK courts in relation to aspects of a child's upbringing.

Family life

The research findings of developmental psychologists generated a widespread acceptance – at least among child-care professionals – that children, particularly

69 Application No. 17383/90, (1996).

70 Ibid, at para 78.

71 Application No. 45071/09, (2012).

72 See, also, *C v. Finland*, Application No. 18249/02, (2006).

73 See, *Maumousseau and Washington v. France*, Application No. 41615/07, (2011) where "the Court notes that since the adoption of the [CRC], 'the best interests of the child' in all matters concerning it. . . have been paramount in child protection issues".

74 Application No. 41615/07, (2010).

young children, had a right to be cared for in a family environment where they would have the opportunity to form the secure attachments necessary for their emotional development and future ability to form safe and sustainable relationships. This was reinforced by UN CROC, Article 9, which declared that such care should be provided by the birth parents unless, as in the U.S., prevented by exceptional circumstances. The importance of such attachments did much to raise awareness regarding the limitations of residential care, to legitimate foster care and to strengthen the case of those who believed that every child should have a family (see, also, Chapter 8).

Protection for family life

Recognition of a child's right to family life has been upheld by the ECtHR in cases such as *Y.C. v. United Kingdom*[75] when, in reference to "the parent's right under Article 8 to enjoy a family life with their child," the Court stressed that only exceptional circumstances would "justify a compulsory measure of removal of the care from biological parents".[76] This right is valid regardless of whether the family concerned is marital or non-marital, and this has also provided the rationale for its many rulings reminding domestic authorities that they are required to expedite the return of a child in state care to his or her family of origin whenever feasible. Moreover, while the paramountcy principle applies to both public and private family law cases, the *YC* case is public law, and although the statements relating to private family life would appear to be intended to have a generic application – as might be understood from the absence of any restrictive qualifications in the judgment – it is probably best to treat the scope of the principles stated as confined to public family law. That being the case, there would appear to be a fairly basic contradiction between the role of welfare interests in the paramountcy principle as represented in UK caselaw (and perhaps also that of Australia and New Zealand) and its corresponding role in Article 8 as represented in ECtHR caselaw. The jurisdictional differences in these matters are examined more closely in Part II.

Transitioning from welfare interests to rights: private family law

Traditionally, the law has presumed that the welfare interests of children were subsumed within the rights of their parents and appropriately represented by them; not until that authority had been displaced, or good reason shown for such displacement, would the welfare interests of their child warrant separate consideration. This more conciliatory approach to parents in private family law disputes – where the issues are likely to be in relation to matters of custody and contact – continues to influence ECtHR judgments in ways that are less likely in public family law disputes where there is a graver risk to the welfare of a child.

75 Application No. 4547/10, (2012).
76 Ibid, at para 134.

Proceedings: welfare interests and rights

In a private family law context, the proceedings for divorce and judicial separation determine the welfare interests of most children. As a broad generalisation, it can be said that in all eight jurisdictions presently being studied, the marriage rates are declining, divorce rates are increasing and a growing proportion of those forming and dissolving families are doing so without recourse to matrimonial formalities. All of this generates more family breakdowns and more permutations of parental contests for child custody.[77]

Jurisdictional differences

As Thorpe LJ noted in *A v. B and C*,[78] cases are “fact specific and generalised guidance was not possible. The immutable principle was that the child’s welfare should be the court’s paramount consideration in determining issues such as residence, contact and parental responsibility”. In some jurisdictions, legislation provides that ‘the child’s welfare’ is to be determined in accordance with a welfare checklist that identifies with a high degree of specificity, factors which require the child’s views and preferences to be considered ‘giving due weight to the child’s age and maturity, unless they cannot be ascertained’. The latter requirement repeats a traditional standard formula, entirely discretionary in application, which fails to import any concrete recognition of a child’s rights and which retains the subjective clause. While ‘the child’s welfare test’ is necessarily applied in a manner that takes account of the particular child’s age, character and circumstances, there is no requirement that it be treated as a matter of paramount importance, and it leaves the judiciary with wide discretionary powers to determine what, in any particular set of circumstances, constitutes ‘the child’s welfare’. Significantly, the test does not require the child’s consent, nor is there any suggestion that he or she has any rights in relation to the decision (see, further, Chapter 2).

Guardianship, this most ancient of family law orders, continues to serve its traditional function of vesting parental responsibility for a child in someone other than the child’s parents. While ‘the child’s welfare’ test will almost certainly be applied, this will not be interpreted as giving a child the right to consent or withhold consent to a proposed guardianship order, nor does the test imply that the child’s welfare interests be treated as being of paramount importance. Wardship, a similarly ancient procedure but one in which a child had the right to have their welfare interests treated as the matter of paramount importance, is generally resorted to when statutory procedures are inappropriate or insufficient to cope with complex and/or urgent cases where the welfare interests of a child are at serious risk. Once

77 See, further, Koivula, T., ‘What Makes a Father: Differentiation of Unmarried and Divorced Fathers in the Context of Custody under the Jurisprudence of the European Court of Human Rights’, *International Journal of Law, Policy and the Family*, Vol. 38, No. 1, 2024, https://doi.org/10.1093/lawfam/ebae002

78 [2012] EWCA Civ 285.

a child has been made a ward of court, that court is then empowered to apply the paramountcy principle when making any decision regarding the child's upbringing: in effect, the court can use that power to override the wishes of all other parties, including the parents and the wishes of the child (see, further, Chapter 2).

Adoption, traditionally the most private of family law orders, has broadened in legal function – in all jurisdictions currently being studied – as it adapts to address the social changes affecting the family. In many, the child concerned has a right to consent or withhold their consent to the proposed adoption. By the early years of the 21st century, in both common law and civil law jurisdictions, step-adoptions had become the single most common type of adoption. However, it is now viewed – mainly in some common law jurisdictions – as compromising for the welfare interests of the children involved due to an awareness that such adoptions can lack transparency: a child may grow up with a distorted perspective of actual family relationships. The new sensitivity to the rights of a child – to have and maintain a real connectedness with birth parents – gradually acquired recognition and priority over the discretionary right of a parent to use adoption as a means of legally repairing family boundaries. Consequently, legislators in some jurisdictions have, in recent years, introduced a requirement that the courts give preference to alternative orders, such as guardianship or special guardianship, when considering the appropriateness of step-parent adoption applications. As regards intercountry adoption (ICA), there has long been ambivalence surrounding the issue of whether this is compatible with the welfare principle because of its potential to sever a child's sense of cultural identity and a child's connections with their family and community of origin, and because it often, seemingly, meets the needs of adopters rather than those of children. Therefore, it is suggested that there is a probability that it breaches UN CROC, Article 20(3), which states that 'due regard shall be paid to the desirability of continuity in a child's upbringing and to the child's ethnic, religious, cultural and linguistic background'. Arguably, this may be countered by the right of a child with a disability to have as full a family life as possible, rather than be consigned to institutional care in the countries of eastern Europe.

Finally, in all CANZUS nations, it is the adoption of Indigenous children by non-Indigenous couples that generates most contention. This is considered to be non-compliant with the welfare interests of the children concerned as it forecloses their right to retain a cultural identity determined at birth.

Proceedings in an Indigenous context

Extended family and community networks, a strong characteristic of tribal societies, have traditionally played a significant role in providing support to vulnerable family units and preventing family breakdown. This, however, is less the case than formerly as the majority of Indigenous families are now living in urban settings.

Matrimonial

Rates of divorce and separation among Indigenous couples are higher than in the rest of the population. While marriage and divorce ceremonies may be conducted in accordance with customary practice, if they are to be formally recognised in law, they must also meet statutory and regulatory requirements.

Custody and guardianship

These are the main court orders available in respect of Indigenous children who become the subjects of parental divorce proceedings in either tribal or state courts. The grounds for granting these orders and the responsibilities they vest in those to whom they are granted are the same as for non-Indigenous applicants.

Custody issues generate greatest political and legal contention when one of the parents of the child concerned is not a tribal member. Again, responsibility for determining custody issues will fall to the tribal courts in respect of couples living on reservation and to state/province courts when they are not, or when the custodial parent is non-Indigenous, though this may be challenged by tribal authorities who may at least assign a tribal member to assist the court and advise on cultural matters. When the child concerned is identified as Indigenous, then the court will take into account the proposed arrangements to protect the child's cultural identity as this is held to constitute a critical component of the child's welfare interests.

Guardianship is intended for use by those relatives who may not wish to see a complete severance of ties between child and family and is particularly appropriate in relation to older children who have a right to maintain established relationships with parents and siblings. The courts are having more frequent recourse to this order in circumstances where previously an adoption order might have been sought, because it is less permanent and absolute and affords greater scope for preserving an Indigenous child's cultural identity.

Adoption

For Indigenous people there are three types of adoptions: customary, private and departmental. Although these parallel systems are in place, customary adoption has traditionally dominated and is integral to the family life of all Indigenous communities.

Customary

This arrangement for the care of a child, made between the birth parent(s) and the adoptive parent(s), who are usually relatives or members of the same community, has long been practised among the Indigenous people in the CANZUS nations and elsewhere.

While customary adoptions have gained legal recognition in most jurisdictions, they have been known to give rise to difficulties, usually in relation to inheritance claims, particularly where land is involved. From the perspective of the welfare of the child, customary adoption offers complete transparency, not just between the two families but the exposure extends to the tribe as a whole: this reduces the probability of identity issues for the adopted child, and it also means that if welfare issues become apparent, support from tribal members will be readily available, and the adoption can be promptly terminated if necessary.

Private

This form of adoption, common to the tribal communities of both countries, usually refers to the personal and direct placing of a child for adoption by his or her parents, most usually the mother. It can also refer to the involvement of private or commercial agencies, a particular characteristic of the U.S. adoption process, in arranging adoption placements. Either way the placement is authorised by the birth parent. The profit motive associated with private adoptions can add to the contention when the adoption being arranged is that of an Indigenous child by a non-Indigenous couple (see, also, Chapter 3).

Departmental

As the name suggests, this refers to adoptions conducted in accordance with statutory law in which all stages of the process are subject to regulatory controls and to independent professional assessment and monitoring; it is finalised in a court hearing, where the welfare interests of the child will determine whether an adoption order will be made.

Transitioning from welfare interests to rights: public family law, civil jurisdiction

Legally, a child's need for protection has always been interwoven with the child's capacity to consent: the two are correlated according to age; the stronger the need for the first, the lesser is the need for the second (see, also, Chapter 3).

Child protection

Any understanding of what is meant by 'children's rights' starts from this most basic principle: a child, because of his or her innate vulnerability, has an inherent right to protection which extends to include physical, moral and psychological welfare (see, further, Chapters 2 and 8). The principle of the welfare interests of a child, and the right to require others to provide protection for that welfare – as initially proclaimed in the Declaration on the Rights of the Child 1924 – paved the way for an incremental recognition of other legal rights.

General right to protection

The clearly established legal duty to protect children falls first on their parents, then on those in *loco parentis*, which can be any person or other entity appointed formally or informally by the parents as guardians to undertake parental responsibilities on their behalf, and finally, though to a varying extent, there is a duty of care on all third parties in relation to any dealings they may have with a child, which in some countries includes a mandatory public duty to report any evidence of child abuse or neglect. The duty may, by default, ultimately rest on the state 'as carer of last resort' (see, further, Chapter 2).

Direct duty

National legislation, directly and explicitly, gives effect to the right of a child to protection by prohibiting any form of child abuse or neglect: in some jurisdictions this extends to prohibiting parental chastisement. Such negative, prohibitive injunctions are supplemented by other more positive and specific legislative provisions of lesser gravity that impose duties on parents – such as in relation to ensuring attendance at school and for dental treatment, etc. – or on employers, manufacturers or service providers – usually in respect of health and safety requirements, etc. These, the primary direct constituent elements in a child's right to protection, are relatively uncontroversial, unlike the provision of 'baby hatches' which – though proven to save the lives of many babies and are legally permissible throughout the U.S., France and Germany and in as many as nine other European countries – are prohibited in others such as the UK[79] and condemned by the CRC as contravening a child's right, under Article 7 of UN CROC, to be known and cared for by their parents.

However, while a child's right to protection undoubtedly includes protection from threats that could seriously impact the child's health and safety, that right is subject to the degree of serious harm presented by the threat: not all threats are irredeemably harmful; a level of risk is a developmental necessity. Arguably, the right to take risks, and suffer the consequences, is also a right of childhood and one equally entitled to respect from parents and state. Like 'welfare interests', the right to take risks can only be sensibly interpreted and applied in respect of the strengths and weaknesses of each individual child relative to the gravity of the challenge (see, further, school shootings, Chapter 2).

Indirect duty

In many instances, while the legislative intent of a statute is to directly pursue objectives other than securing or promoting child welfare, it may also have an indirect welfare relevance.

Legislation may deal with welfare in the present tense and in relatively objective and precise terms as when it addresses abandonment, parental unfitness and dangers to children's health and safety. Legislation may also deal with welfare in the future tense, though with less precision, as when the judiciary are required to have regard for the welfare of a child during the course of divorce proceedings or to take into account the lifelong welfare interests of a child before granting an order for the child's adoption (which, as has been pointed out, could conceivably mean projecting welfare considerations into the 22nd century).

79 See, the Offences Against the Persons Act 1861, s 27, which makes it a criminal offence to abandon a baby.

Indirect state consensual intervention is also represented in the framework of public service provision, the nature and extent of which has the potential to offset adverse environmental factors. This is most crucial in relation to education and health services: the quality and levels of which, combined with ease of access, have been shown to strategically improve the lives and opportunities of children from socially disadvantaged families.

Prevention and promotion

State child protection duties, while prioritising the safety of children from possible harm inflicted by parents or others, have ostensibly evolved to accommodate the ancillary legal functions of 'prevention' and 'promotion'. However, it often seems that 'prevention' fails to function as a state duty – a legally enforceable aspect of a child's right to protection – but is more likely to be treated as a discretionary state power, the resources for which are liable to be redirected into more pressing priorities arising from the consequences of a failure to protect. Similarly, but to an even greater degree, the same applies to 'promotion': the state obligation to promote the welfare interests of children in public family law is mainly aspirational; in private law it is largely restricted to guiding judicial choices in respect of parenting arrangements and contact (see, also, Chapter 2).

State protective duties: domestic law

Domestic law relating to a state's duty to ensure a child's right to protection is a mix of consensual and coercive provisions culminating, ultimately, in the duty to act as a substitute parent by assuming full parental responsibility.

Consensual

Unlike its coercive counterpart, consensual state intervention in support of vulnerable families is susceptible to political context: it is likely to be viewed as a state duty with a reciprocal public expectation in the more social welfare–oriented liberal democracies such as the UK and France but eschewed as state meddling in private family matters in rights-oriented democracies such as the U.S.

The state duty to offer services designed to protect welfare interests and strengthen family support for children is an acknowledgment of a child's right to a safe level of care – to at least 'good enough parenting' – and of the state's responsibility to underpin this vicariously by resourcing the parents. It begins with a requirement that the appropriate authorities first identify children in need, or at risk of becoming so, rather than wait for requests for assistance. This necessitates adopting proactive measures to locate vulnerable families, assess their needs and determine appropriate services. It then entails the delivery of appropriate and sufficient services.

Coercive

The legislative prohibitions against child abuse and neglect provide the most explicit specification of duties owed by others to ensure the right to safety of children and to safeguard their health and welfare interests. While obviously including physical, sexual and emotional abuse, this also references or otherwise accommodates the trauma that may be experienced by a child when in the presence of domestic violence. To a varying extent, jurisdictions may legislate to reinforce a child's right to protection by measures such as prohibiting the physical punishment of children by parents and/or others and to provide for the mandatory reporting – by members of the general public or by professionals working with children – of instances of child abuse or neglect. The ultimate exercise of state child protection is the removal of child and parental rights, followed by the child being maintained in out-of-home accommodation provided or regulated by the state.

One of the most significant developments in modern family law has been the ratcheting up of state coercive intervention in families on child protection grounds. In most of the countries studied, admissions to state child-care systems have greatly increased over the past decade: in Australia, for example, the numbers practically doubled during the period 2011–21.[80] Much of the general increase has been due to the admission of unaccompanied migrant minors: in the UK such young persons constituted 21% of the children taken into care in 2022–23 (7,090 out of 33,000), more than double their proportion in 2020–21 (10%).[81]

Unfortunately, the increase in state coercive intervention has not necessarily translated into more effective child protection: in France, for example, the number of child protection cases steadily increased in the period 2013–20 (from 318, 710 to 370, 200),[82] but the CRC, in its 2016 report, expressed deep concern about reports estimating that two children die each day, potentially attributable to domestic violence.[83] The failing efforts of state child protection services are highlighted by the experience in New Zealand which is reported to have the world's highest teenage suicide rate[84] and one of the highest rates of child abuse.[85] The U.S. has the singular jurisdictional characteristic of being unable to protect children from school shootings, of which there have

80 See, Australian Institute of Health and Welfare, www.aihw.gov.au/child-protection/

81 See, further, www.communitycare.co.uk/2023/11/20/15th-rise-in-care-population-england/#:~:text=Unaccompanied%20young%20people%20made%20up,year%20has%20remained%20relatively%20static

82 See, further, www.statista.com/statistics/468238/numbers-child-protection-benefit-recipients-france/

83 See, further, CRC/C/FRA/CO/5.

84 New Zealand's youth suicide rate at 14.9 deaths per 100,000 adolescents is more than twice the average among the 41 Organization for Economic Cooperation and Development countries surveyed by UNICEF in 2018. See, further, www.unicef.org.nz/media-releases/new-report-card-shows-that-new-zealand-is-failing-its-children#

85 See further, for example, www.theguardian.com/world/2018/mar/08/study-one-in-four-new-zealand-children-reported-welfare-agencies

been some 2,032 since 1970.[86] In 2022 alone, by May there had been 119[87] (see, further, Chapter 3).

While to some degree these differences may be attributable to cultural context, as a broad generalisation it would seem that law and practice are failing to keep pace with the rising numbers and range of child protection issues. Inevitably, therefore, it can be predicted that family law will have to accommodate a larger and more refined block of child protection provisions if the state duty to ensure the right of its children to a safe upbringing is to be more effective.

Regulating exposure to harmful media transmission

UN CROC, Article 17(e), requires State parties to 'encourage the development of appropriate guidelines for the protection of the child from information and material injurious to his or her well-being', bearing in mind the provisions of Articles 13 and 18.

The contemporary relevance of this provision is in relation to protecting a child's welfare from possible harm emanating from international social media platforms that may expose children to pornography, grooming, cyber-bullying, violent images, etc. A child's right to protection from this form of harm, while acknowledged at a policy level in all jurisdictions, remains imperfectly regulated in most, though the French initiative to establish a child's 'right to be forgotten' on the internet and on social media platforms deserves more attention. The General Comment No. 25 on the Rights of Children in the Digital Environment, adopted by the CRC in February 2021, established guidelines for addressing these increasingly pressing issues. The domestic regulatory authorities in the EU, as elsewhere, are in the process of formulating policies for controlling the dissemination of material harmful to children. Presently the only known government initiative is that taken in Germany to deal with violent video games (*Killerspiele*) which prohibits the sale or the advertising of video games, movies or other forms of media depicting extreme violence.[88]

State protective duties: international law

The state's protective duties towards the welfare of children were first internationally proclaimed in the earlier-mentioned 1924 Declaration, as followed by the Declaration on the Rights of the Child 1959, both of which have been criticised for being 'largely protective and paternalistic in nature'.[89]

Since then, and in all jurisdictions studied, as in many others, the benchmark standards giving effect to child protection – endorsed, ratified and often incorporated into domestic legislation – as interpreted and applied by such international

86 See, further, www.sandyhookpromise.org/blog/gun-violence/16-facts-about-gun-violence-and-school-shootings/

87 See, further, www.statista.com/statistics/971473/number-k-12-school-shootings-us/

88 See, the Youth Protection Act, as amended in 2008.

89 See, Kilkelly, U., *Children's Rights in Ireland: Law, Policy and Practice*, Tottel, 2008, at p 2.

bodies as the ECtHR and the CRC, have done much to firmly establish and elucidate the right of the child to protection. The threshold for such protection – the point at which concerns for child welfare justify state intervention in family affairs – is loosely governed by Articles 1, 3 and 8 of the ECHR requiring, respectively, respect for human rights, prohibition of inhuman or degrading treatment and respect for private and family life.[90] These provisions are reinforced by the UN CROC,[91] in particular by Articles 3 and 19 which declare, respectively, the best interests of the child to be the primary consideration in all decisions concerning children and that all appropriate legislative, administrative, social and educational measures should be taken to protect a child from all forms of harm. (UN CROC remains unratified by the U.S.) Many decades of ECtHR rulings, drawing from these articles, have clarified the scope of the duty to enforce a child's particular right to protection in the ECHR Member States while also setting general benchmarks for state protective duties in other countries.

Duty to be proactive in protecting children

The fact that the ECtHR has, in a number of cases, found a state to be culpable for failing to effect rapid intervention resulting in preventable harm, clearly illustrates the Court's understanding that a child has a legal right to prompt and effective state protection. So, for example, in the UK the authorities were found to have breached Articles 3 (prohibition of inhuman or degrading treatment) and 13 (right to an effective remedy) when – despite receiving reports of child abuse or of being in possession of information that should have alerted them to the risk of such abuse – they failed to promptly institute protective measures.[92]

Having intervened, a state may nonetheless still fail in its obligation to provide effective protection. For example, *X. and Others v. Bulgaria*[93] concerned allegations by three Bulgarian children that they were sexually abused in an orphanage. The ECtHR found that although a satisfactory legislative and regulatory framework was in place for preventing child sexual abuse, the authorities had failed to use all reasonable investigative measures. In particular, no attempt had been made to examine the applicants medically or interview them or other children named by them, nor had there been any use of the covert investigative measures expressly mentioned in the Lanzarote Convention.[94]

90 See, further, O'Halloran, K., *Children, the Law and the Welfare Principle: European Judicial Perspectives*, Routledge, 2023.

91 Also, note the three UN CROC protocols: the Optional Protocol on the Involvement of Children in Armed Conflict; the Optional Protocol to the Convention on the Sale of Children, Child Prostitution and Child Pornography; and the Optional Protocol on a Communications Procedure.

92 *Z and Others v. the United Kingdom*, Application No. 29392/95, (2001), *TP and KM v. UK* [2001] 2 FLR 549 and *E and Others v. the United Kingdom*, Application No. 33218/96, (2002). See, also, *O'Keeffe v. Ireland* [GC], Op. cit.

93 Application No. 22457/16, (2021).

94 Council of Europe Convention on the Protection of Children against Sexual Exploitation and Sexual Abuse 2007 (the 'Lanzarotte Convention') was introduced in order to promote national and international co-operation against sexual exploitation and sexual abuse of children.

Duty to protect from neglect

The ECtHR addressed this theme in *Olsson v. Sweden*[95] when it stressed that the mere fact a child would be better off if placed in care was insufficient. So also in *Saviny v. Ukraine*,[96] where it found that children had been placed in care due to the parents' lack of financial means, and in the absence of evidence that the authorities had attempted to provide relevant social assistance, it held that they had violated their Article 8 duty to maintain family unity. Again, in *Khan v. France*,[97] the Court found the state itself was responsible for making a child homeless by dismantling the makeshift camps outside Calais housing migrants hoping to cross the channel to England.

It might be added that parental neglect is more likely to trigger coercive than consensual intervention in some countries, such as the U.S., where ensuring that basic standards of child welfare are met is usually viewed as the responsibility of the family rather than the state, and failure to meet those standards is liable to be interpreted as evidence of a breach of the parental duty of care warranting child removal rather than family assistance. This approach might help explain the alarming infant mortality rate: in 2023, this reached 5.48 per 1,000 live births (the first rise in 20 years),[98] making the U.S. 51st in the world (significantly higher than in dozens of other developed countries such as Sweden 2.15, Japan 1.82, and Australia 3.14).[99]

Duty to protect from abuse

The ECtHR has examined the states' protective duties in relation to a wide range of acts constituting child abuse, mainly through proceedings under Articles 2, 3 and 8 of the ECHR. Under Article 3, for example, it has ruled that long-term neglect by parents,[100] repeated sexual abuse by schoolteachers,[101] rape[102] and corporal punishments[103] all fall within the definition of 'cruel and degrading treatment'. In C.*A.S. and C.S. v. Romania*,[104] the ECtHR established that Article 3 imposes an obligation on state authorities to conduct effective investigations into allegations of child abuse, while in *X. and Others v. Bulgaria*,[105] it stressed that

95 Application No. 10465/83, (1988).
96 Application No. 39948/06, (2008).
97 Application No. 12267/16, (2019).
98 See, further, the BMJ, www.bmj.com/content/383/bmj.p2569
99 See, the Centers for Disease Control and Prevention's National Vital Statistics System.
100 *Z and Others v. the United Kingdom* [GC], Application No. 29392/95, (2001).
101 *O'Keeffe v. Ireland* [GC], Application No. 35810/09, (2014).
102 *M.C. v. Bulgaria*, Application No. 39272/98, (2003); *M.G.C. v. Romania*, Application No. 61495/11, (2016), para 58.
103 *Tyrer v. the United Kingdom*, Application No. 5856/72, (1978); *M.C. v. Bulgaria*, Application No. 39272/98, (2003), para 150; *O'Keeffe v. Ireland* [GC], Op. cit., at para 146.
104 Application No. 26692/05, (2012). See, also, *E v. United Kingdom*, Application No. 33218/96, (2002).
105 Application No. 22457/16, (2021).

Article 3 has to be interpreted in the light of other applicable international instruments, in particular the Lanzarote Convention[106] and the state duty with regards to investigation and procedural requirements. In *F.O. v. Croatia*,[107] the alleged harassment of a pupil by a teacher in a public school – calling the applicant "a moron, an idiot, a fool, hillbilly" – and the failure on the part of the state authorities to effectively respond to his allegation, was held to infringe Article 8. The ECtHR found that teachers should be aware that any form of violence, including verbal abuse, towards students, however mild, is not acceptable in an educational setting.

Duty to protect from corporal punishment

The ECtHR has found that chastising a child for unacceptable behaviour, by administering corporal punishment, constitutes a violation of Article 3. This is the case whether it is administered[108] officially (by teachers[109] or police officers[110]), privately (by a stepfather),[111] or is an accepted aspect of community life (by a religious organisation).[112]

Out-of-home placements

The impact of research in the field of developmental child psychology, combined with the many official reports on child abuse and deprivation in children's homes, led to a recognition that a child in state care had the right to a safe and nurturing environment which in turn led to the withdrawal of the residential care provision for most children in the developed nations during the latter half of the 20th century. Instead, foster care was generally developed as a replacement for residential institutions, though to a lesser extent in Germany.

Residential care

Once the mainstay of statutory child-care systems, the use of residential placements has in recent years greatly diminished. In the CANZUS nations, the main reason for the decline in use of such facilities was their association with an assimilation policy that saw generations of Indigenous children being removed from their

106 Council of Europe Convention on the Protection of Children against Sexual Exploitation and Sexual Abuse 2007.

107 Application No. 29555/13, (2021).

108 Ursula Kilkelly comments that these cases were determined more in accordance with matters of procedure than strictly as breaches of the Convention (note to author, June 9, 2023).

109 See, *Campbell and Cosans v. the United Kingdom*, Application Nos. 7511/76 and 7743/76, (1982) and *Costello-Roberts v. the United Kingdom*, Application No. 13134/87, (1993).

110 *Tyrer v. the United Kingdom*, Application No. 5856/72, (1987).

111 *A. v. the United Kingdom*, Application No. 25599/94, (1998).

112 *Tlapak and Others v. Germany*, Application Nos. 11308/16 and 11344/16, and *Wetjen and Others v. Germany*, Application Nos. 68125/14 and 72204/14, (2018).

families of origin to residential schools, triggering intergenerational trauma for the Indigenous people and undermining the legitimacy of state residential facilities as a contemporary form of provision for children.

The growing awareness of a child's need for a family environment, rather than an institutional setting, has generally been a driving force for change. In France and Germany, however, a relatively high proportion of out-of-home placements are still consistently made in favour of residential facilities which may correlate with both a strong state deference to parental status/family unity and to the, at best, marginal relevance of the paramountcy principle.

Foster care

From the outset, foster care was found to have at least two serious faults: there were never enough foster parents, so matching the skills of foster carers with the particular needs of a child was seldom possible, leading to placement disruption and children being shuttled from one foster home to another; alternatively, foster care was liable to become a victim of its own success, as a close bond between a child and their foster carer could readily displace the child/birth parent relationship and undermine any prospect of rehabilitation. These difficulties are now threatening the future of foster care which, like residential care, may be largely abandoned and used only in exceptional circumstances.

Kinship care

Arrangements for the out-of-home care of a child with his or her relatives – as long practised in the Indigenous communities of the CANZUS nations – has in recent years become accepted as the preferred option for state placements in most developed countries. Such placements are more compliant with UN CROC principles as they offer the best opportunity for a child to retain direct links with their family and culture of origin, thereby preserving an authentic sense of belonging and of personal identity. They are often reinforced by guardianship orders. The policy emphasis on kinship placements often leads to adoption with many children being returned through that process to their kinship networks. This has the added advantage for the state of positioning ongoing child-care responsibilities in a private rather than a public setting; albeit supplemented with public funding.

An interesting point of difference between France and Germany is their respective use of kinship placements: while this is a strong feature of child-care policy in Germany, there is comparatively little reliance on the extended family for such purposes in France. While in Germany the majority of children in foster care are placed with a relative (60% in 2005), this is true for only a small minority in France (7% in 2007). This is unusual, given the use of kinship in all the common law countries, and constitutes an interesting aspect of jurisdictional difference but one that may compromise a French child's identity rights.

Secure accommodation

Safeguarding the welfare interests of children requires the provision of secure residential facilities to ensure the protection of those whose behaviour presents a threat to themselves or to others. While both Ireland and the UK rely to some degree on such provision, the scale of need is greatest in the latter. In the U.S., it has been estimated that approximately 35,000 children are being held in solitary confinement in the juvenile system alone,[113] and such treatment is also imposed on children in custody in adult facilities. In a civil law context, treatment with behaviour modification programmes in a structured setting is preferred to confinement.

Family rehabilitation

Such is the strength of the ECtHR defence of a child's right to parental care that it has stressed in *YC v. the United Kingdom* that

> family ties may only be severed in very exceptional circumstances and that everything must be done to preserve personal relations and, where appropriate, to 'rebuild' the family. It is not enough to show that a child could be placed in a more beneficial environment for his upbringing.[114]

Further, *Gorgulu v. Germany*[115] provides authority for the view that the child's welfare must be seen in a long-term context, and this may even require terminating a third-party adoption placement, however satisfactory, if state intervention is to meet the test of 'proportionality'.

Unlike residential care, the presumption in foster care has been that the child has a right to be cared for by their family of origin; therefore, in most cases, preparation for rehabilitation to safe parental care is generally understood to be the objective. However, in Ireland, partnership with parents and rehabilitative work may have been something of a forced option, due to constitutional constraints that favoured state protection and support for the birth family, but this has now become established practice and is unlikely to change radically.

In practice foster care often turns into a permanent alternative to birth family care, either because standards in the birth family fail to improve sufficiently or because the child has bonded so closely to the foster parents that to break that bond would be detrimental to their welfare interests. This places the state in a position of being unable to rehabilitate the child, thereby breaching Articles 5, 18 and 27 of UN CROC which require it to support parental care. In order to avoid

113 U.S. Department of Justice, Office of Juvenile Justice and Delinquency Prevention, Conditions of Confinement: Findings from the Survey of Youth in Residential Placement 9 (2010).

114 (2012) 55 EHRR 33, at para 35.

115 Application No. 74969/01, (February 26, 2004) ECtHR. Also, see, *P, C and S v. UK* (2002) 35 EHRR 31, *K and T v. Finland* [2001] 2 FLR 707 and *Johansen v. Norway* (1996) 23 EHRR 33.

permanency planning for a child in state care becoming, by default, consigned to long-term foster care or adoption, the authorities in many countries have switched from preferencing foster care to kinship care. This provides the same opportunity for rehabilitation to parental care while offering the safety net of continued family and cultural connection in the event of rehabilitation being unrealistic.

Intercountry adoption

While UN CROC, Article 21, declares that 'States Parties that recognize and/or permit the system of adoption shall ensure that the best interests of the child shall be the paramount consideration', it is often claimed that ICA is adverse to the long-term welfare interests of the children concerned, because it compromises their sense of personal and cultural identity.[116] However, it must be conceded that as the recipient developed nations become increasingly multicultural, it is probable that this claim is diminishing in significance.

Transitioning from welfare interests to rights: public family law, criminal jurisdiction

In the context of proceedings where an offence involving a child has been or is alleged to have been committed, the legal issues are usually relatively uncomplicated and will dictate the separation of a child's interests from those of any first or third parties. Where the child is of an age and understanding to express views on the issues, then he or she will be encouraged to do so.

Juvenile crime

For most of the 19th century, juveniles who committed crimes were treated by the legal system in much the same way as adults. Liability for the consequences of a child's criminal behaviour was traditionally held to rest solely with that child; unless parental involvement, as accomplice or through the usual rules governing the acts of principal and agent, could be proven. This was illustrated, as mentioned in an earlier book in this series, by the hanging, one day in England in 1814, of five children between eight and twelve years old for petty larceny.[117] Only if a clear differentiation could be made, defining a child's conduct as falling more within the category of 'care' than 'offence', would the court favour a welfare-oriented rather than a punishment-oriented disposal option.

Juvenile justice systems

By the end of the 20th century, a common jurisdictional emphasis in juvenile justice had evolved with a focus which was less on the welfare interests and rights

116 See, for example, Hubinette, T., 'Adopted Koreans and the Development of Identity in the Third Space', *Adoption & Fostering, London, BAAF*, Vol. 28, No. 1, 2004, pp 16–24.

117 See, Morris, A. and Giller, H., *Understanding Juvenile Justice*, London, Croom Helm, 1987, at p 6.

of child offenders and more on safeguarding the public, blended with a mix of training and rehabilitation measures. A differentiating jurisdictional characteristic had, however, begun to acquire salience in the U.S. as the 'due process' clause in the Constitution was applied to ensure that processes and outcomes of juvenile justice conformed to constitutionally protected standards. Arguably, juvenile court proceedings in the U.S. have since become more adversarial in nature than in other common law jurisdictions: requiring all the normal components and safeguards of an adult trial, tending to transfer juveniles into the adult criminal justice system, while also adopting a similarly punitive approach when it comes to disposal options.

The French system is singularly different. The dual civil/criminal jurisdiction administered by the *juge des enfants* represents an approach, long since abandoned elsewhere, of maintaining a legal focus on welfare interests while addressing criminal activity. The Civil Code directive that the *juge des enfants* should 'always strive to obtain family's consent to the measure envisaged' highlights the importance given to considerations of welfare rather than justice and is indicative of underlying state deference to family integrity.

In an Indigenous context

The fact that Indigenous children are grossly over-represented in their respective justice systems is undoubtedly the single strongest shared jurisdictional characteristic of the law as it relates to offending children in the CANZUS nations. The rising rate of violent crimes committed by and upon Indigenous youth is consistently much higher than that committed among non-Indigenous youth. The disparity between the two groups raises questions as to whether the justice systems contain structural biases prejudicial to the welfare interests and rights of Indigenous youth.

The system

Authorities and academics are in agreement that the present system is failing Indigenous youth. Consequently, a new and distinctive policy is underway: to develop restorative justice as a possible strategy for addressing the common over-representation problem with a focus on exploring ways of transferring more of the administration and adjudication of justice issues from the present system into tribal control. This would seem to be at a more advanced stage in Canada, thanks to the Indigenous Justice program launched in 1996.

Tribal/state juvenile court

The authorities in the CANZUS nations have openly admitted that existing preventative strategies are not working, that the over-representation of Indigenous youth in the justice system is a serious indictment of governmental failure to address their needs, and that consequently a new approach must be devised. The common jurisdictional answer would seem to be to vest more responsibility in the tribal authorities, enabling them to implement culturally appropriate preventative programs, police a range of antisocial and criminal behaviour, adjudicate on breaches of the law in tribal courts, and impose non-custodial penalties.

Sentencing

Despite the existence of government policy and legislative provisions that facilitate non-custodial options, the end result is a consistent judicial reliance on custody for Indigenous youth. Canadian research findings indicate[118] that the output of the youth justice system simply reflects the systemic racism channelling more Indigenous children into that system. Again, a policy is now emerging of giving tribal authorities more responsibility for developing culturally appropriate, non-custodial options that may more effectively engage Indigenous youth and address recidivism.

Transitioning from welfare interests to rights: hybrid

For many generations, the binary division between public and private proceedings remained a clearly understood and accepted structure for family law in the jurisdictions being considered, as in others. Except in theocratic states, or in those where secularism has not wholly displaced religious influence, family law has now largely shed its traditional polarisation and become reorganised around distinct functions. Of these functions the most dominant is protection, often indirectly as in the threat of domestic violence. While restraining orders are most frequently sought in a private family law context, they are also relevant in the public arena as foster parents and adopters may on occasion be applicants in circumstances where protection is needed from members of a child's birth family.

Other such hybrid orders, such as non-consensual adoptions from state care and parental abduction, which transect public and private sectors of family law, are on the increase in all jurisdictions studied and are the subject of analysis in Part II.

Conclusion

The journey from a concern for the welfare of children to respect for their legal rights has some way to go. Indicators of the distance yet to be travelled are many and varied. One such is the obdurate retention in the U.S. and in England and Wales of what is probably the lowest age of criminal responsibility for children in the developed western world.[119] England also continues to uphold a parent's 'right' to

118 See, among others, Luo, D., 'The Overrepresentation of Indigenous Youth in the Criminal Justice System; Exposing a Problematic Reality of Imprisoned Marginalized Groups in Canada', *The Society: Sociology & Criminology Undergraduate Review*, pp 69–74, https://jps.library.utoronto.ca

119 Set at ten years of age by the Children and Young Persons Act 1933 (as amended), s 50. See, for example, comments of the CRC, *Concluding Observations: United Kingdom of Great Britain and Northern Ireland*, United Nations, 2008, at para 78. Note that in Sweden, Finland and Norway, the age of criminal responsibility is set at 15 years.

physically chastise their child and declines to mandate the public reporting of suspected child abuse. In Ireland, the latter is mandatory,[120] the age of criminal responsibility is set slightly higher[121] but the court system remains unmodernised – an 'outlier of poor practice' – and inimical to the welfare interests of children.[122] These indices, representative of traditional state/family relationships, would seem non-compliant with contemporary international principles as stated primarily in the United Nations Convention on the Rights of the Child 1989 (UN CROC), the European Convention for the Protection of Human Rights and Fundamental Freedoms 1950 and as elucidated in associated caselaw.

120 Children First Act 2015, s 14.

121 Set at 12 years of age by the Children Act 2001, s 52, as amended by the Criminal Justice Act 2006, s 129.

122 Corbett, M. and Coulter, C., *Child Care Proceedings: A Thematic Review of Irish and International Practice*, Department of Children and Youth Affairs, 2019, as cited in Annual Report of the Special Rapporteur on Child Protection 2020, at p 144.

2 Child as a legal entity

Introduction

In 2011 'the status of the child as a subject of rights' was reaffirmed by the UN Committee on the Rights of the Child (CRC) in an Optional Protocol which came into effect in 2014.[1] The European Court of Human Rights (ECtHR) was very aware of this when, a year later in *M and M v. Croatia*,[2] it advised that even though children "lack the full autonomy of adults, [they] are, nevertheless, subjects of rights". These pronouncements highlight just how recent has been the law's transformation of the child as a legal entity: first, recognising the child as the object of proceedings most usually to provide protection for them or their property; and subsequently, as the subject, designating the child a party to proceedings – and therefore entitled to representation – if only for specific and limited purposes.

This chapter has a twin focus: on the extent to which the child, in certain circumstances, has acquired the attributes of a legal entity, particularly by being able to give a valid consent; and on the extent to which the child is then able to demonstrate that capacity in a courtroom setting. Beginning with the law governing the legal capacity of a child, it examines how the evolution of the child as a legal entity has changed the child's role in proceedings and considers the resulting impact on family law.

Legal capacity

The circumstances in which a child may legally give or withhold their consent – thereby becoming personally responsible and accountable for a decision and not have it and its consequences challenged on the basis of a lack of competence – have varied across many centuries and cultural contexts. An essential component of any contractual arrangement, the validity of consent has probably been most contentious in relation to sexual relations but has also played an

1 See, Committee on the Rights of the Child, *Optional Protocol to the Convention on the Rights of the Child on a Communications Procedure*, December 19, 2011, https://www.ohchr.org/en/instruments-mechanisms/instruments/optional-protocol-convention-rights-child-communications

2 Application No. 55597/09, (2015) para 171.

DOI: 10.4324/9781003510383-4

important role in matters such as determining responsibility for criminal offences and capacity to act as a credible witness. Always the basic underlying issue is as follows: what is the determining factor or factors in any decision-making process that entitles a child to have his or her welfare interests protected by others or, instead, require such others to respect and act upon the rights exercised by that child?

Identity

Legal recognition of a child as a 'person' brought with it an acknowledgment of a bundle of associated rights including to family life, to an identity, and to retain meaningful links with their family and culture of birth. The United Nations Convention on the Rights of the Child (UN CROC), Article 9, specifically recognises a child's right 'to preserve his or her identity' while Article 20(3), states that when considering child-care measures, 'due regard shall be paid to the desirability of continuity in a child's upbringing and to the child's ethnic, religious, cultural and linguistic background'. In some countries (e.g. Canada and Germany), children are recognised as legal entities independent of their parents, and are allowed, for example, to hold residence permits in their own right.

Personal and cultural

The ability of a child to develop a confident sense of personal identity will owe much to the opportunity the child has had to form close attachments and to the experience of being 'psychologically parented'. This concept emphasised that what was important, and crucial to the welfare of every child, was that the child had a sufficiently close and trusting relationship with a caregiver – parent or not and of either gender – that would allow an emotional bond to develop between them. Without that bonding experience, there is a risk that a child may grow into adulthood with what has been described as a tendency to become a "psychological vagrant" or someone with an inability to form and sustain the trusting relationships that enable others to affirm their sense of identity (see, also, Chapter 8).

Privacy

Much of contemporary family law relating to privacy rights has been a consequence of the ECtHR development of Article 8 of the European Convention on Human Rights (ECHR) and Article 16 of UN CROC. Increasingly, in recent years, the law can be seen to be giving considerable attention to matters of privacy, in which context the right to an 'identity' and to a cultural affiliation has acquired a particular prominence.

Child's right to give or withhold consent

There has probably always been a tacit acknowledgment that when children reach a particular developmental stage, they then become more mature, discerning and correspondingly more capable of contributing to decisions affecting them and of being held responsible for their consequences. The age at which this occurs varies from child to child but has come to be loosely associated with the time after puberty. There are many references to such a process in the religious texts of Christianity and Islam, but more pragmatically, the law's initial interest in the decision-making capacity of children was to hold them accountable for criminal conduct. A crude indicator of jurisdictional difference in the law's respect for the rights of children is whether or not parental chastisement is permissible: there can be fewer instances that demonstrate as clearly where the distribution of rights lies than the lawfulness of a parent physically beating a submissive child. In England and Wales, Canada, some Australian states and the U.S., the law permits a parent to use corporal punishment to chastise their child, subject to the condition that the degree of physical force is 'reasonable'. It is legally prohibited in Ireland, New Zealand, France and Germany.

There is probably no greater indicator of the transition from welfare interests to rights than the broadening range of matters in respect of which the law is prepared to recognise the capacity of a child to give or withhold their consent. That capacity demonstrates the *locus standi* of an autonomous and independent legal entity. Although UN CROC does not directly address this matter, in Article 12 it does require States Parties to ensure that a child who is capable of forming views on issues affecting them has the right to express those views and that they are given due consideration in accordance with their age and maturity. Indeed, a fundamental principle of UN CROC, as elaborated in the General Comments, is that an 'adult's judgment of a child's best interests cannot override the obligation to respect all of the child's rights under the Convention'.[3]

Views of a child

It might be expected that by now there would be some cross-jurisdictional consistency regarding the subject matters on which a child has an independent legal right to give or withhold a valid consent, and on the age at which the child can do so. This is not the case, though there is a degree of jurisdictional convergence in some subject areas. The greatest consistency lies in the broad consensus that the wishes of a child in relation to the matter at issue should always be ascertained and taken into account, the child should be listened to, and the older the child, the greater is the weight that should be given to those wishes. The age threshold is most often further conditioned by a maturity requirement: the younger the child, the stronger is the probability that the law will require evidence of capacity for discernment, and the greater the likelihood that it will otherwise assume that the parent may act on the child's behalf. The fact that in some jurisdictions reference is made in constitutional or legislative provisions to the rights of the child should not deflect from

3 Committee on the Rights of the Children, *General Comment No. 14 (2013) on the Right of the Child to have His or Her Best Interests Taken as a Primary Consideration (article 3, para 1)**, CRC/C/GC/14, at para 4.

a recognition that the circumstances in which the judiciary are prepared to endorse and enforce such rights are few in number and disparate in nature.[4]

'Age of discernment'

By the latter decades of the 20th century, judicial notice was being taken of the fact that a child of sufficient maturity and discernment to understand the issues at stake could have a right to independently make a decision on a matter affecting his or her welfare. In the UK, and thereafter more generally in the common law world, it was the ruling in *Gillick*[5] that established the right of a child at the 'age of discernment' to take unilateral decisions on some matters affecting their welfare, whether defined as falling within public or private family law (a child's right to consent being accompanied by a duty to be accountable; neither necessarily excluding parental responsibility). In Ireland, Article 42A established a constitutional duty, resting on the court, to ascertain the views of children, though for some years there had been a recognition that under Article 40.3 children had a procedural right to be heard in cases affecting them.[6] In fact the courts have a solid record of defending the right of a child to be heard on matters affecting their welfare. So, for example, when deciding to hear from a six-year-old child, Finlay Geoghegan J stressed that "anyone who has had contact with normal six year olds knows that they are capable of forming their own views about many matters of direct relevance to them in their ordinary everyday life".[7] In *RP v. SD*,[8] a child of four years and eleven months of average maturity was found *prima facie* not to be of an age where she was capable of forming her own views in relation to relevant matters. More recently, the Child Care (Amendment) Act 2022, s 5, inserted a new provision into the 1991 Act to provide that the court must have due regard to the views of the child in proceedings relating to child or special care. The court must give due weight to these views according to the child's age and maturity.

In the civil law countries, perhaps most clearly in France, much the same judicial recognition was established by the *juges des enfants*.

The Gillick test

The 'gold standard' on the legal validity of a child's consent is provided by the landmark decision *Gillick v. West Norfolk and Wisbech Area Health Authority*.[9] In that case, the House of Lords ruled that in some circumstances a doctor

4 Compare, for example, the declaration in article 42A of the Irish Constitution that 'the State recognises and affirms the natural and imprescriptible rights of all children and shall, as far as practicable, by its laws protect and vindicate those rights' with the very few specific rights that have ever been judicially recognised.

5 [1986] I AC 112, HL.

6 See, *FN v. CO* [2004] 4 I.R. 311, per Finlay Geoghegan J, at p 322.

7 *N v. N* [2008] IEHC 382.

8 [2012] IEHC 188.

9 Ibid.

could prescribe contraceptives for a child under the age of 16 years without consulting the child's parents. Since then the legal standing of a child in any decision-making process affecting his or her interests has depended upon their age and their understanding of the issues involved. As Lord Scarman explained,

> a minor's capacity to make his or her decision depends upon the minor having sufficient understanding and intelligence to make the decision and is not to be determined by reference to any judicially fixed age limit.

In effect, the rationale of the *Gillick* test or of any similar rule is that there should be a tapered relationship between a child (according to their age/maturity) and the child's parents regarding the right to take decisions relating to that child's welfare interests. The wishes of an older child, usually not less than 16 years of age, will be presumptively determinative; but much will turn on the gravity of the matter at issue, the child's understanding of the context, of the options available and of the related arguments for choosing; and also their grasp of the likely consequences of any decision made. Additionally, there are some entirely anomalous circumstances – due, perhaps, to a lacuna in the law – in which it would seem neither age nor maturity are factors: the law has preordained a transition from welfare interests to rights.

Jurisdictional differences and their significance

Where a child is aged 16 years, or though younger is deemed to be '*Gillick* competent', the law in the UK now requires that the child's consent be sought in relation to the matter at issue. In Ireland, the traditional rule requiring the views to be sought and taken into account prevails: there is neither statutory provision nor caselaw granting a child the right to make legally binding decisions. The *Gillick* ruling is loosely followed in many common law jurisdictions where it permits a degree of legal decision-making by older children. In Ireland, there is no requirement in any legislation for a child's consent on a matter affecting the child's welfare though the consent of a child aged 16 years or over will most usually be sought in respect of a surgical, medical or dental procedure. In neither France nor Germany is there any equivalent to that ruling: there are very few matters in relation to which a child, aged 16 years or younger, can unilaterally give a legally binding consent; in both it generally serves as little more than a judicial reference point and has little if any application to children in Indigenous communities.

In the U.S. the age of consent is not federally determined, it varies from state to state from age 16 to 18 years, and it varies again according to whether the issue arises in a civil or criminal context. While the concept of an 'emancipated minor' is relevant, it requires evidence of a good deal more independence than is necessitated by the '*Gillick* test'.[10] Some statutes stipulate that this concept needs to be

10 *Gillick v. West Norfolk and Wisbech Area Health Authority* (1985) 2 A11 ER 402.

substantiated by minors demonstrating their independence by living and supporting themselves away from their parents. Otherwise, in general, only in the absence of conflict with parental authority are U.S. courts willing to permit minors to make independent decisions.[11] There is, however, caselaw indicating a level of equivalence with the *Gillick* test: an unemancipated mature minor may give a valid consent to medical treatment where the procedure is for the benefit of the minor and, in the judgment of the treating physician, the minor has sufficient intelligence to understand its nature and consequences.[12] Alternatively, in *re E.G.*,[13] the Illinois Supreme Court seemed to give precedence to the importance of parental authority when it asserted that if a parent were to oppose a child's refusal of life-saving treatment, "this opposition would weigh heavily against the minor's right to refuse". Whether this statement of principle would transcend the gravity of such circumstances may be open to question.

In both the U.S. and Canada, the capacity of a child aged less than 18 years to give valid consent to sex, to accessing contraceptives or abortion, is determined by a combination of age and maturity; if 16 years of age or older, there woud be a presumption of capacity.[14] In Canada the consent of a child aged 12 years or older is a requirement for his or her adoption. Many states in the U.S. accept as legally valid the consent of an underage child to medical treatment, the giving or refusal of consent from a child aged 12 years or older to post-adoption contact arrangements with birth family, and the right of a mother of any age to place her child for adoption. In both jurisdictions the caselaw shows a definite judicial reluctance to let adolescents, under the age of 16 years, take decisions that may result in their death. As Abella J for the SCC explained in *A.C. v. Manitoba (Director of Child and Family Services)*,[15] 'mature adolescents . . . have strong claims to autonomy, but these claims exist in tension with a protective duty on the part of the state that is justified by the difficulty of defining and identifying *maturity*'. She went on to express a view with which the judiciary in other jurisdictions would most likely concur: the ability of adolescents to make treatment decisions "is ultimately calibrated in accordance with maturity, not age".[16] When the decision to be taken is in relation to abortion, in the face of parental opposition, the judiciary have less difficulty in respecting the adolescent's decision. In Australia, New Zealand and elsewhere, until a child reaches the age of 16 years, the law will seek the child's views in relation to matters such as medical treatment,[17] but it does not usually require their consent.

11 See, *Bakker v. Welsh*, 108 N.W. 94, 96 (Mich. 1906) and *Younts v. St. Francis Hosp. & Sch. of Nursing*, 469 P. 2d 330, 333 (Kan. 1970).

12 *Bishop v. Shurley*, 237 Mich. 76, 211 N.W. 75 (1926), *Lacey v. Laird*, 166 Ohio St. 12, 139 N.E. 2d 25 (1956) and *Younts v. St. Francis Hospital*, 205 Kan. 292, 469 P. 2d 330 (1970).

13 549 N.E. 2d 322, 328 (Ill. 1989).

14 *Carey v. Population Services International*, 431 U.S. 678 (1977).

15 *2009 SCC 30* [2009] 2 SCR 181, at para 86.

16 Ibid, at [111].

17 *Auckland Healthcare Services Ltd v. Liu*, High Court, Auckland, M812/96, (July 11, 1996).

Child's consent and the paramountcy principle

There is, clearly, a conflict between the legal effect of a child's consent and that of the paramountcy principle. In any legal proceedings where the principle is determinative, while the child concerned may wish to give or withhold their consent to an issue, it will fall to the court to decide whether such wishes satisfy the requirements of the principle. If the court, taking a long-term more holistic view, should determine that an alternative course of action that does not comply with the child's wishes is on balance the better option, then it is bound to set aside the child's consent, or lack thereof, and direct compliance with its preferred option. The paramountcy principle requires the court or other decision maker to stand aside from all other opinions, including the child's, and, after identifying and weighing the relative merits of all the options, to make such decision as it considers most conducive to furthering the welfare interests of that particular child, with or without the latter's consent.

Determination of interests by child

Judicial recognition of a child's capacity to contribute to, or in some cases determine, decisions affecting their upbringing, while in itself an improvement in their legal status, lacked functionality until legal and other forms of representation became available. Not until the mandatory appointment of guardians *ad litem* to 'give voice' to the child's wishes and to advocate on their behalf, did the child's welfare interests begin to impact proceedings; not until granted full party status in certain proceedings did the child then have the opportunity to assert their welfare interests, instruct a lawyer and play a more effective role in determining proceedings (see, further, later).

Circumstances in which a child's consent is determinative

There are few issues or areas of law on which there is jurisdictional consistency regarding the right of a child to give a legally binding consent. However, there are some circumstances which seem to attract much the same jurisdictional response such as sexual relationships and minor medical treatment (dentistry, etc.) to which a child aged 14 years or less cannot give a valid legal consent. Only in certain circumstances – such as sexual intercourse, access to contraceptives and medical/dental treatment – would the consent of a child aged 16 years be legally valid. Until they reach that age, then in Australia, New Zealand and elsewhere, while the law seeks a child's views in relation to matters such as medical treatment,[18] it does not, usually, require their consent. Given such restrictions, it seems somewhat of an anomaly that in adoption proceedings some Australian states require the consent of a child aged 12 years or older as a prerequisite for their adoption. There are also a scattering of seemingly random matters on which various jurisdictions require or

18 Ibid.

permit a child's consent to authorise a process. So, for example, in France, if the child is older than 13 years, then the child's personal consent is mandatory for both a plenary[19] and a simple adoption.[20]

SEXUAL RELATIONS

Most commonly the law permits a child of not less than 16 years of age to give a valid consent to sexual relations. In England and Wales, for example, the Sexual Offences Act 2003 expressly recognises that a child, aged between 16 and 18 years, can give such consent. In both France and Germany, once a child has attained the age of 15 years, then the child can normally give or withhold a valid legal consent in a range of situations – such as to dental treatment and to a sexual relationship – but any younger and their consent alone would be insufficient.

ADOPTION

In neither England and Wales nor in Ireland is there any statutory requirement that the consent of a child be obtained for their adoption, though this is a necessity in some U.S. states and in all Canadian provinces and territories where it is most usually a prerequisite for any child aged 12 years or older. It is not a requirement in New Zealand, but in some Australian states the consent of a child aged 12 years or older must be obtained. In France a child's legal right to give or withhold consent to their adoption (whether plenary or simple) is conditional upon their being 13 years of age or older, and a similar right is available to a German child aged 14 years or older.

GUARDIANSHIP

In Australia, the consent of the child concerned, if aged 12 years or older, is a prerequisite for a guardianship order.

RESPITE CARE

In New Zealand, the provision of state respite care is conditional upon the consent of the child concerned, if aged 12 years or older, if the respite is for an extended period.

STATE CARE

In England and Wales, under s 20 of the 1989 Act, if a child is aged 16 years or more and consents to being accommodated (and this is judged to be necessary on welfare grounds), or to being discharged from accommodation, then a local

19 See, article 345 of the Civil Code.

20 See Art. 360 *in fine* of the Civil Code: L'adoption simple est permise quel que soit l'âge de l'adopté. (. . .) Si l'adopté est âgé de plus de treize ans, il doit consentir personnellement à l'adoption.

authority is obliged to give effect to that consent. A child of that age may not be removed from such accommodation without his or her consent.[21] In Germany a child of any age – even if aged seven years or younger – can request and require the *Jugendamt* to take him or her into care.[22]

GENDER TRANSITIONING

The age at which children can give a valid legal consent to irreversible puberty blockers is 18 years in France and Australia where at medical discretion it could be younger; 16 years in Ireland and New Zealand, and much the same in Germany depending on maturity; but is now 18 years or older in England and Wales.[23] In Canada there is no consensus, a child of 15 years of age was judged entitled to give consent in 2020 despite his father's wishes, but later that year a mother challenged the right of her 17-year-old daughter to undergo trans surgery. In the U.S. the age threshold varies from state to state, but it is generally argued that it is unlawful to prescribe puberty-blocking drugs to children under the age of 18 years as they lack competence to give a valid consent.

The ancillary issue of how old a child needs to be before a parent's consent will be sufficient to authorise such treatment is another matter.

Courts and regulatory framework

As the child acquired the status of a legal entity, so the legal system and family law more broadly were required to adapt to accommodate this new role. The ways in which the legal system has shaped and, more recently, been shaped by the principle of the welfare of the child is an important dimension to the transition from welfare to rights and one which reflects the principle's capacity to also generate structural change and contribute to a fundamental reconfiguration of family law.

The legislative framework

As France and Germany belong to the civil law tradition, the main body of domestic law lies in their respective Civil Codes and, also in both cases, the Codes together with other legislation and regulations shelter under constitutional umbrellas as reinforced by international treaties and conventions, etc. While amendments to the Civil Codes of both countries have provided a modernised body of law relating to children, it should be noted that the CRC in 2022 found the German Code to be weighted in favour of parents and recommended that the government 'strengthen efforts to incorporate children's rights explicitly into the Basic Law'.[24] The common law nations rely on a domestic body of subject-specific legislation, amended

21 The Children's Act 1989, s 20(11).
22 Op. cit., s 42(1).
23 *ABCD v. Tavistock*, EWCA Civ 1363.
24 CRC/C/DEU/CO/5-6, at para 6.

or replaced as necessary, and in some cases additional protection is provided by constitutions that state broad principles and by the same international treaties and conventions, etc. By the closing decades of the 20th century, the common law nations currently being studied had introduced or were preparing to introduce legislation to reform their laws relating to children: prioritising their welfare interests, giving recognition to the UN CROC principles, and firmly separating the civil and criminal jurisdictions.

The courts

Both France and Germany have a similar hierarchy of national courts and ancillary regulatory bodies, etc., are subject to the ECtHR appeal process and to CRC monitoring in respect of children's welfare interests and rights. This is not dissimilar to the equivalent common law hierarchy. By the turn of the century, the traditional civil and common law court hierarchies had made room for new child-specific forums such as the Children's Ombudsman, Children's Commissions, Special Rapporteurs, etc. In tandem with these structural innovations, new government posts, such as Minister for Children, were introduced for the similar purpose of ensuring the prioritisation of children's welfare interests and rights at all levels.

Child participation

The courtroom is obviously the most critical forum for decisions affecting the welfare interests of a child and for the exercise of their rights. The formalities and conduct of proceedings can be intimidating, and to many incomprehensible, which detracts from children's ability to participate and therefore from their perception of having had a fair hearing. As a general rule, proceedings should ensure that a child's age, level of maturity and emotional capacities are taken into account,[25] while the Lanzarote Convention adds that the effective participation of children in proceedings must be 'treated as priority and carried out without any unjustified delay', advice that is reiterated in CRC General Comment No. 10. It also provides rules for interviews with the child, which must be carried out, again without unjustified delay, by professionals trained and in premises designed for this purpose (see, also, Chapter 3).

Right to be heard

The extent to which a child is authorised to participate in proceedings affecting their welfare interests – to have legal or other representation, to give consent to validate decisions taken relating to those interests – and whether their participation is age dependent, are matters that determine whether the child is being treated as the subject of, or as a party to, those proceedings. UN CROC, Article 12, states that

25 See, *T. v. the United Kingdom* [GC], Application No. 24724/94, (1999), at para 61.

a child has the right to express his or her opinions freely and the right to have those opinions taken into account in any matter or procedure affecting the child. This is subject to the caveat that the child concerned must be capable of forming his or her own views. Due weight, commensurate with the age and maturity of the child, must be given to those views. ECHR, Article 8, implicitly requires that a child be involved in any decision-making process related to the child's family and private life.[26] Depending on the age and maturity of the child concerned, the child must be provided with the right to be consulted and heard in order to protect his or her best interests: due weight must be given to the child's views and feelings as well as to the child's right to respect for his or her private life;[27] as regards very young children, the courts must rely on an expert assessment.[28]

It is probable that, whenever possible, the judiciary have generally sought to engage directly with children in the course of proceedings concerning their welfare, perhaps by inviting comments from the child and very often by retiring from the courtroom, de-robing and informally chatting to the child. The more formal involvement of a child in proceedings, at the latter's initiative, was a development endorsed in 1985 by the Beijing Rules, Rule 14(2), which by emphasising that proceedings were to be carried out in 'an atmosphere of understanding' encouraged child participation.

Consent and legal representation

UN CROC, Articles 13 and 14, state the right of a child to self-determination, dignity, respect, non-interference and the right to make informed decisions. The Oviedo Convention, Article 6 (2),[29] provides that the opinion of the child must be taken into consideration 'as an increasingly determining factor in proportion to his or her age and degree of maturity'. The Council of Europe *Guidelines on Child Friendly Justice* advise that children should have their own legal representation in proceedings where there is a potential conflict between their welfare interests and the interests of others.

Just as there is no jurisdictional consensus on whether a child should be entitled to directly address the court, there is none on which proceedings or legal representation for such a child should be mandatory. There are also very few circumstances in as few countries where a child's consent is absolutely necessary (the adoption of a child aged 14 years or older being generally an exception) or has absolute independent validity. Nonetheless, where a child of more than 12 years of age and of sufficient maturity to understand the matter at issue and its significance wishes to give or withhold consent to a decision in relation to that issue, the courts will

26 See, *Sahin v. Germany*, Application No. 30943/96, (2003) and *Sommerfield v. Germany*, Application No. 31871/96, (2003).

27 See, *N.TS. and Others v. Georgia*, Application No. 71776/12, (2016).

28 See, *Neves Caratão Pinto v. Portugal*, Application No. 28443/19, (2021).

29 Convention for the Protection of Human Rights and Dignity of the Human Being with Regard to the Application of Biology and Medicine (Convention on Human Rights and Biomedicine), 1979.

generally at least take the child's views into account. Further, at least in the context of civil proceedings, a court is unlikely to make a determination that is in direct opposition to a child's declared preference.

Jurisdictional differences and their significance

The right to be heard has generated official guidance[30] in England and Wales, and there is judicial recognition of a child's right to be heard in proceedings affecting their upbringing.[31] In Ireland, although Article 42A.4.2. of the Constitution provides similar recognition, it is inadequately addressed. The U.S. Supreme Court has declared that:[32]

> the Juvenile Court is theoretically engaged in determining the needs of the child and of society rather than adjudicating criminal conduct. The objectives are to provide measures of guidance and rehabilitation for the child and protection for society, not to fix criminal responsibility, guilt and punishment.

However, there does not appear to be any hard and fast rules on the right of a child to be heard on matters affecting their interests in either the U.S. or the Canadian courts: though in the U.S. there is a long-standing attempt to lend judicial authority in support of allowing a child to directly and in person address the court on matters of importance during the course of proceedings, but that minority opinion has never been unequivocally endorsed,[33] nor has it in Canada, where the lack of firm judicial recognition of this right has attracted criticism from the UN Committee on the Rights of the Child.[34] In New Zealand, the Family Court (Supporting Children in Court) Legislation Act 2021, s 5(g), introduced a new principle requiring ("must") a child to be given reasonable opportunities to participate in decisions. In Australia, the child's right to be heard is at the judge's discretion though the Family Law Act 1975, s 60CC(3)(a), does impose a requirement that the court 'consider any views expressed by a child in deciding whether to make a particular parenting order in relation to the child'. France has a singular approach to children who, for whatever reason, come before the courts. Their needs and deeds are then viewed as symptomatic of family vulnerability or dysfunction which requires 'education' in the form of assistance from social workers, psychologists and other state-employed experts in family dynamics. Accordingly, the *juge des enfants* exercises both a civil

30 See, the Family Justice Council, *Guidelines for Judges Meeting Children who are Subject to Family Proceedings*, April 2010 [2010] 2 FLR 1872 and *Guidelines in Relation to Children Giving Evidence in Family Proceedings*, December 2011 [2012] Fam Law 70.

31 *Re D (A Child) Abduction; Rights of Custody* [2007] IAC 619 and *Re D (A Child) (International Recognition)* [2016] EWCA Civ 12, per Lady Hale, at para 44.

32 *Kent v. United States*, 383 U.S. 541, 544 (1966).

33 *Wisconsin v. Yoder*, 406 U.S. 205, 241–249 (1972), per Douglas J, at pp 244–245.

34 See, the U.N. Committee on the Rights of the Child, 61st session, C/CAN/CO/3-4, October 2012, at paras 36 and 37.

and criminal jurisdiction, and since the extension of the judicial remit in 1958, this includes a discretion to authorise *assistance educative.*[35] The French approach is also singular in the way the legal system relates to children. The *juge des enfants* has a duty to hear directly from any child who wishes to be heard and is *capable de discernement* unless their age or state of mind does not allow it.[36] In Germany, a child of any age has a constitutional right to be heard in the Family Court on a matter concerning them.[37] Moreover, if aged 14 years or older, the child may, if the child so wishes, represent themselves without the need of a legal representative. This includes the right of a child of that age to bring a maintenance claim against their parent(s) before the Family Court,[38] and the child may also file an application for interim measures in all matters affecting them.[39]

As regards representation, not until the mandatory appointment of guardians *ad litem* in the UK to 'give voice' to the child's wishes and to advocate on their behalf in Family Court proceedings in all matters concerning the child, when necessary to protect their welfare interests,[40] did the child's welfare interests begin to impact proceedings and not until granted full party status in certain proceedings did the child then have the opportunity to assert their welfare interests, instruct a lawyer and play a more effective role in determining proceedings. The Children and Family Court Advisory and Support Service (Cafcass), established in 2001, revolutionalised court services by amalgamating all those relating to children into one body. Further change occurred in 2014 with the introduction of the Family Court. While the child in the UK is now a party in public law proceedings, and the appointment of a children's guardian and a lawyer is the norm,[41] in private law proceedings they are rarely parties and are therefore without representation, though this may be directed[42] where there is 'an issue of significant difficulty'. In Ireland, the Child Care Act 1991 confers a discretionary power, rather than a duty, on the court to appoint a solicitor and otherwise leaves the guardian *ad litem* (GAL) to act as the child's representative.[43] There is therefore less probability of a child being granted representation in Irish than in equivalent English proceedings. In the U.S., 'due process' in theory requires that a child be represented by a lawyer, but in practice many child offenders are not represented: in child protection cases only

35 The *Cour de Cassation* has ruled that jurisdiction in respect of *assistance éducative* proceedings is exclusive to the *juge des enfants* and has denied the *juge aux affaires familiales* any jurisdiction to order educational measures.

36 The Civil Code, article 388–1.

37 The Act on Court Procedure in family Matters and Non-Litigious Matters, ss 9(1) and 167(3).

38 The Act on Court Procedure in family Matters and Non-Litigious Matters, ss 9(1), 60 and 167(3).

39 Ibid, ss 9(1) and 167(3).

40 The Act on Court Procedure in Family Matters and Non-Litigious Matters, s 50.

41 A guardian must be appointed for the child unless the court is 'satisfied that it is not necessary to do so in order to safeguard his interests' (Children Act 1989, s 41(1)).

42 The Family Procedure Rules 2010, Practice Direction 16A.

43 The Child Care (Amendment) Bill 2021 proposes to clarify, consolidate and extend the role of the GAL as child advocate in care and protection proceedings and to provide a GAL with an entitlement, in certain circumstances, to legal representation.

32 states make provision for such representation. In general the practice is to assign a GAL to provide a report on welfare interests of the child but not representation for the child's rights. In both the U.S. and Canada, the requirement to ensure that a child has the right to make informed decisions is subject to the view of a judge or regulator that any such decision is compatible with what the judge or regulator considers is in the best interests of that child. As Canadian children do not normally have party status in family law generally, let alone in child protection proceedings, they therefore do not automatically qualify for legal representation, nor indeed for the legal aid often necessary to pay for it;[44] but in a number of provinces (Alberta, Ontario and Québec), lawyers are commonly appointed to represent the interests of children in child protection cases and may advocate for the outcome desired by the child. In New Zealand, under the Care of Children Act 2004, s 7, a lawyer is to be appointed for a child in all proceedings under the act, unless there are exceptional circumstances rendering that appointment inappropriate.[45] The corresponding Australian provisions seem more permissive: the Family Law Act 1975 leaves the crucial matter of legal representation to be determined by an exercise of judicial discretion, even if this is subsequently expanded by a directive that requires 'the independent children's lawyer for the child to ensure that the child's views are fully put before the court'. In France, as in Germany, a parent is their child's legal representative but, unlike a similar child in Germany, a child has party status in proceedings regarding their welfare and may, therefore, elect to be legally represented. In Germany, unlike France, the child subject of proceedings will mostly be supported by a GAL who will elicit their views, ascertain their welfare interests and advocate on their behalf before the judge. However, in neither country does a child have an automatic right to legal representation. German law provides for the mandatory appointment of a GAL in Family Court proceedings in all matters concerning the child,[46] whenever necessary to protect their welfare interests,[47] unless those interests are adequately represented by a lawyer or another appropriate legal representative. There is no equivalent requirement in France where the approach may offer informality at the price of due process. In all jurisdictions, as mentioned previously, the law relating to the consent of a child at best tends to be guarded.

Access to justice: civil proceedings

As guaranteed under Article 6 of the ECHR and more broadly in the U.S. under the Constitution's 'due process' clause, access to justice is a composite right of

44 Note that 'in some jurisdictions, such as British Columbia, the government gives no funding for legal representation for children and has actively opposed this prospect' as reported in the Canadian Bar Association (Child and Youth Law Section), *Alternative Report to the UN Committee on the Rights of the Child*, 2020, Op. cit., at p 33.

45 See, further, Practice Note: Lawyer for the Child: Code of Conduct, 2007, www.justice.govt.nz/courts/family-court/practice-and-procedure/practice-notes/lawyer-for-the-child

46 The prompt appointment of a guardian to advise and support an unaccompanied migrant child is also mandatory in Germany.

47 The Act on Court Procedure in family Matters and Non-Litigious Matters, s 50.

fundamental importance, encompassing an entitlement to equality before the law and to equality of protection by it. Access to a legal system that complies with the principles of child-friendly justice[48]: ensures the right of children to express their views freely and for those views to be heard[49] and taken into account on matters that concern them, in accordance with their age and maturity; is attentive to the child's right to dignity and psychological integrity if they are to avoid further victimisation,[50] especially in respect of those who have been sexually abused as they are particularly vulnerable; adheres to a presumption of innocence and a fair trial; respects due process; and provides an effective remedy.

Generally, of the eight jurisdictions presently being considered, seven make a clear distinction between public child care and protection and the criminal justice systems, and in the latter the role and weighting of the welfare principle tends to be quite marginal. Only France would seem, as a matter of public policy, to blur the distinction between behaviour that is criminal and warranting prosecution with its particular set of disposal options and behaviour indicative of a troubled child in need of supportive services.

Again, of the eight jurisdictions, seven have ratified UN CROC (the U.S. being the exception) and have struggled with the uncertainty surrounding 'paramountcy'. At times, the ECtHR links paramountcy to public family law (child protection), other times it seems to suggest a private law linkage (rights of parents and child) but on several occasions it has ruled that the paramountcy principle should apply to "all decisions concerning children".[51] There are problems with the latter proposition. One is that there are definite circumstances in which children's welfare interests are not accorded a paramount weighting in law.[52] Another is that the welfare interests of a child may be so entangled with those of a parent (most often mother and baby) that separating their interests is not feasible: the symbiotic relationship of mutual attachment is the natural and primary vehicle that determines the child's welfare interests; intervention risks reversing the desired outcome and causing long-term damage to the child's welfare interests.

48 See, 'Guidelines of the Committee of Ministers of the Council of Europe on child-friendly justice', Council of Europe Publishing, 2010, https://rm.coe.int/16804b2cf3

49 This right is recognised not just by article 12 of UN CROC but also by both article 24(1) of the EU Charter of Fundamental Rights and by article 21 of the Brussels IIa Regulation (recast).

50 See, *G.U. v. Turkey*, Application No. 16143/10, (2016).

51 See, also, the *CRC General Comment No. 14 (2013) on the Right of the Child to have His or Her Best Interests Taken as a Primary Consideration.*

52 Most obviously, in a criminal context the welfare interests of a child are clearly subordinate to the interests of justice: judicial attention focuses on accountability, punishment, proportionality, reparation and social rehabilitation rather than on the indicators of welfare. In the context of illegal migration, priority is given to upholding the government's immigration laws rather than welfare interests, while under the Hague Convention priority is given to upholding comity between nations. Welfare interests are also not prioritised in matters such as choice of out-of-home placements, conditions in asylum and secure accommodation, and decisions regarding refugee status. Moreover, they have no relevance to uncontested divorce and separation proceedings where, by far, the majority of judicial decisions affecting welfare interests are taken.

Right to a 'child-friendly' legal system

A child has the right – under Article 6 of the Council of Europe Convention on the Exercise of Children's Rights[53] – to proceedings conducted in an age-appropriate manner that engages the child and confirms their understanding of the law and its significance.

Generally, the modern approach to children in court is one that endeavours to be holistic in nature, one that fully takes into account their particular needs and perceptions. This requires a child-friendly legal system, the key objective of which, according to Article 40 of UN CROC, is to reintegrate children into society. The younger the child is, the more difficult – and the more necessary – it will be to ensure the legal system functions in a child-friendly manner. The need for such a system was illustrated in *R.B. v. Estonia*[54] which concerned a four-year-old sexually abused child, R.B., who alleged a violation of her rights under Articles 3 (prohibition of torture) and 8 (right to respect of private and family life). The ECtHR agreed. Estonia's law had not been adapted to meet the Court's requirements, which required less strict rules for the testimony of children. It found that the Estonian justice system failed to be child-friendly as, in relation to the questioning of witnesses, it did not distinguish between procedural rules for adults and children.

Representation/participation: jurisdictional differences

As a general rule, proceedings should ensure that the child's age, level of maturity and emotional capacities are taken into account,[55] while the Lanzarote Convention adds that the effective participation of children in proceedings must be 'treated as priority and carried out without any unjustified delay', advice that is reiterated in CRC General Comment No. 10. It also provides rules for interviews with the child, which must be carried out without unjustified delays, by professionals trained for this purpose and in premises designed for this purpose.

One aspect of effective participation is the child's right to be heard, and the CRC have drawn attention to the need for this right to be exercised.[56] It is probable that judicial willingness to allow for this right would be strongest in the U.S.[57] In Ireland, Article 42A established a constitutional duty, resting on the court, to ascertain the views of children, though for some years there had been a recognition that under Article 40.3 children had a procedural right to be heard in cases affecting them.[58] In England and Wales a child's views, his or her evidence, and how these

53 CETS No. 160, 1996.

54 Application No. 22597/16, (2021). See, also, *G.U. v. Turkey*, Application No. 16143/10, (2016).

55 See, *T. v. the United Kingdom* [GC], Application No. 24724/94, (1999), at para 61.

56 United Nations, Committee on the Rights of the Child (CRC), *General Comment No. 12 (2009) on the Right of the Child to be Heard*, CRC/C/GC/12, July 1, 2009.

57 See, *Kent v. United States*, 383 U.S. 541, 544 (1966).

58 See, *FN v. CO* [2004] 4 IR 311, per Finlay Geoghegan J, at p 322.

are brought before the court, have been the subject of a range of judicial rulings[59] and guidance[60] over the last decade or two. In New Zealand, since the turn of the century, the statutory law[61] has required that a child's views should be brought before the court;[62] which, of course, does not necessarily mean that the child, rather than their legal representative, will be permitted to do so in person. There is no similarly worded concession in Australian law.

France has a singular approach to children who, for whatever reason, come before the courts. Their needs and deeds are then viewed as symptomatic of family vulnerability or dysfunction which requires 'education' in the form of assistance from social workers, psychologists and other state-employed experts in family dynamics. Accordingly, the *juge des enfants* exercises both a civil and criminal jurisdiction, and since the extension of the judicial remit in 1958, this includes a discretion to authorise *assistance éducative*.[63] The French approach is also singular in the way the legal system relates to children. There is no courtroom as such, the judge conducts proceedings in their office where all parties, including the child, are encouraged to speak directly to the judge. Legal representation is rare, and the judge's role is less adjudicative but more that of a mediator whose aim is to encourage parents and child to consent to the appropriate steps needed to address the presenting issues. The Civil Code directive that the *juge des enfants* should 'always strive to obtain family's consent to the measure envisaged' highlights the importance given to considerations of welfare rather than justice and is indicative of underlying state deference to family integrity.

In Germany, children aged 14 years or older can act in all matters affecting them without the participation of their legal representative.[64] This includes the right of a child of that age to bring a maintenance claim against their parent(s) before the Family Court,[65] and the child may also file an application for interim measures in all matters affecting them, without the need for a legal representative.[66] The appointment of a GAL is mandatory in Family Court proceedings in all matters concerning the child, when necessary to protect their welfare interests,[67] There are no specific

59 See, for example, *Re D (A Child) (Abduction: Rights of Custody)* [2006] UKHL 51, [2007] 1 FLR 961, per Lady Hale and *Re D (A Child) (International Recognition)* [2016] EWCA Civ 12; [2016] 2 FLR 347, per Ryder LJ.

60 See, the Family Justice Council, *Guidelines for Judges Meeting Children Who are Subject to Family Proceedings*, April 2010 [2010] 2 FLR 1872 and *Guidelines in Relation to Children Giving Evidence in Family Proceedings*, December 2011 [2012] Fam Law 70.

61 Oranga Tamariki Act 1989, s 11, and the Care of Children Act 2004, s 6(2).

62 Now, in New Zealand, under the Family Court (Supporting Children in Court) Legislation Act 2021, s 59(g), a child 'must' be given reasonable opportunities to participate in decisions.

63 The *Cour de Cassation* has ruled that jurisdiction in respect of *assistance éducative* proceedings is exclusive to the *juge des enfants* and has denied the *juge aux affaires familiales* any jurisdiction to order educational measures.

64 The Act on Court Procedure in family Matters and Non-Litigious Matters, s 112.

65 Ibid, ss 9(1), 60 and 167(3).

66 Ibid, ss 9(1) and 167(3).

67 The Act on Court Procedure in family Matters and Non-Litigious Matters, s 50.

rules requiring a child-friendly court environment, nor are there any legal measures explicitly stipulating that a child can be examined *in camera*, behind a screen or through a video link. However, as far as possible, the child has to be informed in an appropriate manner about the subject matter, the issues and the possible results of the proceedings,[68] and a child of any age has a constitutional right to be heard in the Family Court on a matter concerning them, but only if older than 14 years of age can the child act on all matters affecting them without necessarily having a legal representative.[69]

Right to have welfare interests protected: primary/paramount

There is a sense in which the welfare interests of a child have become a right. Even though the Convention does not explicitly list the child's best interests as one of the rights and freedoms it proclaims, the concept of the child's best interests is implicitly present in Article 8 of the ECHR, which guarantees the right to respect for one's private and family life. This is supported by a number of ECtHR rulings which maintain that states have a duty to protect the best interests of the child.[70]

The question remains, however, as to the weighting that should be given to welfare interests relative to other matters: primary or paramount? dependent upon context? upon the gravity of the issue? Article 3(1) of UN CROC and Article 24(2) of the European Social Charter have declared in favour of 'primary consideration', while the Convention on the Elimination of All Forms of Discrimination against Women requires states to ensure that 'in all cases the interests of the children shall be paramount' (see, also, Chapter 1), and the CRC has issued guidance to aid interpretation.[71] The ECtHR, however, has equivocated. The Court has noted that "since the adoption of the [CRC], 'the best interests of the child' in all matters concerning it . . . have been paramount in child protection issues",[72] "it was a principle of good law to hold that the interests of the child were paramount";[73] "the Court reiterates that in judicial decisions where the rights under Article 8 of parents and those of a child are at stake, the child's rights must be the paramount consideration";[74] and that "there is currently a broad consensus – including in international law – in support of the idea that in all decisions concerning children, their best interests must be paramount";[75] but three years later, while the Court repeated the latter form of words, it added the caveat "whilst alone they cannot be decisive, such

68 The Act on Voluntary Jurisdiction, s 50b(2).

69 The Act on Court Procedure in Family Matters and Non-litigious Matters, ss 9(1) and 167(3).

70 See, for example, *Maumousseau and Washington v. France,* Application No. 41615/07, (2011) where "the Court notes that since the adoption of the [CRC], 'the best interests of the child' in all matters concerning it . . . have been paramount in child protection issues".

71 *General Comment No. 14 (2013) on the Right of the Child to have His or Her Best Interests Taken as a Primary Consideration.*

72 *Maumousseau and Washington v. France*, Op. cit.

73 *Kroon v. The Netherlands* (1994) Series A No 297 – C, 19 EHRR 263.

74 *Yousef v. The Netherlands* [2003] 1 FLR 210, at para 73.

75 *Neulinger and Shuruk v. Switzerland,* Application No. 41615/07, (2010).

interests certainly must be afforded significant weight".[76] Leaving aside for the present, whether these statements hold true in respect of 'all decisions concerning children',[77] why the consensus supports an 'idea' rather than a 'right', how 'best interests' can be both paramount but not decisive and what exactly is meant by 'significant weight', they clearly all imply a corresponding reduction in the relative significance of other factors. In particular, they serve to devalue the rights of parents and thereby, arguably, undermine from within the fundamental premise of family law that the integrity of the family unit is entitled to protection.

Right to prompt decision-making

Delay in the decision-making processes of court or other authority can be particularly harmful to children who – because of their need to form the attachments crucial for emotional and psychological development – require settled and trusted boundaries sooner rather than later. The welfare interests of a child, subject to protracted processes, may be compromised because of the "danger that any procedural delay will result in the *de facto* determination of the issue submitted to the court before it has held its hearing".[78] The ECtHR has cited particular circumstances giving rise to delay that had been prejudicial to welfare interests: the complexity of the case,[79] the conduct of the applicant and the other parties,[80] the conduct of the relevant authorities,[81] and the nature of matters at stake for the applicant in the litigation.[82] More recently, in *K.B. and Others v. Croatia*,[83] the ECtHR found that delays in the proceedings, resulting in a failure to secure a mother's regular contact with her sons, violated her right to respect for family life. These cases, and many others in a similar vein, indicate that in recent years the judiciary have become much more cognisant of the possible damaging psychosocial implications of decision-making delays affecting the welfare interests of children

Jurisdictional differences and their significance

In England and Wales, the volume of public and private family proceedings generated a need for a more coherent family court system, with specially trained judiciary

76 *Jeunesse v. the Netherlands,* Application No. 12738/10, (2014).

77 The accuracy of this statement must, surely, be questionable at the very least in the context of juvenile justice.

78 See, *W. v. The UK,* Application No. 9749/82, (1987), at para 65.

79 See *Glasser v. United Kingdom* [2001] 1 FLR 153.

80 See *Glasser* (Ibid), and *Hokkanen v. Finland* [1944] 19 EHRR 139, [1996] 1 FLR 289, where, in both cases, the delay was attributable to the party awarded custody refusing to comply with the terms of contact orders. More recently, see *Pini and Others v. Romania* [2004] EHRR 275.

81 See *Bock v. Germany* [1990] 12 EHRR 247, where the court held that there had been a breach of article 6 by the delay resulting from domestic courts seeking an unnecessary number of reports.

82 See *H v. United Kingdom* [1988] 10 EHRR 95, where the court noted that the irreversibility of adoption proceedings was a factor in the adopters' failure to apply promptly. Also, see, *Mikulic v. Croatia,* Application No. 53176/99, (2002).

83 Application No. 36216/13, (2017).

and other staff. This represents a significant differentiating jurisdictional characteristic, one reinforced by a sophisticated menu of court orders, many equally applicable across both public and private sectors. In that jurisdiction, unlike Ireland, there is now a legislative framework and a range of professionals and facilities specifically designated to separately address the civil and criminal conduct of children. In Ireland, as Kilkelly has noted, 'research into the operation of the Children Court has found serious problems, from a child's perspective, with the way the court operates . . . the proceedings themselves generally take place without the direct involvement of the children concerned'.[84]

Ensuring that children experience a 'child-friendly' legal system is an important aspect of giving effect to the welfare principle. This has become standard policy in most European countries. The court hearings in both France and Germany strive to be child friendly. This is most obvious in France where there is no courtroom as such, the judge conducts proceedings in their office, and the parties and the child are all encouraged to speak directly to the judge without the customary procedural stages. Legal representation is rare, and the judge's role is less adjudicative, more that of a mediator whose aim is to encourage parents and child to consent to the appropriate steps needed to address the presenting issues. In the CANZUS nations (Canada, Australia, New Zealand, United States), new tribal courts are beginning to be established to give Indigenous people, including children, a culturally appropriate context within which to consider the significance and consequences of their breaches of the law.

Decision-making processes can be slow. In *H v. United Kingdom*,[85] for example, the parent complained of the "deplorable delay" of almost two years in court proceedings concerning her contact application in relation to her child in local authority care. By the time the matter was brought before the court, almost three and a half years had elapsed since she had last seen her child who was by then well settled with prospective adopters. The ECtHR warned that "in cases of this kind the authorities are under a duty to exercise exceptional diligence". In Ireland, the shortage of adequate placements for troubled teenagers leads to delayed decision-making. This was illustrated in the case of *AF (a minor) v. Child and Family Agency*[86] when O'Regan J was faced with the respondent agency's claim that it had no placement available for AF and was unable to give any indication as to when a placement would be available, despite the acknowledged ongoing immediate risk to AF. In the U.S, following introduction of the Family First legislation, the court now requires stronger evidence than formerly that the issue of a termination of parental rights (TPR) order – totally severing parental ties – would necessarily be wholly compliant with a child's welfare interests. Raising the welfare threshold in this way leads to delays as judges now require 'compelling evidence'

84 See, Kilkelly, U., *Children's Rights in Ireland: Law, Policy and Practice*, Dublin, Tottel, 2008, at p 543.

85 Ibid., See, also, *Paulsen-Medalen and Svenson v. Sweden* (1998) 26 EHRR 260 and *Z.M. and K.P. v. Slovakia*, Application No. 50232/99, (May 11, 2005).

86 [2019] IEHC 435.

that a TPR is necessary. In Canada, the Charter, s 7, would seem to extend constitutional protection to the liberty of 'the person' – which could be interpreted as including family life – from any state intervention that does not derive from 'principles of fundamental justice', and the Supreme Court of Canada has ruled that the welfare principle cannot come within that definition.[87] As in the UK, there are concerns regarding the length of time unaccompanied minors seeking asylum wait in detention centres while their applications are processed. In New Zealand slow decision-making processes may help account for the fact that once any child is admitted to state care, there is a strong likelihood that the child will remain there: the percentage of children and young people in 'return to home' placements is low (less than 10%)[88] and is decreasing. Much the same policy prevails in Australia: the average child remains in foster care for approximately 12 years: consequently, for some one-third of those children, the links with their family of origin become so attenuated that they do not return home on discharge from foster care, indeed many are rendered homeless. The ECtHR has found the French state to be culpable for failing to effect prompt intervention resulting in preventable harm.[89] For example, in *Association Innocence en Danger v. France and Association Enfance et Partage v. France*,[90] when it was severely censored for not providing unaccompanied migrant minors with access to healthcare services (see, further, later). So, also, in *Affaire A.L, c. France*,[91] which concerned a child who was only four months old when contested proceedings began but was six-and-a-half years old when they concluded. In Germany, where the problem of unaccompanied migrant minors has been particularly acute, the CRC in its 2022 report was critical of the decision-making process for determining their status and expressed concern regarding 'lengthy stays by some asylum-seeking and refugee children in reception centres and collective accommodation facilities'.[92]

Of all eight jurisdictions, England and Wales has for some years had the strongest legislative commitment to upholding the paramountcy principle. In neither Canada nor the U.S. can the principle be said to have much of a role in domestic law. As the Inter-American Commission on Human Rights has commented in respect of the U.S., 'the principle of the best interests of the child is restricted to certain areas of the law that are related to child welfare and the family . . . it has not been made effective in all federal and state legislation and policies involving children'.[93] In Ireland and France, the principle has recently

87 *Canadian Foundation for Children, Youth and the Law v. Canada (Attorney General)* [2004] 1 SCR 76, [2004] SCC 4.

88 'Return to home' meaning return to a biological parent.

89 Note, however, that France launched a Global Action Plan 2015–2017 for the protection of children.

90 Application No. 15343/15, (2020).

91 Application No. 13344/20, (2022).

92 See, CRC/C/DEU/CO/5-6, at para 39.

93 See, the Inter-American Commission on Human Rights, *Children and Adolescents in the United States' Adult Criminal Justice System*, 2018, at p 136. See, further, www.oas.org/en/iachr/reports/pdfs/Children-USA.pdf

been incorporated into their constitutions, though it remains to be seen what effect that has. In both Australia and New Zealand, legislation applies the paramountcy principle to matters affecting the welfare of a child; the Family Law Act 1975, s 60CA, governing applications for parenting orders; and the *Oranga Tamariki* Act 1989, s 4A, in respect of any matter affecting 'the well-being and best interests of the child or young person'. In the former country, the Care of Children Act 2004, s 4, specifies that the welfare and best interests of a child must be the first and paramount considerations, and it provides, in s 5, a list of welfare indicators to aid interpretation and application of the principle. Much the same approach is evident in the latter country where the Children Act 2004, s 5, specifies a list of welfare indicators to aid interpretation and application of the principle (see, also, Chapter 8). In Australia, paramount weighting is given to a child's welfare interests in all applications for parenting orders[94] but is not applied, as in the UK, to every matter affecting a child's upbringing.[95] Similarly in New Zealand the paramountcy principle was asserted early and repeatedly in several domestic statutes. Although it has to be said that, legislative and UN CROC commitments notwithstanding, the principle would not seem to have positively changed the disproportionate flow of Indigenous and Māori children into the child welfare and juvenile justice systems nor the inordinate numbers of children in both jurisdictions who enter the child welfare system due to exposure to domestic violence. As regards Germany, where there is no unequivocal statement in law declaring that the welfare interests of the child must be treated as of paramount importance, the CRC has expressed concern 'that the principle of the best interests of the child is not being applied in all proceedings affecting children' and recommended that it be consistently applied 'in all policies, programmes and legislative, administrative and judicial proceedings affecting children, including in relation to trafficking and migration and asylum procedures'.[96]

Access to justice: criminal proceedings

International instruments have contributed to establishing a framework of principles for the guidance of national law and policy in relation to child offenders. So, for example, UN CROC has stated a number of governing principles including that states ensure the separation of juvenile and adult detainees and keep deprivation of liberty to a minimum (Article 37) and that states promote the rehabilitation of offenders in the community (Article 40). In addition, provisions of the European Convention on Human Rights and the Lanzarote Convention rules are also relevant.

94 Family Law Act 1975, s 60CA.

95 See, further, Young, L, 'Mature Minors and Parenting Disputes in Australia: Engaging with the Debate on Best Interests v. Autonomy', *UNSW Law Journal*, Vol. 42, No. 4, 2019.

96 CRC/C/DEU/CO/5-6, at para 16.

Justice systems: jurisdictional differences and their significance

The era when the justice system interpreted the unlawful deeds of children as symptomatic of psychosocial needs has long gone. In all jurisdictions – if to a lesser degree in France – the primary aim of the system is no longer oriented toward welfare but on protection of the public and the prevention of further offences.

In England and Wales, welfare in a justice context lost the paramountcy status assigned to it under the 1989 Act and indeed has little relevance as a threshold criterion at points of either entry or exit in criminal proceedings. This is not dissimilar to Irish policy which has been stated as focussed on 'diverting children from crime and the criminal justice system, promoting restorative justice, enforcing community sanctions, facilitating rehabilitation and, as a last resort, providing for detention'.[97]

In the U.S., there has been ongoing concern regarding the fact that states are not required to separate youths from adults in adult facilities and that 'a significant number of children are being consistently treated as adults in the U.S. criminal justice system'.[98] Moreover, children of African American descent are wholly disproportionately represented in the number of children processed by the U.S. juvenile justice system.[99] In sharp contrast to comparable practice elsewhere in the developed nations, the U.S. courtroom culture is one of oppressiveness for reasons that include the following: the child may be a good deal younger than elsewhere (possibly as young as six years old in North Carolina); the child may be deliberately treated in a demeaning manner, by being required to do 'the perp walk' and remaining shackled in court; and the child may not have the reassurance and guidance of a legal representative. In none of the other jurisdictions currently being studied is the court regime so calculatingly disrespectful of a child's welfare interests and so disregarding of their rights to privacy and dignity, most simply fail to make the adjustments necessary to respect the child and facilitate his or her understanding of court processes. This pronounced jurisdictional characteristic is compliant with neither the welfare principle nor with international standards. The Inter-American Commission on Human Rights, in its 2018 report, deplored[100]

> the consistent use of full restraints, including handcuffs and belly- and ankle-shackles on youth. This practice, known as "shackling," is uniformly applied to all youth in the justice system, regardless of whether they represent a risk of danger or escape. Its use is mandated for all courtroom appearances,

97 See, Irish Youth Justice Service, *Report on the Implementation of the National Youth Justice Strategy 2008–2010*, https://www.iprt.ie/youth-justice/report-published-on-the-implementation-of-national-youth-justice-strategy-2008-2010/

98 See, the Inter-American Commission on Human Rights, *Children and Adolescents in the United States Adult Criminal Justice System*, 2018, at pp 9 and 32. See, further, www.oas.org/en/iachr/reports/pdfs/Children-USA.pdf

99 See, Office of Juvenile Justice and Delinquency Prevention, https://ojjdp.ojp.gov/model-programs-guide/literature-reviews/racial-and-ethnic-disparity

100 See, Inter-American Commission on Human Rights, 2018 report, Op. cit.

where youth are especially affected in their ability to participate in the hearing that involves them.

Moreover, the U.S. legal system is unique in that in many states, children can be sentenced to life in prison without the chance of parole: currently, more than 3,000 people are serving such sentences for crimes committed when they were children.[101] They may also be later executed for crimes committed when minors.[102] In Canada, the system has been found to be deficient and Indigenous children to be over-represented in it.[103] In June 2022, the CRC expressed concern about juveniles being put on trial and sentenced as adults. It advised that juveniles should have access to juvenile justice both at the trial and at sentencing stages.

In Australia the juvenile justice system operates on the basis, ostensibly, that the welfare interests of the child is the matter of paramount importance (an assertion not borne out by the experiences of many Indigenous children). However, in New Zealand this principle – being confined to determining issues of guardianship and care – does not override justice considerations.

In France, the ordinance of 2 February 1945 introduced the first *juges des enfants* who exercised both civil and criminal jurisdictions,[104] based on the principle that educative measures, or welfare considerations, had to take precedence over punitive ones. This welfare orientation continues in the 21st century. The equivalent German legal system has been praised for being 'particularly instructive' because it 'responds to crimes committed by young people in ways that are age appropriate, centre on rehabilitation, and resort to incarceration only in limited circumstances and when absolutely necessary'.[105] The law relating to children continues to emphasise the welfare dimension with its diversion, educational and restorative justice measures.

Age of criminal responsibility

A key indicator of the priority given to the welfare interests of children entering the criminal justice system is the age at which they are eligible to do so, which varies considerably, representing the lack of a coherent policy towards the welfare/justice balance among the eight countries presently being studied. Another indicator is the importance attached to welfare considerations by the CRC which recommends certain procedural guarantees including the presence of parents at court hearings

101 See, further, https://eji.org/issues/children-in-prison/

102 A total of 38 states permit the use of the death penalty of which 23 authorise its use in respect of those who were juveniles when they committed the crime.

103 See, further, www.justice.gc.ca/eng/rp-pr/jr/jf-pf/2019/may01.html

104 The criminal and civil jurisdictions being authorized by the 1945 Ordinance and articles 375 ff. of the French Civil Code, respectively.

105 See, Fair and Just Prosecution Report, *Lessons Learned from Germany: Promoting Developmentally Appropriate and Rehabilitative Youth and Young Adult Justice*, 2022, https://fairandjustprosecution.org/wp-content/uploads/2022/06/FJP-Germany-Youth-Justice-Brief.pdf

for penal matters involving children in conflict with the law[106] and the right of the child to be heard.[107]

The younger the age of criminal responsibility – as in the UK and the U.S. – the greater is the risk to welfare interests. A child will be held criminally liable for their actions between 6 (North Carolina) and 14 years in various states in the U.S.; at 10 years of age in England and Wales, Australia and New Zealand; at age 12 years in Ireland and Canada; and at age 14 years in Germany. In France this is dependent upon each individual child's age of discernment', generally held to lie between 10 and 13 years of age. Given that the CRC has often stated that the minimum limit should be 'at least 14 years',[108] it is remarkable that all but one of the eight jurisdictions being studied – among the world's most developed nations – should choose to continue criminalising much younger children. Jurisdictional age differences are not confined to the lower limit. While for most purposes and in most jurisdictions children are defined as such until they reach 18 years of age, when it comes to criminal liability this is stretched to 21 years in Germany and in New Zealand.

Prevention

The CRC advise, in General Comment No 10, that deprivation of liberty must be used as a measure of last resort and for the shortest appropriate period of time; instead preference should be given to the use of diversion and to the prevention of juvenile delinquency.[109]

The most important indicator that prevention is having a positive role in relation to juveniles is when the evidence shows that fewer of them are entering their national justice systems.[110] Certain strategies have been important in this context. For example, there is now considerable jurisdictional consistency in reliance upon the 'family group conference' – pioneered in New Zealand – as a model for engaging the family and wider community in the process of determining how to respond to the child offender and his or her offence. Its effect is to leverage welfare interests into disposal options for youth offenders while also removing the 'Chinese wall' that traditionally separated the offender from the offence by now requiring the offender to account directly to their victim and to hear the response from that person and from the wider community. Also, a range of community-based measures

106 *CRC General Comment No. 14: On the Right of the Child to Have His or Her Best Interests Taken as a Primary Consideration*, 2013, at para 15.

107 *CRC General Comment No. 12: On the Right of the Child to be Heard*, 2009, at para 2.

108 United Nations, Committee on the Rights of the Child, *General Comment No. 24 (2019) on Children's Rights in the Child Justice System*, CRC/C/GC/24, September 18, 2019, section C.

109 See, Committee on the Rights of the Child, *General Comment No. 10 (2007) Children's Rights in Juvenile Justice*, CRC/C/GC/10, https://www2.ohchr.org/english/bodies/crc/docs/CRC.C.GC.10.pdf

110 See: for Australia, Australian Bureau of Statistics, *Recorded Crime – Offenders, 2019–202;* for New Zealand, Ministry of Social Development, 'Child and youth offending patterns – research reports', www.msd.govt.nz/about-msd-and-our-work/publications-resources/research/child-and-youth-offending-patterns/index.html

have evolved to give effect to policies designed to keep offenders out of custodial facilities. These have increased in all jurisdictions, and by far the majority of offenders are now supervised, usually by probation officers, in their communities.

In England and Wales the statutory requirement that local authorities take reasonable steps to reduce the need to bring criminal proceedings against children and to encourage them not to commit criminal offences, seems quite bland.[111] In Ireland, the Youth Justice Strategy 2021–2027 aims to maximise opportunities to promote positive behavioural change in 'at-risk' youths and to supplement the work of the Garda Youth Diversion Programme in preventing young offenders and children involved in antisocial behaviour in Ireland from committing further offences and entering into the adult criminal justice system.

The U.S., which has some of the highest levels of youth violence and crime in the developed world, was criticised in a 2018 report that detailed at length the many ways in which the juvenile justice system was currently failing youth who commit offences and 'highlighted the need to prioritise prevention policies'.[112] The Canadian juvenile justice system has been found to be deficient and Indigenous children to be over-represented in it,[113] nevertheless prevention programmes focus on encouraging and supporting local community initiatives that, for example, help youth learn new social skills and channel their energies into positive activities; ensure that youths are educated and trained for constructive careers that contribute to their communities; ensure that youths receive good nutrition, housing, and health care; and protect children from physical, emotional or sexual abuse.

In Australia the juvenile justice system operates on the basis that the welfare interests of the child are the matter of paramount importance, whereas in New Zealand the principle – being confined to determining issues of guardianship and care – does not override justice considerations. In both, a high proportion of offenders are channelled towards community rather than detention options, and the negative role of the principle is apparent in its weak preventative function which allows a high proportion of children to transfer from the care system to the justice system, and fails to prevent the consistent over-representation of Indigenous and Māori children in that transfer.[114]

In France the long-established reliance on educative measures to correct tendencies toward criminal behaviour is apparent in the recourse in recent years to restorative justice, which

> constitutes any measure allowing a victim along with the perpetrator of the offence to participate actively in the resolution of the difficulties resulting

111 See, the Children Act 1989, s 2, para 7, and the Crime and Disorder Act 1998, ss 38–41.

112 See, the Inter-American Commission on Human Rights, *Children and Adolescents in the United States Adult Criminal Justice System*, Op. cit., at p 75.

113 See, further, www.justice.gc.ca/eng/rp-pr/jr/jf-pf/2019/may01.html

114 See, further, for Australia at: The Australian Institute of Health and Welfare, *Youth Justice in Australia 2020–21*, www.aihw.gov.au/reports/youth-justice/youth-justice-in-australia-2020-21/contents/summary for New Zealand, www.1news.co.nz/2022/08/24/startling-link-revealed-between-state-care-and-prison/

> from the offence, and in particular in reparation for the harms of any kind resulting from its commission.[115]

This was initially introduced in 2014, subsequently amended by successive judicial reforms and young offender management policies[116] and provides an alternative to criminal proceedings by offering a more welfare-oriented approach to offending, allowing a child to avoid being burdened by a criminal record. The German juvenile justice system has been commended for prioritising social rehabilitation rather than punishment, its limited use of incarceration and its success in maintaining consistently low rates of recidivism.[117] Significantly, it has been estimated that the incarceration rate in Germany is nine times less than in the U.S. (76 per 100,000 versus 693 per 100,000).[118] It also has an emphasis on educative measures which include the issuing of instructions and the requirement that the offender accept certain forms of educative assistance – socio-educational input – or residential accommodation with backup support from social workers.

Responsibility for criminal conduct: parent and child

Traditionally, the law has presumed that the responsibility for children's actions was subsumed within, and appropriately represented by, the rights of their parents. Recently, in many developed countries, this has changed: the responsibilities of child and parent have become separable (arguably, too readily) and seen in legal terms as distinctly apart.

While all school shootings are tragic and harrowing – the loss, suffering and bewilderment being obviously deeply traumatising – the 2024 Michigan case,[119] when the court held the separated parents of a 15-year-old criminally responsible for his 2021 killings of four fellow high school pupils, was of particular legal interest. The mother's conviction in February of involuntary manslaughter was the first time in very many such shootings that a parent had been convicted of such charges, and this was followed in March by the similar conviction of the father. There were circumstantial aspects to the case which assisted proof of parental liability: they had bought the gun as a Christmas present for their son; the mother had accompanied him to a firing range where he learned to use it; they had failed to properly secure the weapon; and they had refused to take him from school on

115 *Gouvernement de la République française*, 2020, article 10–1. See, also, Circular of March 15, 2017 (*Ministère de la justice*, 2017).

116 See, *Code de la justice pénale des mineurs*, articles L13–4 and L112–8.

117 See, Dünkel, F., 'Criminology and Criminal Justice, Juvenile Justice and Juvenile Delinquency', *International and Comparative Criminology*, 2016, https://doi.org/10.1093/oxfordhb/9780199935383.013.68

118 See, The Crime Report, 2018, https://thecrimereport.org/2018/04/10/in-germany-its-hard-to-find-a-young-adult-in-prison/

119 The boy, Ethan Crumbley, killed four in the attack and wounded seven others, including a teacher. He was sentenced to life in prison without the possibility of parole. See, further, www.bbc.co.uk/news/world-us-canada-67571551

the day of the shooting, as school officials suggested, after finding his drawings of a gun and bloody figures. The case raises questions as to the potential liability of others in similar cases (under the principles of contributory negligence, common enterprise or wilful recklessness), such as gun shop proprietors, school officials and law enforcement officers.

For present purposes, certain aspects of this case would seem to be particularly relevant: the fact that the 15-year-old, being deemed to be responsible for his actions, was tried and convicted as an adult, and that his conviction did not detract from additional parental responsibility for his actions. Arguably, when contrasted with the 2024 conviction of two 12-year-old boys for the machete killing of a young man in England,[120] interesting questions arise as to jurisdictional differences regarding the legal autonomy of a child in the latter jurisdiction as opposed to some level of shared parent/child responsibility for criminal conduct in the U.S. While both cases are fact sensitive, the weapons used were, self-evidently, made to kill and kept in the family home without any parental safeguards. In both cases the children, as such, were not fully fledged legal entities; a duty of care, if not some level of legal responsibility for their child's actions, presumably remained with the parents. The *Gillick* rationale – and the French discernment approach – being based on an understanding of shared parent/child legal responsibility, tapering towards mutual independence as the child matures into adulthood, would suggest that the younger the child, the greater is the level of parental responsibility. Indeed, it is worth remembering that UN CROC, Article 15, declares that 'States Parties shall respect the responsibilities, rights and duties of parents'. At this point, however, there does not seem to be any indication that the English parents of a 12-year-old with a machete will bear a level of legal accountability, similar, if not greater, to that of American parents of a 15-year-old with a gun, for the resulting use of those weapons by their children.

Access to justice in an Indigenous context

The fact that in all CANZUS nations, Indigenous children are over-represented in their respective justice systems is probably the single strongest shared jurisdictional characteristic of the law as it relates to children. They have historically shared this same intergenerational trend: over-representation in the criminal justice system being, very often, a continuation of their similar over-representation in the child welfare system. These nations are now exploring ways of transferring more of the administration and adjudication of justice issues from the present system into tribal control. The common jurisdictional strategy would seem to be to vest more responsibility in the tribal authorities, enabling them to implement culturally appropriate preventative programs,

120 See, further, www.birminghamworld.uk/news/crime/two-boys-12-found-guilty-of-murdering-birmingham-resident-4660271

police a range of antisocial and criminal behaviour, adjudicate on breaches of the law in tribal courts and impose non-custodial penalties. This would seem to be at a more advanced stage in Canada, following the Indigenous Justice program launched in 1996.

Right to representation

Both the U.S. and Canada are required to ensure that an Indigenous child – whether appearing before a tribal or state/province court – is represented by a lawyer. In addition, a tribal representative should be present, or someone 'culturally competent', to safeguard the child's cultural heritage by mediating between the child and court officials, interpreting and explaining the cultural implications of any matters arising, particularly as regards disposal options. Where a child, more than 12 years of age and of sufficient maturity to understand the matter at issue and its significance, wishes to give or withhold consent to a decision in relation to that issue, the court will at least take their views into account but will reserve to itself the final responsibility for determining what it considers to be in the child's best interests. Similarly, Indigenous and Māori youth in Australia and New Zealand respectively, are assured of representation by a lawyer and by a community representative who will advise the court on the cultural implications of the offender's conduct and provide him or her with a sense of community support and solidarity.

Right to recognition of cultural identity

International recognition of the protection needed for Indigenous culture is provided by UN CROC, Article 20, which requires the state when considering a foster or adoption placement to have due regard to the desirability of continuity in a child's upbringing and to the child's ethnic, religious, cultural and linguistic background. This is supported by Article 30 requiring it to ensure that a child who is Indigenous shall not be denied the right, in community with other members of his or her group, to enjoy his or her own culture, to profess and practise his or her own religion, or to use his or her own language. Further reinforcement is available in the UN Declaration on the Rights of Indigenous Peoples, Article 8, which states that Indigenous peoples and individuals have the right not to be subjected to forced assimilation or destruction of their culture.

Any proposed adoption of an Indigenous child by non-Indigenous applicants must satisfy the 'best interests' of the child test which requires that consideration be given to the cultural identity of the child; their cultural heritage; and his or her cultural, racial and religious background. Whether, having done so, a holistic view of the welfare interests of the child indicates that all other welfare-related factors outweigh culture-specific factors and justify an adoption must, most probably, turn on the facts presented in each individual case, like all other decisions taken to protect and promote the welfare interests of a child.

Conclusion

Family law is shaped by cultural context.[121] This is well illustrated by the jurisdictional contrasts provided in this chapter, perhaps most starkly in the differences between Indigenous and non-Indigenous communities. The opportunities for an Indigenous child to avail of the rights promised by UN CROC are so much less than those of a non-Indigenous child, and that disparity long preceded the introduction of the Convention. However, there are some signs – the introduction of tribal courts for example – that indicate a recognition of the adverse effects of cultural dissonance.

Not until the early years of the 21st century were there some indications of jurisdictional convergence in respect of the legal status of the child and towards a more 'child-friendly' court setting. These developments were probably due to a shared exposure to an array of influences that shaped a common response. Among the more potent of these were the inexorable demographic trends forcing a contraction in public spending; a rise in the rate of family breakdown, creating an ever-growing pool of vulnerable children with rights to protection and security; the emergence of a body of academic research – particularly in the field of developmental psychology – which greatly enhanced and informed a professional understanding of child welfare–related matters; and the steady pressure from international judicial and regulatory bodies – particularly rulings of the ECtHR – encouraging national compliance with principles of international jurisprudence. The first two resulted in jurisdictions prioritising coercive over consensual state intervention and directing it primarily towards child protection and criminality. The third and fourth generated a recognition that family-based care, where safe and permanent attachments could flourish, was preferable to both residential care and to successive short-term foster placements. The combination of all four has led to the state generally retreating from engagement in family disruption, unless there is evidence of child protection concerns to which most resources are now deployed in a co-ordinated multidisciplinary response.

121 A conclusion reflected in the majority ruling of the ECtHR in *A, B, and C v. Ireland*, Application No. 25579/05, (2010).

3 Family life and family breakdown

Introduction

Family law begins with the relationships – the reciprocal rights and duties – of family members as regards each other, their needs and property. This nuclear family unit was initially understood as parents and the child or children born of their relationship, collectively sheltering under the legal and religious status of marriage. It is an interpretation that has since changed fundamentally and in many different ways (see, further, Chapter 8). This is of little consequence to the majority of families (except in relation to matters such as religious ceremonies, the registration requirements of various public bodies and the drawing up of wills). Not unless and until family breakdown occurs do legal issues regarding the reciprocal rights and duties of family members become activated.

This chapter has a twin focus on family life and on family breakdown. In relation to both, it is concerned to identify important developments and significant jurisdictional differences as regards the welfare interests and rights of children and to consider their implications for the future of family law.

Family life

> The existence or non-existence of 'family life' for the purposes of Article 8 is essentially a question of fact depending upon the real existence in practice of close personal ties.

So stated the ECtHR in *K&T v. Finland*.[1] On both sides of the Atlantic, recognition of 'family life' is now grounded on notions of the privacy and respect that individuals are entitled to from the state, coupled with a recognition that the welfare interests have primacy and must be protected. How family life was established – the form it has taken and the presence or absence of any genetic or legal links between its members – is of lesser importance than the quality of their relationships and of the attachments developed by the child. This was demonstrated more than a decade

1 Application No. 25702/94, (2001), at 150.

DOI: 10.4324/9781003510383-5

ago in *Saleck Bardi v. Spain*[2] when the ECtHR found that the applicant's Article 8 rights had been infringed by a lack of due process in the way the Spanish conducted proceedings. This case concerned a stateless single mother in an Algerian refugee camp who, in 2002, gave permission for a charity to organise a holiday for her nine-year-old daughter in Spain, where she was found to have health problems. Proceedings were initiated to extend her stay in Spain, and the child continued to stay with the host family. In March 2004 the Spanish authorities were informed that the mother was seeking her child's return. In May 2004 the Spanish child protection service declared the child abandoned, and in September 2005 custody was provisionally awarded to the Spanish foster family, pending enquiries to identify her biological family and to determine whether she had been subjected to ill treatment in her place of origin. The mother was not informed of these proceedings, but in June 2006 she went to Spain and appeared before the same family affairs judge in an unsuccessful effort to secure her daughter's return. In April 2007, the judge award guardianship to the host family, on the grounds that the child, now aged 15 years, had expressed her wish to remain with them and claimed she had been treated as a slave in the refugee camps. In April 2008, the mother's appeal was dismissed and the guardianship awarded to the host family was confirmed, on the grounds that the interests of the child, who had established emotional ties with that family and did not wish to see her mother again, prevailed over those of her mother. The European Court of Human Rights (ECtHR) condemned the Spanish procedures: awarding guardianship to a foster family was unjustified, given the mother's clear intent on re-establishing contact with her daughter. Nevertheless, the fact of a faulty process could not be allowed to prejudice the outcome. In its examination of how the child's best interests were considered, the Court was satisfied that it had been accorded weight as a *substantive right*: it found that the Spanish authorities had given thorough and appropriate consideration to the best interests. It was satisfied that when the Spanish authorities awarded custody to the foster family, they accorded decisive importance to the child's best interests as they recognised that she had established strong ties with that family throughout the years of her stay, and she expressed her wish to not stay with her biological mother.

In Europe, the presumption underpinning Article 8 is that the entitlement of parent and child to the mutual enjoyment of each other's company constitutes a fundamental element of family life and should be protected against arbitrary action by public authorities according to Council of Europe guidance[3] and rulings of the ECtHR in cases such as *K A v. Finland*[4] and *Kutzner v. Germany*.[5] In the U.S., the deference shown by the state to the constitutionally protected individual liberty of a parent to exercise care and control over their children has been affirmed by the U.S.

2 Application No. 66167/09, (2011).

3 See, Council of Europe, *Parenting in Contemporary Europe: A Positive Approach*, 2007, www.coe.int/t/dg3/children/publications/ParentingContempory_en.asp

4 (2003) 1 FCR 201.

5 (2003) 1 FCR 249.

Supreme Court (USSC).[6] This has centred on the right to custody but now extends to determining education (including home-schooling), religious upbringing and includes reasonable chastisement.[7] It has been evident in cases such as *Eisenstadt v. Baird*[8] when the USSC extended the protection of privacy – initially confined to the marital family unit – to the individual.[9]

Family life and legal status

Personal identity, and social recognition of such, is very much bound up with legal status. As the ECtHR explained, in *C.E. and Others v. France*,[10] a legal parent/child relationship constitutes "an essential aspect of the [child's] identity"[11] and "an essential aspect of the individual's identity is at stake when the parent/child relationship is affected",[12] especially when it is sought to be established in respect of minors[13] (see, also, Chapter 8).

Marriage

The ECtHR has been clear that marriage is not a legal prerequisite for family life but, equally, that marriage itself offers no guarantee that the subsequent presence of children will necessarily constitute family life.

Jurisdictional differences and their significance

In England and Wales, affirmation for the legal importance of 'parental responsibility' came with the introduction of the Children Act 1989 when the term was defined as 'as all the rights, duties, powers, responsibilities and authority which by law a parent of a child has in relation to the child and [their] property'. In the intervening decades, the emphasis has been on developing the 'responsibilities' of birth parents who may separate, may establish and terminate successive family units, but will always take with them their responsibilities for any child they have conceived; the reciprocal rights of the children involved – to contact with both birth parents, etc. – regardless of the latter's choices; with the welfare interests of the child always being of paramount importance in any issue affecting their upbringing.

In Ireland – not unlike Germany, Canada and federal authority in the U.S. – there has been less legislative initiative to emphasise the relative rights

6 *Pierce v. Soc'y of Sisters*, 268 U.S. 510 (1925) and *Meyer v. Nebraska*, 262 U.S. 390, 399 (1923).
7 *Pierce v. Soc'y of Sisters*, Ibid, at 534–535.
8 405 U.S. 438 (1972).
9 See, *Stenberg v. Carhart*, 530 U.S. 914, 921 (2000), *Planned Parenthood of Se. Pa. v. Casey*, 505 U.S. 833, 847 (1992) and *Griswold v. Connecticut*, 381 U.S. 479, 485–486 (1965).
10 Application No. 29775/18.
11 Ibid, at para 54.
12 *Mennesson v. France*, Application No. 65192/11, (2014), at para 96.
13 Ibid, at paras 88–89.

of children and more reliance on constitutional provisions framing traditional family values.

In the joint application *Mennesson v. France* and *Labassee v. France*,[14] the Court distinguished between the references to 'family life' and 'private life' in Article 8(1). The two French married couples – the Mennessons and the Labassees – had acquired children through commercial surrogacy arrangements in the U.S., but on their return to France, the Registrar for births, marriages and deaths had refused to register the children as commercial surrogacy was prohibited in France. As regards the 'family life' of the Mennessons, the ECtHR found no evidence of state interference (the children went to school, attended healthcare check-ups, etc., as did other French children). As regards 'respect for private life', the Court found that this required the right to establish details of one's identity, which formed part of the legal parent/child relationship.[15] The domestic authorities had interfered with this but had not established that the interference had been 'in accordance with the law', 'pursuing a legitimate aim(s)', and 'necessary in a democratic society'.[16] Ultimately, while the ECtHR found that the children's right to respect for private life had been infringed by the French authorities, it held that there had been no violation of Article 8 with regard to the intended parents' right to respect for their family life.

In *C.E. and Others*[17] the Court again distinguished between 'family life' and 'private life'. Evidence that ex-partners have been engaged in raising the biological parents' children, participating in their education and sharing maintenance costs demonstrates the existence of family life, as do arrangements for rights of contact, overnight visits, etc. 'Private life', on the other hand, refers to the emotional ties – the parent/child bond – created and developed between an adult and a child, which is legally presumed to exist for the child of a marital relationship but which needs to be proven in a non-marital context. The Court considered that the main issue was the establishment of a legal parent/child relationship between, on the one hand, a child born from a "friendly sperm donation" in France or by medically assisted procreation carried out abroad and, on the other hand, a woman who is the former partner of the child's biological mother. Following family breakdown, both former partners had expressed the wish to go on with their parental project and been playing a meaningful role in the child's education and identity development by exercising some parental rights. The ECtHR found that for technical reasons, French law at that time prevented applicants from same-sex relationships from establishing legal rights in respect of a child and held that the French authorities' refusal to allow the establishment of a legal parent/child relationship between a child and a woman who is the former partner of their biological mother – also the child's legal parent – whether by full adoption (*l'adoption plénière*) or by

14 Ibid.

15 Ibid, at para 96.

16 Ibid, at para 50.

17 *C.E. and Others v. France*, Application Nos. 29775/18 and 29693/19, (2022).

recognised enjoyment of a status (*possession d'état*) did not violate Article 8 of the Convention (right to respect for private and family life).

Adoption and family life

By the early years of the 21st century, adoption had greatly changed.[18] Not only had it decreased considerably in volume, but it had very largely taken the form of adoption of a child by a person or persons known and related to him or her – most often step-parents – and termed a 'family adoption'. This was and continues to be the most common type in all jurisdictions being studied, though indications are that this will not continue indefinitely, leaving intercountry adoption (ICA) as the rapidly shrinking residual form of the traditional 'stranger adoption' and non-consensual adoption from state care (see, further, Chapter 5) to become potentially more mainstream.

Types of adoption involving consensual birth parent

Accouchement sous X, the traditional woman's right, under Article 341 of France's Civil code, to give birth and relinquish her child anonymously as demonstrated in in *Odièvre v. France*,[19] continues to represent the most radical form of consensual adoption. This contrasts markedly with ICA – an aspect of private adoption – in which there is often doubt as to whether full and informed parental consent had really been given, or if the child is a genuine orphan, as opposed to the child being simply placed in state care by impoverished parents. As in surrogacy and in other forms of private adoption, profit-making intermediaries may be involved, and there may be grounds for suspicion that the voluntary relinquishment of birth parents has been induced by the prospect of financial reward.

Private adoption

The right of a birth mother to place her child for adoption with whomsoever she chooses, or to authorise another person to do so on her behalf, while traditionally a characteristic feature of adoption – and one consistently practised within Indigenous communities – has now largely been prohibited in most developed nations or is restricted to placements with close relatives. This right was indicative of the legal reality that perceived adoption as the most private, radical, absolute and exclusive order known to private family law. There were other such indicators such as birth parent's right to anonymity, adopter's right to veto post-adoption birth parent contact and to the permanent confidentiality of adoption records. The growing public dimension to adoption, coupled with equality rights and the greater weighting

18 See, for example, the right of transexuals to adopt in *Frette v. France*, Application No. 36515/97, (2002).

19 [2003] 1 FCR 621. Also, see, *Kearns v. France*, Application No. 35991/04, (January 10, 2008) ECHR.

given to a child's welfare interests, has greatly diluted the relative importance of birth parents' rights in the adoption process.

However, private adoption remains prominent in the U.S. and to a lesser extent in Canada. The placement right of a birth mother is asserted in the laws of most states; only four restrict placement to agencies in non-relative adoptions.[20] Such placements are often conducted on a for-profit basis: 'accredited agencies' must be non-profit; but in an ICA context, 'approved persons' or 'facilitators' – a category that may include large organisations as well as lawyers, social workers and independent consultants – are entitled to operate on a fees for service basis. The fact that some 45% of U.S. adoptions originate in private arrangements,[21] and may be influenced by profit considerations, would seem less likely to be in the best interests of the children concerned and in some cases may well be detrimental.[22]

Step-adoption

From the perspective of the welfare interests of a child, the disadvantages of this form of adoption remain: it completely severs all legal links between the child and their birth father together with his extended family; it changes the child's legal identity; and it obscures the biological links between the parties concerned. Nonetheless, the assumption of welfare compatibility was upheld in *Eski v. Austria*[23] when the ECtHR ruled that a step-adoption could proceed despite objections from the birth father who had maintained irregular contact with the eight-year-old child following family breakdown six years earlier. In several countries, such as Ireland, the adoption process has mainly attracted step-parent, intercountry applicants and foster parents, in that order.

Kinship adoption

These adoptions are an attractive option in respect of children in state care because they provide for minimal disruption to a child's sense of belonging within the family, class, culture and locality of their birth. It is also open to interpretation as a strand in a broader state policy to retreat from taking responsibility for family matters by returning children through that process to their kinship networks.

The common law jurisdictions – Ireland, the UK, the U.S., Canada, Australia and New Zealand – all now rely heavily on kinship placements for children admitted by care order to the public care system. This contrasts with some civil law jurisdictions; while such placements are a strong feature of child-care

20 Colorado, Connecticut, Delaware and Massachusetts.

21 In 2000–2001, it was estimated that 45% of adoptions were initiated by private arrangement. See, further, U.S. Child Welfare Information Gateway, *How Many Children Were Adopted in 2000 and 2001?* www.childwelfare.gov/pubs/s_adopted/s_adopteda.cfm

22 See, further, www.childwelfare.gov/pubPDFs/s_adopted.pdf#page=6&view=Findings:%20Children%20Adopted

23 Application No. 21949/03, (2007).

policy in Germany (in 2005, 60% of all children in the public care system were placed with a relative), there is comparatively little reliance on the extended family for such purposes in France (in 2007, only 7% of such children were so placed).

This form of adoption has been growing so rapidly, as the placement of choice for children admitted to the public care systems in most of the jurisdictions being studied, that it may ultimately displace foster care which has been the mainstay of those systems for many decades. It has found approval in ECtHR rulings which include, for example, a finding that a close caring relationship between grandparents and a child is sufficient for an adoption.[24]

Intercountry adoption

In all developed nations, the correlation between increased recourse to ICA and decreased domestic availability of voluntarily relinquished adoptable children, particularly babies, is unmistakable. In Ireland, for example, ICA has always been proportionately more significant than in neighbouring jurisdictions[25] due, in all probability to resistance – in law, policy and social values – to non-consensual adoption from the Irish public care system. Clearly, recourse to ICA has considerable implications for the welfare of the children concerned; on the one hand, as it is increasingly restricted to children with health and social care needs that cannot be catered for in their countries of birth, ICA is providing a route to medical care and family life that would not otherwise be available; on the other, it may well be diverting adopters away from those children who are older and/or have complex needs that languish in their domestic public care systems.

Cultural/religious affinity

Articles 8, 9 and 11 of the European Convention on Human Rights (ECHR) and Article 27 of the International Covenant on Civil and Political Rights specifically recognise the right of minorities to maintain their own culture, language and religion. This is reinforced by Article 20(3) of the United Nations Convention on the Rights of the Child (UN CROC) which states that 'due regard shall be paid to the desirability of continuity in a child's upbringing and to the child's ethnic, religious, cultural and linguistic background'. International law now places a high priority on identity rights and requires preference to be given to adoptions that provide for cultural affinity between adopters and child as this – in the absence of other critical factors – accords with what is best for the latter's long-term welfare.

24 *Marckx v. Belgium* (1979) Series A No. 31, 2 EHRR 330, at para 31.

25 For example, in 2004 the Adoption Authority made 648 adoption orders, of which 375 (58%) were entries in the Register of Foreign Adoptions, a high rate of foreign adoptions by international standards. In 2022, although only 102 adoption orders were made, there were 170 entries in the Register.

Jurisdictional differences and their significance

The strongest jurisdictional characteristic is not one of difference but of similarity. All eight jurisdictions have in common the fact that in recent decades the main use of adoption has been the opposite for which it was initially intended: being used by a birth mother (acting jointly with a child's stepfather) to legally acquire rather than to relinquish parental responsibility. Such has been the growth in step-parent adoptions – accompanied by policy reservations as to their compliance with welfare interests due to their tendency to skew an adopted child's perception of actual family structure and relationships – that some jurisdictions have taken legislative steps to divert step-applicants towards alternative and less extreme proceedings (note that in France step-parents are confined to the 'simple' form of adoption). So, England and Wales, New Zealand and some states in Australia have introduced 'special guardianship' orders explicitly for that purpose, an initiative that other jurisdictions may well follow. Should this, the main use of adoption, be curtailed, along with the continued decline in third-party adoptions and ICA, then questions may well arise as to its future, if indeed it has one.

One aspect of the general decline in adoption orders in all eight jurisdictions is the particular slump in recourse to overseas sources. All jurisdictions now share the experience of a rapidly shrinking ICA market as countries traditionally relied upon cease to make children available, the constraints imposed by the Hague Convention take effect, while surrogacy and assisted reproductive technology make it increasingly possible to bypass adoption as a means of creating a family. It would seem probable that ICA will continue to decline – except as an international response to national disasters and in some circumstances as an adjunct to commercial surrogacy – and that the practice of non-consensual adoption from state care will spread to fill that gap and to defray state care costs (see, further, Chapter 5).

Although the role of the paramountcy principle is claimed to be another shared feature of adoption law among the jurisdictions, this is not necessarily the case. The ECtHR assertion that "there is currently a broad consensus – including in international law in support of the idea that in all decisions concerning children, their best interests must be paramount"[26] – is not always evident in national adoption legislation. In the U.S., the Adoption and Safe Families Act 1997 declares the health and safety of children to be the paramount concern of state child welfare service, and in the UK this principle is similarly legislatively stated but extended to apply to the welfare of the child throughout childhood. The principle is also of paramount importance in Ireland[27] and in Australia[28] but not in Canada nor New Zealand[29] and

26 *Neulinger and Shuruk v. Switzerland*, Application No. 41615/07, (2011), at para 135.

27 Constitution, article 42A.4.1(ii): in proceedings concerning the adoption, guardianship or custody of, or access to, any child, the best interests of the child shall be the paramount consideration.

28 Adoption of Children Ordinance 1965 (Act No. 15/1965).

29 Section 11(b) of the Adoption Act merely requires that 'the welfare and interests of the child will be promoted by the adoption', though the paramountcy principle is stated in s 6 of the CYP&F Act.

is not so stated in either French or German adoption law. There is similar jurisdictional disparity as regards the necessity for a child's consent to be available for their adoption.[30] There is no such requirement in the UK,[31] Ireland or New Zealand. In Canada all provinces and territories require an adoption order to be conditional upon the consent of the child concerned above a certain age; in most jurisdictions, that age is 12 years. Similarly, in the U.S. where the minimum age of a consenting child varies between 10 and 14 years, and so also in France in respect of a child not less than 13 years of age. In Australia, the consent of a child aged 12 years or older should be obtained if they are deemed '*Gillick* competent'. In Germany, a child's consent is required from the age of 14 years.

While the latter part of the 20th century was a period when adoption changed from being largely a means of regulating the non-kinship placements of voluntarily relinquished illegitimate babies and became more a means of sanctioning the private family arrangements of birth parents – almost always mothers, in respect of their own children – it would seem likely that the 21st century will see a sharp fall in the consensual role of birth parents in the adoption process as both step-adoptions and ICA decline and non-consensual adoptions from state care increase. The U.S., in this as in many other respects, is an outlier. In the ethos of a free-market economy – where the freedom of the individual and entrepreneurship are greatly valued – it is likely that private adoption will retain its position at the heart of that process, reinforced by a discretionary parental veto on information disclosure to adoptees; a veto which also applies in parts of Canada.[32] Moreover, as a succession of rulings by the Health and Human Services grant exemptions from the requirements of equality and non-discrimination legislation[33] to faith-based foster care and adoption agencies, enabling them to refuse to engage with the LGBT community including same-sex foster carers and adopters, it would seem inevitable that this will become another culture wars battleground.

In vitro fertilisation, surrogacy and family life

In vitro fertilisation (IVF) treatment emerged in the 1970s and, since then, some seven million children have been born as a consequence of such treatment which has improved considerably in effectiveness in recent years. As has been pointed

30 The child's consent to be adopted is required from the age of 12 years in eleven EU Member States (Belgium, Croatia, Czechia, Denmark, Finland, Greece, Latvia, the Netherlands, Portugal, Spain and Sweden).

31 Excepting Scotland where the consent of a child aged 12 or older is required.

32 See, *Ontario v. Marchand* (2006) 81 O.R. (3d) 172 where the court ruled that the right "to know one's past" was not to a principle of fundamental justice within s 7 of the Charter. See, also, *Canadian Foundation for Children*, at paras 8–11, *R. v. Malmo-Levine* [2003] 3 SCR 571, at para 113 and *Cheskes v. Ontario (Attorney General)* (2007) 288 D.L.R. (4th) 449, at para 116 (Ont. SCJ).

33 For example, on January 23, 2019, the HHS ruled that in South Carolina the Miracle Hill Ministries and other taxpayer-funded faith-based foster care agencies could maintain their rejection of all foster parents other than those who subscribed to Miracle Hill's particular interpretation of Protestant Christianity.

out, "IVF used to be around 7% successful and now it is around 30%. So, as a choice, adoption is competing with lots of other ways of having children".[34] The greater its efficiency, the greater is the freedom of choice available to initiate family life.

While surrogacy in its altruistic form has been practised for many generations, the commercial variant has only become popular, for those who can afford it, since around the turn of the century. It has since grown in effectiveness – with a 60% success rate – and exponentially in volume[35] becoming almost industrialised in some countries, but it gives rise to much controversy and inconsistency in regulatory policy: partly because of difficulties in relation to ascertaining what might be a reasonable financial recompense for the surrogate, partly because of how to legally differentiate the implications arising from gestational as opposed to traditional surrogacy and partly due to uncertainty as to how best to secure the rights of the children involved (see, further, Chapter 4).

Jurisdictional differences and their significance

As Kirsty Horsey has noted: 'In some countries, surrogacy is prohibited in any form, although this does not stop people using it. In others, it is unregulated but still practised. In some nations it is regulated in either a "commercial" or an "altruistic" model'.[36]

In England and Wales, the law currently favours surrogate mothers: agreements are unenforceable and create insecurity for commissioning couples by allowing surrogate mothers to choose to keep the child after birth; the courts ensure that surrogacy arrangements are altruistic and that no improper payments have been made. In Ireland, where there is no specific legislation governing surrogacy,[37] the UN Committee on the Rights of the Child (CRC) has expressed concern that insufficient attention is being given 'to the rights and interests of children born as a result of assisted reproduction technologies.'[38]

Commercial surrogacy is prohibited in Canada where it is illegal to pay a surrogate mother, egg donor or sperm donor[39] but is generally legal in the U.S. and in some states is so developed as to make that country a top destination resort in international health tourism, while in others the 'culture wars' is an inhibiting

34 See, further, www.theguardian.com/society/2018/nov/03/england-adoption-rates-falling-as-ivf-improves-says-senior-official

35 See, further, *Global Surrogacy Market Grows at a Staggering CAGR of 6.25%*, https://straitsresearch.com/press-release/global-surrogacy-market-size

36 See, Horsey, K., 'The Future of Surrogacy: A Review of Current Global Trends and National Landscapes', *Reproductive BioMedicine Online*, Vol. 48, No. 5, 2024, www.sciencedirect.com/science/article/pii/S1472648323008635

37 See, further, www.citizensinformation.ie/en/birth_family_relationships/adoption_and_fostering/surrogacy.html

38 UN Committee on the Rights of the Child, Concluding Observations of the Committee on the combined third and fourth periodic reports of Ireland, 2016, at para 33.

39 See, the Assisted Reproduction Act 2004.

factor. Throughout Australia, surrogacy is prohibited on a commercial basis, but altruistic surrogacy is permitted as is reimbursement for some of the surrogate's costs. The Family Court of Australia in the leading case of *Re Evelyn*[40] upheld the ruling of the court at first instance which had broadly decided in favour of the biological mother who had reneged on the surrogacy arrangement; a decision based squarely on the paramount welfare interests of the child and the court reiterated its ruling in *Rice v. Miller*[41] that there could be no presumption favouring a birth parent. Most states now automatically recognise the commissioning parent as fully vested with parental rights and status – to the complete exclusion of the birth mother. In New Zealand altruistic surrogacy is legal but commercial surrogacy is not, and in any event the commissioning parent must adopt the child in order to legitimate their parental status. The increase in commissioning couples returning home to New Zealand with their babies has given rise to jurisdiction issues.[42]

In France, surrogacy is not merely unavailable but since 1991 it has been legally prohibited,[43] a position that has hardened in recent years: a surrogacy contract is null and void, and violations are punished by civil and criminal sanctions. As in New Zealand, this has given rise to jurisdiction issues for those returning home with babies born elsewhere: since 2010, French courts have consistently denied recognition for surrogate contracts and for any right to adopt children born abroad from surrogate mothers. However, in *Mennesson v. France*[44] the ECtHR considered the refusal of French authorities to register children in such circumstances violated the children's right to family life. In Germany, surrogacy is illegal[45]: the mother of a child is the woman who gave birth to that child.[46] A commissioning male may be recognised in law as the father only if he is either genetically linked and initiates court proceedings to obtain legal recognition or obtains the consent of the surrogate who acknowledges that he is the father.[47]

Welfare interests

IVF and other such advances in medical science are almost always beneficial for the welfare interests of children as those born by such means are very much wanted, the parenting they experience is likely to be of a high standard and their welfare interests must benefit accordingly.

40 (1998) FLC 92–807. See, also, *Re Evelyn (No. 2)* (1998) FLC 92–187 where the High Court of Australia considered and dismissed the issue of appeal.
41 (1993) FLC 92–807, at pp 85 and 106.
42 See, for example, *In Re Application of L* [2003] NZFLR 529 and *Punter v. Secretary for Justice*, 2 NZLR 28 (CA).
43 Under article 16.5 of the Civil Code, such contracts are null and void. The *Cour de cassation* in 1991 invalidated a decision of lower jurisdictions giving effect to surrogacy by creating a filiation link between the child and the wife of the biological father after the completion of such a contract.
44 Op. cit.
45 The Embryo Protection Act 1991, s 1(1)(7).
46 Civil Code, s 1591.
47 The Civil Code, s 1595(1).

However, there can be a downside: the child may have an unknown genetic predisposition to particular health issues; any origin information the child receives will be entirely at parental discretion with resulting crucial implications for the development of his or her identity and cultural affiliation; and due to the anonymity surrounding the use of genetic material, a child may never know their true genetic origins. More immediately, there may be legal issues regarding the child's parentage and nationality.[48] Surrogacy can be combined with genetic editing – whether involving an embryo implanted in a surrogate or birth mother – to eliminate a genetic predisposition towards particular diseases or to enhance an innate attribute. This has given rise to a concern that we could be on the verge of entering an era of 'designer babies'.

Surrogacy arrangements are, clearly, not without their problems. Perhaps the most significant issue is represented by the Latin maxim *mater semper certa est* (the mother is always certain) which creates a legal presumption that the woman who gave birth (the surrogate) is the mother of that child. Should the terms of the transaction be renounced by one of the parties – either by the surrogate because she has chosen to keep the child or the commissioning couple because, as in a recent Australian case, the child was perceived to have a defect – then in law the surrogate may well be recognised as the mother and be entitled, or required, to assume parental responsibilities. However, that legal presumption was countered by the approach adopted in the 1988 New Jersey case of *In re Baby M*[49] as consolidated in the 1993 Californian Supreme Court decision in *Johnson v. Calvert*.[50] The latter case essentially determined that the surrogate, who had no genetic link with the baby, was therefore unrelated to the child, and instead the commissioning woman, who was genetically linked to the baby, could be construed as the legal mother. This decision cleared the way for non-altruistic surrogacy arrangements in the U.S. and laid the ground for much contemporary international caselaw which centres on the presence or absence of a genetic link between child and a commissioning party (see, further, Chapter 4).

There can be no doubt that international commercial surrogacy is set to continue growing exponentially for the foreseeable future, displacing third-party adoption, whether domestic or ICA, and will almost certainly become subject to international regulation. Family law must adjust accordingly with provisions for securing the rights of the children involved, at the very least by ensuring a right of access to origins information.

Trans/sexual orientation and gender identity issues and family life

Requests for gender transition, reflecting much distress among the children concerned and their parents, have greatly increased in recent years in Europe and elsewhere, perhaps constituting what has been described as 'this epidemic-like

48 See, Pascoe, C.J., *Issues of Forced Adoption and International Commercial Surrogacy*, Melbourne, Federal Court of Australia, October 2, 2013, www.law.monash.edu.au/about-us/events/chie-judge-pascoe-dpeech-notes.pdf

49 537 A. 2d 1227 (NJ 1988).

50 851 P. 2d 776 (Cal. 1993).

phenomenon'.[51] In the U.S., for example, as of 2022, there were an estimated 300,000 teenagers aged 13 to 17 years who identified as trans, double the number recorded in 2017.[52] Many children begin the transition process with clinical guidance and counselling before moving on to puberty blockers and hormonal treatment around the age of 10 to 12 years, sometimes younger, on the basis of parental consent. The fact that children can be permitted to enter a process with such lifelong consequences for their welfare long before they are of an age to exercise their right to give or withhold their consent to it is highly contentious and, to some, constitutes a form of child abuse.[53]

Child's consent

In England, a *Gillick* competent minor, or a person aged 16 years, was able to give a valid consent to embarking on medical treatment leading to a change in gender identity but, under the Gender Recognition Act 2004, was denied a GR certificate until he or she reached 18 years of age. However, the capacity of minors to give a valid consent on such a grave, complex matter was challenged and – following whistleblower disclosures, a High Court case[54] and an NHS commissioned review of the service (the Cass review) in 2021[55] – the clinic facilities were closed because of growing public and professional disquiet regarding their ability to ensure a holistic treatment response to the increasing numbers of 16-year-old adolescents presenting with gender identity issues and ostensibly consenting to irreversible puberty-blocking treatment. The final Cass report in 2024 found that

> the rationale for early puberty suppression remains unclear, with weak evidence regarding the impact on gender dysphoria, mental or psychosocial health . . . The use of masculinising/feminising hormones in those under the age of 18 also presents many unknowns . . . The effect on cognitive and psychosexual development remains unknown'.

Following the report, such treatment is no longer available in the NHS to those under age 18 years (though there are concerns regarding availability in private clinics). In Ireland, Article 42A established a constitutional duty, resting on the court, to ascertain the views of children, though for some years there had been a recognition that under Article 40.3 children had a procedural right to be heard in cases

51 The National Academy of Medicine Report, *Medicine and Gender Trans Identity in Children and Adolescents*, 2022, www.academie-medecine.fr/la-medecine-face-a-la-transidentite-de-genre-chez-les-enfants-et-les-adolescents/?lang=en

52 See, further, https://williamsinstitute.law.ucla.edu/press/transgender-estimate-press-release/

53 See, Latham, A., 'Puberty Blockers for Children: Can They Consent?', *The New Bioethics*, Vol. 28, No. 3, pp 268–291.

54 *Bell v. Tavistock* [2020] EWHC 3274 (Admin).

55 See, the Cass Final Report, 2024, https://cass.independent-review.uk/home/publications/final-report/

affecting them.[56] Nonetheless, a young Irish person under 16 years of age cannot give legal consent to a gender identity change.

In the U.S. gender transitioning requires an initial medical diagnosis of 'gender dysphoria' followed by medical treatment. A child may give a valid legal consent in most states when he or she has reached 16 years of age, though in some they must be at least 17 or 18 years of age. The opinion of the USSC several decades ago that "most children, even in adolescence, simply are not able to make sound judgments concerning many decisions, including their need for medical care or treatment"[57] probably continues to weigh heavily on medical practitioners in this context. In Canada – as in Ireland, France and Germany – self-certification rather than medical intervention is sufficient to validate gender identity. The Australian courts, on the other hand, underwent a good deal of equivocation[58] regarding authorisation for a child to commence trans treatment before deciding, in *Re Matthew*,[59] that a *Gillick* competent minor could make such a decision provided there was no controversy between parents and medical professionals. In New Zealand, the Care of Children Act 2004, s 6, requires the court to take into account the views of a child on matters concerning their welfare, but there is no requirement to comply with their wishes.

In France, children may access puberty blockers and hormone replacement treatment at any age on the basis of their consent, though accessing surgical procedures will require parental consent until the child concerned is at least 14 years of age. This was reinforced in 2022 by a law weighted in favour of children's consent and singularly punitive towards parents: it prohibits parents and professionals from refusing to facilitate a child's decision to undergo a gender transitioning process, and it heavily penalises those who do so. This law, which seems harsh and is without any known equivalent elsewhere, provides for 'the total or partial revocation of parental authority' of any parent who attempts to prevent their child's gender transition. In Germany, new legislation will provide children aged 14 to 17 years, with the right to change their gender marker on their birth certificate and their first name(s) in the civil registration office with the support of their parents or guardians. The fact that a 16-year-old child is debarred from taking an independent decision on this matter – but not on other matters such as accessing contraceptives – is likely to attract controversy. Children, 13 years of age or less, will be entitled to do so only if they have a signed declaration of approval from their parents or guardians. All of this raises questions as to where and why the child's consent or withholding of consent fits in the process.[60]

56 See, *FN v. CO* [2004] 4 I.R. 311, per Finlay Geoghegan J, at p 322.

57 See, *Parham, Commissioner, Department of Human Resources of Georgia v. J. R.*, 442 U.S. 584 (1979), at p 603.

58 See, for example, *Re Lucy (Gender Dysphoria)* [2013] FamCA 518 when a 13 year old girl was found not to be *Gillick* competent.

59 [2018] FamCA 161.

60 Jörg Reinhardt comments 'this will be the same as in s 1746 of the Civil Code in terms of a minor´s consent to his or her adoption' (note to author, August 4, 2023).

Welfare interests

The fact that children – in France, Germany, Ireland and Canada – will no longer be required to undergo irreversible, life-changing, medical intervention in order to legally change their name and gender, although many will want physiological transformation, must be viewed as the least detrimental way of addressing their gender identity issues; particularly given the numbers who later de-transition, a few repeatedly. Interestingly, in Canada the court sought the views – though not the consent – of an 11-year-old when considering a parental dispute regarding his eligibility for gender transitioning treatment as "these issues cannot be properly considered without J.K.'s direct participation, nor would it be fair to J.K. for the court to attempt to do so".[61]

Needless to say, for those who do come to have regrets following completion of their gender reassignment treatment, the adverse impact on their welfare interests can be devastating.

Jurisdictional differences and their significance

In 2023, Dr Riittakerttu Kaltiala, a leading psychiatrist who has presided over youth gender transition treatments for more than a decade, expressed the view that 'four out of five' gender-questioning children eventually accept their bodies if no medical interventions are carried out, citing in support data from 12 separate studies.[62] Such acceptance, however, is probably more readily made in the absence of medical intervention.

In England, as in Ireland, official recognition of gender change can only be issued to someone aged 18 years or older so, in effect, a child's legal and biological gender will always be synonymous. However, there is a significant difference between the two countries: in England and Wales an applicant for a Gender Recognition Certificate must have a diagnosis of gender dysphoria, have been living in the desired gender for at least two years and intend to do so on a lifelong basis; in Ireland, self-identification of gender is all that is necessary without any requirement for medical intervention or any form of assessment. In Ireland, those aged between 16 and 17 years can undergo gender transition if they have the consent of both parents, the agreement of the family doctor and that of an endocrinologist or psychiatrist, together with a court order. In the U.S., gender transition requires medical corroboration: the person must first be diagnosed as suffering from gender dysphoria; they must then undergo medical treatment. Canada, like Ireland, permits self-identification of gender identity, without the need for surgery.[63] In Aus-

61 *K. (N.) v. H. (A.)*, 2016 BCSC 744, per Skolrood J.

62 Described as 'Finland's leading expert on paediatric gender medicine and chief psychiatrist at its largest gender clinic' – made the claim in an interview with the liberal newspaper *Helsingin Sanomat*. See, further, https://nypost.com/2023/02/22/four-out-of-five-kids-who-question-their-gender-grow-out-of-it-trans-expert/

63 *C.F. v. Alberta* [2014] ABQB 237.

tralia, the requirements for gender recognition vary depending on the jurisdiction, but national guidelines now recognise that gender diverse people are no longer required to undergo surgery to formally register a change in their gender identity. In New Zealand – where the rate of gender transitioning children is reported to be 11 times that of Britain[64] – evidence of medical surgery to align physical characteristics with perceived gender identity has been unnecessary since the ruling in *Michael v. Registrar-General of Births*.[65]

France, in 2010, became the first country in the world to declassify gender dysphoria as a mental illness, meaning that a child expressing a wish to change their gender no longer had to receive psychiatric assessment and treatment. Further, since 2017 it has been possible to change gender identity without undergoing sex reassignment surgery, enforced sterilisation or receiving any medical diagnosis. In June 2023, the German parliament (*Bundestag*) introduced draft legislation to provide a right to gender self-identification, that is, without any need for medical involvement. The more 'affirmative' French approach must ease the pressure on uncertain children facing the challenge of transitioning and the scepticism of others. However, the relative ease with which the process may be commenced – with puberty blockers perhaps being authorised for those aged as young as ten years and hormone bombardment and surgical operations as early as 15 years – may well lead more to commit to the process, including some who may later regret having done so. In contrast, the U.S. approach requiring surgical intervention seems harsh and, given the rapidly increasing rate at which children are declaring sexual orientation and gender identity (SOGI) issues, it can only result in many with regrets and with seriously compromised welfare interests.[66]

Family breakdown

Family breakdown – whether marital or not – constitutes by far the greatest risk to the welfare interests of children and is the main focus of contemporary family law. The ECtHR has been clear that – whether occurring in circumstances governed by public or private law – family breakdown should not result in a breakup of a parent/child relationship: "only exceptional circumstances may lead to a severing of the family ties and that everything must be done to preserve personal relations and family unity or to 'rebuild' the family". Moreover, mutating families are a phenomenon of modern society; many families are now reconfigured more than once as adult relationships fracture, children are redistributed and serial or intergenerational parenting comes into play.

64 See, further, https://tatou.health.govt.nz/achieving-pae-ora-healthy-future/transing-children-1

65 (2008) 27 FRNZ 58.

66 See, further, Jorgensen, S., 'Transition Regret and Detransition: Meanings and Uncertainties', *Archives of Sexual Behavior*, Vol. 52, No. 5, pp 2173–2184, 2023.

Family breakdown and the welfare principle: private family law

In all jurisdictions studied, where there are children involved in proceedings for divorce, judicial separation or nullity, the court will require an assurance regarding the proposed arrangements for their future care, and information will need to be submitted to the court for it to be satisfied that their welfare interests will be safeguarded. This is generally addressed in a fairly perfunctory manner where the parties are not contesting future care arrangements.

Proposed arrangements for the future care of children will also arise in circumstances where, following family breakdown and reconfiguration, a non-citizen parent or step-parent seeks to effect family reunification by joining the birth parent who has care responsibility for their child.

Jurisdictional differences and their significance

In the UK, family breakdown has risen by 8% over the past decade – largely in the context of non-marital families.[67] It is estimated that this jurisdiction has the highest rate of family instability in the developed world, in particular among cohabiting couples with children under 12 years of age,[68] and this has become a settled and accepted characteristic of social life. In Ireland, where the rate of family breakdown is a great deal lower, with divorce rates at approximately half that in England and Wales,[69] there is a correspondingly stronger expectation of stability in family life. In both the UK[70] and Ireland[71] the welfare of a child, in this context, is treated in law as being the matter of paramount importance, and in both the views of the child must be ascertained and taken into account and the respective welfare checklists applied. However, there is some doubt – particularly following *YC v. United Kingdom*[72] (see, also, Chapter 5) – as to whether, in England and Wales, the interpretation and application of paramountcy in a private family law context is the same as in public family law. This has been the focus of discussion and some contention among academics and the judiciary for the past two decades. It may be that while interesting, it is not very important as the ECtHR has yet to make a definitive finding that the UK approach resting on welfare interests and paramountcy in a public or private family law context, if different, is in some way fundamentally incompatible with Article 8 requirements.

67 See, further, https://marriagefoundation.org.uk/wp-content/uploads/2017/03/MF-paper-Annual-family-breakdown.pdf

68 DeRose, L., et al., *The Cohabitation Go-Round: Cohabitation and Family Instability Across the Globe*, New York, Social Trends Institute, 2017.

69 See, further, https://ionainstitute.ie/marriage-breakdown-in-ireland-higher-than-we-think/

70 The Children's Act 1989, s 1(1) and *In Re G (Children) (Residence: Same Sex Partner)* [2006] UKHL 43.

71 The Child Care Act 1991, s 24, and the Guardianship of Infants Act 1964, s 42A.

72 Application No. 4547/10, (2012), at p 138. For further analysis of this case and related issues see George, R., *The Child's Welfare in a European Perspective*, Welfare%20in%20a%20European%20 Perspective.pdf

In the U.S., parental rights and the autonomy of the nuclear family unit are traditional benchmarks of the state/family relationship which emerge most clearly at times of family breakdown. This is very much in keeping with the legacy of the constitutional rights of birth parents under the Fourteenth Amendment as established by the ruling in *Santosky v. Kramer*[73] and also with the U.S. failure to ratify UN CROC and the Convention on the Elimination of All Forms of Discrimination against Women. The state must show compelling reason if it is to infringe rights of family privacy and parental autonomy: the welfare interests of children are best assured by the parental right to custody, and state intervention – if it is to further those interests – should focus on supporting the parents. In the event of family breakdown, then – despite the presumptive rule that a fit parent has a right to custody of their child – when there is a contest between two equally entitled parents, the rule gives way to the best interests principle and instead of the paramountcy principle, "the trial court must apply the 'best interest of the child' standard to determine custody and visitation questions".[74] Notably, however, the child's interpretation of what would constitute their best interests might then prevail as in *Custody of Vaughn*[75] when the judge was of the view that the 11-year-old child's preference in having his custody awarded to the father was enough to tip the balance in favour of the father, all else being equal (though ultimately the hearing was remanded to allow for further enquiries). Similarly in Canada, under the Divorce Act 1985, s 16(1), the court in making a decision about a child must apply only the 'best interests' test rather than the paramountcy principle and be guided by the welfare checklist as set out in s 16(3). In Australia, as the Family Court of Australia has stated "as the best interests of the child are the paramount consideration, the court may consider making such orders whenever it would be in the best interests of the child to do so after affording procedural fairness to the parties".[76] In New Zealand the court is similarly required, under the Care of Children Act 2004, s 4, to always regard the welfare and best interests of the child as the paramount consideration and to apply the welfare checklist as itemised in s 5.

In France, unlike many of the previously discussed common law countries, there is no welfare checklist to guide the judiciary, though the best interest test must be applied (Civil Code, Article 373–2) when making decisions regarding contested parental care arrangements or on other matters affecting the upbringing of a child. Based on the history of each parent's direct care of their child, the relative merits of their proposed future care arrangements and the wishes of the child, the judge will first establish that both parents must retain contact with the child and continue to discharge their parental responsibilities throughout his or her childhood. The judge will then make decisions regarding the child's future residence, the visiting rights and shared care arrangements of the non-custodial

73 455 U.S. 745 (1982).

74 *Routten v. Routten*, 843 S.E. 2d 154, 159 (2020), at 159.

75 664 N.E. 2d 434, 438–440 & n 11 (Mass. 1996).

76 *Goode & Goode* [2006] FamCA 1346, at para 65.

parent, maintenance and other ancillary matters. In Germany – as in the previously discussed common law countries – since the introduction of the Child Law Reform Act 1998 in proceedings for divorce (there are no judicial separations), the Family Court will only hear and determine issues relating to the future care of children if one of the parties files a motion accordingly. Married parents are equally vested with joint parental responsibility and will continue to be so even after a divorce, when the best interests test will be applied to determine future care arrangements (s 1671 of the Civil Code), unless there is evidence that one or both of the parents present a risk to the welfare interests of their child.[77] The advice given by the ECtHR in *Ahrens*, and not intended to be restricted to Germany, was that "consideration of what lies in the best interests of the child concerned is of paramount importance in every case of this kind; depending on their nature and seriousness, the child's best interests may override that of the parents".[78] Arguably, however, the equivocation implied in the conditioning clause "depending on their nature and seriousness" is important. It indicates a difference between the interpretation given to the paramountcy principle in the UK and several other common law nations (excluding the U.S. and Canada), and that of the ECtHR. The Article 8 caselaw, which holds that a "child's best interests *may* override that of the parents", is not quite what is meant by 'paramountcy' in the former countries. Additionally, while the "nature and seriousness" of the circumstances does condition the role and weighting of a child's welfare interests and rights in the U.S. and Canada, for example, and can be seen to do so in some ECtHR rulings,[79] it cannot be said to have that effect in the UK.

The most obvious finding from the previous discussion is not the jurisdictional differences but the similarities: the volume of cases; the restrictions on state interference – 'compelling reason' in the U.S. and 'necessary in a democratic society' in Europe – in family affairs; the fact that only a small proportion are contested, providing few opportunities to apply welfare interests and rights; the variety of parenting models coming before the courts; and the very few references in the judgments to the views of the children concerned, let alone to their rights. The differences include the fact that the role of the paramountcy principle in most of the common law jurisdictions does not seem to have any equivalent in the civil law jurisdictions, and the virtual absence of written judgments in the latter. Perhaps a major jurisdictional difference – though hard to evaluate – is whether the interpretation and application of a child's welfare interests and rights in many ECtHR rulings conform to the same standards as those of the paramountcy principle. On balance, it would seem probable that the paramountcy principle – as developed particularly in England and Wales to bridge the laws of adoption and of care and protection – is more uncompromising than its Article 8 counterpart.

77 *Neulinger and Suruk v. Switzerland*, Application No. 41615/07, (2011), at para 135.

78 *Ahrens v. Germay*, Application No. 45071/09, (2012), at para 63.

79 See, for example, *Johansen v. Norway*, Application No. 17383/90, (1996) and *K and T v. Finland*, Application No. 25702/94, (2001).

Family reunification

The ECtHR has pointed out that the national authorities obligation 'to take measures to facilitate reunion is not absolute'.[80] In *Hokkanen v. Finland*,[81] for example, a widower was unable to persuade grandparents to return his children – placed with them on a temporary respite basis – and the local authorities had not only failed repeatedly over several years to have the children returned, but the courts ultimately transferred legal custody to the grandparents. While the Court acknowledged that there were difficulties arranging contact as a result of the animosity between the parties, it took the view that because the inaction of the authorities placed a burden on the father to have "constant recourse to a succession of time-consuming and ultimately ineffectual remedies to enforce his rights", his right to respect for family life under Article 8 had been violated. Further, on a practical basis, "there may indeed come a stage where it becomes futile, if not counterproductive and harmful, to attempt to force a child to conform to a situation which, for whatever reasons, he or she resists"[82] (see, further, Chapter 8).

It is important to note that in recent years several family reunification[83] cases, involving foreign national parents or step-parents of EU children, have caused Advocates General to issue opinions and the Court of Justice of the European Union (CJEU) to determine issues in which the role of the welfare interests of the children concerned played a significant part in balancing the right to family life against immigration rules and regulations.

Case C – 540/03 *European Parliament v. Council of the European Union*[84] was one such case in which the CJEU took judicial notice of the fact that the right to family life – as established by the ECtHR in its developing caselaw on Article 8 – is now a general principle of EU law as confirmed by the Directive on Family Reunification which stated that 'measures concerning family reunification should be adopted in conformity with the obligation to protect the family and respect family life enshrined in many instruments of international law'.[85] Six years later, two joined cases were determined on the basis of evidence of an attachment between child and non-citizen step-parent applicant that would constitute 'family life'.[86] Both applications for residence permits failed for lack of any such evidence. (There was no biological link nor any legal, financial or emotional linkage between the children and applicants.) However, where – as in *Alfredo Rendon Marin* and *C.S.*[87] – the evidence supported the applicant's claim to be the biological parent and

80 See, *Suur v. Estonia*, Application No. 41736/18, (2021), at para 94.
81 (1994) 19 EHRR 139.
82 Ibid, at para 96.
83 See, *Directive 2003/86/EC of 22 September 2003 on the Right to Family Reunification* [2003] OJL 251.
84 ECLI:EU:C:2006:429, at para 30.
85 See, Preamble to Directive 2003/86/EC, Op. cit., at p 12.
86 Cases C-356/11 and C-357/11 *O, S & L* ECLI:EU:C:2012:776.
87 Case C-165/14 *Alfredo Rendón Marín v. Administración del Estado* ECLI:EU:C:2016:675; Case C-304/14 *Secretary of State for the Home Department v. CS* ECLI:EU:C:2016:674.

the primary carer of an EU citizen child, then that was sufficient to demonstrate the existence of 'family life', which the child had a right to, and sufficient also to prevent the deportation of the applicant. The same if stronger argument grounded the decision in *Chavez-Vilchez and Others*[88] where the court found that the fact that an EU citizen parent is "able and willing to assume sole responsibility for the primary day-to-day care of the child is a relevant factor, but it is not in itself a sufficient ground" for concluding that if the non-citizen parent was refused a right of residence then the child's right to respect for family life would nevertheless remain secure.[89] This was a case that concerned eight mothers of one or more Dutch children whose fathers were also Dutch. All the children lived mainly or exclusively with their mothers who sought rights of residence as this would enable them to acquire, where appropriate, social assistance or child benefits under Dutch law. The domestic authorities needed to know whether it mattered that the children were entirely legally, financially and/or emotionally dependent on their mothers as it could not be excluded that the Dutch national fathers might, in fact, be able to care for the children. The Court considered that, prior to any decision, an assessment was needed that would take into account

> in the best interests of the child concerned, all the specific circumstances, including the age of the child, the child's physical and emotional development, the extent of his emotional ties both to the Union citizen parent and to the third-country national parent, and the risks which separation from the latter might entail for the child's equilibrium.[90]

If depriving the non-citizen parent of a right of residence would be against the child's best interests, due to the child's dependency on that parent, then the latter has a derived right of residence in the EU, based on the child's right to family life.[91]

Welfare interests

In all jurisdictions there is a legislative requirement that when determining disputed custody/contact arrangements following family breakdown, the court must apply a 'welfare test' to ensure that the proposed child care arrangements are satisfactory. In many this is achieved by applying a statutory 'welfare checklist' to determine whether or not – or to what extent – the proposed arrangements comply with child welfare indicators, and in some, but not all, the paramountcy principle has a role to play.

However, the problem remains that in by far the majority of divorce and judicial separation cases following marriage breakdown, there is no judicial scrutiny of

88 Case C-133/15 *Chavez-Vilchez and Others* ECLI:EU:C:2017:354.

89 Ibid, at para 72.

90 Ibid.

91 See, also, Case C-82/16 *K.A. and Others* ECLI:EU:C:2018:308.

future parental arrangements. (There is oversight but, in the absence of dispute, this is very superficial in nature.)

Family breakdown and the welfare principle: public family law; civil

The policy, principles and law governing the civil jurisdiction of public family law as it relates to children remains anchored on the same functions in the 21st century as it had for most of the 20th century. As identified earlier, these are 'prevention' and 'promotion', which constitute the grounds for consensual state intervention in family affairs; and 'protection', most often accompanied by 'control' leading to variants of 'state care/custody', following coercive intervention. All functions are required to be applied in accordance with UN CROC provisions to which the eight jurisdictions of this study subscribe (even if not yet ratified by the U.S.).

Jurisdictional differences and their significance

In the early part of the last half of the 20th century, changes in the law relating to the family and the welfare of children seemed to reflect an important policy shift in the role of the state: away from a general investment in public services in support of parental responsibilities and the maintenance of family unity and towards an investment in the professional and institutional resources necessary to protect children and hold their parents accountable for breaches in statutorily specified thresholds of parental responsibility. As this series has shown, there were several different reasons prompting such a shift: in part it was simply an acknowledgment that supporting family unity, marital or not, had become untenable; while advances in the field of child psychiatry and behavioural psychology had generated a recognition that the formative years of child development – as regards opportunities for attachment, emotional and physical security, etc. – were crucial for a child's welfare, so early child focussed intervention was the priority; and of course the inescapable logic of demographic trends, together with the cost of government responses to international exigencies – war, economic recession, climate change, large-scale migration, an enduring cost-of-living crisis, etc. – meant that tax revenues could no longer stretch to accommodate generic public service provision, which had to be either franchised out to private companies or prioritised and targeted accordingly.

Consensual state intervention

By the turn of the last century, while all eight jurisdictions had in place legislation detailing state responsibility to provide family support services, a disconnect had become apparent between the duty to provide and the actual provision. There was some jurisdictional variation in this misalignment.

PREVENTION

In those countries where traditional family values and the presumption favouring the autonomy and responsibility of birth parents are strongest – Germany, Ireland, parts of the U.S. and Australia – the lack of state supportive intervention is weakest, though not so much in Ireland where the constitutional guarantees in Articles 41 and 42 require the state to protect 'the inalienable and imprescriptible rights of the family' and the 'inalienable right and duty of parents', implying that the state will provide special protection for the status of parents and family. The same implication would also be true of France if, as Eglin claims, the role of the judge 'makes the French system close to a defence of the birth family and parents' rights ideology',[92] a perception corroborated by the perpetuation of the '*accouchement sous X*' practice which allows for an absolute and permanent renunciation of all parental rights and responsibilities, indicating a state reluctance to radically intervene in matters integral to parental status. It would seem less the case in England and Wales where the ethos, if not so much the practice, of a national health and welfare system – with the inference that public services will bear some responsibility for supporting the parental role – still prevails. In Ireland, family support has largely been left to religious and secular voluntary organisations and to the non-profit sector more generally. Given the particularly worrying health outcomes for many children in New Zealand, where there are statutory provisions placing specific duties on the authorities to provide support services to vulnerable families, the gap between legislatively required family support and appropriate service provision is most noticeable. In this country, as in its fellow CANZUS nations (Canada, Australia, New Zealand, United States), the consistent over-representation of Indigenous children in the child-care and juvenile justice systems clearly demonstrates a failure of state consensual preventative intervention on their behalf.

The significance of 'prevention' in this context is the same as it is in any other: its absence or ineffectiveness results in the deterioration of a known risk situation and the infliction of otherwise avoidable damage or loss. It can also have a procedural significance. Article 8 of the ECHR – particularly as interpreted in *YC v. United Kingdom*[93] – requires substantive evidence that preventative measures have been taken before state coercive intervention can justifiably proceed. In that case, the fact that the local authority had sought to 'rebuild the family through the provision of support for alcohol abuse and opportunities for parenting assistance' provided the necessary evidence to satisfy the procedural requirement (see, further, Chapter 5). Arguably, judging from the statistics relating to deteriorating children's health and increased admissions to the care and justice systems, this function – not unlike 'promotion' – remains largely aspirational. Its tendency towards spuriousness is perhaps most obvious in the alarming U.S.

92 Eglin, M., *Judicial Child Protection in France and England: A Comparative Approach*, June 2001, www.afmif.fr/Judicial-child-protection-in.html

93 Application No. 4547/10, (2012), at p 138.

infant mortality rates[94]: the fact that the world's richest nation has one of the world's poorest rates for keeping infants alive (33rd out of 38 in 2019, according to the Organization for Economic Cooperation and Development),[95] says a lot about 'prevention'.

PROMOTION

In terms of its functionality and its defining characteristics as a legal term, 'promotion' is an elusive concept. While there is a high level of jurisdictional consistency in the legislative references made to the need to promote the welfare interests of children, the lack of specificity in the related statutory provisions leaves little scope for measuring the effectiveness of state interventions to that end, let alone determining any jurisdictional differentiation in relative achievements.

In an Indigenous context

Given the research findings,[96] it might have been anticipated that an investment of more resources would be channelled in the direction suggested by the predictive indicators of out-of-home care – poverty, lack of basic needs, etc. – with the objective of relieving pressure and preventing the necessity for admission to the child welfare system. In fact, neither those findings nor the explicit preventative legislative principles (such as those found in Jordan's Principle and the Indian Child Welfare Act) have increased effective service provision nor reduced the over-representation of Indigenous children in the welfare and justice systems of the CANZUS nations.

Coercive state intervention

Within the broad boundaries of family law, the most basic contemporary indicator of the welfare interests of the child lies in the statutory grounds for child abuse and neglect. Evidence of state-inflicted historical abuse can be found in the many official reports testifying to the fact that hundreds of thousands of children suffered as a direct result of government policy in the CANZUS nations and as a consequence of the English government policy of transporting children to those nations (colonies at the time).

PROTECTION

There is some degree of jurisdictional variation in the threshold for state intervention in family affairs on child protection grounds. The Irish threshold is higher

94 The provisional infant mortality rate for the U.S. in 2022 was 5.60 infant deaths per 1,000 live births, 3% higher than the rate in 2021 (5.44). See, further, www.cdc.gov/nchs/data/vsrr/vsrr033.pdf

95 See, further, www.americashealthrankings.org/learn/reports/2021-annual-report/international-comparison

96 See, for example the Pew Charitable Trust report 'Time for Reform: A Matter of Justice for American Indian and Alaskan Native Children', 2007.

than most: there must be compelling reasons why the child cannot remain within parental care, and the child must require care or protection which they are otherwise unlikely to receive. Only slightly lower is that of the U.S. and Canada where the drive to protect children by removing them from an abusing or neglectful parent would seem to be considerably stronger than in the UK and on a par with the rising rates of removal in Australia. This is similar to France and Germany, more so in the latter where children can only be removed from parental care if there is no other option. The indisputable evidence of the scale and breadth of state failure to protect children in New Zealand would seem to suggest that the threshold is highest in that jurisdiction.[97]

The requirement for the state to be proactive in intervening to ensure the protection of children is a statutory requirement in England and Wales (though parental chastisement continues to be lawful, there is no mandatory public duty to report abuse, and non-consensual adoption from the care system has long been a priority policy objective) but not in the jurisdictions where the state maintains its traditional respect for family autonomy.

It is also worthy of note that in Canada and the U.S., neglect rather than abuse provides the main grounds relied upon for the issue of court orders transferring care responsibility from parents to state. That this is also the case in relation to the Māori in New Zealand and the Indigenous communities in Australia is significant as it raises the possibility that the level of poverty – endemic in Indigenous communities – rather than parental conduct is the primary cause of children being removed from their family homes in all CANZUS nations, and the probability that Indigenous children are disproportionately represented in the relevant care order statistics.

The state care system

In all jurisdictions, children are either admitted to state care with parental consent or are committed without it by judicial order. Children are then placed in residential care, with family members in 'kinship care'; in foster care; or in an adoption placement. Significantly, there is a marked difference in the jurisdictional rate at which children enter the state care system.

97 See, for example: the Organization for Economic Cooperation and Development report that rates of child abuse and neglect are high in New Zealand relative to other developed nations (Gilbert, R., et al., 'Child Maltreatment: Variation in Trends and Policies in Six Developed Countries', *Lancet*, 2011, https://scholar.google.com/scholar_lookup?hl=en&publication_year=2011&author=R+Gilbert&author=J+Fluke&author=M+O%27Donnell&author=A+Gonzalez-Izquierdo&author=M+Brownell&author=P+Gulliver&title=Child+maltreatment%3A+variation+in+trends+and+policies+in+six+developed+countries); the UNICEF report that this country has one of the worst rates of child abuse in the developed world (of the 41 developed countries included in the 2020 UNICEF Innocenti Report Card, New Zealand ranks 35th overall for child well-being); and the Youth Health and Wellbeing chart, which ranks this country as having the highest rate of teen suicides in the developed world (www.newstalkzb.co.nz/on-air/kerre-woodham-mornings/audio/nathan-wallis-new-zealand-ranks-bottom-of-developed-countries-on-youth-mortality-rates).

RESIDENTIAL CARE

The use of such placements has greatly diminished in recent years, following many national child abuse reports – particularly in Ireland, Canada, New Zealand and Australia – where care was most often in facilities owned and staffed by religious organisations that have since been found to be responsible for perpetuating institutional child abuse. So, also, in the CANZUS nations where the assimilation policy saw generations of Indigenous children being removed from their families of origin to residential schools and taught to abandon their Indigenous culture in favour of westernised cultural norms. In contrast, contemporary policy and practice in France and Germany favour residential care in preference to foster families, particularly in Germany. This preference may reflect both a strong state deference to parental status/family unity in both countries and to the, at best, marginal relevance of the paramountcy principle. In England and Wales the reliance on residential care would seem to be a forced option. The CRC commented in its 2023 report:

> With regard to children in the care system, the Committee was deeply concerned about the large number of children still in care, including in unregulated accommodation such as hotels . . . also concerned at the placement of children in situations of vulnerability, in secure and residential care homes, sometimes amounting to depriving children of their liberty.[98]

Much the same critique could now be levelled at Ireland.

There will always be a need for small residential facilities, professionally staffed and catering for children with particularly complex health and social care issues. These are gradually becoming an integrated part of the state care system in all jurisdictions. They all also share a growing need for secure accommodation that offers safe but closed treatment facilities for those troubled children who are at risk of harming themselves or others. The reliance on such facilities is greatest in the U.S.

FOSTER CARE

This form of state care has for many decades been viewed as most conducive to promoting a child's welfare interests because it provides a substitute family life and a protective environment that allows for safe attachments and developmental growth; it also enables the child to retain links with their parents, facilitated by contact arrangements, which best ensure that the child maintains an authentic sense of identity and of belonging to their family and community of origin. All six common law jurisdictions rely heavily on foster parent placements, whereas the two from the civil law tradition – while certainly using such placements – do so to a markedly lesser extent. Indeed, the CRC has expressed concern in its 2023 report on France regarding the use of foster care stating – in a comment perhaps intended

98 CRC/C/GBR/CO/6-7, 2023, https://childrenslegalcentre.wales/un-committee-on-rights-of-child-uk-concluding-observations-2023/#

to have a wider application – that the 'placement of children in foster families is disruptive, and changes in foster families are frequent, disregarding children's attachments to foster parents'.[99]

In the U.S., where foster care services – along with adoption – are largely franchised out to for-profit organisations, there would appear to be a pushback on the established commitment to this form of state care. It may be that this is due largely or in part to the expense involved, but it might also, perhaps, be attributable to a conflict between the above two objectives. Foster care may be on the verge of facing rejection as the preferred form of state care, having become a victim of its own success. There would seem to be a growing acknowledgment that a child removed from failing or unsafe parental care and placed in an approved family, where paid carers are encouraged and incentivised to behave as model substitute parents, creates an attractive caring environment in which the child wants to remain and which tends to intimidate birth parents, resulting in a loosening of ties between the two. Inevitably, this undermines the likelihood of the state achieving its ordained objectives: of rehabilitating the child to parental care – as required by international law – and avoiding where possible the retention of the child in foster care for the duration of his or her childhood. It remains to be seen how this develops, but it might explain the relatively sudden attractiveness of kinship placements (which were once considered not to be compliant with a child's welfare interests because they were viewed as likely to expose a child to a confused sense of family relationships and to the risk of being returned to the circumstances which had prompted their initial removal) in all jurisdictions.

KINSHIP CARE

In recent decades there has been a pronounced shift away from the former orthodoxy that children in need of out-of-home care should be wholly removed from the troublesome context of their birth families and placed in a professionally managed care service. In a reversal of earlier policy, previous weaknesses are now viewed as strengths: it is seen as an attractive state option precisely because it retains a child's links with his or her birth family, providing for minimal disruption to a child's sense of belonging within the family, class, culture and locality of their birth. It often leads to adoption with many children being legally returned through that process to their kinship networks. This policy, reinforced by the use of guardianship orders, has been positively developed for some years by public child-care agencies in the U.S. and Canada. In Australia, as of 2021, the majority of children in state care were placed with relatives or kinship carers rather than with foster carers (54% and 36%, respectively).[100] At the same time in New Zealand, 88% were living with family/whānau or with a caregiver of the same

99 CRC/C/FRA/CO/6-7, at para 32(b).

100 Note that in 2018–19, all states and territories adopted a standardised national system for defining 'out-of-home care' and for related data collection.

ethnicity.[101] Both Ireland and England and Wales also now rely heavily on kinship placements.

An interesting point of difference between France and Germany is their respective use of kinship placements: in Germany the majority of children in foster care are placed with a relative (60% in 2005); in France, this is true for only a small minority (7% in 2007).

In an Indigenous context

The cultural dissonance between the Indigenous and non-Indigenous communities is particularly acute at times of family disruption. Tribal coherence, whereby members are bound by mutual ties of loyalty and belonging, and intergenerational networks of relatives, is threatened by family breakdown.

Coercive state intervention

Coercive state intervention in family affairs, on grounds of child neglect or abuse, is governed by statute, and the grounds are equally applicable to Indigenous and all other children. In practice that intervention may be conducted by tribal authorities and be determined by a hearing before a tribal or state/province court (in respect of an off-the-reservation child).

Exiting the state care system

For some time there has been a distinct jurisdictional difference in the response to the ECtHR statement of principle that "everything must be done to preserve personal relations and, where appropriate, to 'rebuild' the family. It is not enough to show that a child could be placed in a more beneficial environment for his upbringing".[102]

REHABILITATION

Article 10(1) of UN CROC requires that all applications for family reunification involving children be dealt with 'in a positive, humane and expeditious manner'.

The ECtHR has repeatedly reminded states of the principle that they should do all they can to maintain relationships between a child in its care and the birth family, and work towards their reunification: even in cases where parent and child are separated by hundreds of miles and have been apart for several years; their relationship remains covered by the definition of family life, and a parent's right

101 See, further, www.orangatamariki.govt.nz/assets/Uploads/About-us/Performance-and-monitoring/Quarterly-report/September-2021/Oranga-Tamariki-Quarterly-Performance-Report-as-at-September-2021.pdf

102 *YC v. the United Kingdom*, at para 35.

to be reunited with his or her child creates for states a "positive obligation" to take measures to fulfil that objective.[103] However, the principle is more often violated than upheld. Foster care, intended to be a temporary solution, has instead become the default destination for tens of thousands of children for the duration of their childhood, despite rehabilitation to parental care being the declared objective in international and domestic law.

In Australia, New Zealand and Ireland, the preferred policy has been to work towards family reunification[104] rather than impose the permanent severance effects of non-consensual adoption, though in parts of Australia during the last few years there have been indications that in some states this policy may now be changing to one of promoting adoption. In France and Germany, the Civil Codes require the authorities to prioritise the safe rehabilitation of a child in state care to their family of origin.[105] In France, this is reinforced by statutes that necessitate planning for family reunification, wherever feasible, for every child taken into state care, and in practice there is considerable investment in 'the ideology of maintaining the parent-infant relationship at all costs'.[106] In Germany, there is no explicit equivalent legal obligation: rehabilitation would seem to be largely aspirational; family reunification is achieved for no more than 4% to 5% of the child-care population. In France, judging from the CRC recommendation to the authorities that they should 'facilitate the rehabilitation and social reintegration of children', the rate of successful rehabilitation is not much better.[107]

NON-CONSENSUAL ADOPTION

Current UK judicial guidance[108] diverges from ECtHR benchmark cases,[109] and from practice in most other common law and civil law jurisdictions, but is in keeping with practice in the U.S., in that it has firmly established a policy preference for adoption rather than long-term foster care. This policy is facilitated by legislative provisions aligning the grounds for care orders and adoption orders, by the practice of concurrent placements, by the use of freeing and placement orders and by significant government financial grants. In Ireland, Canada, New Zealand and most of Australia, while there is no corresponding established policy, a few children do currently exit public care by way of adoption; those that do tend to be adolescents being adopted by their long-term foster parents (see, further, Chapter 8).

103 *Saleck Bardi v. Spain*, Application No. 66167/09, (2011).

104 Note, however, that there is no nationally agreed definition of what constitutes 'family re-unification'.

105 For France, see Civil Code, article 3750–2. For Germany, see the Civil Code, s 1673 et seq.

106 See, Berger, M., *The Failure of Child Protection Services*, Paris, Dunod, 2003.

107 CRC/C/FRA/CO/5, at para 54.

108 See, *Seddon v. Oldham MBC* [2015] EWHC 2609 (Fam) and *Re W (A Child)* [2016] EWCA Civ 793.

109 *YC v. the United Kingdom*, at para 35.

AGEING OUT

This has traditionally been the fate of most of the child-care population in all jurisdictions, but in recent years, as noted earlier, some have developed affirmative policies to return children to their families of origin whenever feasible or, failing that, to actively pursue non-consensual adoption.

The civil law countries – France and Germany – have a well-established record of retaining by far the majority of their child-care populations in state care for the duration of childhood. While, admittedly, the common law countries also provide state care for many children until they age out at 18 years of age, the proportion is much lower, and there is a stronger likelihood that the retention is due to failed efforts to rehabilitate or find adopters. Ireland would be an exception as a far higher proportion of its child-care population remain in long-term foster care than is the case in other common law jurisdictions.

In an Indigenous context

The most striking jurisdictional difference between the Indigenous children of the CANZUS nations and other children – as regards their experience of the state care system – is the wholly disproportionate number of Indigenous children entering that system.

Regardless of the parallel care routes – state or tribal – by which an Indigenous child is admitted to state care, the disposal options are much the same and subject to the mandatory hierarchy of placement choices and the explicit requirement that the professionals involved – from probation service or the child welfare authorities – ensure that members of the child's family and tribe are engaged in formulating the care plan.

FOSTER CARE

In all CANZUS nations, there are clear statutory directives requiring that when an Indigenous child requires out-of-home care, preference in order of priority should be given to foster care with birth family, a relative, or other tribal member. Nonetheless, the shortage of Indigenous foster carers results in children often being placed with non-Indigenous foster parents, often located far from the birth family and other tribal connections. Once placed, every effort must be made to maintain the child's relationships with birth family members, tribe and culture.

PARENT/CHILD RELATIONSHIP

Maintaining the bonds of attachment between a child in foster care and members of his or her family of origin can be more difficult when that child is from an Indigenous community: the shortage of Indigenous foster parents, the distances involved and quite often the poverty constraints affecting the child's family and community all present real obstacles. However, the parent/child bond is looser in an Indigenous context, where traditionally parenting was not exclusive to the nuclear family unit but, to a varying extent, is a responsibility shared among the community, with the result that rehabilitation from state care need not be interpreted as a return to birth family care. So, while the legal obligation requiring child welfare authorities to work towards rehabilitating the child is the same, and as most placements are with relatives, this is more easily achieved even if the rehabilitation is to the community and not necessarily to the birth parents.

Family breakdown and the welfare principle: public family law: criminal

For child welfare purposes, family breakdown in the context of private and public civil law – as outlined earlier – is where the greatest volume of cases occur and where the widest range of child welfare–related principles are applied. However, it may also occur as the cause or effect of juvenile crime, a context in which welfare considerations must be balanced against those of justice and where personal accountability and the prevention of future harm to the public will weigh heavily with the court. While in all jurisdictions there is a general duty to take into account the welfare of children, their justice systems are generally focussed primarily on protecting the public, promoting accountability and preventing re-offending. The French system is singular in that the dual civil/criminal jurisdiction administered by the *juge des enfants* represents an approach long since abandoned elsewhere in favour of keeping a legal focus on welfare interests quite separate from that on criminal activity (see, further, Chapter 2).

Conclusion

As family life becomes more diversified, unstable, prone to breakdown and reconfiguration, so family law is having to be adjusted accordingly. This chapter has shown just how far that body of law has been stretched in structure and content as its form is reshaped to accommodate new functions alongside those of a more traditional nature.

The contemporary focus on the rights of the child – as distinct from the traditional concern for welfare interests – is probably attributable to several different causal factors. One such has been the trickle-down effect of human rights that inevitably isolates the individual and emphasises their particular claim to victim status. Another prominent factor is the demographic trends that have forced a contraction in public spending, leading to the state being more ready to adopt a 'child rescue' rather than a holistic family support role. The willingness to contemplate a child's welfare needs as detachable from birth family relationships would seem to owe much to the emergence of a body of academic research – particularly in the field of developmental psychology – which has greatly enhanced and informed professional understanding of child welfare–related matters and strengthened an awareness of a child's right to a close nurturing attachment to someone who need not be a birth parent. In addition, the steady pressure from international judicial and regulatory bodies – particularly the rulings of the ECtHR – encourage national compliance with principles of international jurisprudence, including those that reinforce a child's sense of personal and cultural identity.

The change in legal emphasis, from prioritising parental rights and support for the nuclear family unit to instead prioritising the recognition of a child's rights, has necessitated what may turn out to be a 'root and branch' overhaul of the law relating to children: one with a central focus on the child, which has necessitated making the court a more amenable and effective setting that facilitates child participation. A notable feature of this reform has been a move away from the rigid structuring of the law into distinct sets of proceedings, each determined by a final and absolute order, towards a more flexible or 'hybrid' approach that anticipates probable ongoing state involvement (for example in adoption). This will be explored in the following Part II.

Part II

Hybrid family law and implications for children's rights

4 Commercial surrogacy and parental abduction

Introduction

Surrogacy and the abduction of a child by their parent are both facets of contemporary family life that have in common their hybrid nature and an exponential rate of increase. As they expand their proportion of family law cases, the principles now being worked out in relation to both will in time require adjustments to be made in family law as a whole. The purpose of this chapter is to examine jurisdictional differences in approach to commercial surrogacy and parental abduction with a view to assessing the significance of such differences and their associated principles.

Surrogacy

The advances in medical science that have made surrogacy available have not been viewed by everyone as an unmitigated benefit. It has been consistently opposed by religious organisations, particularly by Catholicsm and Judaism. Opposition has not been confined to theologians and other religious adherents. Those with an interest in ethics and morality have protested against what has been termed the 'rent a womb' approach to procreation as have those with human rights concerns who object to the exploitation of women in socially disadvantaged circumstances being used as surrogates by the wealthy who can afford such disposable income options. Consequently, recognising a legal parent/child relationship established through surrogacy or alternative reproductive technology can be challenging, especially where there are explicit or implicit bans on surrogacy, as is the case for the majority of Council of Europe states. Given this lack of consensus on the lawfulness of surrogacy, or as regards the legal recognition of the intended child/parent relationship, the European Court of Human Rights (ECtHR) is of the view that states must in principle be afforded a wide margin of appreciation: both as regards the regulation of surrogacy and as regards the recognition of such child/parent relationships.

Definitions, principles and international law

Initially surrogacy was a matter of private family law, confined as it most usually was to an arrangement made between family members or close friends. When it was largely transformed from being based on altruism to commerce, to that extent

DOI: 10.4324/9781003510383-7

surrogacy was thereby also transformed into a matter of public family law. As both the altruistic and the commercial variants now continue in tandem, surrogacy may fairly be viewed as a hybrid public/private aspect of family law.

Definitions

Surrogacy is complicated. The most readily understood definition is the distinction drawn between gestational and traditional surrogacy. In gestational, the surrogate has no biological link with the child, as the eggs of another (most usually the commissioning mother) have been implanted in her womb using in vitro fertilisation (IVF) which enables the eggs to be fertilised (most usually by the commissioning father, or another donor) to create the embryo the surrogate then carries; same-sex couples, single men and heterosexual couples and women who cannot produce healthy eggs commonly resort to egg donors in the gestational form of surrogacy. On the other hand, in traditional surrogacy, the surrogate's own eggs are used, making her the biological mother; and intrauterine insemination, or artificial insemination, is employed for fertilisation purposes. Many countries – including the UK, Australia and Canada – permit altruistic but prohibit commercial surrogacy. Others – including some U.S. states – permit both; yet others – including France and Germany – prohibit both.

Differentiation between altruistic and commercial surrogacy

Surrogacy – commercial rather than altruistic – has greatly increased in recent years[1] and, for those who can afford to make that choice, is now rapidly displacing adoption as the preferred means of achieving parenthood. It is particularly attractive to same-sex couples and to those for whom a genetic link to the child is wanted and possible. For those unable to start a family by normal means, surrogacy – whether commercial or altruistic – offers an alternative means to achieve the same end result. The motivation required to make, sustain and possibly to pay for a surrogacy arrangement ensures that the resulting child is very much planned for and 'wanted', with a high probability that the child's welfare interests will be safeguarded and promoted.

ALTRUISTIC SURROGACY

This form of surrogacy occurs when one woman, motivated by altruism, has a baby on behalf of another – who is unable to give birth – for the latter to rear as her own. Not unlike blood or organ donation, this is often viewed as an aspect of 'the gift relationship'.[2] The fact that the surrogate providing such a service may receive a

1 See, How Many Surrogate Births Per Year? 2022, https://worldcenterofbaby.com/blog/how-many-surrogate-births-per-year-statistics-of-newborn-babies/

2 See, Titmus, R., *The Gift Relationship: from Human Blood to Social Policy*, The New Press, 1997.

sum of money to compensate for her role in the process will not detract from the definition of 'altruism', provided the amount is not excessive.[3]

From the perspective of the welfare interests and rights of the child, an altruistic surrogacy arrangement between family members, even if extended, may give rise to issues: there may be genetic complications as a consequence of consanguinity, and insecurity and anxiety for the child due to uncertainties as to who is the 'real' mother and a distorted perception as to where the child 'fits' in the family.

COMMERCIAL SURROGACY

Commercial surrogacy, as a route to becoming a parent, would seem on the face of it to be a straightforward contractual transaction for services rendered: 'both parties are motivated by personal gain to enter a legally enforceable agreement, which stipulates that the contract mother or "surrogate" is to bear a child of the intending parents in exchange for a fee';[4] it is treated as such in many jurisdictions including most U.S. states; but it is also prohibited in many others, including France, Germany, Ireland, Australia and the UK.

Gestational surrogacy

This occurs when a surrogate is impregnated with the genetic material of another – usually through IVF – and carries the resulting foetus to full term when the child is handed over to that other or to someone else. A gestational surrogate mother is not related to the baby she carries: there is no biological link between the surrogate and the child she is carrying.

GENETIC LINK

Surrogacy, whether altruistic or commercial, can include a genetic link between the child and one of the prospective 'parents'. In such circumstances, the courts tend to lean more favourably towards finding that the unit satisfies the definition of 'family life'. Interestingly, the ECtHR has accepted that Article 8 can extend to the potential relationship which may develop between intended parents and a child, even if family life has not yet been fully established,[5] and has ruled that Article 8 is applicable to the relationship between the applicant and her embryos as they contained part of her genetic material and therefore constitute part of her identity.[6]

3 In the UK, for example, reasonable expenses under £12,000 are allowed, and, according to a report by Surrogacy UK (2015), altruistic surrogates typically receive £10,000 to £15,000. See, further, Horsey K., *Surrogacy in the UK: Myth Busting and Reform: Report of the Surrogacy UK Working Group on Surrogacy Law Reform*, Surrogacy UK (Publishers), 2015, www.familylaw.co.uk/docs/pdf-files/Surrogacy_in_the_UK_report.pdf

4 See, Walker, R. and van Zyl, L., *Towards a Professional Model of Surrogate Motherhood*, London, UK, Palgrave Macmillan, 2017.

5 *D. and Others v. Belgium*, Application No. 29176/13, (2014).

6 *Parrillo v. Italy*, Application No. 46470/11, (2015).

In *Paradiso and Campanelli v. Italy*,[7] the Court considered the case of an Italian couple who, having made surrogacy arrangements with a Russian clinic and paid 50,000 euros, took delivery of a baby and were issued with a birth certificate which indicated that they were the parents. On their return with the child to Italy, they sought to have the child registered as theirs at which point DNA testing ordered by the Court showed that the applicant was not the biological father of the child. The authorities determined that as the applicants had violated both domestic surrogacy law and international adoption law, the child would be removed and taken into state care. As the birth parents were unknown, the child was considered 'abandoned' for all legal purposes and had been placed in a foster home before being placed in a family with a view to adoption. In 2015, at an initial hearing, the Court found that a *de facto* family life had existed, taking into account that the applicants had lived in Italy with the child for six months and had "acted as parents" towards the child. It held that the applicants' Article 8 right to private and family life had been violated by the irreversible removal of the child. At a second hearing, the Grand Chamber, as previously explained, reversed the earlier findings. It found that the applicants wish to become parents had been operationalized with such disregard for the law that their "parental project" had been vitiated: they deliberately acted with premeditation in order to circumvent domestic and international legislations as regards medically assisted reproduction techniques and adoption. In so doing they left the Italian authorities with the

> difficult choice between allowing the applicants to continue their relationship with the child, thereby legalising the unlawful situation created by them as a *fait accompli*, or taking measures with a view to providing the child with a family in accordance with the legislation on adoption.[8]

The recklessness of their methods was such that the end result could not have provided the secure framework necessary to satisfy the legal definition of "family life". The ruling provides authority for the proposition that the existence of family life for the purposes of Article 8 is a question of fact in which the court will have regard to the emotional ties between the members of the family, the period of time spent in a familial relationship, and the existence or non-existence of a biological link between the persons concerned. In the absence of any biological link, the duration of shared cohabitation necessary to establish family life will be longer.

A noteworthy factor in this judgment is that the prompt intervention of the state authorities in removing the child was credited as having pre-empted the development of a bonding relationship which could have been determinative in entitling the applicants to Article 8 protection for their "family life". This finding has clear implications for practices such as the pre-emptory removal of babies from maternal care in hospitals and from short-term foster care placements.

7 Application No. 25358/12, (2017), at para 197.
8 Ibid, at para 209.

Principles

The "principle of sanctity of life"[9] finds explicit protection under many international instruments including the Universal Declaration on Human Rights, the European Convention on Human Rights, the International Covenant on Civil and Political Rights and in the Preamble of the 1989 Convention on the Rights of the Child. Consequently, it is unsurprising that commercial surrogacy, genetic editing and other forms of intervention that may be perceived as interfering with the "sanctity of life" have been and continue to be highly contentious on both sides of the Atlantic.[10]

Protection of privacy

Like adoption, surrogacy was once a matter that belonged firmly in private family law. In recent decades, as the commercial variant of surrogacy has swollen in volume, there has been a corresponding shrinking in that of adoption: while the two are connected, the relationship is not solely one of cause and effect; other factors have played a part. The right of a child to enjoy respect for his or her private life has grown in salience as the courts deal with the increased complexity of surrogacy cases.

THE EUROPEAN CONVENTION ON HUMAN RIGHTS, ARTICLE 8

The Article 8 right to private life has been found to extend to respect for decisions to become a parent or not.[11]

Because of the uncertainties that can accompany surrogacy arrangements, the courts when faced with custody contests will consider the thorny question – is it the welfare interests of a child or the acquisitive interests of a childless couple that are being prioritised? In that context, the child's right to respect for his or her private life, within the meaning of Article 8 of the European Convention on Human Rights (ECHR), will have a strong bearing on the outcome and may well be determinative. In *Mennesson v. France*,[12] *Labassée v. France*[13] and others,[14] for example, the ECtHR considered the refusal of the French authorities to recognise the legal relationship between children born as a result of surrogacy treatment abroad and the commissioning couples. It extended protection to the children concerned by ruling that state intervention had caused a violation of Article 8 as regards the right to respect for their private lives.

9 *Reeve v. The United Kingdom*, Application No. 24844/94, (2002).
10 See, for example, Gozdecka, D.A., 'Backlash or Widening the Gap? Women's Reproductive Rights in the Twenty-First Century', *Laws*, Vol. 9, No. 1, 2020, https://doi.org/10.3390/laws9010008
11 *Evans v. the United Kingdom*, Application No. 6339/05, (2007).
12 Application No. 65192/11, (2014).
13 Application No. 65941/11, (2014).
14 For example, *Foulon and Bouvet v. France*, Application Nos. 9063/14 and 10410/14, (2016) and *Laborie v. France*, Application No. 44024/13, (2017).

THE U.S. CONSTITUTION

In the U.S., the judicial rationale in relation to contraception[15] – as being protected by the right of privacy – paved the way for an extension of a similar recognition in respect of abortion which was duly affirmed by the U.S. Supreme Court (USSC) in *Roe v. Wade*[16] and which for the next 50 years established a federal right of access to abortion, a ruling that also served as an iconic benchmark for judiciary and legislatures elsewhere.[17] However, in fact this ruling was less about establishing a right to abortion and more to do with recognition of the importance of personal autonomy which itself was anchored on the right to privacy.[18]

Prevention of exploitation

As noted by Justice Ryan in *Mason v. Mason*,[19] surrogacy can lead to "rampant forum shopping by couples seeking the best surrogacy prices and conditions". Such a marketing approach to starting a family – which has included rejection of babies that failed to meet expectations – would seem exploitive and may well be damaging for the infants and birth parents involved. Undoubtedly there are issues regarding the commodification of children and the exploitation of women.

COMMODIFICATION OF CHILDREN

The legal uncertainties that accompany surrogacy arrangements – and are most apparent in commercial arrangements made overseas in respect of children who return to be domiciled in the surrogacy prohibiting jurisdiction of the commissioning 'parents' – must clearly be adverse to the welfare interests of the children concerned. The scope for exploitation in surrogacy arrangements, and the consequent vulnerability of a child's welfare interests, were highlighted in a recent U.S. case in which a same-sex couple pre-ordered an unborn baby for $8,000 who was duly handed over immediately after birth.[20] The child subsequently suffered serious sexual abuse at the hands of his paedophile parents undergoing what was described by the U.S. Attorney's Office as "some of the most heinous acts of exploitation that this Office has ever seen".[21]

15 See, *Griswold v. Connecticut*, 381 U.S. 479 (1965) and *Eisenstadt v. Baird*, 405 U.S. 438 (1972).

16 410 U.S. 113. 1973.

17 See, for example, Ginsburg, R.B., 'Some Thoughts on Autonomy and Equality in Relation to Roe v. Wade', *North Carolina Law Review*, Vol. 63, pp 375–386, 1985. Also, see, Siegel, R. and Greenhouse, L., 'The Unfinished Story of Roe V. Wade', in Murray, M., Shaw, K. and Siegel, R. (eds.), *Reproductive Rights and Justice Stories*, St. Paul, Foundation Press, 2018.

18 See, *Planned Parenthood of Southeastern Pennsylvania v. Casey*, 505 U.S. 833 (1991). See, further, O'Halloran, K., *Reproductive Rights & the Law: Dissent and Democracy*, Elgar Publishing, forthcoming.

19 [2013] FamCA 424, at para 4.

20 See, *United States of America v. Mark Jonathan Newton*, United States District Court, 1: 12-CR-0121-SEB-DKL, per Barker J (June 25, 2013) 8.

21 Department of Justice, *Hogsett Announces Charges Against Four Men in International Child Exploitation Conspiracy*, Press Release, June 28, 2013, www.usdoj.gov/usao/ins

SURROGATES

Surrogacy 'tourism' is now becoming something of a moral dilemma as prospective parents shop among the less developed nations and among the socially disadvantaged in the developed western nations for the best deal available. The socio-economic reality of the circumstances of surrogates in India, Thailand, Ukraine and elsewhere detracts from the argument that

> prohibiting surrogacy restricts the freedom of women to use their reproductive capacity as they choose and that it is an affront to the autonomy of women to make their own choices about the way they will spend their time and their talents.[22]

Mater semper certa est

The principle that the mother is always certain has been a legal benchmark in family law for centuries, but its continuing shelf-life is beginning to look a bit dubious. The rule creates a legal presumption that the woman who gave birth (the surrogate) is the mother of that child. Should the terms of the transaction be renounced by one of the parties – either by the surrogate because she has chosen to keep the child or the commissioning couple because, as in a recent Australian case, the child had what was perceived to be a defect – then in law the surrogate may well be recognised as the mother and be entitled, or required, to assume parental responsibilities.

Cases such as *S. H. and others v. Austria*[23] and *H. v. the United Kingdom*,[24] have confirmed that the ECtHR will continue to regard this as the governing principle, thus hoping to avoid the possibility of multiple parents claiming legal rights or responsibilities in respect of a child born by means of IVF.

PRESUMPTION FAVOURING CARE BY BIRTH PARENT/S

Speaking for the current law in England and Wales, Lindblom LJ has warned the following:[25]

> The repeated reference to a 'right' for a child to be brought up by his or her natural family, or the assumption that there is a presumption to that effect, needs to be firmly and clearly laid to rest. No such 'right' or presumption exists.

Arguably, though, some support for an alternative view that the *locus standi* of birth parents does give them some degree of priority – all other factors being

22 See, Shapiro, J., 'For a Feminist Considering Surrogacy, Is Compensation Really the Key Question?', *Washington Law Review*, Vol. 89, No. 1345, pp 1352–1353, 2014; cited in Finkelstein, *supra* note 183, at p 25.

23 Application No. 57813/00, (2011).

24 Application No. 32185/20, (2022).

25 *Re W (A child)* [2016] EWCA Civ 793, at para 71. A refrain reiterated by McFarlane LJ and others: see, for example, *Re H (A Child)* [2015] EWCA Civ 1284, per McFarlane LJ, at paras 89–94.

equal – when it comes to balancing their right to state recognition as presumptive primary carers, against the claims of all others, can be found in United Nations Convention on the Rights of the Child (UN CROC): Article 5 directs that that

> States Parties shall respect the responsibilities, rights and duties of parents, . . . to provide, in a manner consistent with the evolving capacities of the child, appropriate direction and guidance in the exercise by the child of the rights recognised in the present Convention.

Article 9 states that a child shall not be separated from his or her parents against his or her will, and that all parties must be given the opportunity to participate in any proceedings relating to this situation.

Jus sanguinis

The law relating to blood relationships has been profoundly destabilised by recent advances in reproductive medicine. Among the casualties is the principle that the nationality of children is the same as that of their parents, irrespective of their places of birth. In the context of commercial surrogacy, where anonymous donor genetic material may be involved and where the birth parent and the social parent may not be synonymous, there is often difficulty in establishing who, in law, is the parent of the child. This may give rise to a conflict of jurisdiction in states where the *jus sanguinis* principle applies – for example, France and Germany – when a child is born of parents who are citizens of another state. In fact a number of such cases have been heard by the ECtHR.[26]

Welfare interests of the child

The ECtHR has been clear that when issues arise in relation to surrogacy – as in any other situation concerning a child – then the best interests of that child are paramount,[27] especially where there is a genetic link between the child and one of the commissioning 'parents'.[28]

Surrogacy is yet another aspect of private family law where practice has generated concerns not just regarding children's welfare interests, but also as regards their rights – perhaps, particularly in relation to a child's right to an identity and access to the personal origins information necessary for the development of that identity. The legal uncertainties that accompany surrogacy arrangements and are most apparent in commercial arrangements made overseas in respect of children who return with commissioning 'parents' to be domiciled in the latter's home jurisdiction, must clearly be adverse to the welfare interests of the children concerned.

26 For example, *C. v. Italy,* Application No. 47196/21, (2023).
27 *A.L. v. France*, Application No. 13344/20, (2022).
28 *Mennesson v. France*, Application No. 65192/11, (2014).

PROMPT AND EFFECTIVE PROCESSES

Proceedings concerning the relationship between prospective parents and a child born through a surrogacy arrangement must be carried out with exceptional diligence to prevent the legal issues from being determined on the basis of a *fait accompli.*[29] Further, states must provide rapid and effective processes to establish the parent/child relationship between the biological parent and the child born as a result of surrogacy abroad, ensuring that decision-making processes are sufficiently focussed on the best interests of the child, free from excessive formalism and capable of achieving this interest independently of possible procedural defects.

CITIZENSHIP RIGHTS

As mentioned earlier, the ECtHR, in *C. v. Italy*,[30] drew attention to the significance of the *jus sanguinis* principle and its implications for the citizenship rights of children born as a result of commercial surrogacy. That case concerned a four-year-old girl, born of a surrogacy arrangement in Ukraine to an Italian married couple, the husband having a genetic link to the child. On their return to Italy, where surrogacy is prohibited, the couple's efforts to have the child's birth registered and themselves recorded as her parents were denied on the grounds that it was contrary to public policy, and their successive appeals were unsuccessful. This refusal in effect rendered the child stateless. The Court ruled that the Italian authorities' refusal to transcribe the birth certificate, even in part, prevented the establishment of a legal parent/child relationship between the applicant and her biological father, which violated Article 8. It found that the state must avoid leaving the child in a situation of legal uncertainty and that it bore a positive obligation to uphold the child's right to private life. By failing to balance the different interests at stake, the domestic courts had overlooked the procedural requirements of effectiveness and promptness. It also pointed out that the decision-making process had to be free from excessive formalism but instead should further the child's best interests irrespective of any procedural flaws and regardless of the specific requests of the parties. The domestic courts cannot remain passive in the face of a child's legal uncertainty but must explore potential solutions within the national legal framework, even if the parties do not suggest these solutions. Ultimately, the Court's decision seemed to be based less on the merits of the case and more on procedural matters: the inordinate length of time the domestic courts had taken to come to its conclusion had left the child stateless for a period that was not compliant with her right to respect for her private and family life.

IDENTITY INFORMATION RIGHTS

As the ECtHR has advised, "respect for private life requires that everyone should be able to establish details of their identity as [an] individual human being".[31]

29 *A.L. v. France*, Op. cit., and *D.B. and Others v. Switzerland*, Application No. 58817/15, (2022).
30 Application No. 47196/21, (2023).
31 See, *Mennesson v. France*, Op. cit., at para 96.

Among the problems associated with surrogacy is that the information the child receives will be entirely at parental discretion with resulting crucial implications for the development of the child's identity and cultural affiliation; due to the anonymity surrounding the use of genetic material, a child may never know their true genetic origins. There may also be health issues: the use of anonymous genetic material to generate conception may mean that the child has an unknown genetic predisposition to a particular illness or disease. More immediately, as has been pointed out, issues may arise as to the child's parentage and nationality.[32]

TRAFFICKING

Children born of surrogacy arrangements are potentially vulnerable. The risks of an overlap between surrogacy, trafficking and slavery – especially in some African countries – are considerable. Issues as to the legal standing and identity of the child, parental status, and the child's rights to links with birth parents and to cultural roots, make this an area where international regulation is overdue. Commercial surrogacy has become a high growth 'industry', displacing intercountry adoption (ICA) and undercutting domestic adoption, where profit margins already play a significant role. Should it diversify by accommodating genetic editing for a niche market of 'designer babies', the welfare interests of many more children could then be at risk should they fail to meet 'buyers' expectations.

Arguably, in principle, the Hague Convention and UN CROC – which both prohibit trafficking in children – in so doing could also be interpreted as prohibiting transnational commercial surrogacy, as this might be similarly construed as "represent(ing) a human rights violation for the child"[33] by objectifying children and exposing the welfare interests of some to an unregulated risk. The Optional Protocol to UN CROC on the Sale of Children, Child Prostitution and Child Pornography (OPSC) draws attention to this danger,[34] and Article 2, prohibiting the sale of children, could be engaged where excessive remuneration is offered to a surrogate in arrangements that purport to be 'altruistiic'.

International law

A number of international instruments contribute to a framework of legal provisions that variously impact upon surrogacy.

32 See, Pascoe, CJ., *Issues of Forced Adoption and International Commercial Surrogacy*, Melbourne, Federal Court of Australia, October 2, 2013, www.law.monash.edu.au/about-us/events/chie-judge-pascoe-dpeech-notes.pdf

33 See, Finkelstein, A., 'Surrogacy Law and Policy in the U.S.', *Columbia Law School*, p 20, 2016, https://web.law.columbia.edu/sites/default/files/microsites/gender-sexuality/files/columbia_sexuality_and_gender_law_clinic_-_surrogacy_law_and_policy_report_-_june_2016.pdf

34 See, further, www.ohchr.org/en/ohchr_homepage

European Convention on Human Rights

Surrogacy is somewhat constrained by the ECtHR ruling in *Sijakova v. The Former Yugoslav Republic of Macedonia*,[35] which stated that neither the right to marry and to found a family, nor the right to private and family life, nor any other right guaranteed by the Convention implies a right to procreation. This would seem to be out of step with the commitment given to reproductive rights at the UN-sponsored International Conference on Population and Development in Cairo in 1994 and at its Fourth World Conference on Women in Beijing in 1995, to the assurances proclaimed two decades ago in the Van Lancker report[36] and indeed to the legislative intent underpinning the Convention on the Elimination of All Forms of Discrimination against Women.

PROHIBITION

The ECtHR has taken judicial notice of the fact that surrogacy is expressly prohibited in 14 of the 35 member states of the Council of Europe, in ten of which it is either prohibited under general provisions or not tolerated, or the question of its lawfulness is uncertain, but is expressly authorised in seven member states and appears to be tolerated in four others.[37] It therefore allows states a wide margin of appreciation when making decisions relating to surrogacy. This was illustrated in *K. K. and Others v. Denmark*[38] when four of seven judges voted for the judgment upholding the rights of children born though commercial surrogacy. The remaining three judges' joint dissenting opinion was that Denmark had not violated any ECHR rights. Emphasising that there is no consensus within the member states of the Council of Europe on the sensitive matter of commercial surrogacy, the dissenters took the view that there must be a margin of appreciation for states to strike a balance between private and public interests. According to the minority, the judgment "practically eliminate[s] altogether, in substance, the margin of appreciation" for foreign commercial surrogacy arrangements.[39]

This approach is counterbalanced by a much narrower margin of appreciation when it comes to determining parentage, because this involves a key aspect of an individual's identity. The approach of the Court and its primary concern for the welfare interests of the children involved was apparent in its treatment of *Mennesson v. France*,[40] *Labassee v. France*,[41] and others (see, further, later).[42]

35 Application No. 67914/01, (2003).
36 See, European Parliament, Committee on Women's Rights and Equal Opportunities, *Report on Sexual and Reproductive Health and Rights*, Brussels, European Parliament, 2002.
37 *K. K. and Others v. Denmark*, Ibid, at para 78.
38 Application No. 25212/21, (2022).
39 Ibid, at para 88.
40 Application No. 65192/11, (2014).
41 Application No. 65941/11, (2014).
42 The following cases were similarly concluded: *Foulon and Bouvet v. France*, Application No. 9063/14, (2016); *Laborie v. France*, Application No. 44024/13, (2017); *C and E v. France*, Application Nos. 1462/18 and 17348/18, (2019); and *D v. France*, Application No. 11288/18, (2020).

Convention on the Elimination of All Forms of Discrimination against Women

Article 12 requires states to 'take all appropriate measures to eliminate discrimination against women in the field of healthcare in order to ensure . . . access to health care services, including those related to family planning', while Article 16 explicitly states that women ought to have not only the possibility, but also equality, in deciding on the number and spacing of their children.

United Nations Convention on the Rights of the Child

The rights of a child recognised in UN CROC apply to all children, including those born by surrogacy. In particular, Articles 7 and 8 – protecting rights to registration at birth, to a name and identity, and to a later right of access to origins information – can be placed at risk in respect of a child born through a surrogacy arrangement and could lead to statelessness. However, currently neither UN CROC nor any other international instrument specifically provides protection for such children, and few states do so in relation to domestic or international surrogacy.[43]

Jurisdictional differences and their significance

In Ireland,[44] there is no specific legislation governing surrogacy which has led to the CRC expressing concern that insufficient attention is being given 'to the rights and interests of children born as a result of assisted reproduction technologies.'[45] As in England and Wales, there are broadly relevant legislative provisions, and although there is no regulatory oversight in the former jurisdiction, there is some in the latter where the law currently favours surrogate mothers: agreements are unenforceable and create insecurity for commissioning couples by allowing surrogate mothers to choose to keep the child after birth; the courts ensure that surrogacy arrangements are altruistic and that no improper payments have been made; while an amendment to the 1989 Act established a presumption that the involvement of a birth parent in the life of the child concerned would further that child's welfare.[46] In both, however, there are many hundreds if not thousands of children born by surrogacy arrangements, mostly contracted overseas, for whom there are often issues regarding their legal status. Moreover, Ireland is one of six of the 43 European countries that have failed to introduce specific legislative provisions to regulate assisted reproduction techniques,[47] and although improved contracep-

43 See, UNICEF, *Key Considerations: Children's Rights and Surrogacy*, www.unicef.org/media/115331/file#:~:text=Children%20born%20through%20surrogacy%20have,of%20the%20Child%20(CRC)

44 See, further, www.citizensinformation.ie/en/birth_family_relationships/adoption_and_fostering/surrogacy.html

45 UN Committee on the Rights of the Child, *Concluding Observations of the Committee on the Combined Third and Fourth Periodic Reports of Ireland*, 2016, at para 33.

46 See, *in Re H (A Child) (Surrogacy Breakdown)* [2017] EWCA Civ 1798.

47 See, further, www.eurekalert.org/pub_releases/2020-02/esoh-emt020320.php

tives are more available,[48] and abortion services have now been legalised, access remains problematic (as of 2021, 9 of the nation's 19 hospitals did not provide such procedures).

In the U.S., while there are no federal laws governing surrogacy, most states have legislated for surrogacy contracts and tend to be broadly facilitative;[49] almost all allow the surrogate to be financially compensated,[50] but in some the 'culture wars' is an inhibiting factor. It is probable that the evolution of the law and practice relating to surrogacy owes a good deal to the 1988 New Jersey case of *In re Baby M*[51] as consolidated in the 1993 Californian Supreme Court decision *Johnson v. Calvert*.[52] The latter case essentially determined that the surrogate – who had no genetic link with the baby – was therefore unrelated to the child, and instead the commissioning woman, who was genetically linked to the baby, could be construed as the legal mother. This decision seemed to clear the way for non-altruistic surrogacy arrangements in the U.S. which, thereafter, greatly increased in volume, perhaps particularly due to its attraction for same-sex couples. Commercial surrogacy is illegal in Canada, but altruistic surrogacy has generally been legal since 2004; both altruistic and commercial surrogacy are prohibited in Québec. Along with other assisted reproductive technology procedures, surrogacy is subject to federal regulation – but can give rise to issues such as in the 2009 Ontario case of *C (M.A.) v. K. (M.)*.[53] Cohen J then denied an adoption application by a lesbian in respect of her partner's birth child. Finding that the sperm donor father had sustained a close and caring relationship with the six-year-old child since her birth, and that the applicant had in place a written agreement addressing the parties' respective roles and rights, Cohen J ruled that the effect of an adoption order would be contrary to the child's best interests as it would undermine her "sense of place in the world, her confidence in her experience of the world and her understanding of who her family is".[54] This view is clearly applicable in other contexts such as step-adoptions.

In Australia, surrogacy is regulated at the state and territory level.[55] Although prohibited throughout the country on a commercial basis, altruistic surrogacy is permitted, and some reimbursement of the surrogate's costs is allowed. In *Re*

48 *McGee v. Attorney General* [1974] IR 284.

49 See, for example, Finkelstein, A., et al., 'Surrogacy Law and Policy in the U.S.', *Columbia Law School*, 2016, https://web.law.columbia.edu/sites/default/files/microsites/gender-sexuality/files/columbia_sexuality_and_gender_law_clinic_-_surrogacy_law_and_policy_report_-_june_2016.pdf

50 See, further, www.modamily.com/blog/us-surrogacy-laws-by-state

51 537 A. 2d 1227 (NJ 1988).

52 851 P. 2d 776 (Cal. 1993).

53 *M.A.C. v. M.K.* [2009] ONCJ 18 (Can. Ont. Ct. J.). A full account of this case can be found in Bala, N. and Ashbourne, C., 'The Widening Concept of Parent in Canada', *Journal of Gender, Social Policy & the Law*, Vol. 20, No. 3, pp 13–14, 2012.

54 Ibid, at para 64.

55 See Parentage Act 2004 (ACT); Surrogacy Act 2010 (NSW); Surrogacy Act 2010 (Qld); Surrogacy Act 2012 (Tas); Assisted Reproductive Treatment Act 2008 (Vic); Surrogacy Act 2008 (WA). There is no legislation in the Northern Territory.

Evelyn,[56] a leading case, the Family Court of Australia upheld the ruling of the court at first instance which had broadly decided in favour of the biological mother who had reneged on the surrogacy arrangement, though both parties were ordered to share responsibility for long-term decisions regarding the child's health, welfare and development. Most states will now usually automatically recognise the commissioning parent as fully vested with parental rights and status – to the complete exclusion of the birth mother. In New Zealand, where there is an absence of surrogacy-specific legislation,[57] altruistic surrogacy is legal, but commercial surrogacy is not. Whether the surrogacy arrangement is concluded within or without the jurisdiction, the commissioning parent must adopt the child in order to legitimate their parental status.

Surrogacy remains firmly contrary to law and public policy in both France and Germany. Since 2010, French courts have consistently denied recognition to surrogate contracts and to any right to adopt children born abroad from surrogate mothers, which causes problems when the children resulting from such contracts accompany the commissioning 'parents' on their return home to France. Recently, in *Affaire A.L, c. France*,[58] the ECtHR considered a domestic, and therefore illegal, surrogacy arrangement which had resulted in the surrogate mother giving the child not as agreed to the unmarried same-sex couple (one with a genetic link to the child) with whom she had an arrangement, but to a married heterosexual couple – one of whom promptly registered himself as the child's father – for financial profit. Eventually, the genetically linked applicant's claim was rejected on the grounds that – six years later – the child now had an established family life with the heterosexual couple. In contrast to the earlier *Mennesson* case,[59] the child's right to a genetically validated identity was not deemed to be a core component of their best interests, and those best interests could only be secured by translating the married couple's parental status from *de facto* to *de jure*. In Germany, to make a human being the subject of a contract is legally impermissible: surrogacy is therefore illegal;[60] the mother of a child is the woman who gave birth to that child.[61] Assisted reproductive technology services are regulated by some of the most restrictive legislation in the western world,[62] and surrogacy is not only illegal but it is a criminal offence for health professionals to assist someone in need of such a service.

56 (1998) FLC 92–807. See, also, *Re Evelyn (No. 2)* (1998) FLC 92–187 where the High Court of Australia considered and dismissed the issue of appeal.

57 Note, however, the relevance of the Human Assisted Reproductive Technology Act 2004, the Adoption Act 1955 and the Status of Children Act 1969.

58 Application No. 13344/20, (2022).

59 *Mennesson v. France*, Application No. 65192/11, (2014).

60 The Embryo Protection Act 1991, s 1(1)(7).

61 Civil Code, s 1591.

62 See, further, Robertson, J.A., 'Reproductive Technology in Germany and the United States: An Essay in Comparative Law and Bioethics', *Columbia Journal of Transnational Law*, pp 189–227, 2004.

In practice, surrogacy has long outgrown its initial parameters as 'altruistic' and solely a matter for domestic regulation. By far the majority of surrogacy arrangements must now be defined as commercial and international.

Parental abduction

There would seem to be a correlation between the current high levels of population movement both from the 'global south' into the western developed nations and within those nations, with the rising number of parental child abductions. Increasingly, the unauthorised removal of a child by a non-custodial parent is international in nature and particularly prevalent in England and Wales,[63] France – some 1500 cases every year – Canada, the U.S. and in Australia where the rate is reputed to be perhaps the highest in the world.[64]

Definitions, principles and international law

Initially, parental abduction of a child, like surrogacy, was a matter of private family law, confined as it was to a dispute between birth parents and most usually to the parties' jurisdiction of habitual residence. Its transformation into a matter of public policy and public family law was due to the increased proportion of abductions that involved a removal of the child to another jurisdiction, the complex intra-jurisdictional legal litigation involved and infringements of the criminal law.

Definitions

The term 'abduction' is open to misinterpretation: the third-party removal of a child without permission of the parent, guardian or authorised other, which had not been a pronounced feature of life in modern western nations, is now becoming more so as the scale and spread of the trafficking of children – often associated with large-scale migration, ICA and surrogacy – increasingly attracts public concern; while in the background, the occasional and often random 'snatches' of children by 'strangers' with mental health issues continue in many countries.

Abduction

Parental child abduction is the taking, concealing or detaining of a child by one parent – or authorising a person to do so on their behalf – without the other parent's

63 The Foreign Office estimates that the number of parental child abduction cases has risen by 88% in under a decade. See, further, www.familylaw.co.uk/news_and_comment/Parental-child-abductions-cases-rise-141212-654

64 Child Recovery Australia estimates that more than 250 children are abducted into or out of Australia by parents every year, while the 'Australia: Bringing Them Home' documentary, aired in 2015 on Al Jazeera's 101 East, cites the number at closer to 400.

consent or that of a court. When a child is so removed from a parent or person vested with legal custody, without their permission, this is invariably accompanied by contention if not trauma regarding the welfare interests of the child concerned. With increasing frequency, as globalisation accelerates the volume and rate of travel, such abduction involves the legal systems of more than one country, and the parties concerned find their actions and legal proceedings governed by international law.

Principles

Unlike other forms of abduction of a child, when undertaken by the child's parent, it is most usually motivated by love, and the child, while confused, may quite often be relieved as the abducting parent may well be fleeing with the child from domestic violence. When the matter reaches court, certain principles come into play before a judicial determination can be made regarding the child's future.

The comity of nations

The Hague Convention is premised on the principle that nations should, wherever possible, demonstrate reciprocal respect for each other's laws and institutions. This is given effect by the Article 12 provision requiring signatory states to ensure the prompt return of an abducted child to their country of origin. In practice, however, such return depends on the judicial interpretation given to the grounds providing exceptions to that requirement. Of particular importance in this context is Article 13(b) which provides that when to do so would expose the child to a 'grave risk of harm' or otherwise place the child in an 'intolerable situation', then an abducted child should not be returned to their country of habitual residence.

The welfare of the child

The Article 12 directive expresses the legislative intent of the Hague Convention, thereby legally reducing the significance of the welfare principle in all Convention cases, though the principle continues to have its customary overriding effect in all non-Convention cases, where this is compatible with domestic legislation.

Clearly this is a context in which the rights as well as the welfare interests of a child are of importance. Article 12 of the 1989 Convention, requiring that the views of a child be heard 'in any judicial and administrative proceedings affecting the child,' is very relevant as is the Hague Convention, Article 13, under which a court is not obliged to order the return of a child if it finds that the child objects and has attained an age and degree of maturity at which it is appropriate to take account of his or her views. Also relevant is the Brussels Regulation which provides for the right of the child to be heard during the procedure unless the judge considers it inappropriate due to the child's age and degree of maturity.

The proportionality principle

The Hague Conference on Private International Law, in its guide to implementation of the Convention, advises that 'where safeguards or guarantees are applied which place limits or restraints on the exercise of contact, these should be proportionate to the risks of abuse and no more than are necessary to achieve the protection of the child'. It suggests that 'the principle expressed here is one of proportionality, reminding authorities that limits on parental contact should be justifiable in terms of the child's interests'.[65]

Where there is doubt as to whether an abducted child can be safely returned to their country of habitual residence – as when the country of origin does present a degree of risk or of exposure to an intolerable situation – then some jurisdictions will err on the side of caution and decide on the basis of the welfare interests of the child. When doing so, and conducting such a balancing exercise, the jurisdictions are relying on the proportionality principle – weighing the welfare of the child against the gravity of the risk – in accordance with the established domestic caselaw of many such jurisdictions.

International law

By far the most important international instrument relating to the parental abduction of children is the Hague Convention on the Civil Aspects of Child Abduction 1980, but there are other international laws which also have a bearing on such matters.

The Hague Convention on the Civil Aspects of Child Abduction 1980

As of 2022, 101 nations were parties to this multilateral treaty which – together with the Brussels II Regulation[66] – requires the prompt return of any child wrongfully removed from, or wrongfully retained in, a country that is not their country of habitual residence. Any contention regarding the abduction of a child from one of those 101 nations, where they are habitually resident, and taken to another country in that group is therefore intended to be adjudicated in accordance with Convention provisions.

The Hague Convention is primarily concerned with jurisdictional issues, it provides a mechanism for facilitating the comity of nations, treats the welfare interests of the child as a matter of secondary concern,[67] and provides clear and fixed rules for the return of an abducted child. This differs from the approach adopted in similar circumstances involving a non-Convention country where the welfare of the child can be accorded a greater weighting, as conditioned by the cultural context prevailing in that

65 The Hague Conference on Private International Law, 'Transfrontier Contact Concerning Children', *Family Law*, 2008, at para 1.2.

66 EU Council Regulation (EC) No. 2201/2003 (the "Revised Brussels II Regulation").

67 See, for example, *X v. Latvia*, Application No. 27853/09, (2013).

country,[68] thus allowing for more flexibility and uncertainty as regards the return of an abducted child. It also quite often differs from the approach adopted by signatory parties to the Convention when its requirements clash with those of the welfare interests of the child concerned. Nonetheless, the majority of international child abduction cases fail to be determined in accordance with the Hague Convention.

The European Convention on Recognition and Enforcement of Decisions Concerning Custody of Children 1980

Though limited to Europe, this Convention together with its Hague counterpart directly influence law and practice, and both provide the primary legal response to international child abduction.

The United Nations Convention on the Rights of the Child 1989

Articles 3 and 19 of the Convention declare, respectively, the best interests of the child to be the primary consideration in all decisions concerning children and that all appropriate legislative, administrative, social and educational measures should be taken to protect a child from all forms of harm.

EC Regulation No. 1347 (Brussels II)

Now known as Brussels II b (having been recast in 2022), this requires that judgments issued and enforcible in any EU state – on matters of parental responsibility of spouses (custody, access, etc.) – be recognised and enforced in all other EU states.

Jurisdictional differences and their significance

As is apparent from the caselaw, this is an area of family law in which the rights of a child are very constrained and in which their welfare interests may be subordinated to the Hague rights of their parents.

Returning an abducted child

The welfare approach of the court in England and Wales is to undertake a "global holistic evaluation" by weighing all the relevant factors, looking at the case as a whole and determining the course that best meets the need to protect the child's welfare.[69] Similarly in Ireland, the courts have tended to look more towards its domestic custody laws than to Hague requirements as was apparent, for example, in *HI v.*

68 *Re J (A Child) (Return to Foreign Jurisdiction: Convention Rights)* [2005] UKHL 40.
69 See, *Re F (A Child) (International Relocation Cases)* [2015] EWCA Civ 882.

MG.[70] It was also evident in *WPP v. SRW*,[71] which concerned a mother who had legal custody but took the two children from the U.S., where they had lived their entire lives, to her native Ireland, thereby breaching court orders granting the father visitation rights, the Irish Supreme Court dismissed the latter's appeal. It ruled that to order the return of the children to their place of habitual residence, merely so as to entitle the non-custodial parent to exercise his rights of access, was not warranted.

In the U.S., which is a Hague signatory state, *Abbott v. Abbott*[72] illustrates the courts' approach. This case concerned a mother's removal of her son, for whom she had been awarded legal custody, from Chile without permission from either the father or the court. The U.S. Supreme Court found that the father shared a right of custody with the mother – a U.S. citizen – and that as "the Convention is based on the principle that the best interests of the child are well served when decisions regarding custody rights are made in the country of habitual residence", then ordering the return of the child "does not alter the existing allocation of custody rights . . . but does allow the courts of the home country to decide what is in the child's best interests". So, fortuitously finding congruency between Hague, the child's welfare interests and domestic custody laws, the child was returned.

In Australia – a signatory state to the Hague Convention – although estimates of the number of children involved vary greatly,[73] there is consensus that the rate of annual parental abductions is one of the highest in the world. If a child has been abducted to Australia, there is authority to suggest that – notwithstanding the Convention – the domestic court will apply the best interests of the child principle to determine whether the child should be returned,[74] although the paramountcy principle does not apply.[75] Where a child and their abductor have relocated from another country to New Zealand – a signatory state – then it is not a given that the child will be expeditiously returned. If, by the time the application is heard, there is evidence that the child has well settled in their new environment for a year or more, then the Convention presumption that the welfare interests of the child require his or her prompt return no longer applies.[76] If the applicant was not exercising rights of custody at the time of removal, then also the court may not order the child's

70 (1999) 2 IRLM 22.

71 [2000] IESC 11.

72 130 S.Ct. 1983 (2010).

73 According to Coalition of Parents of Abducted Children (COPAC), the number is approximately 170. Child Recovery Australia estimates that more than 250 children are abducted into or out of Australia by a parent every year. The 'Australia: Bringing Them Home' documentary, aired in 2015 on Al Jazeera's 101 East, cites the number at closer to 400. It is estimated that less than 50% of these children are recovered and returned by authorities to the custodial parent. See, further, www.australianmissingpersonsregister.com/ParentalAbductions.htm; also, https://ramsdenlaw.com.au/news/the-hidden-crisis-of-international-parental-child-abduction-in-australia/

74 *ZP & PS* (1994) FLC 92–480 and *Pascarl & Oxley* [2013] FamCAFC 47.

75 This is because such proceedings are not 'proceedings for a parenting order' as required by s 65E of the Family Law Act.

76 *Secretary of Justice v. HJ* (2006) NZFLR 195.

return, though "a right of intermittent possession and care of a child will fall within the definition of rights of custody".[77] Similarly, this is the case if the applicant consented or acquiesced in the child's removal, though the consent must be "real, positive and unequivocal".[78]

In France, neither the Hague Convention nor Brussels IIa is applicable if the child has been abducted from their habitual residence in a country that is not a Hague signatory state, or from a similar such country, immediately prior to the abduction. In those circumstances the parent seeking the return of the child must contact the local judicial and diplomatic authorities of the country in which the child has been abducted. In Germany, the tardiness of the judicial process, its prejudicial effect on the claims of a wronged parent and its capacity to compromise the welfare interests of an abducted child, were illustrated in a recently concluded case which had begun with the abduction in 2014 of a one-year-old child by his unmarried mother from the family home in Spain and ended with the 2022 decision of the *Bundesverfassungsgericht* in respect of the now nine-year-old German child. As time passed it became increasingly obvious that transferring the child to Spain into the custody of a father he hardly knew (and with whom he did not even share a common language) was likely to result in severe trauma, as would removal from the parent who had provided exclusive care for most of his life, the loss of his *de facto* father (the mother having married) and his family, uprooting from school and friends and being immersed in a foreign language and culture. Throughout this prolonged muddle, in which the provisions of Hague and Brussels II *bis* were not always compatible, there is no evidence that the child's welfare interests – nor indeed his fundamental rights – were given independent legal representation.[79]

Return and 'risk of harm'

Article 13 of the Hague Convention allows the authorities of the country to which the child has been abducted to refuse to order the return of the child if there is a grave risk that such return would expose the child to physical or psychological harm or otherwise place the child in an intolerable situation. In England and Wales, the court in *Re K (A Child: Hague Convention: Child Abduction)(REV 1)*[80] explained that the gravity of the risk must reach a level of demonstrable seriousness and that "intolerable" must be such as the particular child placed in the particular circumstances could not be expected to tolerate.[81] This approach – termed the

77 *Gross v. Boda* (1994) 12 FRNZ 564, at p 4.
78 *KMA v. Secretary of Justice* [2007] NZCA 223.
79 See, further, the editors of the EAPIL blog, https://eapil.org/2022/11/24/german-constitutional-court-stays-enforcement-of-a-spanish-child-return-order/
80 [2020] NIFam 9.
81 Citing *Re D* [2007] 1 AC 619, at para 52.

"grave risk" defence – has also been followed in Ireland[82] and in France. In New Zealand, a grave risk of harm/intolerable situation may persuade a court not to order a child's return, but there must be evidence that the risk is serious.[83]

In France, the courts in case n°18–23916[84] considered that the return of the children concerned would expose them to a serious risk of physical or psychological danger because of the father's alcoholism and the depressive and suicidal disorders from which he suffered, which made him "very irritable" towards his children. Moreover, if the mother returned then, because of the arrest warrant issued against her by the American authorities, she risked being arrested and would not be in a position to ensure the welfare of the children. So the court rejected the application for the child's return to the U.S. On the other hand, in the recent case of *Bhadauria v. Côté*,[85] a mother had taken her 16-month-old child to France, without telling the father, and while the French court accepted that if she had acted due to domestic violence then she might legitimately claim that her actions – though unlawful – together with her request to remain in France, were justified by the best interests of the child. However, on the facts, the court found that she was unable to meet the burden of proof in relation to the allegations of family violence and was ordered to return the child.

Welfare interests

The law in England and Wales has been explained by Baroness Hale:

> In all non-Convention cases the courts have consistently held that they must act in accordance with the welfare of the individual child. If they did decide to return the child, that is because it is in the best interests to do so, not because the welfare principle has been superseded by some other consideration.[86]

This is in contrast to Convention cases when the court must abide by the Article 12 requirement to promptly return the child, though the court should bear in mind that the Convention contains no express requirement to make the best interests of the child its primary consideration.

82 *K (R) v. K (J) (Child Abduction: Acquiescence)* [2000] 2 IR 416 when Barron J cited with approval the formulation given in *Friedrich v. Friedrich*, 78 F. 3d 1060 (6th Cir. 1996): first, there is a grave risk of harm when return of the child puts the child in imminent danger prior to the resolution of the custody dispute, e.g. returning the child to a zone of war, famine or disease; second, there is a grave risk of harm in cases of serious abuse or neglect, or extraordinary emotional dependence, when the court in the country of habitual residence, for whatever reason, may be incapable or unwilling to give the child adequate protection.

83 *A v. A* (1996) FRNZ 348, at 355.

84 Civ 1, February 14, 2019.

85 2022 ONSC 2476 (CanLII).

86 See, *Re J (A Child) (Return to Foreign Jurisdiction: Convention Rights)* [2005] UKHL 40.

In France, the courts have approached this issue by examining in some detail – as in the previously mentioned *Bhadauria v. Côté* – the consequences for the child concerned should he or she be returned to their place of habitual residence. In a fairly recent case it was expressly stated that the French courts are not bound by the reasons for the decisions issued by the judicial and administrative courts of the state in which the child had his habitual residence prior to the abduction.[87] In Germany, the courts' alleged non–Hague compliant approach has been a repeated cause for complaint from the U.S.,[88] and the European Commission has also received official complaints that Germany 'takes a highly questionable view of the best interests of "its" children in its territory following an abduction' and 'that Germany was the most reluctant of the European countries to apply the terms of the Convention'.[89] These complaints have centred on the inappropriate use by German courts of certain provisions of the Hague Convention to justify retaining abducted children in Germany, the length of time it has taken to adjudicate cases, and the failure to enforce left-behind parents' visitation rights. The previously mentioned 2022 decision of the *Bundesverfassungsgericht*, in respect of a prolonged legal tussle between a German mother and Spanish father regarding their child whom she had abducted, would seem to support the U.S. complaints.

Child's wishes

In England and Wales, as in Ireland, the child has at least a right to be heard. The court will take into account any objection of a child to his or her return to their country of origin, even if that child is no more than six years of age.[90] While in Ireland the requirement to do so is subject to the 'take into account' caveat, in England and Wales the *Gillick* ruling ensures that a child, even if aged 16 years or less will, if of sufficient maturity and discernment, have an actual right to decide whether it is in their interests to return or not. However, their objection to being returned must be a forceful rejection as "the word 'objects' imports a strength of feeling which goes far beyond the usual ascertainment of the wishes of the child in a custody dispute".[91] In Canada, as the Canadian Bar Association has noted, the judicial approach of heavily conditioning a child's views was one that 'could undermine the due weight accorded to the objections of a child of sufficient age and

87 See, Case n°18-23916, Civ. 1, February 14, 2019.

88 See, further, www.gao.gov/products/gao-01-423

89 See, Child Abductions in Germany, *Parliamentary Question – E-006436/2020*, www.europarl.europa.eu/doceo/document/E-9-2020-006436_EN.html

90 See: in Ireland, *MN v. RN* [2008] IEHC 382; and in England and Wales, *W v. W (Abduction: Acquiescence: Children's Objections)* [2010] England and Wales High Court 332 (Family Division).

91 *Re R (A Minor: Abduction)* [1992] 1 FLR 105 *per* Bracewell J, at 107–108.

maturity, a concern which has been borne out in subsequent decisions'.[92] It adds that 'objections to return expressed by children are often given less than due weight in the judicial exercise of discretion even when sufficient age and maturity are established, which minimizes children's effective participation'.[93]

In Australia, in *Department of Family and Community Services & Tamlin*,[94] the protests of an eight-year-old child abducted by her mother from Thailand were insufficient to prevent an order for her return. This would seem consistent with the fact that in this country, the consent of the child concerned is not a defence to a charge of abduction[95] and is reflective of a more traditional approach to the parent/child relationship. In New Zealand, the objection of the child concerned to being returned can be persuasive. In *White v. Northumberland*[96] the court applied the test: has the child attained an age and degree of maturity at which it is appropriate to give weight to the child's views; and, if so, what weight should be given to the child's views and how should any residual judicial discretion be exercised? Importantly, in a Hague Convention case, a child's views will only be ascertained if the abductor is presenting them in defence, whereas in a non-Hague case, the courts are bound to take the child's views into account, though those views will not be determinative.

Conclusion

Commercial surrogacy and parental abduction are aspects of contemporary society that have rather suddenly become prominent features of family life with each presenting its own challenges for family law. They have both emerged from their previous private family law context to become hybrid public/private proceedings as public policy concerns – regarding the opportunities for adult exploitation, uncertainties as to the relative legal status of the parties and a need to identify and protect the welfare interests/rights of children – required changes in domestic law. The resulting cases demonstrate that both are currently inadequately addressed by existing international law.

The rights and welfare interests of the children involved are of concern in both sets of proceedings.

92 The Canadian Bar Association (Child and Youth Law Section), *Alternative Report to the UN Committee on the Rights of the Child*, 2020, Op. cit., at p 27 citing: *Andegiorgis v. Giorgis*, 2018 ONCJ 965, at paras 65–68, 76; *Cormier v. Borsk*, 2019 ONCJ 889, at paras 42, 48, 50; *Children's Aid Society of Toronto v. P.B.*, 2019 ONCJ 683, at para 56(1).

93 Ibid, at p 28, citing multiple sources in support of that view.

94 [2019] FamCA 157.

95 See, *R v. Mejac* [1954] Tas SR 26.

96 (2006) 26 FRNZ 189.

5 Adoption from state care and intercountry adoption

Introduction

While starting a family is taken for granted by most people, for whom it is no more difficult than it ever was, for increasing numbers of couples – including the growing proportion of those with fertility issues or in same-sex relationships – parenting opportunities are not readily available. Paradoxically, the growing number of those with unfulfilled needs to parent would seem to be matched by the growing number of children in the public care in those same nations who need parenting. In addition, the effects of poverty in many under-developed nations is leading to a situation where many children, for whom neither parental or state care is affordable, are entering the intercountry adoption (ICA) process. This is occurring in a context where a growing proportion of child-oriented services in the western nations would seem to be in the process of being outsourced from the public to the private sector. All of this may lead – as in any situation of scare resources, private agencies and profit margins – to market manipulation by competing interests: a situation where, without effective regulation, children may well be at risk.

This chapter deals with two supplementary opportunities for parenting in contemporary western society: adoption from state care and ICA. The first is illustrative of the issues that accompany the outsourcing of child-oriented services from the public to the private sector: an already well-established U.S. jurisdictional characteristic where many services – from adoption to custodial facilities – are now delivered on a for-profit basis. The second considers a reverse flow from the private to the public sector: where private enterprise services, ostensibly altruistic, give rise to public policy issues that require regulatory intervention. Because they are, arguably, informed by much the same principles, ethical dilemmas and – if to a lesser extent – governed by not dissimilar laws relating to issues such as parental rights, the first section of this chapter provides a composite framework or guide to such matters as they relate to both adoption from state care and ICA.

DOI: 10.4324/9781003510383-8

Composite framework: adoption from state care and intercountry adoption

In a warning that applies equally to both forms of adoption, the European Court of Human Rights (ECtHR)[1] has advised that only after every effort has been made to explore the feasibility of returning a child in the public care system to their birth family will recourse to adoption be compliant with Article 8 of the European Convention on Human Rights (ECHR).

Definitions, principles, ethical issues and international law

The law and principles governing both adoption from state care and ICA are largely provided by the provisions of the ECHR and the United Nations Convention on the Rights of the Child (UN CROC), as interpreted and applied by the ECtHR. This has since been supplemented by other international instruments such as the Declaration on Social and Legal Principles relating to the Protection and Welfare of Children, with special reference to Foster Placement and Adoption Nationally and Internationally 1986, the Optional Protocol on the Sale of Children, Child Prostitution, and Child Pornography 2000 and the United Nations Guidelines for the Alternative Care of Children (see, further, later). The Guidelines, introduced in 2009, were intended to enhance UN CROC implementation "regarding the protection and well-being of children deprived of parental care or who are at risk of being so" (para 3).

Definitions

Adoption is a complex social phenomenon, intimately knitted into its family law framework and shaped by pressures affecting the family in its local social context. It is a mirror reflecting the changes in our family life and the efforts of family law to address those changes. This has caused it to be variously defined in different societies, in the same society at different times and across a range of contemporary societies. There are significant definitional differences in relation to simple and plenary adoption, between both and customary adoption as practised by the Indigenous communities of the CANZUS nations (Canada, Australia, New Zealand, United States), domestic and intercountry adoption – and between adoption and *kafalah*.

Adoption

In legal terms, adoption has been defined as a legal method of creating between the child and one who is not the birth parent of the child an artificial family relationship analogous to that of parent and child;[2] or, more bluntly,[3] providing homes for children

1 *Haase v. Germany*, Application No. 11057/02, (2005).
2 See, Tomlin Committee Report (Cmnd 2401) 1925.
3 See, Houghton Committee, *Report of the Departmental Committee on the Adoption of Children, (Cmnd 5107)*, London, HMSO, 1972.

who need them is its primary purpose. It should be noted that while most usually associated with children, in fact many countries permit the adoption of adults.

In law adoption may be either 'full' or 'simple': in the former the legal relationship between the birth parent and their child is terminated; in the latter this relationship is not completely severed. Countries such as the UK, the U.S. and Australia only give legal recognition to full adoptions, while such others as France and many other civil law countries also recognise the simple form. Article 26 of the Hague Convention in its governance of ICA gives recognition to both, and Article 27 empowers a receiving country to convert a simple adoption into a full adoption if the law of that country permits such a conversion and if the appropriate consents are available.

Jurisdictional differences in contemporary adoption law and policy, theoretically ironed out by such international legislation as UN CROC and the Hague Convention, in fact continue to strongly differentiate national approaches to adoption. For example, in France and more generally in Europe, the absence of statutory powers to remove all parental rights and totally dispense with the need for parental consent means that the adoption experience is virtually entirely a consensual process and a matter for private family law. The corollary is that public child care institutions in those countries have a high investment in family support and long-term foster care services. In the UK and the U.S., by way of contrast, the non-consensual use of adoption in relation to children in the public care system has mainstreamed adoption into the national child protection system, making it much more part of public family law. This has brought with it significant features that are becoming distinguishing characteristics of their adoption experience. The children involved are often old enough to have their views taken into consideration, for their consent to be relevant and to have a sense of personal and cultural identity; to be adopted in sibling groups; to experience significant health and/or social care problems; to be committed to ongoing post-adoption contact with their birth parents/siblings; and to be adopted by persons qualifying for ongoing state financial and professional assistance.

Abandonment

In ICA, the term 'abandonment' like 'orphan' can be used flexibly: both may be loosely interpreted in some countries to include children placed in institutional care by a parent unable to cope with care costs but who might visit the child occasionally and whose whereabouts could well be known to the authorities.

Intercountry adoption

This phenomenon is currently largely defined and regulated by the Hague Convention on Protection of Children and Co-operation in Respect of Intercountry Adoption 1993 (as amended in 2008). ICA is defined by the Hague Convention as occurring when

> a child habitually resident in one Contracting State ("the State of origin") has been, is being, or is to be moved to another Contracting State ("the receiving State") either after his or her adoption in the State of Origin by spouses or a

> person habitually resident in the receiving State, or for the purposes of such an adoption in the receiving State or in the State of origin.

ICA was and is associated with the disruption to normal family life caused by war, civil unrest and natural disaster in the global south. The subjects are sometimes but not always orphans or refugees fleeing danger for sanctuary in any country offering safety and protection. Increasingly, however, disruptions to care arrangements in the family of origin are now more likely to have their roots in chronic poverty, climate change or other forms of socio-economic deprivation. It is a context within which much controversy has swirled around definitions such as 'orphan' and ethical issues such as 'maintaining cultural integrity'. Whether they are orphans; victims of war, disease or natural disasters; or are simply from deprived backgrounds, abandoned in institutional care, with or without parental consent, the children become available for ICA due to inadequate domestic child care and adoption options. Such domestic failure is further complicated by the political complicity of western nations choosing to facilitate the removal of children rather than resource the care and protection infrastructure in the child's country of origin.

Realistically, ICA can no longer be seen in terms of an altruistic child rescue response to circumstances such as those mentioned earlier, nor merely as an adjunct to traditional adoption, that most private of private family law proceedings. More often than not, it now functions to facilitate the demand-led pressure to satisfy the parenting needs of infertile couples in modern western societies. Increasingly, it overlaps with surrogacy and can become entangled in child trafficking. It may now be viewed more broadly as just one aspect of the accelerating pace of change that is internationalising the functions of family law: adoption in common with marriage, divorce, child maintenance and abduction, is now liable to be conducted across the traditional divides of jurisdiction, race and gender; belonging to neither the 'public' or 'private' sectors of family law but relocating to the middle ground as a hybrid.

Kafalah

Shari'a law prohibits adoption. However, the practice of *kafalah*, a form of long-term foster care, has long been used instead. This is a form of simple adoption, widely used in Islamic countries or by Muslims living elsewhere, which circumvents the *Quor'an* prohibition[4] on legally mixing bloodlines by facilitating the raising of another's child as the carer's own while providing safeguards to prevent full legal assimilation into the carer's family: the birth parent can never be replaced by adopters as the former retain important rights. Duncan explains the difference between the two as follows[5]:

> *Kafalah* does not have the effect of integrating the child into the new family. The child remains in name a member of the birth family and there are

4 *Quor'an*, v. 33 and the Sura, v. 4 and 5.

5 See, Duncan, W., 'Children's Rights, Cultural Diversity and Private International Law', in Douglas, G. and Sebba, L. (eds.), *Children's Rights and Traditional Values*, Aldershot, Ashgate, 1998, at p 32.

> no inheritance rights in respect of the new family. However, *kafala* may if necessary involve delegation of guardianship in respect of the person and property of the child and in an intercountry situation it may result in a change in the child's nationality.

The gap between statutory adoption and *kafalah* is one which continues to jeopardise the human rights of those involved, particularly the children, many of whom have been taken into public care due to the concern of authorities about their uncertain legal status and the absence of a parent within the jurisdiction. These Muslim children, together with others who from time to time are swept into the ICA process, may initially be entrusted to prospective adopters and brought into western society where their adopters arrange the conversion of a *kafalah* guardianship into a statutory domestic adoption.

State care

According to the previously mentioned guidelines, state care can take the form of 'foster placement . . . adoption or, if necessary, placements in suitable institutions for the care of children' (UN CROC, Article 20(3)). Decisions regarding children in alternative care should have due regard for the importance of ensuring they have a stable home that meets their basic need for safe and continuous attachment to their caregivers, with permanency generally being a key goal (para 12). In accordance with the predominant opinion of experts, alternative care for young children, especially those under the age of three years, should be provided in family-based settings (para 22). 'Where such arrangements are not possible or are not in the best interests of the child, efforts should be made to find a permanent family placement within a reasonable period' (para 44). This will entail a child leaving state care by way of either non-consensual domestic adoption or by ICA.

Where such arrangements have been made, then that period of tenure may well place the carer in a position to claim that their adoption of the child should be legally sanctioned as this was now the best way to secure the child's welfare interests. So, for example, in *Moretti and Benedetti v. Italy*,[6] the Court determined that by providing foster care for 19 months, during the initial important stages of a child's life, the conditions of "family life" had been satisfied, enabling an application by the carers to adopt the child to go ahead instead of that of another couple who had sought to adopt her. Again, in *Kopf and Liberda v. Austria*,[7] a period of 46 months of foster care was similarly recognised.

Principles

A central principle, embedded in both Hague and UN CROC and applying equally to adoption from state care and ICA, is that adoption is generally a service for

6 Application No. 16318/07, (2010).
7 Application No. 1598/06, (2012).

children, rather than for an adult seeking to acquire a child. Other principles also have roles to play.

The ECtHR, for example, is guided by principles such as 'proportionality', 'compatibility with democracy' and 'a margin of appreciation'. The first requires a fair balance to be struck[8] between the demands of the general interests of the community and the requirements of the protection of the individual's fundamental rights.[9] The second imports a liberal measure of balance and tolerance.[10] Frequently the ECtHR can be seen applying the test – is this form of state intervention necessary in a democratic society?[11] The third permits states a degree of latitude in the interpretation of human rights obligations[12] and assists the ECtHR to cope with the somewhat disparate national experience of adoption, particularly between the UK and the rest of continental Europe. The doctrine of a 'margin of appreciation' declares that individual states are entitled to act with a level of discretion in accordance with their particular legal tradition. However, in relation to adoption from state care, this doctrine has had a strictly limited application. As was explained in *Saviny v. Ukraine*,[13]

> notwithstanding a margin of appreciation enjoyed by the domestic authorities in deciding on placing a child into public care, severing family ties means cutting a child off from its roots, which can only be justified in very exceptional circumstances . . . A relevant decision must therefore be supported by sufficiently sound and weighty considerations in the interests of the child, and it is for the respondent State to establish that a careful assessment of the impact of the proposed care measure on the parents and the child has been made.

Parental rights

The ECtHR has stressed the importance of remembering that the principle of the best interests of a child is not opposed to the fundamental right of parents to live a family life with their children[14]: "where the existence of a family tie with a child

8 See: *Huang v. Secretary of State for the Home Department* [2007] 2 AC 167, at para 19; *R (Quila) v. Secretary of State for the Home Department* [2012] 1 AC 621, at para 45; and *Bank Mellat v. HM Treasury (No 2)* [2013] UKSC 39, [2013] 3 WLR 179, 222, at para 20.

9 See: *Olson v. Sweden (No 1)* (1988) 11 EHRR 299; *Sporrong v. Sweden* [1982] 5 EHRR 35, at para 69; *Tsirlis and Kouloumpas v. Greece* (1997) 25 EHRR 198, at para 116; *Razgar v. Secretary of State for Home Department* [2004] UKHL 27, at para 20; and see, *Kozac v. Poland* [2010] ECHR 280, (2010) 51 EHRR 16.

10 See, *Refah Partisi v. Turkey* (2003) 37 EHRR 1, [2003] ECHR 87.

11 See, *Olson v. Sweden (No 1)*, Op. cit., where it is explained that to be justifiable such interference must be "relevant and sufficient; it must meet a pressing social need; and it must be proportionate to the need".

12 See, for example, *Lithgow v. United Kingdom* (1986) 8 EHRR 329, *Fredin v. Sweden* (1991) 13 EHRR 784, *Abdulaziz, Cabales and Balkandali v. United Kingdom* (1985) 7 EHRR 471.

13 Application No. 39948/06, (2008), at para 49. See also: *Kutzner v. Germany,* Application No. 46544/99, (2002), at paras 67 and 81; *Moser v. Austria,* Application No. 12643/02, (2006); *Kurochkin v. Ukraine,* Application No. 42276/08, (2010); *Schalk and Kopf v. Austria*, Application No. 30141/04, (2010); and *Burden v. the United Kingdom* [GC], Application No. 13378/05, (2008).

14 See, *Melo Soares v. Portugal*, Application No. 72850/14, (2017).

has been established, the state must act to enable that tie to develop and provide legal protection making possible the integration of the child in his family".[15] The frequently repeated claim – primarily by UK judiciary – that there is no legal presumption favouring the upbringing of a child by their birth parent needs to be seen in the light of such ECtHR rulings: "where the existence of a family tie with a child has been established, the state must act to enable that tie to develop and provide legal protection making possible the integration of the child in his family".[16]

Clearly this principle is equally applicable to both adoptions from state care and ICA, as in both cases an available but neglecting birth parent may be incapacitated – more by poverty than wilfulness – from providing 'good enough' parenting due to insufficient state support. In relation to an overseas adoption, the Hague Convention, Article 4(b), provides that this will only be lawful 'if the competent authorities of the State of origin have determined, after the possibilities of placement within the State of origin have been given due consideration, that intercountry adoption is in the child's best interests'. If the authorities – following a consideration of the alternatives – should so determine, then they must give the parents an opportunity to consent to the adoption plan. If the parents refuse to consent, steps must be taken to judicially terminate parental rights; in either case, discussions must be held to identify the type of adoption placement best suited to cater for the child's particular needs.

Both parents are entitled to make decisions about their child, including consenting to the child's adoption and participating in the selection of approved prospective adopters. The ECtHR has assiduously established the principle that those whose interests are at stake in any decision-making process must be afforded every opportunity to fully engage in that process. This is an aspect of the 'equality of arms' principle whereby both parties to proceedings must be placed in a position where they have equal knowledge of and be permitted to comment on evidence held by the other.[17] So, for example, in *Case Soares de Melo v. Portugal*,[18] among many violations of Article 8, the ECtHR listed "the decision-making process that led to the placement of children in institutions for their adoption, which was not conducted fairly saw the lack of effective involvement of the applicant".[19]

Involvement in decision-making

This principle reflects the emphasis now placed on procedural rights, which have developed to become a crucial aspect of Strasbourg jurisprudence, especially under Article 8.

15 Ibid, per Judge Sajo, President at concluding paras, citing *Kroon and others v. the Netherlands*, Application No. 18535/91, (1995) 19 EHRR 263, [1994] ECHR 35, and *Wagner and JMWL v. Luxembourg*, Application No. 76240/01, (2007).

16 Citing *Kroon and others v. the Netherlands*, Application No. 18535/91, (1995) 19 EHRR 263, [1994] ECHR 35, and *Wagner and JMWL v. Luxembourg*, Application No. 76240/01, (2007).

17 See *P, C and S v. United Kingdom*, Op. cit.

18 Application No. 72850/14, (2017).

19 Ibid, at para 123.

In *Buchberger v. Austria*,[20] the ECtHR found that Article 8 rights had been breached by the failure of a local authority to sufficiently involve the claimant in its decision-making process. The case concerned a mother whose children had been taken into care because she had arrived home 45 minutes late from work having left them unsupervised. When she sought through court proceedings to retrieve her children, the local authority failed to provide a statement of reasons for their action and failed to give her copies of documents upon which it relied but which had not been communicated to her. In practice, this principle must be breached more often than not in respect of ICAs where the children concerned are rarely full orphans and the authorities' engagement with their parents is often reduced to a dismissive 'whereabouts unknown' note in the file.

A capacity to participate effectively in decision-making is dependent upon access to all relevant information. The ECtHR has made a number of rulings in which it has emphasised the importance of ensuring that defendants are not disadvantaged by a non-disclosure of documents that may have a material bearing on the outcome of their case. In *TP and KM v. United Kingdom*,[21] for example, the court ruled that the non-disclosure by a psychiatrist to the defendant of a tape recording adverse to the latter's interests was wrong.

This principle is not confined to parents. The right of children to also be involved is established in both the Hague Convention and in UN CROC, Article 12. It recognises that on issues relating to his or her adoption and upbringing, the child's views must be sought, must be taken into consideration and may be determinative depending upon their maturity. As mentioned earlier, some jurisdictions require the consent of the child concerned as a prerequisite for their adoption.

The paramountcy principle

Article 21 of UN CROC established the best interests of the child as the paramount consideration in all matters relating to adoption,[22] while the ECtHR has done so in several cases.[23] For example, in *Hendricks v. The Netherlands*,[24] the court interpreted Article 8(2) to mean that where there is a conflict between the rights and interests of the child and those of a parent, which can only be resolved to the disadvantage of one of them, then the interests of the child must prevail. In

20 Application No. 32899/96, (2001).

21 [2001] 2 FLR 549. Also, see, *Re M (Care: Challenging Decision by Local Authority)* [2002] FLR 1300.

22 Also established by article 24 of the African Charter on the Rights and Welfare of the Child and article 4 of the European Convention on the Adoption of Children (Revised).

23 See: *Sahin v. Germany, Sommerfield v. Germany, Hoffmann v. Germany* [2002] 1 FLR 119; *K and T v. Finland* [2000] 2 FLR 79; and *Pini and Others v. Romania* [2004] EHRR 275.

24 (1982) 5 EHRR 223. See also *Kroon v. The Netherlands* (1994) Series A No. 297–C, 19 EHRR 263 where the court commented that it was a principle of good law to hold that the interests of the child were paramount.

Yousef v. The Netherlands,[25] the ECtHR for the first time used the phrase "paramountcy of welfare" when comparing the interests of a child with those of the parent[26]:

> The Court reiterates that in judicial decisions where the rights under Article 8 of parents and those of a child are at stake, the child's rights must be the paramount consideration.

In *Neulinger and Shuruk v. Switzerland*,[27] the ECtHR found that treating a child's welfare interests as paramount, as required under Article 21 of UN CROC, did not mean ignoring the Article 8 rights of their parents; these too must be taken into account and full consideration given to the principle that in general a child's welfare is best assured by parental care. Arguably, practice developments in nations such as the UK are pushing at the boundaries established by ECtHR caselaw and at the requirements of Articles 3 and 21 of the Convention on the Rights of the Child.

The proportionality principle

The 'principle of proportionality', as the ECtHR declared 40 years ago, means that any state interference must correspond to a pressing social need, and be proportionate to the legitimate aim pursued, if it is to be "necessary in a democratic society".[28] More recently, the ECtHR decision in *Gorgulu v. Germany*[29] provides authority for the view that the child's welfare must be seen in a long-term context, and this may even require terminating an adoption placement, however satisfactory, if local authority intervention is to meet the test of 'proportionality'. Again, the decision in *Zhou v. Italy*[30] demonstrated that any progression from intervention in respect of a vulnerable parent/child relationship to a non-consensual adoption placement will only be human rights compliant if the intervening authorities have first offered appropriate supportive services and, when this has clearly failed, have then proceeded in a manner that gives the parent every opportunity to engage in decision-making and legally challenge the authorities' course of action. In *KA v. Finland*,[31] the Court stressed that, to be compliant with Article 8(2), the making of a public care order must involve a careful and unprejudiced assessment of all relevant evidence held on file and be justified by a recorded statement of specified reasons. The latter should be made available to the parent or guardian so as to ensure that they are in a position to participate in any further decision-making, including

25 [2003] 1 FLR 210.
26 Ibid, at para 73. Also, see: *R and H v. United Kingdom* (2012) 54 EHRR 2, [2011] 2 FLR 1236.
27 [2010] ECHR 1053.
28 *The Sunday Times v. United Kingdom*, Application No. 6538/74, (1979).
29 Application No. 74969/01, (2004).
30 Application No. 33773/11, (2014). Also, see, *Akinnibosun v. Italy* [2015] ECHR 697.
31 [2003] 1 FCR 201.

lodging an appeal. The principle is perhaps most fully stretched when applied to the removal of a newborn baby from maternal care in a hospital (an act which is often a precursor to an adoption placement). This has been held to be a disproportionate response to the level of risk presented by the mother and breached the latter's rights under Article 8. The ECtHR has explored this practice in a number of cases, mostly involving the UK.[32]

The proportionality principle is central to Article 8 of the ECHR, and the judiciary are required to take it into account in their decision-making. However, arguably, the experience of the Indigenous communities in the CANZUS nations indicates that in practice the interpretation and application of the principle is subject to cultural context considerations.

The subsidiarity principle

This principle lies at the heart of the EU project, is crucial to the working of the ECHR and operates in conjunction with the doctrine of the margin of appreciation to invert the 'authority pyramid' by protecting the right of states to determine their domestic issues in accordance with domestic laws. Only after that stage has been completed should a matter be referred to the ECtHR or other EU institution for a reconciliation of differences arising between interpretations of domestic law and Convention provisions.[33]

The Hague Conference Permanent Bureau in its *Good Practice Guide* recognised a need for the stricter accreditation and authorisation of agencies involved in ICA, with special attention to the professional quality and scope of the services they provide and to ensuring that their numbers are not greater than those needed. In an important policy statement, the *Guide* also explains the role to be played by the subsidiarity principle:[34]

> The subsidiarity principle is central to the success of the Convention. It implies that efforts should be made to . . . ensure that a child has the opportunity to be adopted or cared for nationally. It implies also that intercountry adoption procedures should be set within an integrated child protection and care system which maintains these priorities. However, States should also ensure that efforts to achieve this goal do not unintentionally harm children by delaying unduly a permanent solution through intercountry adoption.

32 See, for example: *O v. the United Kingdom*, Application No. 9276/81, (1987); *H v. the United Kingdom*, Application No. 9580/81, (July 8, 1987); *W v. the United Kingdom*, Application No. 9749/82, (1987); and *B v. the United Kingdom*, Application No. 9840/82, (1987).

33 See, Glas, L.R., 'The Age of Subsidiarity? The ECtHR's Approach to the Admissibility Requirement that Applicants Raise Their Convention Complaint before Domestic Courts', *The Netherlands Quarterly of Human Rights*, Vol. 41, No. 2, 2023, https://journals.sagepub.com/doi/10.1177/09240519231169837?icid=int.sj-full-text.similar-articles

34 'A Guide to Good Practice', The Hague, 2008, Ibid, at p 22.

> States should guarantee permanency planning in the shortest time possible for each child deprived of his/her parents. Policies should work to promote family preservation and national solutions, rather than to hinder intercountry adoption.

Poverty relief is crucial to reducing child availability for adoption

Article 7 of UN CROC provides for the right of a child 'to be known cared for by his or her own parents'. This is supported by Articles 18 and 19, which reinforce the principle that the state should give priority to measures that keep children in their families and culture of origin, and by Article 11(1) which requires measures to be taken to combat the 'illicit transfer and non-return of children abroad'. However, whether as a consequence of being in state care in a developed nation or of abandonment in a less developed one, the route to adoption is very often dictated by poverty: in both cases the flow of children is almost invariably from circumstances of social disadvantage to one of relative well-being. For governments in many under-developed countries and for some in the developed western nations, ICA and adoption from state care, respectively, provide a safety valve, enabling it to transfer the care costs of children it cannot afford to maintain in public care to the private sector. Once the socio-economic circumstances of families or of a country improve – as has been the case with South Korea – then children cease to be readily available.

For the poorer citizens of countries in the 'global south', the lack of any support services and exposure to unremitting poverty increases the likelihood of parental relinquishment or abandonment of children. In some cases, the benefit to poverty-stricken birth parents in places such as South America and Africa derives not only from the ending of care responsibility and the comfort of knowing that their child will be better cared for by others but from the direct or indirect payments made by intermediaries seeking to arrange adoption placements. To some this equation presents as just another instance of the west 'outsourcing' its production requirements to third world countries. Parallels may be drawn with the effects of poverty in the developed nations where, as Patricia Strowbridge of Adoption Professionals has claimed[35],

> Take Florida, which has 5,000 to 7,000 adoptions a year. Over 80% of them are private and most of these involve young women. In many cases they simply can't afford to keep their babies because income is so low and welfare is so poor. So they get in touch with an adoption agency.

In such circumstances, if a failure to cope due to poverty does not lead to the initiation of voluntary relinquishment, it may ultimately result in the children concerned being admitted to state care on grounds of child neglect. It is difficult to

35 See, *The Independent Review*, January 5, 2005, as cited by Hilpern, K., in her feature article 'The Daddy of All Game Shows', at p 3.

avoid the conclusion that the provision of appropriate and sufficient family support services – in compliance with Articles 18 and 19 of UN CROC – would do much to reduce the availability of children through both the ICA and adoption from state care routes and allow – in compliance with Article 7 of UN CROC – more children 'to be known and cared for by his or her own parents'.

Intercountry adoption is only justified after all other options have been discounted

The principle that ICA 'shall only take place if the competent authorities of the State of origin have determined after the possibilities for placement within the State of origin have been given due consideration that intercountry adoption is in the child's best interests' is expressed in the Preamble to the Hague Convention and in Article 4(b). This principle clearly places an obligation on both potential sending and receiving countries to invest in the resources necessary to retain a child within his or her country of origin as a first option. It is a principle that seldom seems to guide the political choice as to whether government resources should be invested in providing safe care for children within their families of origin or in providing alternative permanency arrangements through non-consensual adoption.

Rehabilitation principle

Articles 7, 8 and 9 of the Convention on the Rights of the Child declare that children have, as far as possible, the right to know and be cared for by their parents, the right to preserve their identity, including family relations, and the right not to be separated from their parents against their will unless to do so is in their best interests. An admission to the public child care system, therefore, should be time limited and conclude with a return to parental care as soon as the problems that gave rise to the admission have been resolved: there is an onus, assumed or statutory, on the public authorities to be proactive in working towards a speedy family reunification; an onus which necessitates nurturing the parent/child relationship, while the latter remains in care, in preparation for their return home. When a child enters the public care system, the birth parent should be promptly offered a rehabilitation training program. The role of the authorities at this stage is critical for the human rights of both child and birth parent and the support provided can determine whether or not a child is placed for adoption.[36]

The ECtHR has advised that every effort should be made to explore rehabilitation if a subsequent recourse to adoption is to be compliant with Article 8 of the ECHR.[37] In *Johansen v. Norway*,[38] it considered the decision of a Norwegian court which had directed that a child be taken into care, placed in a foster placement with a view to adoption and refused contact between the child and her applicant mother. The ECtHR

36 See, UN General Assembly, Guidelines for the Alternative Care of Children, (February 24, 2010), A/RES/64/142, at paras 155–156.

37 *Haase v. Germany*, Application No. 11057/02, (2005).

38 (1996) 23 EHRR 33.

viewed these measures as "particularly far reaching in that they totally deprived the applicant of her family life with the child and were inconsistent with the aim of reuniting them". It stressed the importance to be attached to the continuing interest of birth parents in the future upbringing of their child. As has been said,[39]

> The leading case of *Johansen v. Norway* makes clear that deprivation of parental rights and access should only occur in exceptional circumstances. It would be justified if motivated by an overriding requirement pertaining to the child's best interests . . . The opposite of a trivial test.

The appropriateness of this approach was confirmed by the ECtHR in *K and T v. Finland*[40] and in *Neulinger and Shuruk v. Switzerland.*[41] The court returned to this theme in *YC v. United Kingdom*[42] when it warned that[43]

> family ties may only be severed in very exceptional circumstances and that everything must be done to preserve personal relations and, where appropriate, to 'rebuild' the family. It is not enough to show that a child could be placed in a more beneficial environment for his upbringing.[44]

The birth parent must use the rehabilitation opportunity to demonstrate a capacity to achieve an improved standard of parental care that is significant and sustainable, while the authorities must make genuine efforts to assist the parents, which they had failed to do in *Kutzner v. Germany.*[45] From the outset, it must be made clear to the parent what exactly is required of them: they must be fully part of the decision-making process. The caveat being, as noted in *Pini and Others v. Romania,*[46] that:

> Article 8 does not require that domestic authorities make endless attempts at family reunification; it only requires that they take all the necessary steps that can be reasonably demanded to facilitate the reunion of the child and his or her parents.

Delay in establishing and maintaining contact arrangements between parent and child can be fatal to any prospect of rehabilitation. In *H v. United Kingdom,*[47] for

39 See, Houses of Parliament, England: Hansard, Lords, 16.10.02, Col. 929.
40 [2000] 2 FLR 79, at para 178.
41 See, *Neulinger and Shuruk v. Switzerland* [GC], Application No. 41615/07, (2010).
42 (2012) 55 EHRR 967.
43 Ibid, at para 134.
44 Op. cit., at para 35.
45 (2002) 35 EHRR 25.
46 [2004] EHRR 275.
47 Application No. 9580/81, (1987). See, also, *Paulsen-Medalen and Svenson v. Sweden* (1998) 26 EHRR 260 and *Z.M. and K.P. v. Slovakia*, Application No. 50232/99, (2005).

example, by the time the matter was brought before the court, almost three and a half years had elapsed since the mother had last seen her child who was by then well settled with prospective adopters. The ECtHR stressed that

> In cases of this kind the authorities are under a duty to exercise exceptional diligence since . . . there is always the danger that any procedural delay will result in the *de facto* determination of the issue submitted to the court before it has held the hearing.

The ruling, that any "excessive delay" breached Article 6(1), established the important duty to expedite proceedings in such circumstances. Again, in *K.A.B. v. Spain*,[48] the ECtHR was concerned with the adoption – despite the father's opposition – of a child who had been declared abandoned after his mother's deportation. The applicant complained that he had been deprived of all contact with his son and that neither he nor the child's mother had been informed of the proposal to adopt the child. The ECtHR held that there had been a violation of Article 8: in particular, that the passage of time resulting from the authorities' inaction, the deportation of the child's mother without the necessary prior verification, the failure to assist the applicant when his social and financial situation was most fragile at the earlier stage, together with the failure of the courts to give weight to any other responsibility for the child's abandonment and the finding that the applicant had lost interest in his son's welfare, had decisively contributed to preventing the possibility of reunion between father and son.

Ethical issues

For the value systems of modern western nations – the legal structures of which are highly sensitised to issues of equality and non-discrimination as played out in matters of race, class, etc. – both ICA and adoption from state care carry considerable baggage. For third world countries, coming to terms with the legacy of colonialism, ICA reverberates with echoes of their earlier experiences of exploitation. Some take the view that this is simply a modern manifestation of colonialism: seen as not dissimilar to the economic and commercial cultivation of client relationships with third world countries by modern western societies; their viewpoints centring on political interpretations of ICA where the transfer of children is seen as a proxy manifestation of mercenary national interests. Similarly, non-consensual adoption – at least for the CANZUS nations – is strongly associated with the weaponised use of adoption by the state as a means of enforced cultural assimilation. Unsurprisingly, then, ICA and adoption from state care – both resonating with earlier experiences of victimisation by the state – can generate contemporary ethical dilemmas.

48 Application No. 59819/08, (2012).

Altruism

Adoption, whether from state care or ICA may, like blood or organ donation, be viewed as an aspect of 'the gift relationship',[49] but this is not always the dominant motivation. Whether driven by altruism or by personal need, adopters often seek to acquire elsewhere the babies unavailable in modern western society due to the fall in fertility rates, exacerbated by deferred conception to facilitate career choices, an increase in the efficiency and use of birth control techniques together with the modern growth in government support services for single parents. The shortfall in supply relative to demand is well documented, for example, 'in Italy, for every local child eligible for adoption there are an estimated 15 couples wishing to adopt'.[50]

Nonetheless, in many cases, adoption from state care or via ICA is triggered by the compassionate altruistic response of prospective adopters to the plight of children, orphaned by war or abandoned to institutional care. For such children the altruism of adopters often offers them the only opportunity they will have to experience a safe and caring family life. There is much truth in the observation made by Silberman:[51]

> While critics of intercountry adoption view transnational and transracial placement of children as forms of imperialism and genocide, others argue that intercountry adoption offers the only viable opportunity for many of these children.

Because adoption, child-care and foster care services are often so under-developed in the 'global south' countries, ICA is often the easiest way of immediately securing the welfare interests of the children concerned.

Child rescue

The 'child rescue' approach has its origins in a very practical and necessary humanitarian response to the plight of refugee children abandoned or orphaned in the aftermath of the Korean war. Since then tens of thousands of children in such situations have been rescued from the scene of natural disasters such as in Haiti, and from the many theatres of war such as in Bosnia and Ukraine. There are those who argue that this child rescue approach is unwarranted: that every effort should be made to rehabilitate children back into their society and culture of birth as soon as

49 See, Titmus, R., *The Gift Relationship: From Human Blood to Social Policy*, The New Press, 1997.

50 See, Menozzi, C. and Mirkin, B., 'Child Adoption: A Path to Parenthood?', at p 4, https://paa2007.populationassociation.org/papers/70610

51 See, Silberman, L., 'The Hague Children's Conventions: The Internationalization of Child Law', in Katz, S., Eekelaar, J. and Maclean, M. (eds.), *Cross Currents: Family Law and Policy in the United States and England*, Oxford, Oxford University Press, 2000, at p 607; citing D'Amato, A., 'Cross-Country Adoption: A Call to Action', *Notre Dame Law Review*, Vol. 73, p 1239 and Bartholet, E., 'International Adoption: Propriety, Prospect and Pragmatics', *Journal of the American Academy of Matrimonial Lawyers*, Vol. 13, p 181, 1996.

it is safe to do so; to uproot a child from their familiar social context – from family, friends and community – is to risk damaging their sense of personal and cultural identity. They argue that to 'siphon off' such children into the homes of adopters in the very different cultures of western society is to take opportunistic advantage of a crisis and to prioritise the needs of adopters over the long-term best interests of the children.

Diverting adopters from domestic child-care needs

There is an argument that ICA channels adopters away from meeting the needs of children in the domestic public child-care system. All western nations currently involved in ICA also have children in their public care systems whose needs could be more appropriately met by adoption. These children remain unadopted because of factors such as health and social care problems, age, lack of parental consent, lack of sufficient post-adoption support services and because they are in sibling groups. Even in countries where a facilitatory legal and administrative environment exists, the likelihood of such children being adopted is reduced by the counter-attraction to prospective adopters of securing a healthy baby, without ongoing entanglement with members of the baby's birth family, from outside the jurisdiction. The argument is that ICA encourages 'shopping around' which is wholly contrary to the UN CROC principle that adoption is intended to provide a child with a family, not vice versa.

While the research methodology employed by Chou and Browne has generated controversy, it is hard to challenge their finding that a positive correlation exists between the number of incoming international adoptions and the number of young children in institutional care in those receiving countries, and they are surely right to raise the question – why, after decades of international adoption, are there still large numbers of children in institutional care across Europe?[52]

Public/private and costs

From the perspective of cash-strapped governments in most developed nations, the prospect of meeting the needs both of children who require safe parenting and of the many childless couples eager for an opportunity to parent, while simultaneously transferring much of the care costs to the latter, adoption from state care may seem fortuitous even if it does generate much contention.

Adoption from state care is viewed by some as a government strategy to redefine a matter of public policy by privatising its responsibilities through the transfer of child-care costs from the public to the private sector and to assuage the demand, represented by an ever-growing waiting list of approved adopters, for adoptable children. There are those who consider it to be wholly immoral to pay those who

52 See, Chou, S. and Browne, K., 'The Relationship between Institutional Care and the International Adoption of Children in Europe', *Adoption & Fostering*, Vol. 32, No. 1, pp 40–48, 2008, at p 45.

choose to offer a child a family life while also legally cutting that child's ties to their birth family. They argue that it must be preferable for a child to keep the child in a safe home environment while facilitating their links with parents and other family members so as to ensure the child retains an authentic sense of identity and belonging. Others feel that to allow a child, failed by parental care, to drift between foster homes and be deprived of opportunities to develop attachments, trust and a sense of being valued, is to deny the developmental needs of that child, their right to family life and the relevance of the welfare principle.

Many aspects of contemporary adoption reveal how far it has evolved from being the most private of private family law proceedings to something close to a public service. Adoptions are increasingly accompanied by financial assistance, the ongoing involvement of a range of different professions and various forms of intrusive provision. As adoption progressively assumes more of the hallmarks of a public service, so it is required to conform to the standards of transparency, accountability, freedom of information, etc., that are expected of other such services. In so doing it is progressively shedding its characteristic hallmarks of privacy.

Personal and cultural identity

There is no express protection for the right to an identity under Article 8 or any other Convention provision, but both the Hague Convention and UN CROC recognise that due regard must be given to a child's ethnic, religious, cultural and linguistic background when considering adoption. Access to origins information, an essential step towards building a sense of identity, is facilitated by Article 30(1) of the Convention which requires sending countries to preserve information relating to the identity of birth parents and in particular to the child's personal and family history; this is to include information regarding the family's medical history. For an adopted person such information can be crucial. Further, Article 30(2) leaves the issue of access to that information to be determined by the laws of the adoptee's place of residence.

In *Gaskin v. United Kingdom*,[53] the ECtHR first found that the right to private life included an entitlement to access the information necessary to establish an identity. That case concerned a plaintiff who had spent his childhood in care and sought to challenge the refusal of social services to give him access to the confidential records relating to him. The ECtHR endorsed the view of the Commission that

> respect for private life requires that everyone should be able to establish details of their identity as human beings and that in principle they should not be obstructed by the authorities from obtaining such very basic information without specific justification.

53 (1990) 12 EHRR 36.

Again, in *MG v. United Kingdom*,[54] the ECtHR found that the applicant had been wrongfully denied full access to social services files which would have clarified whether his name had been entered on the child protection register and whether his father had ever been convicted of child abuse. Similarly, in *Godelli v. Italy*,[55] the ECtHR held that the applicant's Article 8 rights had been violated by Italian legislation which, in cases where the mother had opted not to disclose her identity, did not allow a child – who had not been formally recognised at birth and was subsequently adopted – to request either non-identifying information about his or her origins or the disclosure of the birth mother's identity without the latter's consent.

Kinship adoption

In keeping with the legal significance now attached to the previously mentioned principles of personal and cultural identity, there has been a relatively recent acceptance that kinship foster care and adoption offer a means for furthering the same end: that of demonstrating respect for private life by retaining and building upon the sense of personal and cultural identity that a child would have assimilated from their parents. Cultural identity is and has long been been a much-prized feature of upbringing in Indigenous communities. In all CANZUS nations great importance is attached to ensuring that as Indigenous children mature, they retain a sense of where and to whom they belong, an awareness of their cultural heritage and family traditions. The value of such links for a child, promoting an orientation towards their birth family and its cultural context, is now strongly endorsed by international conventions for use in the adoption processes of developed societies.

Kinship adoption is now acquiring preferential status in those societies where it functions: in a private family law context, when a relative adopts a child abandoned by their parents or whose parents have died, become disabled or are otherwise unable to cope; and in a public law context when a child in state care is adopted consensually or non-consensually by a relative. In particular, it has become a valued option for children in the public child-care system because its perceived strengths – of maintaining birth family relationships and a sense of continuity with the home environment – are viewed as most likely to be compliant with the Article 8 requirement to demonstrate respect for private life. In the U.S. and Ireland, where the private life dimension to family law finds constitutional protection, there is a well-established reliance on kinship care coupled with a high tolerance for step-adoption. This is now being emulated in countries like the UK and Germany.

There may, however, be consequences for recognising the relative advantages of kinship care. The future of foster care is becoming questionable. Following on from the quiet revolution that saw an end to institutionalisation as the primary – sometimes the sole – state resource for 'out-of-home children', it may be that foster care

54 Application No. 39393/98, (2002).
55 Application No. 33783/09, (2012).

will similarly become largely redundant. Its traditionally valued benefits – removal from home environment, immersion in an approved model of family care and exposure to non-birth parent caring attachments – are coming to be regarded as carrying a risk of non-compliance with the requirement to respect private life. In the CANZUS nations an extra layer has been added to the questioning of foster care: this is now being scorned by some as 'a racist institution' because it functions with systemic cultural asymmetry; almost always white Caucasians fostering children of colour due, for whatever reason, to the gross shortage of Indigenous foster parents; the resulting disconnect alienating the child from their family, community and cultural heritage. All in all, the public child-care systems of the developed nations could be on the cusp of fundamental change as foster care – the backbone of those systems for many generations – is overtaken by kinship care.

Consequences may also follow for the future of the law as it relates to ICA, commercial surrogacy and, if to a lesser extent, child abduction. The ramifications of giving legal recognition to the importance of private family life, and its associated principles of personal and cultural identity, are difficult to predict but will probably very much depend on the context in which they are applied. However, it may be that as social mobility and multiculturalism become more pervasive, the legal significance of a singular sense of cultural affinity will correspondingly weaken.

Commodification of children

ICA is seen by some as just another form of international trade in which children are the 'goods' to be traded,[56] and the pejorative term 'commodification' is applied to activities such as ICA and commercial surrogacy (see, further, Chapter 4). Hayes, who has noted the drift from welfare interests to marketing, comments that 'the demand of potential parents abroad has the effect of creating or maintaining the supply of children, particularly given the inducement of the fees that these parents are willing to pay'.[57] For some academics such as Hubinette, ICA carries 'ugly parallels to contemporary trafficking of women and the historic transatlantic slave trade', not dissimilar to the economic and commercial cultivation of client relationships with third world countries by modern western societies.[58] He argues that this has certainly been the experience of Korea.[59]

International law

Numerous international instruments variously contribute to a framework of legal provisions that impact either or both adoption from state care and ICA.

56 See, further, Triseliotis, J., 'Intercountry Adoption: Global Trade or Global Gift?', *Adoption & Fostering, London, BAAF*, Vol. 24, No. 2, pp 45–54, 2000.

57 See, Hayes, P., 'Intercountry Adoption: A Comparative Analysis of its Effects on Domestic Adoption Rates', in *ESRC End of Award Report, RES-000-22-1840*, Swindon, ESRC, 2009, at p 1.

58 See, Hubinette, T., 'Adopted Koreans and the Development of Identity in the Third Space', *Adoption & Fostering, London, BAAF*, Vol. 28, No. 1, pp 16–24, 2004, at p 19.

59 Ibid, at p 19.

The United Nations Guidelines for the Alternative Care of Children 2009

These start from the general principle that efforts should primarily be directed towards enabling children to remain in or return to the care of their parents. Removing a child from the care of the family should be seen as a measure of last resort and whenever possible be temporary and for the shortest duration possible (para 14). Children temporarily or permanently deprived of their birth family, or in whose best interests cannot be allowed to remain in that environment, are entitled to special government protection and assistance (UN CROC, Article 20(1)).

Provision of alternative care can include "foster placement . . . adoption or, if necessary, placement in suitable institutions for the care of children" (Article 20(3)). Decisions regarding children in alternative care should have due regard for the importance of ensuring children a stable home and meeting their basic need for safe and continuous attachment to their caregivers, with permanency generally being a key goal (Guidelines, para 12).

The European Convention on the Adoption of Children (Revised) 2008

This Convention extends formal recognition to some important principles. It specifies that the father's consent is required in all cases, including when the child was born out of wedlock, and it explicitly covers adopters who are heterosexual unmarried couples in a registered partnership, as well as allowing states to extend adoptions to same-sex couples living together in a stable relationship. It not only reaffirms that the child's consent is necessary if he or she has sufficient understanding to give it, specifying that consent must be required at a minimum as of age 14 years, but also introduces an obligation to consult with the child even where formal consent is not required, reflecting UN CROC Article 12 in an explicit manner. It also places greater emphasis on the right of adopted children to know their identity as opposed to the right of the biological parents to remain anonymous.

Brussels II 2004

This regulation in relation to family law cases with cross-border elements, came into effect on 1 August 2004 and was updated in 2022. Its application to child-care cases, custody and abduction – particularly as regards implementation of Articles 15, 55 and 56 – can make it marginally relevant to ICA

The Hague Convention on Protection of Children and Co-operation in Respect of Intercountry Adoption 1993

In its Preamble the Convention states that – 'intercountry adoption may offer the advantage of a permanent home to a child for whom a suitable family cannot be found in his or her State of origin' – thus tacitly acknowledging the principle that family-based care (even if provided in a different country) is to be preferred to care in an orphanage or similar residential setting.

It declares in Article 1 that its objective is 'to establish safeguards to ensure that intercountry adoptions take place in the best interests of the child and with respect for his fundamental rights as recognised in international law'. In Article 4(b) it provides that a Convention adoption 'shall only take place if the competent authorities of the state of origin have determined after the possibilities for placement within the state of origin have been given due consideration that intercountry adoption is in the child's best interests'.

The Convention is an important statement of principles relating to ICA, but it has no enforcement mechanism, not all relevant countries have ratified it, and even countries that have done so are often also complicit in bilateral agreements that bypass it. Bartholet has challenged Hague on the grounds that "the law poses as protector of children but in the end functions as their enemy".[60] She cites the restrictive constraints requiring children to be orphans before their circumstances entitle them to be eligible for ICA and criticises the Convention for disqualifying children "simply because they appear to have two living parents".[61] Almost three decades after the Hague Convention came into effect (1 May 1995), and despite some 90 states having contracted to abide by it, the majority of ICAs still take place outside the framework it provides.

The United Nations Convention on the Rights of the Child 1989

This Convention (UN CROC) recognises the rights of the child and the corresponding duties of the State. It declares in its Preamble:

> that the family, as the fundamental group of society and the natural environment for the growth and well-being of all its members and particularly children, should be afforded the necessary protection and assistance so that it can fully assume its responsibilities within the community.

The Preamble is underpinned by Articles 18 and 20, which again reinforce the principle that the state should give priority to measures that keep children in their families and culture of origin. In circumstances where a child's family of origin is unable to meet the needs of that child, then Article 20 requires the state to "ensure alternative care for such a child".[62] Article 21 recognises that ICA may be considered as an alternative means of providing for a child's care but only after

60 See, Bartholet, E., 'International Adoption: Current Status and Prospects', *The Future of Children*, Vol. 3, No. 1, 1993, at p 91. A view that lost validity in the U.S. with the introduction of the Intercountry Adoption Universal Accreditation Act 2012 on 14th July 2014.

61 Ibid, at p 92.

62 Subject to the requirement that 'due regard shall be paid to the desirability of continuity in a child's upbringing and to the child's ethnic, religious, cultural and linguistic background'.

all other options for retaining the child within his or her country of origin have been exhausted. In that event, it requires the child's interests to be treated as of paramount importance. In addition, Article 9 provides that children should not be separated from their parents against their will except where this is determined to be in the best interests of the child and in accordance with law. Further, Article 9, para 3, and Article 10, para 2, give formal recognition to a presumption that a child's welfare interests require the maintaining of relationships and regular contact with both their parents, even if the latter are living apart and are in different countries.

Declaration on Social and Legal Principles relating to the Protection and Welfare of Children, with special reference to Foster Placement and Adoption Nationally and Internationally 1986

Article 13 of the Declaration states that the primary aim of adoption should be to provide a permanent family for a child who cannot be cared for by his or her own parents.

Article 17 recognises that ICA is a child-care mechanism of last resort and states that

> If a child cannot be placed in a foster or an adoptive family or cannot in any suitable manner be cared for in the country of origin, intercountry adoption may be considered as an alternative means of providing the child with a family.

It states that the best interests of a child should be paramount, including the right to affection, security and continuing care. Article 24 requires due regard to be given to 'the child's cultural and religious background and interests'.

The Hague Convention on the Civil Aspects of International Child Abduction 1980

The Preamble states that 'the interests of children are of paramount importance in matters relating to their custody'. Despite the reference to 'paramount importance', the approach of the ECtHR is one of balancing conflicting interests rather than applying a presumptive rule that the best interests of the child must prevail.

The European Convention on the Adoption of Children 1967

This Convention – preceded by The Hague Convention on Jurisdiction, etc. – sought to identify some common principles and standards of practice to serve as international benchmarks for the parties involved in adoption. For example, it established the principle that adoption should be in the interests of the child (Article 8, para 1) and should provide the child with a stable and harmonious home (Article 8, para 2).

European Convention for the Protection of Human Rights and Fundamental Freedoms 1950

This Convention (ECHR) established a framework of international rights, the most important of which – for present purposes – is Article 8 stating the right to respect for private and family life. It has generated considerable adoption-related caselaw.

Jurisdictional differences and their significance: adoption from state care

Maternal choice, to retain rather than relinquish a non-marital child, has played a significant role in reducing the number of children now available for domestic adoption in modern western societies. Moreover, many of the latter are enduring protracted retrenchment in government spending on all public services, and provision of long-term state care for children failed by their parents is particularly expensive. Consequently, domestic adoption in some of those societies is changing from being consensually based to coercive in nature, with the availability of children being determined more by the courts than by parental choice.

Law and policy

In England and Wales, government policy has for some decades been to actively pursue the non-consensual adoption of children from state care. Current judicial guidance[63] can diverge from ECtHR benchmark cases,[64] though there is evidence to show that the judiciary are mindful of the need to keep within Article 8 parameters.[65] It can also diverge from practice in most other common law and civil law jurisdictions, but its firmly established policy preference for adoption rather than long-term foster care is in keeping with practice in the U.S. This, it is claimed, is the best way of promoting a child's welfare, and concurrent placements, financial assistance and other forms of support are being used to facilitate it, resulting in 2,960 of the 83,840 children in the care of local authorities (up 2% on the previous year and up 23% since 2013) being adopted during the year ending 31 March 2023 (down 2% on previous year).[66] By way of contrast, adoption in Ireland has been, and very largely remains, a consensual process with only a very small number of children – almost all adolescents – being adopted by their long-term foster parents. Recent changes in the law will facilitate the future possible adoption of children from marital families and from state care, but this is unlikely to develop into a central policy objective. In keeping with its constitutional principles, Ireland has invested instead in maintaining rather than displacing the link between a child in state care and his or her family of origin. This is quite similar to the policy and practice in New Zealand.

Unlike New Zealand, there are indications that in some Australian states, and in Canada, preparations are underway to follow the example set by the U.S. and

63 See, *Seddon v. Oldham MBC* [2015] EWHC 2609 (Fam) and *Re W (A Child)* [2016] EWCA Civ 793.

64 *YC v. the United Kingdom* (2012) 55 EHRR 33, at para 35.

65 See, for example, *EH v. A London Borough Council* [2010] EWCA Civ 344, [2010] 2 FLR 661.

66 See, further, https://corambaaf.org.uk/resources/statistics/statistics-england

the UK: some Australian states are now moving towards policies of statutorily establishing this as the placement of first choice in respect of children who cannot be safely returned to parental care. While there is considerable variation among the provinces and states, the fact that adoption from care is becoming – and in some places has already become – the primary source of adoptees, suggests that in Canada as in the U.S. adoption is now firmly a hybrid public/private family law proceeding. This is heavily supported by state subsidies for the adoption of children from state care and by the recruitment of foster parents who are prepared to adopt. This practice, whereby state responsibilities for neglected and abused children are in effect privatised, has been pursued with particular vigour in the U.S. where authorities are incentivised by reinforcement schemes such as federal bonus payments to those who exceed their prescribed quota of annual adoptions.

The civil law countries – France and Germany – take a markedly different approach. In both, a state deference towards parental status is most clearly apparent in the comparative lack of policy and legislative initiatives to facilitate the non-consensual adoption of children who, failed or abused by their parents, must by default remain in long-term state care.

The proportionality principle and adoption from state care

In England and Wales, the Court of Appeal has stressed that any placement or adoption order made without parental consent must be proportionate to the legitimate aim of protecting the welfare and interests of the child; only in exceptional circumstances could measures totally depriving a parent of family life with a child be justified.[67] In Ireland, the principle would seem to be have been referenced as justification for not pursuing the interventionist measure of non-consensual adoption in respect of children in the public care system, though – following a recent constitutional amendment – that may now change if only to a limited degree. The same issue in England and Wales generates warnings of caution from the judiciary, most notably in *Re B-S*,[68] but this may not slow local authority recourse to pursuing adoption as the preferred exit strategy for children in the public care system. The tension between an embedded cautious judicial approach to adoption from state care – which resolutely requires evidence that this is a proportionate legal response in the light of the particular circumstances and their effect on the welfare of a particular child – and a government policy that strongly advocates such adoption as the preferred option for promoting the welfare of a child in the care system, has been a strong theme in UK child protection for some decades. Irish legislation, which states as a fundamental principle that it is generally in the best interests of the child to be brought up in their own family, perhaps results in a firmer focus of resources to that end than is the case in England and Wales.

Proportionality, in respect of adoption from the state care system, is an issue in the U.S. for two reasons. First, there are proportionately more children in the

67 See, *SB v. A County Council; Re P* [2008] EWCA Civ 535.

68 [2013] EWCA Civ 1146.

system (approximately 74 per 10,000 of children compared, for example, with 47 per 10,000 in England[69]), and therefore, there are more available for adoption from the care system than elsewhere. Second, there is a racial bias factor. While African American children are over-represented in the care system, there is a scarcity of available African American adopters in a context where preference overall is for white children. Consequently, there is a stronger probability that black children will be disproportionately denied access to adoption and retained in the state care system. Some infants, most of whom are black or Asian, leave the U.S. through outgoing adoptions every year.[70] In Canada, as ICA has become more difficult, assertive policies have been initiated to increase adoptions from state care, helped by the fact that from the early years of this century, adoptions by same-sex couples have become legalised in every province and territory. Proportionality is an issue in relation to the availability of culturally compliant adopters for Indigenous children. As in other CANZUS nations, the matching of available Indigenous children and Indigenous prospective adopters is distinctly asymmetrical which disproportionately disadvantages such children relative to their non-Indigenous counterparts. This was highlighted in the seminal case *Racine v. Woods*[71] and the scandal of the 'sixties scoop'.

The Canadian experience in respect of Indigenous children is largely replicated in Australia. The proportionality principle similarly comes into play in relation to both the disproportionate numbers of Indigenous children being admitted to the state care system and to those remaining there due to a lack of culturally matching adopters. Although, as in Ireland, non-consensual adoptions from state care have traditionally been comparatively rare with the policy in most Australian jurisdictions being to keep children with their families of origin whenever possible and not to prioritise adoption for children in care. However, there are signs that this is now beginning to change. In Queensland and in NSW, there have been adoption-related reforms to the child protection legislation which, to a varying degree, include provisions to facilitate the adoption of children from the care system, though in Victoria the reforms excluded any linkage between the child protection and adoption systems. In New Zealand, as in Australia, it is a child's foster parents who are most likely to be his or her adoptors, but unlike Australia – and in keeping with practice in Ireland – the strong traditional resistance to non-consensual adoption results in very few such adoptions: in 2013 there was only one adoption by a foster parent.

Both France and Germany are constrained from impartially applying the principle of proportionality to the relative interests of children in state care and those of their parents by legal traditions establishing the rights of the latter. So, in France, adoption from public care is confined to the small minority of children designated wards of the state – whose parents have been judicially stripped of their rights and

69 See, further, data published by the Performance and Innovation Unit (U.K.), 2000.

70 Buckwalter-Poza, R., 'America's Unseen Export: Children, Most of them Black', *Pacific Standard*, June 24, 2014, www.psmag.com/navigation/politics-and-law/outgoing-adoption-americas-unseen-export-children-black-84084/

71 [1983] 2 SCR 173.

responsibilities – and are fostered with a family approved for adoption or for whom the foster family has submitted an adoption application. The fact that this is not a policy objective is reflected in the statistics: in 2021 of the 310,525 children in care only 613 – *pupilles de l'Etat* – were adopted;[72] instead successful integration into a foster family is viewed as a satisfactory form of permanence. Similarly in Germany, as adoption is essentially a consensual process, there are very few adoptions of children – about 5% – from the care system, even though in many cases the need for parental consent has been judicially removed. Given that foster care provides the legal framework for only one-third of the children in the public care system, a disproportionate number of children – relative to other developed nations – are left to age out in long-term residential care.

The paramountcy principle and adoption from state care

In England and Wales, the paramountcy principle has been embedded in s 1(2) of the Adoption and Children Act 2002 to govern all aspects of the adoption process, including dispensing with parental consent, and a strategic bridge has thus been put in place to link that process with the child-care system. In Irish law, paramountcy is a very recent newcomer having been effectively restrained by the constitutional primacy given to the marital family. Not until 2015, when Article 42A amended the Constitution, did this principle become relevant in relation to public family law as regards the 'safety and welfare of any child'; and to private, 'concerning the adoption, guardianship or custody of, or access to, any child'. It remains to be seen how exactly this constitutionally enshrined principle will be given effect in statutory proceedings and in judicial practice. In particular, it is uncertain whether it will function – as in England and Wales – to bridge the gap between the law of care and protection and adoption law.

Much the same problem would seem to be obstructing policy in Canada. While all provinces and territories more or less share the same agreement in principle that adoption from the public care system should be facilitated, they are handicapped in practice by the lack of any legal requirement that the welfare of the child be accorded paramount importance when determining an adoption application. This leaves adoption not readily accessible for those in the Canadian public care system, resulting in very many children – in respect of whom parental rights have been removed – being consigned to a 'legal limbo' and being left to age out in the care system. This, in effect, is the typical experience of children in all jurisdictions other than for some in the UK and the U.S. In the latter jurisdiction, the paramountcy principle is not known to the law – in the same way as it is in countries such as the UK and Ireland – but a high rate of adoption from state care is achieved by quota setting, bonuses and federal financial incentives to prompt assertive state recruitment of adopters and encourage the placement for adoption of children in

72 See, further, *Les chiffres clés en protection de l'enfance*, https://onpe.gouv.fr/system/files/publication/fs_chiffres_cles_pe_2021.pdf

state care. In 2020, adoption was the route taken by 25% of the children exiting the public care system that year.[73]

Proportionality has a limited role to play in adoption from state care in the CANZUS nations because the historical legacy of abusive state use of 'forced' adoption to expedite government assimilationist policies in respect of its Indigenous population has led to the present situation where non-consensual adoption is so highly sensitive that this option cannot be pursued on an equal basis with both Indigenous and non-Indigenous children. Instead, preference is given to kinship and guardianship as more appropriate for Indigenous and Māori children in Australia and New Zealand, respectively. There is little evidence in the current review of adoption law in New Zealand of any interest in expediting the adoption of children from the care system. In most Australian jurisdictions, the policy has been to keep children with their families of origin whenever possible and not to prioritise adoption for children in care which may account for the fact that although there were 47,000 children in out-of-home care in 2018, only 147 exited by way of adoption in that year. In general, non-consensual adoption from state care is a last resort in New Zealand, only to be used when all efforts at rehabilitation to safe parental care have failed and in practice is extremely rare; in Australia, a similar policy has been in place, but there are now indications that some states and territories – certainly NSW – are moving towards adoption from state care as the preferred option, though others such as Victoria remain firmly resistant to any such policy.

The welfare principle would seem to have less capacity to transcend the private and public divisions in family law and create a middle ground of hybrid public/private proceedings, in Germany more so than in France. That capacity is necessarily closely linked to whether or not the principle is given a paramount weighting and, if so, whether this applies to child protection and/or custody, which is not the case in Germany. Nonetheless, in both countries there is evidence that the principle is to a varying extent bridging the public/private divide and facilitating a flow of matters traditionally regarded as belonging to private family law (e.g. adoption and surrogacy) or to its public counterpart (e.g. foster care and parental abduction) into a new hybrid arena where the previous concern of the law to balance the interests of the parties has been displaced by the welfare principle as the governing standard.

Failed parental rehabilitation

Where there are reasonable grounds for optimism, regarding a possible reunification of parent and child, then the authorities – as required by UN CROC, Articles 9 and 18 – should give first preference to returning the child. Only when this can be discounted as demonstrably too risky are the authorities free to consider the possibility of adoption from state care (see, further, Chapter 3). The parents, however, must be involved in the relevant decision-making process and left in no doubt as to what is expected of them. In England and Wales, for example, the authorities failed

73 See, AFCARS Report FY 2019, www.acf.hhs.gov/sites/default/files/documents/cb/afcarsreport28.pdf

to convince the court that a parent had been fully involved in the decision-making process leading up to a planned rehabilitation programme. She claimed that the authorities had omitted to share crucial information in the preliminary discussions: she had never been informed that she was required to acknowledge responsibility for the death of her first child as a step towards possible rehabilitation with the second.[74] The court found that by not informing the mother of the contents of a report, in which an expert witness had raised the responsibility issue, the local authority may have failed to respect her "right to a fair trial" and thereby breached Article 6.

Again, in England and Wales, *YC v. United Kingdom*[75] concerned an application for a non-consensual adoption placement following failed parental rehabilitation. While there was evidence that various support measures had been tried before commencement of proceedings in the county court, the decision itself was brief and contained little by way of detailed analysis, which was of concern to the ECtHR as it sought to establish whether the requirements of Article 8 had been satisfied. As always, this required evidence that the process was in accordance with the law, pursued a legitimate aim and was necessary in a democratic society. The Court noted that in assessing a child's best interests, and in assessing the proportionality of measures proposed in the pursuit of those interests, many factors would have to be weighed:

> the domestic court must demonstrate that it has had regard to, *inter alia*, the age, maturity and ascertained wishes of the child, the likely effect on the child of ceasing to be a member of his original family and the relationship the child has with relatives.[76]

The Court seemingly suggested that to demonstrate that it had done so, the domestic court judgment should show that all relevant factors (as identified in the welfare checklist) had been expressly considered and weighed in the final analysis. Ultimately, despite finding that "the county court judge did not make express reference to the relevant considerations arising under Article 8 of the European Convention", nor to the factors identified in the statutory checklist, the Court nonetheless concluded – as the judge at first instance had directed his mind to the child's best interests, and had appropriately considered the prospect of rehabilitation, having had regard to various relevant factors and taken note of reports and oral evidence submitted – that the domestic court had not violated Article 8 (see, also, Chapter 3).

Intercountry adoption

ICA has existed for a long time. It was evident, for example, in the practice of sending many tens of thousands, perhaps hundreds of thousands, of orphaned,

74 See, *Re C* (*Care Proceedings: Disclosure of Local Authority's Decision-Making Process*) [2002] 2 FCR 673.

75 Application No. 4547/10, (2012), at p 138. For further analysis of this case and related issues see George, R., *The Child's Welfare in a European Perspective*, Welfare%20in%20a%20European%20Perspective.pdf

76 Ibid, at 135.

abandoned and/or neglected children from the UK[77] and Ireland[78] to Australia,[79] Canada[80] and other British colonial and post-colonial countries in the late 19th and early 20th centuries.[81] Throughout the latter part of the 20th century and currently ongoing, if shrinking in volume, it has played a part in rescuing children from circumstances of war and natural disaster in the 'global south' and transferring them to adopters in the more developed nations. So, for example, from 1956 to 1994 Korea was by far the most important single contributor to ICA,[82] sending a total of some 150,000 children to adoptive homes in other countries, mainly in the U.S. Initially the flow was stimulated by the plight of many children who as orphans or refugees were the casualties of war, but this changed over time as government policy prioritised the use of revenues for poverty relief and developing its industrial base. It facilitated the export of children as a means of avoiding a drain on scarce national resources and only began introducing restrictions in the early 1980s, as national prosperity increased, before ending its involvement with ICA in the 1990s. Political ideology as well as poverty has also played an important role in ICA as illustrated by the government decree in China that only one child per family should be the rule, coupled with the preference for male children, which led to many unwanted female children being absorbed through the ICA process. Again, in Romania under the Ceauşescu regime, the official policy that each family should have a minimum of four children resulted in many being abandoned to ICA by parents who could not provide for them. Also, the current protracted freeze in ICA arrangements between Russia and the U.S. is a consequence of the Russian directive that children could not be sent for adoption to countries that legally tolerated same-sex relationships.

When seen in this light, ICA clearly does not conform to the traditional model of adoption that has always been at the centre of private family law. The public policy dimension is unmistakable: ICA affects the politics of sending and receiving countries, cultural integrity and the long-term welfare of uprooted children; the political reality driving a national policy of sending children overseas remains rooted in poverty; and invariably it is the poor children, whose parents are unavailable or unable to care for them, who are exported by under-resourced state authorities to meet the needs of adopters in other countries. Unmistakable, also are the rights to family life and to privacy of the adopters and children. Whether it is primarily

77 See, for example, Bean, P. and Melville, J., *Lost Children of the Empire*, London, Unwin Hyman Ltd., 1989.

78 See, for example, Robbins, J., *The Lost Children: A Study of Charity Children in Ireland 1700–1900*, Dublin, Institute of Public Administration, 1980.

79 See, for example, Humphreys, M., *Empty Cradles*, Random House, 2009.

80 See, for example, Parker, R., *Uprooted: The Shipment of Poor Children to Canada, 1867–1919*, Bristol, The Policy Press, 2008.

81 See, for example, Milotte, M., *Banished Babies: The Secret History of Ireland's Baby Export Business*, New Island Books, 1997.

82 See, Hubinette, T., 'Adopted Koreans and the Development of Identity in the Third Space', *Adoption & Fostering, London, BAAF*, Vol. 28, No. 1, pp 16–24, 2004, where the author refers to the resulting Korean adoption diaspora.

serving the needs of the children concerned or their adopters, ICA must be recognised as a hybrid form of family law.

Jurisdictional differences and their significance: intercountry adoption

The role and functions of adoption in any society are conditioned by pressures from both the public and private family law proceedings and by the prevailing political ideology governing the state/family relationship at that point in time. It would seem to function as a safety valve: relieving pressure caused by a build-up of children – abandoned, abused or otherwise failed by their birth parents – in the state care system, and similarly doing so in respect of the ever-growing numbers of approved adopters (so many that the waiting lists in many countries are closed) wanting an opportunity to parent such children. As the domestic possibilities of reducing pressure by facilitating a matching of both sets of needs became more constrained, due to a general fall in the number of legally available children relinquished or abandoned by their parents, those prospective adopters – barred from accessing children in the state care system by a lack of parental consent – aided by intermediary agencies, looked to ICA to make up the shortfall. In so doing, they had to negotiate public law requirements relating to matters such as citizenship and immigration but, if successful, could expect to benefit from the traditional private family law privileges of anonymity, privacy and confidentiality no longer available in domestic adoption. It is this amalgam of public/private characteristics that makes ICA – like adoption from state care – a hybrid form of family law proceedings.

Intercountry adoption: a global phenomenon

For children who are orphans, have been abandoned in poorly resourced institutional care, and/or have complex health needs, their removal into the homes of western adopters most often results in an unqualified improvement in their welfare interests and prospects. It must be added that for the very many children in those developed nations who are left in state institutions or in long-term foster care, due to being unadoptable for various reasons, the fact that others have been adopted in their place is disastrous.

ICA, as a global phenomenon, would seem to be shrinking fast. The peak period, 1998–2004, saw annual numbers soar from under 32,000 to over 45,000; since then the overall downward trajectory has been well documented.[83] In the U.S., for example, a 2022 report *Adoption by the Numbers*[84] revealed that they had decreased by 93% since 2004, the year the U.S. had the most incoming ICAs.[85] It

83 See, Selman, P., in Gibbons, J.L. and Rotabi, K.S. (eds.), *Intercountry Adoption: Policies, Practices, and Outcomes*, Ashgate, 2012. Figures from International Social Services (ISS) show a global decline of nearly 50%, from 43,142 adoptions in 2004 to 21,991 adoptions in 2011.

84 See, further, https://adoptioncouncil.org/research/adoption-by-the-numbers/

85 See, further, https://adoptioncouncil.org/blog/new-report-on-international-adoption-highlights-need-for-change/

is considerably ironic that the continued downward trend in U.S. ICA is directly attributable to it having become a signatory state to the Hague Convention; the provisions of which were intended to raise standards of practice and safeguard the welfare of children in international adoption. Instead, U.S. ratification of the Convention in 2008 had the immediate negative effect of stalling very many adoption processes, leaving children and their prospective adopters in limbo, often for years. In Guatemala, approximately 4,000 U.S. adoptions (some at an advanced stage) came to an abrupt halt when the standards of practice governing the legal availability of children were judged to be not compliant with the Hague Convention.[86]

The reasons for the recent global dip in ICA have been the subject of much academic debate.[87] For some, it is to an extent attributable to the economic recession: the expense involved has become a deterrent for many prospective applicants. Others view it as an indicator of the growing effectiveness of the Hague Convention in tightening standards and gradually filtering out those sending countries where standards are suspect. Improvements in methods of assisting conception and the growing use of surrogacy have also played their part. Then there is undoubtedly the role of policy and politics in curtailing the flow from long-established primary sources such as Russia, Korea and China. Certainly, adverse effects followed from the political decision in Russia to terminate ICA arrangements with the U.S.[88] and from the Chinese revision of its adopter eligibility criteria resulting in the exclusion of many prospective U.S. adopters. Perhaps, also, the fact that other jurisdictions would seem to be preparing to follow the example set by the U.S. and the UK and look to domestic sources – specifically to the state child-care system – is having the overall effect of diverting prospective adopters away from ICA.

Jurisdictional differences

This social phenomenon has never been as popular in England and Wales as elsewhere in Europe, largely due to a firm government policy of redirecting prospective adopters towards children in the domestic public care system. This policy has in recent years been considerably reinforced by financial support. Although the annual statistics have not fallen by much since 2014 (2014: 68 and in 2019: 52),[89] ICA is now declining in England and Wales as a proportion of annual adoption orders as a consequence of its social policy and also because of a reversal of government policy in previously well-established 'donor' countries such as China,

86 See, further, 'Stalled Adoption Program in Guatemala Leaves Families in Limbo', *New York Times*, December 8, 2012.

87 See, generally, Gibbons, J.L. and Rotabi, K.S. (eds.), Op. cit.

88 Ostensibly this was in reaction to the ill treatment and deaths of several Russian adoptees in the U.S., but arguably it was a response to the Magnitsky Act and as such had little to do with state concern for the welfare interests of children.

89 See, further, https://static1.squarespace.com/static/61336194b08d594b2a099eeb/t/6134d7699c23732ff69b212d/1630852970201/ICATOTALS1.pdf

Korea, Romania and Russia. In Ireland, ICA has been proportionately more significant than in its neighbouring jurisdictions,[90] so much so that in the previously mentioned global peak period – 1998–2004 – total ICA numbers in Ireland more than doubled. This may well be due to ICA becoming a forced option because of the lack of domestic alternatives. Ireland has seen a drastic reduction in the number of infants voluntarily relinquished by their unmarried mothers because of improved welfare benefits and a reversal of the associated stigma attaching to such mothers. This situation has been exacerbated by the virtual absence of non-consensual adoption from the public care system, together with the non-availability of children from marital families. Interestingly, in Ireland as in other counties such as the U.S., there was a sharp decline in ICA following the ratification of the 1993 Hague Convention: from 395 in 2009 to 242 in 2012, falling to 184 in 2020 and to 174 in 2022.[91]

Once the global leader in recourse to ICA, the U.S. has severely scaled back its involvement in recent years. In 2022, under the terms of the Intercountry Adoption Act 2000, consular officers issued 1,435 immigrant visas to children adopted abroad, or to be adopted in the U.S. by U.S. citizens, which represented a marked fall from the 4,059 adopted the previous year[92] and a dramatic drop in numbers from 22,884 in 2004. In recent years Canada has seen a drop in annual ICAs: in 2022 there were only 414, down from 895 in 2015 and 1,367 in 2012.[93] Prospective adopters in Canada, as elsewhere, have also been similarly adversely impacted by the decision of some sending countries to abruptly terminate long-standing bilateral adoption arrangements.

In Australia, ICA numbers have steadily declined each year from 149 in 2012 to 16 in 2022. A singular jurisdictional characteristic is the role of the Intercountry Adoption Family Support Service, a federal agency established in 2016. This nationwide agency provides counselling support to those engaged in the ICA process and post-placement (including case management) services to intercountry-adopted children and their families, including expatriate adoptions.[94] New Zealand has the distinction of being a global leader in adoption legislation when, in 1881, it became the first nation to introduce a statutory process for adopting children. Adoption in New Zealand has been and continues to be very largely kinship in nature – including ICA – and it may well be where this form of adoption originated. In the early 2000s, for example, of the 500 to 600 annual ICAs, over half were Samoans adopting related older children, mostly so the children could

90 For example, in 2004 the Adoption Board made 273 adoption orders and 484 entries in the Register of Foreign Adoptions, a high rate of foreign adoptions by international standards.

91 See, further, https://aai.gov.ie/images/aai-ar-2022_final_opt.pdf

92 See, further, https://travel.state.gov/content/dam/NEWadoptionassets/pdfs/Tab%201%20Annual%20Report%20on%20Intercountry%20Adoptions.pdf

93 See, further, www.linkedin.com/posts/lynelle-long-8a6399_intercountry-adoption-ica-statistics-2022-activity-7154670406858100737-d8Aq

94 See www.intercountryadoption.gov.au/post-adoption-support/intercountry-adoption-family-support-service/

become New Zealand citizens.[95] In 2013 there were only 24 ICAs of which six were by non-relatives. By 2020, total annual ICAs had fallen to 19 and fell further to 16 by 2022, including a high proportion of kinship adopters.

In France, adoption in domestic law is essentially consensual in nature. The virtual absence of adoption in a child-care context (although a few are adopted, this is almost invariably by their foster parents, with only a handful becoming otherwise available to domestic adopters), together with the dwindling availability of '*sous le secret*' children and wards of the state, has meant that for some time there has been a heavier reliance than elsewhere on ICA.[96] In 1997, for example, a total of 3,528 children were adopted by way of ICA from 70 countries, in 2003, of the 4,500 children adopted, almost 4,000 (90%) were ICA, while in 2022 there were 232 ICAs, a high proportion of which were from non-Hague countries.[97] The fact that due to the constraints of Hague, a growing proportion of ICAs in France and elsewhere are from non–Hague compliant countries, correspondingly increases the risk to the welfare interests of the children and the probability of a public law intrusion into what is otherwise very largely a private law process. Again, in Germany, adoption is essentially consensual and therefore, though to a markedly lesser extent than other countries in Western Europe, domestic sources have been augmented by ICA, but this has been steadily decreasing, from 209 in 2014, to 91 in 2018 and to 81 in 2022.[98]

Trends in recourse to ICA have to take into account the effects of political decisions in former 'sending' countries. In particular, the Russian legislation in July 2013 prohibiting the adoption of children by same-sex couples and single people and also prohibiting adoption from countries that recognise same-sex marriage, regardless of the actual sexual orientation of applicants, has been a serious constraint on international adoption.

Conclusion

Adoption as a private family law process is now greatly reduced in all jurisdictions. This has been due to the overall decline in numbers of voluntarily relinquished children, to the relatively sudden and dramatic rise in commercial surrogacy and to the global contraction of ICA. It has been further diminished by the introduction in some jurisdictions of alternative and less 'draconian' orders, such as special guardianship, specifically designed to divert step-parent applicants away from adoption, though this is offset to an extent in other jurisdictions by the legally

95 See, further, www.teara.govt.nz/en/adoption/page-6

96 See, further, Halifax, J., *Why Are there So Many International Adoptions in France?*, www.uea.ac.uk/swp/icar2/pdf's/Halifax99.pdf

97 See, further, www.diplomatie.gouv.fr/fr/adopter-a-l-etranger/la-mission-de-l-adoption/les-statistiques-de-l-adoption

98 See, further, www.linkedin.com/posts/lynelle-long-8a6399_intercountry-adoption-ica-statistics-2022-activity-7154670406858100737-d8Aq

expedient linking of adoption to surrogacy. As a public family law process, mainstreamed into child protection services, the future of adoption has yet to be decided, but it would seem probable, given the costs of state care together with the steady build-up of children in the care system and the increasing numbers of prospective adopters – particularly same-sex couples – that more jurisdictions will follow the lead established by the U.S. and the UK and incentivise the non-consensual adoption of such children.

6 Unaccompanied migrant minors, detention and trafficking

Introduction

The phenomenon of children travelling long distances without parents – who may be ill, dead or missing – crossing borders, usually with unrelated adult migrants, until eventually arriving in one of the jurisdictions currently being studied, where they are detained, is no longer unusual. Neither, unfortunately, is the ancillary phenomenon of many of those children being recruited – by force or enticement – into activities for which they are underpaid, often punished and from which they are prevented from leaving. Whether orphaned, abandoned or otherwise outside parental control (see, further, Chapter 8), increasing numbers of children are being admitted to the public care systems of the developed nations, far from their countries of birth, while many others fall victim to the predations of traffickers.

This chapter is in three parts: beginning with matters of definition, principle and international law; it then considers the phenomenon of unaccompanied migrant children; and concludes with an analysis of contemporary child trafficking.

Composite framework: unaccompanied migrant minors, detention and trafficking

The lack or collapse of the social infrastructure in some countries of the 'global south', for reasons of chronic poverty, war or socio-economic/political turmoil, has been a significant factor in generating large-scale population movement. In addition, among the developed nations of the northern hemisphere, the increase in family mobility in the latter part of the 20th century was accompanied by ever more cross-jurisdictional disputes concerning matters such as marriage, divorce, child abduction and adoption. In an attempt to substitute international agreement for country-to-country negotiations on the rules and procedures for regulating and protecting the children involved, the Hague Conference on Private International Law held a number of conferences to develop conventions that would state the relevant agreed principles, standards and rules.[1] Eventually four conventions con-

1 See, for example, Dyer, A., 'The Internationalisation of Family Law', *UC Davis Law Review*, Vol. 30, p 625, 1997.

DOI: 10.4324/9781003510383-9

cerning children were produced including the Hague Convention on Protection of Children and Co-operation in Respect of Intercountry Adoption 1993[2] which was specifically concerned with trafficking children.

Definitions, principles and international law

Because the issues in relation to unaccompanied migrant minors, detention and trafficking largely draw from the same body of definitions, principles and international law, it would seem reasonable – as in the preceding chapter – that the first section of this chapter should provide a composite framework or guide to such matters.

Definitions

This area of family law has become a minefield of politically loaded definitional terms: differentiating between 'refugee', 'asylum seeker' and 'illegal migrant' is particularly fraught; while distinguishing between the concepts of a 'safe country of origin', 'first country of asylum' and 'safe third country' is not much easier. For present purposes it seems unwise to delve into the complexities of the law and politics governing migration, so this is referenced only insofar as it relates to the welfare interests of children.

Unaccompanied migrant minors

Defined, under Article 1 of the United Nations Convention on the Rights of the Child (UN CROC), as those 'who have been separated from both parents and other relatives and are not being cared for by an adult who, by law or custom, is responsible for doing so'. Such a child – under 18 years of age – is one travelling across country borders unaccompanied by a parent or a guardian and without legal immigration documents. From 2014 there has been a fairly constant flow of children crossing the borders of South America in order to attempt entry to the U.S. Since 2015 the same phenomenon has been evident on the other side of the Atlantic as many such children journey from countries such as Afghanistan and North Africa with a view to entering northern Europe. In both instances, the children are fleeing adverse social circumstances in their places of birth and hoping to find security and opportunities for employment and for better health and welfare services. The number of unaccompanied minors among asylum applicants in the European Union increased from 11,460 in 2013 to 91,955 in 2015, decreased to 13,550 in 2020, and increased again to 39,515 in 2022.[3]

2 The other two being the Convention on the Civil Aspects of International Child Abduction 1980 and the Convention on Jurisdiction, Applicable Law, Recognition, Enforcement, and Co-operation in Respect of Parental Responsibility and Measures for the Protection of Children 1996.

3 See, Eurostat, *Asylum Applicants Considered to be Unaccompanied Minors by Citizenship, Age and Sex – Annual Data*, https://ec.europa.eu/eurostat/databrowser/view/migr_asyunaa/default/table?lang=en

International protection for migrating children, provided under UN CROC and other instruments,[4] is governed by principles that include non-discrimination (UN CROC, Article 2), best interests of the child (UN CROC, Article 3), life and full development (UN CROC, Article 6), family unity (UN CROC, Articles 12 and 16), non-refoulement (UN CROC, Articles 6 and 37), evolving capacities (UN CROC, Article 5), participation (UN CROC, Article 12) and confidentiality (UN CROC, Article 16).

Refugee

The 1951 UN Convention relating to the Status of Refugees (as amended by its 1967 Protocol) defines a 'refugee' as a person in another country at risk of persecution in her, his or their own country. The Convention sets out certain basic rights of refugees including the right not to be returned to the place where they are at risk of persecution. It also includes the right not to be penalised for being in or entering a country without permission where this is necessary for them to seek and receive asylum.

In 2020, it is estimated that worldwide some 21,000 children claimed refugee status in a country where they had arrived unaccompanied by a parent or guardian.[5]

Asylum

Article 18 of the Charter of Fundamental Rights states that 'the right to asylum shall be guaranteed with due respect for the rules of the Geneva Convention . . . and in accordance with the Treaty on the European Union and the Treaty on the Functioning of the European Union'. Anyone fleeing persecution or serious harm in their own country has the right to ask for protection in another. Whether they have the right to choose the country in which to seek asylum is a moot point. Article 19 prohibits collective expulsions and protects individuals from being removed, expelled or extradited to a state where there is a serious risk of death penalty, torture or other inhuman or degrading treatment or punishment (refoulement). This fundamental human right is recognised as such in the 1951 Geneva Convention on refugees (and its 1967 Protocol) and in Article 14 of the Universal Declaration of Human Rights which states that everyone has the right to seek and enjoy asylum from persecution in other countries. In 1999, the EU established a Common European Asylum System which the European Commission proposed to reform in 2020. The numbers seeking asylum in Europe have varied from over 1.8 million in 2015 to around 142,000 in 2019, a decrease of 92%.

4 Such as Convention Relating to the Status of Refugees 1951; the International Convention on the Protection of the Rights of all Migrant Workers and Members of their Families 1990; and the Convention Against Torture and Other Cruel, Inhuman or Degrading Treatment or Punishment 1984.

5 See, further, www.refugeecouncil.org.uk/get-support/services/childrens-advice/

Detention

Immigration detention is understood by the UN as

> any setting in which a child is deprived of his/her liberty for reasons related to his/her, or his/her parents', migration status, regardless of the name and reason given to the action of depriving a child of his or her liberty, or the name of the facility or location where the child is deprived of liberty. "Reasons related to migration status" is understood to be a person's migratory or residence status, or the lack thereof, whether relating to irregular entry or stay or not, consistent with previous guidance.[6]

Resettlement and relocation

Resettlement is the transfer of a refugee from an asylum country to another state that has agreed to admit him or her and ultimately grant them permanent settlement.[7]

Relocation is the transfer of an asylum seeker who is in clear need of international protection from one jurisdiction to another. Their asylum application will only be determined after relocation.[8]

Non-refoulement

Article 3 of the Convention Against Torture and Other Cruel, Inhuman or Degrading Treatment or Punishment 1987 expressly declares that a state Party cannot expel, return or extradite a person to another state where there are 'substantial grounds' for believing that the person would be at risk of being subjected to torture. The consequences of finding a risk of refoulement were explained by the European Court of Justice[9] when it confirmed that

> it is contrary to EU law to return ('refouler') or expel a person whose refugee status has been revoked or refused due to the fact that there are reasonable grounds for regarding him or her a danger to the security of the host member state or due to the fact that he or she has been convicted of a particularly serious crime, if refoulement or expulsion would expose that individual to the risk of exposure to torture or to other inhuman or degrading treatment or punishment.[10]

This is evident at official EU border-crossing points when Articles 6 and 8 of the Asylum Procedures Directive 2013 and Article 4 of the Schengen Borders Code

6 CMW/C/GC/4-CRC/C/GC/23 at para 6.

7 See, further, www.unhcrc.org/resettlement.htm

8 See, further, www.easo.europa.eu/

9 *M v. Ministry of Interior, Czech Republic M v. Ministry of Interior, Czech Republic*, C-391/16 and *X and X v. Commissioner General for Refugees and Stateless Persons, Belgium*, C-77/17 and C/78/17.

10 Ibid, at paras 95 and 110.

2016 require border guards checking documents at the border-crossing points to respect the principle of non-refoulement. This principle is underpinned by Article 3 of the European Convention on Human Rights (ECHR) which prohibits the subjection of individuals to torture, inhuman or degrading treatment or punishment, and supported by Article 4 of the Charter of Fundamental Rights and by Articles 31 and 33 of the Geneva Convention. The principle was also explicitly endorsed by the European Court of Human Rights (ECtHR) decision in *N.D. and N.T.* v. *Spain*[11] as an absolute right enshrined in Article 3 of the ECHR.

'Trafficked'

'Trafficked' is defined by the UN as the 'recruitment, transportation, transfer, harbouring, and/or receipt" kidnapping of a child for the purpose of slavery, forced labour and exploitation'.[12] This term refers not just to the age-old practice of parents relinquishing their children for financial reward but also to the role played by predatory criminal intermediaries, the purposes for which the children are trafficked, the absence of an objective determination of their welfare interests, the presence or absence of consents (including that of the child), irregular payments, and the abuse of immigration rules and procedures. Although it has only come to prominence in the past decade or so, it is a global problem which, the International Labour Organisation (ILO) estimates, involves some 10,000 children every year;[13] other estimates are much higher.

Principles

Undoubtedly, many developed western states are now experiencing difficulty balancing the rights of refugees to claim asylum with the need to maintain an effective immigrant control mechanism. Some of these difficulties are evident in the policy document *New Pact on Migration and Asylum*.[14]

Deportation of minors or of parents/guardians of minors must be in accordance with the law

The ECtHR has noted that while contracting states have the power to expel an alien convicted of criminal offences, such action will constitute an interference with that person's private or family life and will be in breach of Article 8 of the Convention unless it can be justified under paragraph 2 of that article as being "in accordance with the law", as pursuing one or more of the legitimate aims listed therein, and as

11 Application Nos. 8675/15 and 8697/15, (2020), at para 232.

12 See, Protocol to Prevent, Suppress and Punish Trafficking in Persons, Especially Women and Children (the Palermo Protocol), United Nations, 2000.

13 See, ILO, *Child Trafficking – Essentials*, Geneva, ILO-IPEC, 2010.

14 COM (2020) 609 Final, September 23, 2020, https://ec.europa.eu/info/publications/migration-and-asylum-package-new-pact-migration-and-asylum-documents-adopted-23-september-2020_en

being "necessary in a democratic society" in order to achieve the aim or aims concerned. It must be shown that the interference was supported by relevant and sufficient reasons and was proportionate in that a fair balance was struck between the applicant's right to respect for his family life, on the one hand, and the prevention of disorder or crime, on the other.[15] In several cases,[16] the Court has established the relevant criteria to be applied, in determining whether an interference is necessary in a democratic society including the best interests and well-being of any children, in particular the seriousness of the difficulties which any children of the applicant are likely to encounter in the country to which the applicant is to be expelled. It has advised that

> national decision-making bodies should, in principle, advert to and assess evidence in respect of the practicality, feasibility and proportionality of any removal of a non-national parent in order to give effective protection and sufficient weight to the best interests of the children directly affected by it.[17]

Additionally, the UN Committee on the Rights of the Child (CRC), in General Comment No. 6,[18] prohibits returning a migrant child to her or his country of origin if to do so is not in the best interests of the child, which requires a best interests assessment and determination on the basis of a thorough analysis of the individual circumstances of the child in a holistic manner. Furthermore, general human rights obligations such as the prohibition of refoulement also need to be taken into account as does the *New Pact on Migration and Asylum*.[19]

In *Assem Hassan Ali v. Denmark*,[20] for example, the ECtHR considered the applicant's claim that he should not be deported from Denmark – because of criminal convictions including for drug trafficking – as he had strong links to his six children, one of whom had a mental disability, to his wife and exwife, all of whom had visited him in prison, and that he would lose contact with them if deported. The domestic courts upheld the order for deportation, and the ECtHR noted that in the context of an expulsion based on a crime committed by the parent, the child's best interests still need to be a primary consideration and be accorded effective protection but cannot alone be decisive, as the nature and seriousness of a crime may outweigh other criteria. Accordingly, the ECtHR found that the Danish authorities

15 See, among many others, *Salem v. Denmark*, Application No. 77036/11, (2016); *Hamesevic v. Denmark (dec.)*, Application No. 25748/15, (2017); *Alam v. Denmark (dec.)*, Application No. 33809/15, (2017); and *Ndidi v. the United Kingdom*, Application No. 41215/14, (2017).

16 See, *Üner v. the Netherlands* [GC], Application No. 46410/99, (2006); *Maslov v. Austria* [GC], Application No. 1638/03, (2008); *Balogun v. the United Kingdom*, Application No. 60286/09, (2012); *Samsonnikov v. Estonia*, Application No. 52178/10, (2012); and *Salem v. Denmark*, Op. cit.

17 *Jeunesse v. the Netherlands*, Application No. 12738/10, (2014).

18 At para 84.

19 See, COM(2020) 609 Final, September 23, 2020, https://ec.europa.eu/info/publications/migration-and-asylum-package-new-pact-migration-and-asylum-documents-adopted-23-september-2020_en

20 Application No. 25593/14, (2018).

did not violate the applicant's right to family life, since his children's best interests had been fully taken into account and would not be adversely affected by his deportation to such an extent that their welfare interests should outweigh the state's interest in upholding public order.[21] In such cases the nature and seriousness of the offence committed or the offending history may outweigh other criteria, including a child's best interests.[22]

Best interests are a primary consideration in family reunification

In *Tuquabo-Tekle and Others v. the Netherlands*,[23] the ECtHR identified three elements that need to be taken into account by national authorities if they are to strike a fair balance between the competing interests of the state in immigration control and a child's welfare: the age of the child concerned, the child's situation in their country of origin and the extent to which they are dependent on their parents. In *El Ghatet v. Switzerland*,[24] the applicants' claim for family reunification was dismissed by the Swiss authorities, based on its conclusion that the child had closer family ties in his country of origin, Egypt. The Court stated that the best interests of a child cannot be a 'trump card', which enables children to get accepted into a country where the child's family member is residing and pointed out the importance of carrying out a best interests assessment in each individual case. The authorities should give a detailed reasoning as to how the best interests were taken into account. In this case, the ECtHR concluded that the Swiss authorities' examination was insufficient as it did not enable them to strike a fair balance; therefore, the Court concluded that there was a violation of Article 8.

Detention of a minor must be necessary in a democratic society and should pursue a legitimate aim

The ECtHR has found that the detention of migrant children is compatible with the Convention, where it is strictly necessary and adapted to children's specific needs but has repeatedly warned that the confinement of families with children in detention centres – far from being Convention compliant – constitutes inhuman and degrading treatment.

In immigration detention cases, a frequently occurring dilemma is how to safeguard the right to family life when either the family may be divided as a consequence of a detention order or they may be placed – including children – in a centre established primarily for adults. So, for example, *Mubilanzila Mayeka and Kaniki Mitunga v. Belgium*[25] concerned the detention of a child at Brussels Airport because she did not have the necessary entry documentation. Her application for asylum

21 See, for example, *A.H. Khan v. the United Kingdom*, Application No. 6222/10, (2011).

22 See, for example, *Cömert v. Denmark (dec.)*, Application No. 14474/03, (2006); *Üner v. the Netherlands* [GC], Op. cit.; and *Salem v. Denmark*, Op. cit.

23 Application No. 60665/00, (2005).

24 Application No. 569/71, (2017).

25 Application No. 13178/03, (2006).

was rejected as inadmissible, and an order was issued for her deportation to the Democratic Republic of Congo, where she had no family, but pending removal she was placed in a closed detention centre with adults. Eventually she was reunited with her mother – who had obtained refugee status in Canada – following the intervention of the Belgian and Canadian Prime Ministers. The ECtHR found the form of detention to be completely unnecessary, the authorities should have considered more appropriate alternatives that would have been more in keeping with the best interests of the child. In *Popov v. France*,[26] the issue was whether the detention of a family, including two children born in France, for two weeks in a closed detention facility was compatible with the Convention. The facility had a heavy police presence to monitor the overly stressed inmates, it had no play areas or activities for children, it was equipped with automatic doors which were dangerous for them and the only beds available were for adults. The two children were in a situation of vulnerability heightened by their detention, which was bound to cause them stress and distress and have serious psychological repercussions. In view of their young age, and the duration and conditions of their detention, the authorities should have done more to minimise the inevitably harmful effects on the children. Noting that the aim of confinement must be proportionate with the reasons for it, which in this case was the family's removal from the jurisdiction, it was the authorities' duty when considering the proportionality of the measure to take the children's best interests into account. In this case there had been no particular risk of the applicants absconding that might have justified their detention. The ECtHR considered that two weeks' detention in a closed facility was disproportionate to the aim pursued and amounted to violation of Article 8. More recently, much the same issues arose in *M.S.T. and Others against Poland*[27] which concerned the detention of two adults and their three-year-old child, in a Guarded Centre for Aliens in Kętrzyn for six months pending their deportation. They complained that given the severity of the mother and child's mental health conditions, they should never have been placed in a guarded centre and that such a long detention in very small rooms with a lack of protection from the summer heat, restrictions on outdoor activities, personal inspections and without any privacy to conduct their private and family life, led to a deterioration of their health, in particular that of the child, who began to develop anxiety reactions and stomach problems. This was compounded by the lack of adequate psychological care for the family, including the refusal to consult an independent external psychologist and the lack of a child psychologist in the centre. The case has yet to be resolved, but it has attracted the comment that there seems to be a systemic problem with abusive detention in Poland,[28] as also in France (see, further, later).

In *Rahimi v. Greece*,[29] a landmark judgment concerning the detention of a 15-year-old unaccompanied migrant child in a closed centre for adults with poor

26 Application Nos. 39472/07 and 39474/07 (2012).

27 Application No. 40464/22, (2023).

28 See, further, https://hudoc.echr.coe.int/eng#{%22documentcollectionid2%22:[%22COMMUNICATEDCASES%22],%22itemid%22:[%22001-224596%22]}

29 Application No.8687/06, (2011).

hygiene and infrastructure conditions, the ECtHR found that when national authorities ordered the detention of the applicant, they did not, at any stage, give consideration to his best interests nor to his individual situation as an unaccompanied minor. Furthermore, they had not examined whether it had been necessary as a measure of last resort to place the applicant in the detention centre or whether less drastic action might not have sufficed to secure his deportation. The Court therefore concluded the authorities had failed to strike a fair balance between the competing interests – namely the state's interest in migration control versus the best interests of the child – and accordingly, the latter's best interests could not have functioned as a primary consideration. In highlighting the significance of that lapse, the ECtHR reiterated its finding in *Neulinger and Shuruk v. Switzerland*,[30] that 'there is currently a broad consensus – including in international law – in support of the idea that in all decisions concerning children, their best interests must be paramount'.

Welfare interests and paramountcy

In 2017, the CRC and the Committee on Migrant Workers published their Joint General Comment No.23 and No.4 which emphasised that – despite Article 37 (b) of UN CROC – the detention of children as a measure of last resort is not applicable in an immigration context as this would contravene the best interests principle. This approach echoed the advice of the European Economic and Social Committee that the response of national authorities to unaccompanied migrant minors should be governed by the principle of "the best interests of the child" which should take precedence over all other national and international law[31] and was endorsed by the ECtHR in *Popov v. France*,[32] when, citing previous caselaw,[33] it pointed out that the child's best interests must be *paramount.* In addition, the Court assigns considerable weight to whether less intrusive measures could have been taken. Nikolett Takács has recently sought to translate this formulaic advice into practical steps by identifying four requirements necessary to ensure the priority of the best interests of the child: that detention is a measure of last resort, is for the shortest appropriate period of time, respects the right to family life and that detention facilities are equipped for children.[34]

In *Sh.D. and Others v. Greece et al*,[35] the ECtHR considered the detention of three unaccompanied asylum-seeking children, two of whom were placed in

30 Application No. 41615/07, (2010).

31 See, further, www.eesc.europa.eu/en/our-work/opinions-information-reports/opinions/protection-unaccompanied-migrant-minors-europe-own-initiative-opinion

32 Op. cit.

33 *Rahimi v. Greece and Neulinger and Shuruk v. Switzerland, Op. cit.*

34 See, Takács, N., 'The Threefold Concept of the Best Interests of the Child in the Immigration Case Law of the ECtHR', *Hungarian Journal of Legal Studies*, Vol. 62, No. 1, pp 96–114, 2022, at para 3.2.2.

35 *Sh. D. and Others v. Greece, Austria, Croatia, Hungary, Northern Macedonia, Serbia and Slovenia*, Application No. 14165/16, (2019).

so-called protective custody at a police station and then spent a month living in the *Idomeni* camp in Greece. The ECtHR assigned decisive importance to the best interests of the child when establishing a violation of Article (5) (1) of the ECHR. It reiterated its findings from *H.A. and Others v. Greece*[36] that under Article 3 of UN CROC, states are required to take the best interests of the child into account when making any decision concerning them. The ECtHR was critical of the Greek authorities for placing the children in detention at police stations instead of in temporary accommodation and stated that it was unlawful as their best interests were not taken into account.

Right to family life

'Family life', as the ECtHR has often stated, consists of the mutual enjoyment by parent and child of each other's company.[37] The Court constantly takes this principle into account when balancing a conflict of interests between parent and child or parent and state, even in cases where the child is not the applicant, but the decision concerns the child. This ECtHR approach finds support in UN CROC: Article 5 directs that

> States Parties shall respect the responsibilities, rights and duties of parents, . . . to provide, in a manner consistent with the evolving capacities of the child, appropriate direction and guidance in the exercise by the child of the rights recognised in the present Convention

And Article 9 states that a child shall not be separated from his or her parents against his or her will, and that all parties must be given the opportunity to participate in any proceedings relating to this situation. The CRC recommends that 'states should ensure that their migration policies respect the right of the child to family life and that no child is separated from his/her parents by state action or inaction unless in accordance with his/her best interests'. The UN 'Guidelines on Alternative Care' further substantiate the rights of children in these circumstances and the corresponding duties of the state.[38] However, it is important that this principle should not be abused and used as 'trump card'; therefore, a precise and detailed individualised assessment of all factors – especially the welfare interests of the child concerned – is always crucial. Its relevance in the context of migrant families

36 Application No. 19951/16, (2019).

37 See, *W., B. and R. v. the United Kingdom*, July 8, 1987, Series A No. 121; *Olsson v. Sweden (no. 1)*, March 24, 1988, Series A No. 130; *Eriksson v. Sweden*, June 22, 1989, Series A No. 156; *Margareta and Roger Andersson v. Sweden*, February 25, 1992, Series A No. 226-A; *McMichael v. the United Kingdom*, February 24, 1995, Series A No. 307-B; *Johansen v. Norway*, August 7, 1996, Reports 1996-III; *Bronda v. Italy*, June 9, 1998, Reports 1998-IV; and *Buscemi v. Italy*, Application No. 29569/95, ECHR 1999-VI.

38 UN, Human Rights Council, *UN Guidelines for the Alternative Care of Children*, UN Doc. A/HRC/11/L.13, June 15, 2009.

has a relatively short and thin legal history, but this area of family law has acquired density, has grown in volume over the past decade or so and shows every sign of continuing to build in momentum.

Sen v. the Netherlands,[39] for example, was not untypical. It concerned Turkish parents who, having migrated to the Netherlands, sought to have their daughter, whom they had left with an aunt in Turkey, join them and their two other children, but their application for a residence permit for her was refused. They complained to the ECtHR that this refusal constituted an infringement of their right to respect for their family life. The Court agreed. It found that the restoration of family life could not be achieved by the parents and their two children moving to Turkey, as the latter had always lived in the Netherlands and went to school there while their parents had settled lives in that country. By blocking the possibility of family reunification, through the third child joining them, the Court held that the authorities had violated their Article 8 rights.[40] A similar violation was found in respect of a child who attempted to rejoin her family in Denmark where she had lived with them for most of her life until sent to Kenya by her father to care for the paternal grandfather. The Court found that the child's right to respect for her private and family life could not be ignored. In the circumstances of the case, it could not be said that the applicant's interests had been sufficiently taken into account or balanced fairly against the State's interest in controlling immigration.[41] Again, where migrant parents were lawfully in a country and were refused visas for their children so that their families could be reunited, the ECtHR found that the family reunification procedure had not offered the requisite guarantees of flexibility, promptness and effectiveness to ensure compliance with their right to respect for their family life. For that reason, the state had not struck a fair balance between the applicants' interests on the one hand, and its own interest in controlling immigration on the other, and thereby had violated the applicants' Article 8 rights.[42] Where the children were older adolescents, however, and had not lost their ties with their country of birth – where they grew up and were educated for many years and still had family ties – then the Court was prepared to conclude that the authorities had not overstepped their margin of appreciation under Article 8 in refusing to grant residence permits to the children;[43] particularly as they had never been to the country where their parents now lived and had not lived together with the parent for more than 11 years.[44]

39 Application No. 31465/96, (2001).

40 See, also, *Tuquabo-Tekle and Others v. the Netherlands*, Application No. 31465/96, (2001).

41 See, *Osman v. Denmark*, Application No. 38058/09, (2011).

42 See, *Mugenzi v. France*, *Tanda-Muzinga v. France* and *Senigo Longue and Others v. France*, Application Nos. 52701/09, 2260/10 and 19113/09, (2014).

43 *Berisha v. Switzerland*, Application No. 948/12, (2013).

44 *I.A.A. and Others v. the United Kingdom*, Application No. 25960/13, (2016).

International law

The main pillars of the international legal framework are the Convention Relating to the Status of Refugees 1951, the UN CROC 1989[45] and the European Convention for the Protection of Human Rights and Fundamental Freedoms 1950. Other international treaties, conventions and protocols,[46] certain EU Directives[47] and a guidance publication from the Office of the High Commissioner for Human Rights[48] are also relevant. Further support is provided by assorted international legal instruments and associated advisory publications which variously contribute to a framework of legal provisions – impacting on either or both unaccompanied migrant minors and trafficking – including reports from Special Rapporteurs.[49]

Brussels II

This Regulation in relation to family law cases with cross-border elements, came into effect on 1 August 2004 and was updated in 2022. Articles 15, 55 and 56 have a particular application to child-care, custody and abduction cases.

The United Nations Guidelines for the Alternative Care of Children 2009

Adopted by the UN Human Rights Council in 2009, the Guidelines were intended to enhance implementation of the CRC 'regarding the protection and well-being of children deprived of parental care or who are at risk of being so' (para 3). They start from the general principle that efforts should primarily be directed towards enabling children to remain in or return to the care of their parents. Removing a child from the care of the family should be seen as a measure of last resort and whenever possible be temporary and for the shortest duration possible (para 14). Children temporarily or permanently deprived of their birth family, or in whose best interests cannot be allowed to remain in that environment, are entitled to special government protection and assistance (UN CROC, Article 20(1)).

45 In Ireland the UN CROC is given effect by the National Children's Strategy, launched in 2000, responsibility for the implementation of which rests with the National Children's Office. However, although ratified, this Convention has not yet been incorporated into domestic law. See, further, Horgan, 'The United Nations Convention on the Rights of the Child and Irish Family Law' (1991) 9 ILT 162.

46 In particular: the UN Convention on the Elimination of all forms of Discrimination Against Women with its Optional Protocol; and the International Convention on the Elimination of Race Discrimination.

47 See, in particular, the Equal Pay Directive (75/117/EEC), the Equal Treatment Directive (76/207/EEC) and the General Framework Directive (2000/78/EC).

48 See, the Recommended Principles and Guidelines on Human Rights and Trafficking.

49 Particularly from: the Special Rapporteur on Trafficking in Persons, especially Women and Children; the Special Rapporteur on the Sale of Children, Child Prostitution and Child Pornography; and the Special Rapporteur on Contemporary Forms of Slavery, including its Causes and its Consequences.

Provision of alternative care can include 'foster placement . . . adoption or, if necessary, placement in suitable institutions for the care of children' (Article 20(3)). Decisions regarding children in alternative care should have due regard for the importance of ensuring children a stable home and meeting their basic need for safe and continuous attachment to their caregivers, with permanency generally being a key goal (Guidelines, para 12).

The Protocol to Prevent, Suppress and Punish Trafficking in Persons, Especially Women and Children (the Palermo Protocol) 2000

Effective from 2003, this is an important instrument in the framework of measures designed to combat trafficking.[50] Article 5 requires states to criminalise trafficking, attempted trafficking and any other intentional participation or organisation in a trafficking scheme. Article 7 requires states to consider potential measures for allowing foreign trafficked victims to remain temporarily or permanently in the state to which they were trafficked. Some may be entitled to international refugee protection under the Convention Relating to the Status of Refugees 1951 and its 1967 Protocol. Article 8 deals with the possible repatriation of trafficked victims and requires a state when doing so to have due regard for the safety of that person: repatriation should 'preferably be voluntary'. A right of return to the country of origin is provided under the International Covenant on Civil and Political Rights.

Optional Protocol on the Sale of Children, Child Prostitution, and Child Pornography 2000 (Sex Trafficking Protocol) 2000

This Protocol, appended to UN CROC, defines what constitutes the sale of children and explicitly prohibits the trafficking of children for any purpose including for exploitive and forced labour. It addresses the many purposes for which children are bought and sold.

The Worst Forms of Child Labour Convention (Convention No. 182 of 1999)

This International Labour Organization Convention prohibits perpetrators from using children under 18 years of age for all forms of slavery or practices similar to slavery. Article 7(2)(b) and (c) requires states to take effective and timely measures to provide for the rehabilitation and social integration of former victims of the worst forms of child labour, including trafficking, as well as to ensure their access to free basic education, and, wherever possible and appropriate, vocational training.

European Social Charter (revised in 1996)

The Charter provides for the protection of general social rights, with specific provision for children's rights. It contains some provisions of particular importance

50 See, UN HR, Office of the High Commissioner, *International Instruments Concerning Trafficking in Persons,* www.ohchr.org/sites/default/files/Documents/Issues/Women/WRGS/OnePagers/IntInstrumentsconcerningTraffickingpersons_Aug2014.pdf

for the latter. The European Committee of Social Rights is the body responsible for monitoring compliance by States Parties with the European Social Charter (revised). Article 7 sets out the state responsibility in relation to employment of children, while Article 17 requires states to take all appropriate and necessary measures to ensure that children receive the care, assistance, education and training they need (including free primary and secondary education); to protect children and young persons from negligence, violence or exploitation; and to provide protection for children deprived of family support.

The Hague Convention on Protection of Children and Co-operation in Respect of Intercountry Adoption 1993

This was introduced in response to increased concern regarding trafficking in children, perhaps generated in particular by the international interest in rescuing children from the orphanages of post-Ceauşescu Romania. The Convention provides, at least in theory, protection against 'the abuse, sale of or traffic in children'.

The overlap between lawful adoption and unlawful trafficking of children is well documented in countries as diverse as China, Sri Lanka, Guatemala and Uganda. In recent years there have been a number of cases involving Ugandan children fraudulently removed from birth families and placed with U.S.-based adoption agencies who then facilitated their adoption by U.S. citizens.[51]

The United Nations Convention on the Rights of the Child 1989

This Convention (UN CROC) recognises certain rights of the child and corresponding duties of the state (see, further, at p. 158).

Articles 11 and 35 place duties on states to take measures to prevent child trafficking: Article 11(1) requires measures to be taken to combat the illicit transfer and non-return of children abroad. Article 24 requires states to recognise the right of every child to access 'facilities for the treatment of illness and rehabilitation of health', while Article 28 adds a similar state duty in respect of education. Article 39 requires states to take all appropriate measures 'to promote physical and psychological recovery and social reintegration of a child victim of any form of neglect, exploitation or abuse'.

The Convention Against Torture and Other Cruel, Inhuman or Degrading Treatment or Punishment 1987

Articles 1 and 2 define and prohibit torture. Article 3, the non-refoulement provision, prohibits the removal of a person to another state where he or she would be at risk of being subjected to torture. Article 5 requires detention procedures to be kept under review. Article 16 obliges states to prevent acts of cruel, inhuman or degrading treatment or punishment which do not amount to torture.

51 See, further, www.thenation.com/article/archive/those-kids-are-no-longer-yours-ugandas-adoption-market/

The Hague Convention on the Civil Aspects of International Child Abduction 1980

Entering into force in 1983, the Preamble to this Convention states that 'the interests of children are of paramount importance in matters relating to their custody'.

International Covenant on Civil and Political Rights 1966

This Covenant, which came into force in 1976, is relevant for many reasons including its fair trial and due process guarantees. It has become particularly important because of its wide international application and accompanying monitoring process; the Optional Protocol has now been ratified by 170 countries. Its periodic review process requires signatory states to submit a review of progress on human rights issues. This procedure has a uniform application to all 193 UN member states and provides an opportunity for each to make a periodic declaration to the Human Rights Council regarding the actions it has taken to improve human rights – including the rights and welfare interests of children – to receive comment from its peer signatory states and to agree on goals for the next review.

International Covenant on Economic, Social and Cultural Rights 1966

Signed in 1966, with effect from 1976, this Covenant aims to ensure the protection of economic, social and cultural rights, including the right to self-determination of all peoples and the right to non-discrimination based on race, colour, sex, language, religion, political or other opinion, national or social origin, property, birth or other status. Article 10 provides that children and young persons should be 'protected from economic and social exploitation'.

The Convention Relating to the Status of Refugees 1951

This UN Treaty and its 1967 Protocol define what is meant by 'refugee' and the legal status thereof. It recognises the right of any person – including a child – to claim asylum from persecution, or from the threat of it, in another country. It deals with the central concept of 'refoulement', prohibiting the return of a refugee to a country where he or she might face serious threats. It also states that

> [c]onsidering that the unity of the family . . . is an essential right of the refugee, and that such unity is constantly threatened . . . [the Committee] recommends to Governments to take the necessary measures for the protection of the refugee's family, especially with a view to: (1) Ensuring that the unity of the refugee's family is maintained.

European Convention for the Protection of Human Rights and Fundamental Freedoms 1950

This Convention (ECHR) established a framework of international rights, the most relevant of which is Article 8 stating the right to respect for private and family life.

Jurisdictional differences and their significance: unaccompanied migrant minors

The migrant crisis of 2015–16 triggered a significant increase in migrant children – many unaccompanied – coming into Europe, including into England and Wales, from countries such as Vietnam, Afghanistan, the Middle East, north Africa and most recently from Ukraine. At much the same time, a parallel migrant crisis was building up on the southern border of the U.S. as thousands of migrants from various South American countries travelled to Mexico seeking entry into the U.S. This ongoing mass migration phenomenon has presented the developed western nations with many serious challenges, not least of which has been responding to the needs of tens of thousands of displaced children, many of whom are alone and traumatised.

Migrant minors

Statistics are uncertain but the 2024 report *Lost in Europe*,[52] a cross-border journalism project investigating missing child migrants, estimates that some 51,433 children disappeared after arriving in European countries between 2021 and 2023: some are feared to have fallen into the hands of drug gangs, forced into begging, become victims of human traffickers, or were sold into the sex industry; others may have travelled to family or friends in Europe without reporting it; some have all but disappeared. Unquestionably, as the report points out, 'the plight of unaccompanied child migrants is one of the most pressing issues of our time'. The scale of this problem – which is steadily worsening – questions the sincerity of the debate about children's rights and the capacity or willingness of relevant authorities to give effect to the many national and international provisions ensuring priority for the welfare interests of children.

Jurisdictional differences

It would seem that approximately 24,500 people entered the UK asylum system in 2021, of whom 515 were children, representing a considerable increase from the 87 children admitted the previous year.[53] Because of an asylum backlog[54] which has quadrupled in the last five years from 29,522 individuals waiting for an initial asylum decision in December 2017 to 122,206 in June 2022, more people – of whom a quarter are children – are being retained for longer in the asylum system. Usually, when there are no family members available, the children are taken into the care of the nearest local authority and placed in foster care. Home Office data show that over the last decade, accompanied children made up 16% of all asylum applicants and dependents (60,677), and a further 7% (25,759) were recorded

52 See, further, https://lostineurope.eu

53 See, https://blogs.lse.ac.uk/politicsandpolicy/the-uk-asylum-backlog-and-increased-use-of-immigration-detention-are-negatively-impacting-childrens-welfare/

54 See, www.refugeecouncil.org.uk/latest/news/new-figures-reveal-scale-of-asylum-backlog-crisis/

as unaccompanied child claimants.[55] There are reports that many unaccompanied minors – some trafficked – are still entering this jurisdiction.[56] So, for example, the *Lost in Europe* report mentions that, in 2019, at least 60 Vietnamese children escaped Dutch asylum shelters to be trafficked into Britain where authorities suspected that most ended up working on cannabis farms and nail salons. In Ireland, the 2016 *Child Migration Matters* report[57] detailed the various areas of immigration and child law and policy which negatively affect migrant children but, more recently, the *Lost in Europe* report estimates that in the last 15 months this country has experienced a 500% increase in the number of children arriving alone to claim asylum. It adds that 29 child migrants have disappeared without trace from state care between January 2021 and April 2024, including at least one 13-year-old.

In the U.S. the scale of illegal immigration is a singular jurisdictional characteristic. In 2022, an estimated 152,000 unaccompanied minors were encountered by the immigration authorities at or near the U.S.-Mexico border:[58] an astonishing number. Of this record number, 72% were 15 years of age or older, though also included were infants and toddlers. It has been estimated that, as of 2019, some six million children resident in the U.S. were unauthorised. Of those children who were properly documented citizens: 4.1 million were living with at least one parent who was not, and 5.9 million lived with an undocumented family member.[59] Canada, as has been rightly pointed out 'lacks a clear policy framework consistent with the best interests of unaccompanied minors seeking asylum'[60] but following a landmark Supreme Court of Canada (SCC) decision,[61] it will – if justified by humanitarian and compassionate considerations – grant a foreign national a permanent resident visa after taking into account the best interests of a child directly affected.[62] More recently, the court added that those interests must be "well identified and defined" and examined "with a great deal of attention" in light of all the evidence.[63] In Australia, the Human Right Commission has been a forceful critic of national policies towards unaccompanied migrant minors and notes that the problem peaked in 1999–2000 when 1,923 children were detained: most having arrived by boat with family members and seeking asylum; others having arrived

55 See, www.gov.uk/government/statistical-data-sets/asylum-and-resettlement-datasets#asylum-applications-decisions-and-resettlement

56 See, for example, Every Child Protected Against Trafficking, *Child Trafficking in the UK 2021: A Snapshot*, www.ecpat.org.uk/Handlers/Download.ashx?IDMF=23b51868-f257-49bc-b779-a5059bd65a04

57 See, the Immigrant Council of Ireland, *Child Migration Matters*, www.immigrantcouncil.ie/sites/default/files/2017-10/CMM%202016%20Child%20Migration%20Matters%20SUMMARY.pdf

58 See, www.cbp.gov/newsroom/stats/southwest-land-border-encounters

59 American Immigration Council statistics, https://map.americanimmigrationcouncil.org/locations/national/

60 The Canadian Bar Association (Child and Youth Law section) *Alternative Report to the UN Committee on the Rights of the Child*, 2020, Op. cit., at p 21.

61 *Baker v. Canada (Minister of Citizenship and Immigration)* [1999] 2 SCR 817.

62 Immigration and Refugee Protection Act (SC 2001, c. 27), s 25(1).

63 *Kanthasamy v. Canada (Citizenship and Immigration), 2015 SCC 61* [2015] 3 SCR 909.

unaccompanied. The New Zealand experience of unaccompanied migrant minors is relatively insignificant in relation to that of European and North American countries.[64]

The CRC, in its 2016 report, expressed concern regarding 'the situation of migrant children, particularly unaccompanied migrant children' in France, and questioned the commitment of French authorities to ensuring that a child seeking to obtain refugee status enjoys protection and humanitarian assistance.[65] More recently, French authorities reported to the CRC that it estimated the number of unaccompanied minors in the state in 2022 as approximately 41,000.[66] Germany, of course, has been particularly affected by the scale of the influx of migrants. In 2015 alone, the *Jugendamt* took custody of over 42,300 unaccompanied refugee children,[67] and this country continues to be the most popular European destination for refugee and migrant children. In 2020, some 17% of the total intake of 45,400 children to temporary state care were unaccompanied migrant minors,[68] and the latter doubled in number during the period 2020–2022.[69]

Family reunification

The balancing of competing public policy concerns – children's welfare interests against the integrity of the immigration system – is particularly acute in the context of family reunification. Although many children are *bona fide* independent migrants, some have been sent ahead by their parents in the hope that their child will be able to establish an anchor in a country and so enable the family to follow. Authorities in all western nations are alert to this cynical deployment of children to further the interests of parents because of its potential for private interests to subvert the public interest in maintaining a fair immigration system.

There would appear to be little jurisdictional difference between the UK and Ireland in the approach taken to locate the birth family members of unaccompanied migrant minors and protect them from possible traffickers. In Ireland there is no legislative basis for any requirement that the authorities work towards reuniting a migrant child with their family. Instead, guidance is available in the Family Reunification Policy document, and there is extensive ministerial discretion. The

64 See. Australian Human Rights Commission, *A Last Resort? National Inquiry into Children in Immigration Detention*, 2004, http://humanrights.gov.au/human_rights/children_detention_report/index.html and *Protection of the Rights of the Child in the Context of Migration*, 2010, www.ohchr.org/sites/default/files/Documents/Issues/MHR/Consultation2010/Australian_Human_Rights_Commission.pdf

65 Op. cit., at para 69.

66 See, further, www.ohchr.org/en/news/2023/05/experts-committee-rights-child-praise-france-outreach-patrols-supporting-families

67 See, further, the Federal Statistics Office of Germany.

68 See, further, www.destatis.de/EN/Press/2021/06/PE21_295_225.html

69 See, further, www.infomigrants.net/en/post/49337/germany-number-of-unaccompanied-refugee-minors-more-than-doubles

fact that this matter is not rights based, nor accompanied by an appeal process, are concerning.

In the U.S., under the Trump administration, a "zero-tolerance" policy was pursued to discourage migrants from crossing into the U.S., this included the forcible separation of children and parents; once separated, the children met the definition of 'unaccompanied alien children'[70] and were transferred to the Office of Refugee Resettlement. Between 2017 and 2021, at least 3,900 children – some only a few months old – were separated, and family reunification for many was not achieved until 2023, after President Biden officially rescinded the policy and established the Family Reunification Task Force.[71] However, on the five-year anniversary of the launch of the policy, nearly 1,000 children were still awaiting reunification, according to the U.S. government,[72] which would seem to constitute a cynical disregard for welfare interests and rights of the children concerned. In contrast, the Canadian approach, following the SCC decision in *Singh v. Minister of Employment and Immigration*,[73] was to initiate a new refugee determination system allowing for family reunification of accepted refugees with their dependent family members. The Immigration and Refugee Protection Act 2001, s 3(2)(f), states that the legislative intent is 'to support the self-sufficiency and the social and economic well-being of refugees by facilitating reunification with their family members in Canada'. Successful refugee claimants can then apply for Permanent Residence status, and include their family members in that application, whether their family members are physically in Canada or abroad. In addition, once a refugee is granted permanent residence, they have a 'one year window' to add family members to their application.[74]

In Australia, while most child migrants arrive with their parents, unaccompanied minors – usually adolescent Iraqi or Afghani boys – are placed in detention (despite a UN High Commissioner for Refugees recommendation that unaccompanied children should never be detained), and each is assigned a legal guardian. In 2001, there were over 100 unaccompanied children in detention. The Department states that 'Australia assists, to the extent possible, the process of reunification of unaccompanied minors who are currently seeking asylum in Australia with their families, whether they are in detention or in the community' and works with Australian Red Cross tracing services to achieve this objective. In practice, while contact between detainees and their families is permitted and generally facilitated,

70 As per the Homeland Security Act 2002, s 462(g).

71 See, further, www.bbc.co.uk/news/world-us-canada-64959802

72 See, further, www.dhs.gov/sites/default/files/2023-04/23-03_osec_march_2023_frtf_interim_progress_report_final.pdf

73 [1985] 1 SCR 177, 17 DLR (4th) 422.

74 See, further, www.cba.org/Sections/Child-and-Youth-Law-Section/Resources/Resources/2021/EssayWinnerCYL2021#_ednref42

as they are often in separation detention centres this is not always possible.[75] In New Zealand, the scale of this problem is relatively inconsequential, although laws and policies are stringent and do not include any family reunification responsibilities. This was illustrated in 2023 when it was revealed that among the hundreds of Afghan evacuees that arrived in the aftermath of the Taliban takeover, up to 20 children came without their parents: most with extended family, five without any adult relatives and three had no immediate family members in New Zealand. In the latter instance, the authorities' response would seem to have been to provide foster care rather than pursue family reunification.

In France, the right of unaccompanied migrant minors to be reunited with their parents is well recognised and particularly relevant both when such a child is found in France and when a child's parents are facing deportation.[76] However, this did not prevent the authorities from detaining two children aged five and three years found on French territory, in a centre with adults, before expediting their return to their country of origin, rather than reunite them with their father.[77] The CRC, in its 2016 report, expressed concern regarding 'the situation of migrant children, particularly unaccompanied migrant children'.[78] The German system of issuing visas to permit a parent to join an unaccompanied child migrant – who has been granted protection – was the subject of two decisions by the ECJ in August 2022 which extended the potential for reunification by ruling that the system of denying the right of migrant minors from Syria to reunite with their family in Germany violated the law of the EU: all unaccompanied children who were minors at the time the application for family reunification was lodged had the right to be reunited with their families even if they were now older than 18 years of age.

Detention of minors

The UN Global Study on Children Deprived of Liberty[79] notes that at least 77 countries have laws and policies that allow children to be detained based on their legal or migratory status, and at least 330,000 children globally per year are deprived of their liberty based on their (or their parents') legal or migratory status. Claiming, rightly, that detention is never in the welfare interests of the child – and constitutes a violation of their rights – it maintains that 'all children, regardless of their legal or migratory status or that of their families, have the right to be cared for and protected from violence, abuse and exploitation'. It calls for the ending of such detention.

75 See, further, https://humanrights.gov.au/our-work/projects/14-unaccompanied-children-immigration-detention#endnote194

76 *Mugenzi v. France*, Application No. 52701/09, (2014).

77 *Moustahi v. France*, Application No. 9347/14, (2020).

78 Op. cit., at para 69.

79 See, further, UN Task Force on Children Deprived of Liberty, *Global Study on Children Deprived of Liberty*, 2024, www.unicef.org/media/151371/file/Advocacy%20Brief:%20End%20Child%20Immigration%20Detention%20.pdf

In the UK, as noted earlier, there has been a significant increase in the detention of migrant children in recent years – more entered immigration detention in 2021 than in 2010 – leading to a corresponding increase in the use of contingency accommodation, predominantly commercial hotels. This has been accompanied by an increased tightening of the policy towards migrants.[80] It is reported that hotel stays have meant that 'children have been missing out on vital education, access to healthcare (including routine immunisation programmes) and developmental opportunities' and that 'the increasing reliance on immigration detention as well as unsafe, temporary accommodation, prolonged time spent barred from the labour market and living in deep poverty on Asylum Support all have negative consequences for children's welfare'.[81] Illustrating the extent of dysfunction in the detention system, the government acknowledged in September 2022 that some 222 unaccompanied children were missing from hotel accommodation.[82] Compared with the UK and other European countries, Ireland detains relatively few migrants but has been doing so in prisons and police stations. In 2016 the CRC expressed concern 'at the continued inadequacy of the services framework to address the needs of migrant children'. Not until 2022 did it open the country's first dedicated immigration detention centre at Dublin Airport police station.[83]

Coping with unaccompanied migrant minors is currently at its most acute in the U.S. where many tens of thousands of such children – fleeing socio-economic conditions, violence and drug cartels – arrive at the U.S./Mexico border each year seeking asylum. The government response is largely driven by a policy of detention[84] and resettlement, pursued under s 67 of the Immigration Act 2016, as policed by the Immigration and Customs Enforcement (ICE) agency. The migrants are generally detained close to the border in centres that must conform to standards set by the *Flores* settlement[85] which requires that minors be placed in "the least restrictive setting" – meaning group homes, foster care or other nationwide facilities – three to five days after being apprehended; that they be detained for a maximum of one month; and that they have access to food and water, emergency medical services, bathroom facilities, and ventilated, temperature-controlled surroundings. However, this response has been criticised. It is said that the U.S. has a separate child-caring

80 See, the Illegal Migration Act 2023.

81 See, Pinter, I., *Department of Social Policy, the Centre for Analysis of Social Exclusion, LSE*, https://blogs.lse.ac.uk/politicsandpolicy/the-uk-asylum-backlog-and-increased-use-of-immigration-detention-are-negatively-impacting-childrens-welfare/

82 See, further, www.theguardian.com/uk-news/2022/oct/22/uk-asylum-seekers-home-office-accused-of-catastrop,hic-child-protection-failure#:~:text=More%20than%20220%20unaccompanied%20asylum,"catastrophic%20child%20protection%20failure

83 See, further, www.immigrantcouncil.ie/sites/default/files/2017-10/CMM%202016%20Child%20Migration%20Matters.pdf

84 See, *AAM (A Child) v. Secretary of State for the Home Department* [2012] EWHC 2567 (QB).

85 *Jenny L. Flores et al v. William P. Barr et al.*, CV 85-4544-DMG(AGRx), 2019, U.S. District Court, C.D. CA, Civil Minutes-General. See, further, https://crsreports.congress.gov/product/pdf/IF/IF11799

system for migrant children and families that operates alongside the domestic child welfare systems; it flouts constitutional protections, separates children from parents, and perpetuates a system that is detaining children, warehousing them in large jail-like settings at worst, and sheltering them in large congregate care facilities at best.[86] The overall rate for denial of asylum status and other forms of relief has dropped from about 70% in 2020 to 53% in 2022.[87] In Canada, there have been many protests from organisations such as the CRC, Human Rights Watch and others that have raised objections regarding the detention of immigrant children and families with children.[88] Justification for the concerns of such bodies would seem well supported by recent practice and related caselaw.[89] Following a number of judicial rulings[90] critical of government policy regarding the detention of migrant minors, the Immigration and Refugee Protection Regulations were amended in 2019 to include a requirement that consideration be given to the best interests of a child directly affected by an immigration detention or release decision. A new section was added to affirm the principle in s 60 of the act, stating that a minor child should be detained only as a measure of last resort, and it outlined a non-exhaustive list of factors to consider when determining the best interests of the child.

In Australia, the national system of mandatory immigration detention has been the subject of protests from organisations such as the Australian Human Rights Commission which has expressed concern that it leads to breaches of Australia's obligations under the International Covenant on Civil and Political Rights to ensure that no one is arbitrarily detained, and also to breaches of Australia's obligations under UN CROC.[91] It found that Australia's immigration detention system was fundamentally inconsistent with UN CROC,[92] partly because it failed to ensure

86 See, Mandelbaum, R., 'Why Does the Federal Government Get a Pass? Applying Child Welfare Principles to the Circumstances of Migrant Children and Families', *American University Law Review*, Vol. 71, No. 5, 2022, SSRN, https://ssrn.com/abstract=3926325

87 See, www.acf.hhs.gov/orr/about/ucs/facts-and-data

88 See, also, the *Canada 2016 Human Rights Report*, www.state.gov/documents/organization/265782.pdf

89 See, for example, *Canadian Doctors for Refugee Care v. Canada*, 2014 FC 651.

90 See, for example: *Baker v. Canada (Minister of Citizenship and Immigration)* [1999] 2 SCR 817; *Legault v. Canada (Minister of Citizenship and Immigration)* [2002] 4 F.C. 358 (C.A.); *Canadian Doctors for Refugee Care v. Canada*, 2014 FC 651; *Kanthasamy v. Canada (Minister of Citizenship and Immigration*, 2015 SCC 61; and *B.B. v. Canada (Citizenship and Immigration)*, 2016 FC 1423 (CanLII).

91 See. Australian Human Rights Commission, *A Last Resort? National Inquiry into Children in Immigration Detention*, 2004, http://humanrights.gov.au/human_rights/children_detention_report/index.html and *Protection of the Rights of the Child in the Context of Migration*, 2010, www.ohchr.org/sites/default/files/Documents/Issues/MHR/Consultation2010/Australian_Human_Rights_Commission.pdf

92 Corroborated by the observation made by the UN CRC as to: 'The best interests of the child not being the primary consideration in asylum and refugee determinations and when considered, not consistently undertaken by professionals with adequate training on determination of best interests' (CRC/c/AUS/CO/4, *Concluding Observations: Australia*, 2012, at para 80(b)).

that the welfare interests of the children concerned were the primary consideration and because, if detained for long periods, children were at risk of serious harm to their mental health. New Zealand has no dedicated immigration detention facilities but instead uses its prison system to house illegal immigrants. Nonetheless, it has adopted stringent laws providing for the detention of asylum seekers and child migrants.

In France, according to the UNICEF 2022 report,[93] 'since 2012 at least 33,786 children have been detained', mostly in Mayotte, a French overseas territory. In this country – as in Poland – there would seem to be a systemic problem with the detention of migrant minors. In 2023, the ECtHR delivered three rulings concerning the confinement of families with seven children, aged between seven months and 13 years, who were locked up in 2020 and 2021 at the Mesnil-Amelot and Metz detention centres. This brought to 11 the number of rulings by the ECtHR against France since 2012, involving considerable numbers of children. In 2022, the national report on detention centres and facilities revealed that there had been little change.[94] As regards Germany, the CRC in its 2022 report was critical of the 'lengthy stays by some asylum-seeking and refugee children in reception centres and collective accommodation facilities, including in centres that are not child-friendly, which limit their access to education' and urged that 'their best interests are given primary consideration in all asylum processes and that their views are heard, taken into account and given due weight'.

Welfare interests

Arguably, there is a significant difference between the many domestic and international legislative requirements for states to ensure the prioritisation of a child's welfare interests and the actual arrangements made for accompanied and unaccompanied migrant children. It is probable that the scale of migration into the developed western nations, within such a short period, has been such that the response in those nations has generally been a management one, giving more priority to immigration rules and processes than to the best interests of the children involved.

In England and Wales, both the Children's Act 1989[95] and the Borders, Citizenship and Immigration Act 2009[96] explicitly require the relevant authorities to be guided by the principle of the welfare interests of the child, and similar compliance is required by UN CROC[97] to which this state is a signatory. In cases such as

93 See, *Droits des Enfants en France*, 2022, https://unicef.hosting.augure.com/Augure_UNICEF/r/ContenuEnLigne/Download?id=480588C0-E8CD-4A6A-B8D8-80AAA060B4C4&filename=SynthDroitsEnfantsFrance2022_final_pages.pdf

94 See, further, www.statewatch.org/news/2023/may/detention-of-children-european-court-of-human-rights-rules-against-france-11-times/#:~:text=Since%202012%2C%20the%20ECHR%20has,%22flagrant%20lack%20of%20humanity%22

95 See, the Children's Act 1989, s 3.

96 See, the Borders, Citizenship and Immigration Act 2009, s 55.

97 United Nations Convention on the Rights of the Child, article 3(1).

HH v. Deputy Prosecutor of the Italian Republic, Genoa[98] and *SM and TM and JD and Others v. SSHD*,[99] welfare interests played a key role in decisions preventing removal from the jurisdiction, though failed to do so in subsequent cases.[100] In Ireland, a combination of having incorporated UN CROC into domestic legislation together with a constitutional amendment, has established that the best interests of the child must be the paramount consideration in family law matters, including the detention of migrant children.

In the U.S., the 2020 directive from the Trump administration permitting U.S. Customs and Border Protection to 'promptly expel unaccompanied children at the border', ostensibly due to COVID-19 concerns, though clearly not compliant with the welfare interests of the children concerned, continued until rescinded by the Biden administration. The scale of the problem is apparent from the fact that of the 152,000 unaccompanied children who arrived at the U.S.–Mexico border in 2022, one in six were below the age of 13 years. This formidable challenge has led some to claim that the U.S., the only country that has not ratified the Convention on the Rights of the Child, does not consider a child's best interest in adjudicating immigration proceedings and that detention centres do not always comply with the *Flores* agreement nor with international standards.[101] In Canada, the SCC has emphasised the centrality of the best interests of the child principle to humanitarian and compassionate considerations in applications for permanent residence and noted the need to consider the best interests of a child who is "directly affected" as a "singularly significant focus and perspective".[102] This did not impede the prompt extradition of a mother to the U.S.,[103] notwithstanding a finding that the SCC was required under UN CROC and other instruments to consider the best interests of any children whose future may be adversely affected by decisions regarding their future.[104]

In Australia, as in Germany, an unaccompanied child migrant is automatically allocated a guardian who is inherently obliged to act in the best interests of the child. Unlike Germany, the Australian guardian is the Minister for Immigration and Border Protection who, arguably, is thereby placed in a conflict of interest as the Minister cannot simultaneously give effect to public policy and represent the private interests of someone who may well be compromised by that public policy. In addition, the fact that a policy of mandatory detention is applied to unaccompanied child migrants contravenes the prohibition, in s 37 of UN CROC, on the use

98 [2012] UKSC 25.

99 [2013] EWHC 1144 (Admin).

100 *Alladin v. SSHD* [2014] EEWCA Civ 1334 and *Bibi v. SSHD* [2014] EWHC 3685 (Admin).

101 See, Ramirez, D., 'Comparative Immigration Policies for Unaccompanied Minors: A Shared Challenge', *Loyola University Chicago International Law Review*, Vol. 19, No. 2, pp 157–185.

102 *Kanthasamy v. Canada (Minister of Citizenship and Immigration)*, 2015 SCC 61. Also, see, *Baker v. Canada (Minister of Citizenship and Immigration)* [1999] 2 SCR 817 where L'Heureux-Dubé J held that "the decision-maker should consider children's best interests as an important factor, give them substantial weight, and be alert, alive and sensitive to them" at para 75.

103 *M.M. v. U.S.A.*, 2015 SCC 62.

104 Ibid, at paras 146–147.

of detention except as a last resort, and clearly detracts from their best interests. In New Zealand, the threatened deportation of a married female couple and their child, in *Re Devi Sangeeta*,[105] was stopped when they were able to convince the Tribunal that the difficulties they would experience if they were to be returned to Fiji – in living openly as a gay couple and caring for a teenage daughter – would threaten her welfare interests and make their deportation unjust and unduly harsh.

As regards France, in 2016 the CRC found that the authorities 'do not sufficiently consider the best interests of the child as a guiding principle in all initial assessment processes and subsequent arrangements'. It also noted the

> precarious situation of children and their families in refugee camps . . . such as in Calais and . . . the refusal by authorities to register children and the insufficiency of venues and services to provide them with appropriate and adapted protection.[106]

This was endorsed six years later in a U.S. report that identified significant failings in French efforts to protect the welfare interests of child migrants mentioning that 'police continued to arrest and prosecute child victims of forced begging and forced criminality and deport undocumented migrants'. . . funding for victim assistance decreased compared with the prior year and was generally insufficient. Particularly worrying is the reference to 'the significant increase in children exploited in commercial sex in the past few years, which NGOs [non-governmental organisations] estimated to be between 10,000 and 15,000 predominantly French girls, in April 2021', which caused the national rapporteur to publicly urge the government 'to adopt a clear criminal policy against the sexual exploitation of children'.[107] In this context, the case of *International Federation of Human Rights Leagues (FIDH) v. France*[108] was an important landmark for the rights of migrant children in France and elsewhere. It concerned Articles 13 (the right to social and medical assistance) and 7 (the right of children and young persons to social, legal and economic protection) of the European Social Charter and the prohibition against discrimination. It held that legislation or practices that deny entitlement to medical assistance to foreign nationals, even if they are there illegally, are contrary to the Charter. In effect it placed an obligation on the authorities to ensure that unaccompanied migrant children had equality of access to national social and healthcare services. All children in Germany – including unaccompanied minor migrants – have legal rights to the basic necessities such as health, accommodation, education and protection, although the considerable number of 'missing migrant children' is a matter of concern. The latest records available show that in 2021 some 1,600 were

105 [2015] NZIPT 501973.
106 Ibid, at para 75.
107 Op. cit.
108 Complaint No. 14/2003, (2004).

missing: nearly 1,000 reportedly aged between 14 and 17 years and just over 600 aged 13 years and younger.[109]

Jurisdictional differences and their significance: child trafficking

While all eight countries being considered in this series have recent and ongoing experience of child trafficking, the six common law nations share an additional history of state-driven abusive child trafficking. Mostly this has taken the form of coercive intervention in Indigenous communities entailing the use of enforced adoption and residential schooling to give effect to the states' assimilation policies. It also includes the well-documented history of children exported from England, Wales and Ireland to the colonies of what was then the British Empire.

Contemporary trafficking

According to a recent report, and contrary to popular opinion, more than half of child trafficking victims are trafficked within their own country: child victims trafficked for sexual exploitation were commonly trafficked internationally, those trafficked for forced labour were more likely to be trafficked domestically, and the involvement of family and friends in their recruitment is a prominent trend.[110] For some jurisdictions, however, trafficking continues to be perceived as being first and foremost an immigration problem: borders must be protected; legitimate immigration procedures have to be enforced; and effective policing, detention and deportation are to be prioritised over ease of access to health and welfare benefits. The varying extent to which such prioritisation has marginalised the jurisdictional relevance of UN CROC, and is non-compliant with established caselaw principles, can be seen in the brief summary that follows. It would seem inevitable that family law – on an international and domestic basis – will have to be adjusted to make more room for the prioritisation of the legal functions of prevention and protection in relation to child trafficking and for a right to appropriate service provision including specialised services to address the physical and mental health needs of victims.

Jurisdictional differences

In England and Wales, the so-called county lines cases feature traffickers who target children of separated parents or those looked after by social services, including those with behavioural or developmental disorders. Trafficked children, as well as

109 See, www.infomigrants.net/en/post/29633/hundreds-of-unaccompanied-minors-missing-in-germany

110 See, International Organization for Migration (IOM) and François-Xavier Bagnoud Center for Health and Human Rights at Harvard University (FXB), *From Evidence to Action: Twenty Years of IOM Child Trafficking Data to Inform Policy and Programming*, 2023, https://publications.iom.int/books/evidence-action-twenty-years-iom-child-trafficking-data-inform-policy-and-programming

victims emotionally attached to their traffickers, can also be induced to use drugs or alcohol, thereby increasing the control the traffickers have over them.[111] In this jurisdiction, the leading case of *V.C.L. and A.N. v. the United Kingdom*[112] is of wider significance as it highlighted the importance of ensuring that where there is credible suspicion that someone – in this case, two Vietnamese youths aged 15 and 17 years found working on a cannabis 'farm' – has been trafficked, then the appropriate response from the authorities should be an assessment to determine their eligibility for protection rather for prosecution. In Ireland, it is reported that 'human traffickers exploit domestic and foreign victims in Ireland and traffickers exploit victims from Ireland abroad. Traffickers subject Irish children to sex trafficking within the country'.[113] The report was also highly critical of Ireland's treatment of victims, noting that there was no legally mandated psychological assistance and a lack of specialised services to address the physical and mental health needs of victims. Ireland's system for identifying victims of trafficking is based on Administrative Immigration Arrangements rather than governed by legislation. The Council of Europe Committee has recommended that Ireland establish a specific identification mechanism.

The U.S. is ranked as one of the worst countries globally for human trafficking.[114] According to the annual *Federal Human Trafficking Report*[115] 'in 2018, over half (51.6%) of the criminal human trafficking cases active in the U.S. were sex trafficking cases involving only children'. The introduction of the Trafficking Victims Protection Act 2000 was an important landmark in global trafficking law as it highlighted the primary importance of protecting victims, especially children. Canada has been identified as a source, destination and transit country for victims of human trafficking, including children, for the purposes of sexual exploitation and labour.[116] Although it has legislated to combat human trafficking both domestically and transnationally,[117] there is good reason to believe that Indigenous women and girls have been disproportionality affected by trafficking – as well as other forms of abuse – over past recent decades.[118] A report funded by the Department of Justice which explored the practice of customary adoption gave rise to concerns that links

111 See, the 2020 UNODC report Trafficking in Persons', at p 91, www.unodc.org/documents/data-and-analysis/tip/2021/GLOTiP_2020_15jan_web.pdf

112 Application Nos. 77587/12 and 74603/12, (2021).

113 See, U.S. State Department, *Trafficking in Persons Report*, June 2019, at p 253, www.state.gov/wp-content/uploads/2019/06/2019-Trafficking-in-Persons-Report.pdf

114 See, *Human Trafficking Statistics by State 2022*, https://worldpopulationreview.com/state-rankings/human-trafficking-statistics-by-state

115 See, https://traffickinginstitute.org/federal-human-trafficking-report/

116 See, the International Bureau for Children's Rights, *Child Trafficking in Canada*, www.ibcr.org/en/projets/la-traite-des-enfants-au-canada-2/

117 See: The Criminal Code, s 279; and the Immigration and Refugee Protection Act 2002, s 118.

118 See, Sethi, A., 'Domestic Sex Trafficking of Aboriginal Girls in Canada: Issues and Implications', *First Peoples Child & Family Review*, Vol. 3, No. 3, pp 57–71, 2007. Also, see, Native Women's Association of Canada, *Trafficking of Indigenous Women and Girls in Canada*, 2018, www.ourcommons.ca/Content/Committee/421/JUST/Brief/BR10002955/br-external/NativeWomensAssociationOfCanada-e.pdf

may exist between the practice and the possible human trafficking of Inuit women, girls and children.

In Australia, child sex tourism was identified in the *U.S. 2022 Trafficking in Persons Report: Australia*[119] as a matter requiring a more robust response from the Australian authorities. There is little information on child trafficking in New Zealand.

The U.S. report on trafficking[120] offers an assurance that 'the Government of France fully meets the minimum standards for the elimination of trafficking', while the corresponding report on child trafficking in Germany[121] states that traffickers exploit victims of forced labour primarily at construction sites but also in hotels, seasonal industries like agriculture, entertainment, and restaurants, and in private homes, with reported increases in the number of child victims. It notes that traffickers subject Roma and foreign unaccompanied children to sex trafficking, forced begging and other coerced criminal behaviour and that 'Romani families sometimes force their children, both boys and girls, into commercial sex on the streets'. In its 2022 report, the CRC expressed concern regarding the authorities' treatment of child victims of trafficking and urged that 'their best interests are taken as a primary consideration in decisions regarding their place of stay'.[122]

Conclusion

Relatively suddenly, child trafficking has attracted attention, not just through the media – but legally, socially and politically – as one of the more significant problems of our age, and a likely precursor of worse to come. Closely associated with this global problem, there is another – the phenomenon of unaccompanied child migrants – which also can only get worse as the effects of climate change, war and socio-economic disruption generate more population movement.

119 See, further, www.state.gov/reports/2022-trafficking-in-persons-report/australia/

120 See, U.S. Dept of State, *2023 Trafficking in Persons Report: France*, www.state.gov/reports/2023-trafficking-in-persons-report/france/#:~:text=In%20addition%2C%20Police%20identified%201%2C044,in%202019%20(187%20children)

121 U.S. Government, *2022 Trafficking in Persons Report: Germany*, www.state.gov/reports/2022-trafficking-in-persons-report/germany/

122 CRC/C/DEU/CO/5-6, at para 41.

7 Poverty, discrimination and public services

Introduction

'States Parties recognize the right of every child to a standard of living adequate for the child's physical, mental, spiritual, moral and social development'. So declares Article 27 of the United Nations Convention on the Rights of the Child 1989 (UN CROC). However, for this to happen, children need protection from the effects of poverty, from the risks of abuse, neglect and exploitation in employment and they need access to such basic necessities as health services and education. For many this will not happen without a safety net of public service provision.

This chapter considers the implications of poverty – and the importance of its alleviation by public service provision – for hybrid forms of family law and for the welfare interests/rights of a child. It does so by adopting much the same process in this section as formerly: focusing first on relevant definitions and principles before outlining the international legal framework; second, it considers the relative significance of poverty as a backdrop, or conditioning factor, to the balancing of service provision and child welfare needs; and third, it examines jurisdictional differences and their significance across a range of core areas of public service provision – child protection, health, education and employment – with reference also to their importance for Indigenous children.

Definitions, principles and international law

Poverty and discrimination are, inescapably, factors with potential to distort the effectiveness of law. Allowance must also be made for jurisdictional variations in interpretation of what appear to be standard concepts: welfare services, for example, as understood in the UK are not perceived in quite the same way in the U.S. nor in France. Therefore, the greater the number of countries subscribing to the same international legal instrument – such as the UN CROC – the greater the probability that a common legal language and shared jurisprudence will be established and will in time prevail over cultural context and other jurisdictional differences. The corollary being that this is less likely to happen when significant nations such as the U.S. decline to join all others in ratifying significant international instruments such as UN CROC.

DOI: 10.4324/9781003510383-10

Definitions

There can be no escaping the awkward fact that – despite the best efforts of international bodies such as the Organisation for Economic Co-operation and Development to formulate and apply standard indices of measurement – a degree of relativity continues to distort comparative jurisdictional analysis.

Poverty

The many definitions of poverty reflect the range of different academic, economic and philosophical disciplines for which the concept is of central importance. The 'state of being poor' or of 'being extremely poor' (as 'poverty' is defined by *Oxford* and *Cambridge* dictionaries, respectively) may not add much to our understanding, but they do serve as a reminder that this is a relative concept. Definitions that rely on listing a lack of material resources – food, literacy, and healthcare – are useful, but those that describe its effects would seem more satisfactory, such as that offered by the World Bank:

> poverty is correlated closely with all aspects of a person's life: the world's poor are more likely to be malnourished, they have less access to services like education, electricity, sanitation and healthcare, and they are more vulnerable to conflict and climate change.[1]

The constraints on opportunities and the limitations imposed on choices are clearly key indicators.

Parental responsibilities

Initially, and for many centuries, the health, welfare and safety of a child were viewed as indistinguishable from parental status: to be a parent was to be wholly responsible for a child; accountable for their physical and moral welfare and protector of any entitlement to property, until the child attained adulthood. This proprietal frame of reference, based on parental rights, has been displaced in contemporary family law by the concept of 'parental responsibilities' which implies that parental use of authority is valid only if employed for the benefit of the child. Those attributes of parenting with a functional bearing upon the nurture needs of the child, rather than those traditionally associated with the status of parent, have come to define the latter's legal role in the family. The reframing of this concept has allowed it to play a more consistent role across both public and private sectors of family law.

1 See, further, https://datatopics.worldbank.org/world-development-indicators/themes/poverty-and-inequality.html

Public services

Those services – delivered by government organisations, or by others acting as their agents, and paid for by taxes – universally available to all in any society, are not as readily identifiable or as uniformly accessible as formerly. A differentiating characteristic of modern developed nations is the extent to which each has shed responsibility – and often ownership rights – for the services paid for by the tax revenues of many previous generations. Postal services, residential care for the elderly, utilities including drinking water, prisons and preschool day care for children are among the range of provisions once available from the public sector as of right but now largely only available at a cost from the private sector.

For present purposes, it is those services essential for securing and maintaining the welfare interests of a child (as opposed to furthering a public interest in their compliance with the law) that need to be examined. In the main, the statutory duty to provide these core services continues to rest with government bodies, even if some are franchised out for delivery to charities and to regulated private and non-profit organisations. The responsibility for service standards, availability, sufficiency and accessibility lies with government. Such core services in all countries currently being considered include education, healthcare, protection, housing and terms of employment for adolescent children.

Discrimination

For an act to be discriminatory, it must be shown that an applicant is subject to a difference in treatment from others in a similar situation; in the enjoyment of one of the rights protected by the Convention; which difference cannot be objectively and reasonably justified, having regard to the concepts of legitimate aim, proportionality and margin of appreciation. There is no definitive list of matters constituting discriminatory treatment. Historically, discrimination has been strongly associated with religion, and while this has always been present to a varying degree in Europe, the tensions associated with accommodating the religious affiliations of increased numbers of migrants within the pluralism that now characterises most of modern Europe have caused religious discrimination to increase correspondingly. Much of this surfaces in schools where pupils must sometimes make a stand as proxies for their parents' religious beliefs or lack thereof.

Principles

The principles more generally applicable to the broad socio-legal context, such as 'subsidiarity' and 'margins of appreciation', are examined elsewhere in this series, while for 'welfare interests' and 'paramountcy' see Chapter 1. At present only those with a direct bearing on child welfare interests and rights as applicable in the eight jurisdictions are considered.

Proportionality

The principle requires public body decision-makers to consider the individual's circumstances; choose the least restrictive option; and make a reasoned decision, including why they consider any restriction on human rights to be justifiable. It demands that state intervention in family affairs, on the grounds of protecting the welfare interests of a child, should be proportionate to the risk involved to those interests: such as state intervention in family affairs on child protection grounds. This benchmark principle has been frequently applied and reviewed by the ECtHR over the past several decades. In *Marckx v. Belgium*,[2] for example, it considered the legal distinction between 'legitimate' and 'illegitimate' children in Belgian law, found that the distinction disproportionately disadvantaged the latter, and struck down the inheritance laws making that distinction.

The proportionality principle has played and will continue to play a prominent role in the family law jurisprudence of the ECtHR and in the domestic law of most developed nations.

Preventative state intervention

UN CROC declares in its Preamble that 'the family . . . should be afforded the necessary protection and assistance so that it can fully assume its responsibilities within the community'. This is underpinned by Articles 18 and 20, which reinforce the principle that the state should give priority to measures that keep children in their families and in their culture of origin; Article 24 requires states to recognise the right of every child to access 'facilities for the treatment of illness and rehabilitation of health'; Article 28 adds a similar state duty in respect of education; and finally Article 39 requires states to take 'all appropriate measures to promote physical and psychological recovery and social reintegration of a child victim of any form of neglect, exploitation or abuse'.

Precursor to state coercive intervention

Before a state resorts to coercive intervention in cases of parental neglect, it must first show that every reasonable effort has been made to alleviate the situation by appropriate service provision. *Wallová and Walla v. the Czech Republic*,[3] for example, concerned five siblings taken into public care due to poor community housing facilities and placed by the authorities in two separate children's homes. The Court found that Article 8 had been breached: it ruled that inadequate housing did not justify taking children into state care,[4] the reasons for doing so were relevant but not sufficient and less drastic measures could and should have been used to address the lack of suitable housing.[5] It had articulated the same theme much earlier in *Olsson v. Sweden*[6] when it stressed that the mere fact a child would be better off if placed in care was not sufficient. So also in *Saviny v. Ukraine*,[7] where the ECtHR found that children had been placed in care due to the parents' lack of financial means and

2 Application No. 6833/74, (1979).
3 Application No. 23848/04, (2006).
4 Ibid, at paras 73–74.
5 Note also that s 34(3) of the European Charter of Fundamental Rights provides a right to housing assistance in such circumstances.
6 Application No. 10465/83, (1988).
7 Application No. 39948/06, (2008).

in the absence of evidence that the authorities had attempted to provide relevant social assistance, it held that they had violated their Article 8 duty to maintain family unity. More recently and more graphically, the Court ruled to the same effect in *Soares de Melo v. Portugal*[8] which concerned a single mother unemployed and living in poverty who had six of her ten children, then aged between seven months and six years, taken into care with a view to their adoption, and she was deprived of parental responsibility and denied all contact with them. Domestic authorities had taken the view that she was incapable of performing her role as a mother and noted that she persistently refused to undergo sterilisation, a condition stipulated in an 'agreement' reached with the social services. There was no evidence of mistreatment or abuse, in fact there appeared to be strong bonds of affection between the mother and her children. Ultimately, the ECtHR found that the mother's Article 8 rights had been violated.

Prompt and effective

If the service response is to achieve an alleviation of need, thereby satisfying both a family's entitlement to state support and a child's right to protection for their welfare interests, then delivery must be prompt and effective. The ECtHR has, in a number of cases, found a state to be culpable for failing to effect rapid intervention resulting in preventable harm. Moreover, service delivery must not only be prompt, appropriate and sufficient but also culturally sensitive so as to allow the services to be readily accessed and utilised. This series has disclosed the extent to which the state in the CANZUS (Canada, Australia, New Zealand, United States) nations is consistently failing in its consensual intervention programmes to effectively support Indigenous families and their children due largely to embedded cultural dissonance between service providers and recipients. This may also be a factor in the ineffectiveness of public service engagement with the socially disadvantaged more generally.

Good enough parenting

Establishing clear thresholds for child protection intervention is an imperfect science but in general they would seem to have been lowered since the principle of 'good enough' was judicially accepted and applied.[9]

In England and Wales child protection has become a good deal more stringent in the 17 years since Hedley J stated that "society must be willing to tolerate very diverse standards of parenting, including the eccentric, the barely adequate and the

8 Application No. 72850/14, (2016).

9 This term was first used by the British Psychoanalyst D.W. Winnicott in the 1950s in reference to the majority of parents whom he viewed as being "good enough" at meeting their children's needs. See, further, D. W. Winnicott, *The Child, the Family, and the Outside World,* Penguin, 1973.

inconsistent"[10] while taking into account that "it is not the provenance of the state to spare children all the consequences of defective parenting . . . it simply could not be done".[11] A sentiment not unlike that expressed in the *Sanotsky* case[12] in the U.S. when the court commented that "the fundamental liberty interest of natural parents in the care, custody, and management of their child does not evaporate simply because they have not been model parents".

Parental rights

Although a lynchpin in family law for centuries, this principle has been greatly devalued in England and Wales in recent years, replaced by the alternative concept of 'parental responsibilities'. This has also occurred in other jurisdictions, but not to the same extent. In Ireland, the recognition now given to the paramountcy principle in the Constitution and in statute law must have a correspondingly reductive effect on parental rights. In the U.S., constitutional provisions are to the opposite effect: they require the state to show compelling reason if it is to infringe rights of family privacy and parental autonomy. The argument being that these fundamental liberties, protected by the Fourteenth Amendment, strongly suggest that the welfare interests of children are best assured by the parental right to custody and that state intervention – if it is to further those interests – should focus on supporting the parents.[13] In Canada, traditional values also prevail, and the parental right to chastise a child continues in effect.[14]

In Australia, parental rights – or responsibilities as they are now known in law – are defined in the Family Law Act 1975, s 61B, as 'all the duties, powers, responsibilities and authority which, by law, parents have in relation to children'. There is a strong presumption in Australian family law that birth parents are best placed to bear these responsibilities and thereby safeguard the welfare interests of their child. In New Zealand, the Care of Children Act 2004 clearly states that 'a child's care, development and upbringing should primarily be the responsibility of their parents or guardians' which confirms the long-standing respect that the law in New Zealand has had for parental rights.

In France, the CRC has expressed concern that law continues to refer to 'parental authority' which, as the Committee points out, is not conceptually compliant with the rights of the child and suggested that it be replaced by a term such as 'parental responsibility'.[15] In Germany, parental rights are as defined in ss 1626–1698 of

10 See, *Re L (Care: Threshold Criteria)* [2007] 1 FLR 2050, at para 50.
11 Ibid.
12 455 U.S. 745 (1982).
13 The parental right to custody has been deemed a fundamental right by the USSC: *Santosky v. Kramer*, Ibid.
14 See, *Canadian Foundation for Children, Youth and the Law v. Canada (Attorney General)* [2004] 1 SCR 76, 2004 SCC 4.
15 CRC/C/FRA/CO/5, at para 49.

the Civil Code and protected by the Constitution, resulting in the relatively strong position of birth parents. Although the legislative intent behind the recent amendment of the Basic Law was purportedly to constitutionally embed the welfare interests of the child, the government has offered the puzzling reassurance that this will not affect parental rights: that the rights and responsibility of parents will not be limited, the substance of their rights will continue to be guaranteed and the basic rights of the child are not being expanded to the detriment of others.[16]

Welfare interests of the child

Principle 2 of the UN Declaration of the Rights of the Child 1959 stated that

> [t]he child shall enjoy special protection, and shall be given opportunities and facilities, by law and by other means, to enable him to develop physically, mentally, morally, spiritually and socially in a healthy and normal manner and in conditions of freedom and dignity.

Thirty years later the introduction of UN CROC brought with it the statement that 'in all actions concerning children, whether undertaken by public or private social welfare institutions, courts of law, administrative authorities or legislative bodies, the best interests of the child shall be a primary consideration'. Shortly afterwards Article 24(2) of the European Social Charter, as revised in 1996, proclaimed that 'in all actions relating to children, whether taken by public authorities or private institutions, the child's best interests must be a primary consideration'. In 2013 the CRC issued a comment on interpreting the phrase '*best interests taken as a primary consideration*' in which it identified seven factors held to constitute the best interests of the child: the child's views; the child's identity; preservation of the family environment and maintaining relations; care, protection and safety of the child; situation of vulnerability; the child's right to health; and the child's right to education.[17]

As was explained in the English case *J. v. C.*,[18] "in applying (the welfare principle), the rights and wishes of parents, whether unimpeachable or otherwise, must be assessed and weighed in their bearing on the welfare of the child in conjunction with all other factors relevant to that issue".[19] In Ireland, Article 42A.4.1(ii) of the Constitution now asserts the principle that 'the best interests of the child shall be the paramount consideration' in application to public law proceedings relating to the 'safety and welfare of any child' and private law proceedings 'concerning the adoption, guardianship or custody of, or access to, any child'. However, as in

16 See, further, www.bundesregierung.de/breg-en/service/archive/rights-of-child-in-basic-law-1841338

17 See, Committee on the Rights of the Child, *General Comment No 14: On the Right of the Child to Have His or Her Best Interests Taken as a Primary Consideration (article 3, para 1)* May 29, 2013, pp 52–78.

18 [1970] AC 668 (HL).

19 Ibid, at 719.

Germany and the U.S., it remains to be seen how constricting the more traditional family values – affirming parental status – will be in relation to children's welfare interests/rights.

In the U.S., the court acknowledged in *Parham v. J.R.*[20] that commitment to an institution placed the child's liberty interest at stake but found that the latter's interest was subsumed within the parents' interest in caring for their child and so deferred to the parents' committal decision. This case stands as an indicator of the weak weighting given in U.S. law to the capacity of a child to determine his or her welfare interests relative to the capacity of parents and others to do so on their behalf. However, under the common law an 'emancipated minor' has long been held to be exempt from the normal requirement that their medical treatment be authorised by parental consent.[21] So, judicial notice has been taken of the fact that some minors possess the maturity to make certain specific constitutionally protected decisions, such as the decision to have an abortion.[22] Family First legislation – a significant landmark in U.S. family law – is important because it is anchored on a sense of shared parent/state responsibility for the welfare interests of children. In Canada, given that there is no mention of the paramountcy principle in the Constitution, the Child Care Act 2022, the Child Protection Act 1998 nor in the 2019 changes to federal private family law dealing with matters such as divorce, it would seem that the courts are restricted to applying the best interests of the child test as the only consideration when determining decisions relating to arrangements for children.

In Australia, the court is required to treat the welfare interests of the child as the paramount consideration and, when determining what constitutes those welfare interests, is directed to a checklist of primary and additional considerations, as extensively set out under s 60CC of the Family Law Act 1975. In New Zealand similar checklists are available to aid interpretation and application of welfare interests in the Guardianship Act 1968, s 23; the *Oranga Tamariki* Act 1989, s 4A; and in the Care of Children Act 2004, s 5. These checklists, like the previous UK example and their counterparts elsewhere, are quite alike in content and are not intended to be either prescriptive or exclusive.

The CRC in its 2023 report on France[23] recommended – once again – that the state party strengthen its efforts to ensure that

> the right of the child to have their welfare interests taken as a primary consideration is appropriately integrated and consistently interpreted and applied in all legislative, administrative and judicial proceedings and decisions as well as in all policies, programmes and projects that are relevant to and have an impact on children.

20 141 442 U.S. 584, 606 (1979).

21 See, for example: *State ex. rel. Scott v. Lowell*, 78 Minn. 166, 80 N.W. 877 (1899) and *Smith v. Seibly*, 72 Wash. 2d 66, 431 P. 2d 719 (1967).

22 *Planned Parenthood of Central Missouri v. Danforth, Attorney General of Missouri*, 428 U.S. 52 (1976).

23 CRC/C/FRA/CO/5, at para 17.

In relation to Germany, the CRC expressed similar concerns a year earlier 'that the principle of the best interests of the child is not being applied in all proceedings affecting children' and recommended that it be consistently applied 'in all policies, programmes and legislative, administrative and judicial proceedings affecting children, including in relation to trafficking and migration and asylum procedures'.[24]

Universally applicable, public benefit legislative provisions may also have the ancillary effect of improving life for children. So government initiatives to combat the effects of climate change, for example, or reduce poverty, improve sewage treatment, etc., are also clearly conducive to furthering the welfare interests of children.

Welfare checklists

The use of statutory 'welfare checklists' would seem to be growing more widespread, accompanied by the danger that they may reduce what should be a complex and individualised balancing assessment to a 'tick-box' exercise. In England and Wales the court is required, under s 1(3) Children Act 1989, to apply the welfare checklist in determining all 'family proceedings' which, as this includes matrimonial proceedings, means that the same grid of welfare indicators is being applied across the bulk of proceedings in both the public and private sectors of family law, thereby bringing more consistency to the role and content of welfare interests in the judicial determination of family issues. In Ireland, a new s 24 in the Child Care Act 1991 provides that a non-exhaustive checklist of seven factors is to be taken into account in determining what is in the best interests of a child. Part V of the Children and Family Relationships Act 2015 also provides a welfare checklist.

In the U.S., there is no federal welfare checklist, but in Canada the federal Child Protection Act 1998, s 2, has a mandatory requirement that courts make an order in the 'best interests' of a child which is to be interpreted with reference to a stated list of considerations. In Australia, when determining what constitutes a child's best interests, the court is presently required, as extensively set out under s 60CC of the 1975 Act, to consider a checklist of both primary and additional considerations. In New Zealand, s 5 of the Care of Children Act 2004 provides a list of welfare indicators to aid interpretation and application of the welfare principle.

There is no equivalent in French or German law to the common law 'welfare checklists'.

Paramountcy principle

In England and Wales this principle – drawn initially from caselaw[25] and first statutorily stated[26] in s 1 of the Guardianship of Minors Act 1971 – was asserted

24 CRC/C/DEU/CO/5-6, at para 16.

25 See, *J v. C* [1970] AC 668.

26 Although it had previously appeared in the UN Declaration of the Rights of the Child 1959.

to govern judicial determination of all issues affecting a child's upbringing and administration of the child's property. At first it was confined to judicial decisions in child-care and wardship proceedings but now, like the above-mentioned welfare checklist, it applies across the bulk of proceedings in both the public and private sectors of family law, thereby bringing more consistency to the role and content of welfare interests in the judicial determination of family issues. In Ireland, the requirement that a child's welfare must be the paramount consideration in any decision taken regarding the child's upbringing was first statutorily stated in s 3 of the Guardianship Act 1964 (as substituted by s 45 of the Children and Family Relationships Act 2015) but has always been judicially applied by the High Court in wardship proceedings and, following its constitutional recognition in 2015, is now guaranteed by Article 42A.4.1. The Child Care (Amendment) Act 2021 subsequently inserted a new s 24 into the Child Care Act 1991 to provide that, in proceedings under the Act, the court shall regard the best interests of the child as the paramount consideration. As to whether the constitutional amendment significantly changed the balance in parent/child rights, Humphreys J has noted that "even after the enactment of Article 42A, the principle that best interests presumptively coincide with parental custody applies".[27] Subsequently, O'Donnell J referred to the perception that the pre-existing constitutional position, with its emphasis on the family, might have subordinated the interests of the child to, in effect, those of the parents and that Article 42A could be seen as a restating of the balance,[28] a view endorsed by the majority of the Court of Appeal.[29] Reconciling the state's constitutionally declared special protection for the status of parents and family with the Article 42A iteration of the paramountcy principle would seem to be a judicial work in progress.

In the U.S., as mentioned earlier and first illustrated in *Parham v. J.R.*,[30] the paramountcy cannot be said to play any part in the law relating to children. A decade later, in *re E.G.*,[31] the Illinois Supreme Court recognized the importance of parental authority and asserted that if a parent were to oppose a child's refusal of life-saving treatment, "this opposition would weigh heavily against the minor's right to refuse". Again, in *Bellotti, Attorney General of Massachusetts v. Baird*,[32] the court indicated that adolescents' constitutional rights could not "be equated with those of adults" due to "the particular vulnerability of children; their inability to make critical decisions in an informed, mature manner; and the importance of the parental role in child rearing". An opinion echoed at much the same time by the Supreme Court comment that "most children, even in adolescence, simply are not able to make sound judgments concerning many decisions, including their

27 *Bedford Borough Council v. M* [2017] IEHC 583, *per* Humphreys J, at para 135.
28 In re the Adoption Act 2010, s 49(2) and *JB (a minor)* [2018] IESC 30, [2019] 1 IR 270, at para 5.
29 *Child and Family Agency v. Adoption Authority of Ireland* [2022] IECA 196, at para 87.
30 141 442 U.S. 584, 606 (1979).
31 549 N.E. 2d 322, 328 (Ill. 1989).
32 443 U.S. 622 (1979), at p 634.

need for medical care or treatment".[33] Only in the absence of conflict with parental authority are the U.S. courts usually willing to permit minors to make such decisions.[34] An exception lies in the common law concept of an 'emancipated minor' which holds that such a child is exempt from the normal requirement that their medical treatment be authorised by parental consent.[35] Judicial notice has been taken of the fact that some minors possess the maturity to make certain specific constitutionally protected decisions, such as the decision to have an abortion.[36] The Inter-American Commission on Human Rights points out that U.S. domestic laws do not adequately or consistently reflect the principle of the primacy of the best interests of the child.[37] Indeed, the main reason why the U.S. has declined to become a signatory state to the UN CROC, and why the paramountcy principle does not function in child care law as it does in most other developed western countries, is because of the constitutional protection singled out for the rights of parents[38] as established by the U.S. Supreme Court in cases such as *Santosky v. Kramer*[39] and *Troxel v. Granville.*[40] In that context, the Family First legislation must be viewed as a significant landmark in U.S. family law, anchored as it is on a sense of shared parent/state responsibility for the welfare interests of children. In Canada, as mentioned earlier, the absence of any reference to the paramountcy principle in federal legislation such as the Child Protection Act 1998 and the Divorce Act 1985 or its 2019 amendments, is indicative of a general reticence to establish the welfare interests of a child as the matter of paramount importance in all issues affecting the child's well-being.[41]

In Australia, the paramountcy principle is firmly embedded in the Family Law Act 1975, s 60CA, to govern applications for parenting orders in respect of any Australian child. It is restricted in its application: unlike some other jurisdictions it is not to be applied – as in the UK – to every matter affecting a child's upbringing;[42] under s 60CC, in other contexts it is only required to have regard to the wishes of that child; there is no suggestion that those wishes should then be given any

33 See, *Parham, Commissioner, Department of Human Resources of Georgia v. J. R.*, 442 U.S. 584 (1979), at p 603.

34 See, *Bakker v. Welsh*, 108 N.W. 94, 96 (Mich. 1906) and *Younts v. St. Francis Hosp. & Sch. of Nursing*, 469 P. 2d 330, 333 (Kan. 1970).

35 See, for example: *State ex. rel. Scott v. Lowell,* 78 Minn. 166, 80 N.W. 877 (1899) and *Smith v. Seibly*, 72 Wash. 2d 66, 431 P. 2d 719 (1967).

36 *Planned Parenthood of Central Missouri v. Danforth, Attorney General of Missouri*, 428 U.S. 52 (1976).

37 See, The Inter-American Commission on Human Rights, *Children and Adolescents in the United States' Adult Criminal Justice System*, Op. cit., at p 134.

38 See, Volokh, E., 'Parent-Child Speech and Child Custody Speech Restrictions', *NYU Law Review*, Vol. 81, p 631, 2006.

39 *Santosky v. Kramer*, Op. cit.

40 *Troxel v. Granville*, 530 U.S. 57 (2000).

41 The paramountcy principle is present in some provincial legislation such as the Manitoba Child and Family Services Act 1985, s 2(1).

42 See, further, Young, L., 'Mature Minors and Parenting Disputes in Australia: Engaging with the Debate on Best Interests v. Autonomy', *UNSW Law Journal*, Vol. 42, No. 4, 2019.

particular weighting. Moreover, s 60CA must be read in conjunction with the presumption in s 61DA of 'equal shared parental responsibility' which requires courts to apply the presumption that 'it is in the best interests of the child for the child's parents to have equal shared parental responsibility for the child' when making family orders. In New Zealand, the Guardianship Act 1968 first introduced the principle into statutory law: s 23 then declared that a child's welfare interests were to be regarded as the first and paramount consideration. This was followed by the *Oranga Tamariki* Act 1989, s 4A, which states that 'the well-being and best interests of the child or young person are the first and paramount consideration'.[43]

In France the *Conseil d'Etat* has ruled that Article 3(1) of UN CROC – the child's interest must be a paramount consideration – was directly applicable to French law. However, this conflicts with traditional presumptions favouring family unity and also with Article 375–1 of the Civil Code which states that the *juge des enfants* 'shall always strive to obtain family's consent to the measure envisaged'. More recently, the CRC, in its 2016 report,[44] acknowledged that the principle of the best interests of the child had been raised to the constitutional level and that the *Cour de cassation* and the *Conseil d'Etat* had jointly agreed on its paramountcy weighting. However, the Committee remained concerned that the right was not sufficiently integrated in practice and was not always properly assessed and applied in all government actions and decisions. In Germany, there is no unequivocal statement in the Constitution declaring that the welfare interests of the child must be treated as of paramount importance, though in the Civil Code the best interests of the child are declared to be of paramount importance when determining the child's adoption.[45]

Family law has for centuries, and in all the jurisdictions presently being considered – as well as in many others – revolved around the axis of the marital relationship: marriage formed the legal and social framework for procreation. However, in recent years all major components of that relationship have undergone fundamental change: marriage is no longer necessary; relationships are not necessarily heterosexual, exclusively for two adults nor durable; procreation may occur outside that relationship and the resulting child may not be genetically linked to both or to either of the 'parents'. Given the scale of change in such a short period of time, it would seem unlikely that changes of wording – 'welfare interests' to 'paramountcy', 'parental rights' to 'parental responsibilities' – will cause the axis of family law jurisprudence to dissolve overnight.

International law

The most important international instruments for present purposes are the UN CROC 1989 and the European Convention for the Protection of Human Rights and

43 See, also, the Children, Young Persons, and Their Families Act 1989, s 6, and the Care of Children Act 2004, s 4.

44 CRC/C/FRA/CO/5.

45 The Civil Code, s 1741.

Fundamental Freedoms 1950, but there are many others with a varying degree of relevance.[46]

The United Nations Guidelines for the Alternative Care of Children 2009

The Guidelines were intended to enhance implementation of the CRC 'regarding the protection and well-being of children deprived of parental care or who are at risk of being so' (para 3). Removing a child from the care of the family should be seen as a measure of last resort and whenever possible be temporary and for the shortest duration possible (para 14). Children temporarily or permanently deprived of their birth family, or in whose best interests cannot be allowed to remain in that environment, are entitled to special government protection and assistance (UN CROC, Article 20(1)).

Optional Protocol on the Sale of Children, Child Prostitution, and Child Pornography 2000 (Sex Trafficking Protocol) 2000

This Protocol, appended to UN CROC, addressed the many purposes for which children are bought and sold. It defined and prohibited the sale of children and, in that context, established the principle that improperly inducing consent, as a means of procuring the adoption of a child, violates human rights and is to be treated as a criminal offence.

European Social Charter (revised in 1996)

Article 17 requires states to take all appropriate and necessary measures to ensure that children receive the care, assistance, education and training they need (including free primary and secondary education), to protect children and young persons from negligence, violence or exploitation and to provide protection for children deprived of family support. Article 24(2) requires the child's best interests to be treated as "a primary consideration" in all actions relating to children, no matter whether taken by public or private authorities.

The Hague Convention on Protection of Children and Co-operation in Respect of Intercountry Adoption 1993

The Hague Convention, which entered into force on 1 May 1995, has now been ratified by some 101 contracting states, including the CANZUS nations. Its Preamble declares that 'each state should take, as a matter of priority, appropriate measures to enable the child to remain in the care of his or her family of origin'.

46 See, further, O'Halloran, K., *Children, the Law and the Welfare Principle: European Judicial Perspectives*, Routledge, 2023, at chapter 1.

The United Nations Convention on the Elimination of all forms of Discrimination Against Women with its Optional Protocol

Article 12, requires states to 'take all appropriate measures to eliminate discrimination against women in the field of healthcare in order to ensure . . . access to health care services'.

The UN Convention on the Rights of the Child 1989

This Convention has now been ratified by 196 countries, including all CANZUS nations except the U.S. Its Preamble refers to 'the importance of the traditions and cultural values of each people for the protection and harmonious development of the child'.[47] Article 2 requires the state to take all appropriate measures to ensure that a child is protected against all forms of discrimination or punishment on the basis of the status, activities, expressed opinions or beliefs of the child's parents, legal guardians or family members. It provides for overlapping sources of discrimination. Article 3 requires the state in all actions concerning children, whether undertaken by public or private social welfare institutions, courts of law, administrative authorities or legislative bodies, to treat the best interests of the child as a primary consideration. Article 4 requires the state to provide for the cultural and collective rights of the individual Indigenous child. Articles 6, 7, 18 and 20 are also important in this context, as is Article 30 requiring the state to ensure that a child who is Indigenous shall not be denied the right, in community with other members of his or her group, to enjoy his or her own culture, to profess and practise his or her own religion or to use his or her own language.

The International Covenant on Civil and Political Rights 1966

This commits its parties to respect the civil and political rights of individuals, including children: Articles 1, 24, 26 and 27 are particularly relevant. As of 2018, the Covenant had been ratified by 172 countries; the U.S. and Canada[48] are both parties. It now includes first and second Optional Protocols.

International Covenant on Economic, Social and Cultural Rights 1966

The Covenant commits signatory parties to work towards the granting of economic, social and cultural rights, to the Non-Self Governing and Trust Territories and individuals, including labour rights and the right to health, the right to education and the right to an adequate standard of living. Article 10 provides that children and young persons should be 'protected from economic and social exploitation'.

47 See, also, Articles 5, 20 (particularly 20.3) and 30.
48 Ratified 19.05.1976.

The International Convention on the Elimination of all forms of Racial Discrimination 1965

This UN Convention commits its members to the elimination of racial discrimination and the promotion of understanding among all races. Its impact on national legislation can be seen in the implementation of legislation outlawing racial discrimination by the state, in the workplace or in the provision of services such as housing and education. The definition of 'racial discrimination' in Article 1 is important as it provides that whether a particular action or policy discriminates is judged by its effects, as determined by whether that action has an unjustifiable disparate impact upon a group distinguished by race, colour, descent, or national or ethnic origin.

European Convention for the Protection of Human Rights and Fundamental Freedoms 1950

The European Convention on Human Rights (ECHR) established a framework of international rights, the most relevant of which is Article 8 stating the right to respect for private and family life.

Poverty and non-discrimination: jurisdictional differences and related public service provision

Unquestionably, a society that provides a sufficient platform of public services for all its citizens – healthcare, housing, education, etc. – will, on the 'rising tide floats all boats' principle, thereby also ameliorate child welfare issues. Such a platform will not exist, or not have that effect, in a context of significant poverty when the dynamic is then reversed, nor when public services are distributed on a discriminatory basis. An adequate framework of such services, accessible to all on a needs basis, is essential if the parenting capacity of many socially disadvantaged families is to remain adequate: the correlation seems inescapable.

Jurisdictional differences and their significance: poverty relief

Socio-economic living conditions and indices of poverty will necessarily play a key role in determining the welfare of a nation's children and their future prospects. However, while socio-economic factors are recognised as rights in international law,[49] they remain largely unenforceable, and respect for differences in cultural identity can justify state derogation from rulings that may have particular cultural consequences.

A lack or insufficiency of basic necessities is bad enough in itself, but poverty also acts as a blanket to suppress potential in many areas. Poor health, low

49 See: EU Charter of Fundamental Rights 2000; ECHR, Protocol No. 1, article 2; and the European Social Charter.

levels of academic attainment and weak career/employment prospects are among the adverse effects associated with poverty in childhood.[50] The quality, volume and accessibility of state public services that are available to support families in need – relative to the prevalence of poverty – have the potential to offset social disadvantage and improve the health and welfare of their children. Much international law is now devoted to establishing children's rights to avail of core public services – and to setting benchmarks for standards of service provision – and as such are considered essential to their welfare. For example, both UN CROC[51] and the International Covenant on Economic, Social and Cultural Rights (ICESCR)[52] require states to ensure that specific basic public services are available and accessible to safeguard and promote the rights/welfare of children.

Child's rights: freedom from poverty

UN CROC, Article 6, requires States Parties to 'recognise that every child has the inherent right to life' and to 'ensure to the maximum extent possible the survival and development of the child'.

Poverty and prevention

In England and Wales poverty is steadily becoming a serious social policy issue. As reported in 2019 in a *Lancet* editorial:[53]

> child poverty in the UK has increased year on year since 2011–12. Today, more than 4 million children in the UK – or one in three – live in poverty, an increase of 500,000 in the past 5 years. Strikingly, this rise has been driven almost entirely by the increase in poverty among working families, and child poverty rates are predicted to reach a staggering 40% by 2030.

This situation was not helped by the introduction of 'the two child policy' in 2017 which restricted state child benefits in order to dissuade parents from having large families and enduce them instead to return to employment. The policy failed to achieve the desired objective but did raise poverty levels. Since then, matters have worsened considerably according to a 2024 report on a child health crisis, which claims that 'one of the most important drivers of this crisis is the number of children in the UK living in extreme poverty, which tripled between 2019–2022'.[54]

50 Dornan, P. and Woodhead, M., *How Inequalities Develop through Childhood*, UNICEF, 2015, www.younglives.org.uk/sites/default/files/how-inequalities-develop-through-childhood.pdf

51 See, for example, articles 24, 28/29 and 32 in respect of health, education and employment, respectively.

52 See, for example, articles 10(1), 10(3) and 11.

53 See, 'Britain is Broken: Poor Child Health Proves It', *The Lancet*, Vol. 393, No. 10170, 2019, www.thelancet.com/journals/lancet/article/PIIS0140-6736(19)30162-X/fulltext

54 See, Harron, K., 'Child Health Crisis', *The Academy of Medical Sciences*, https://acmedsci.ac.uk/policy/policy-projects/child-health

Reportedly, 12% of children were in absolute poverty in 2008–9,[55] but this rate is now at 30%. The 2024 report notes that the infant survival rate is worse than in 60% of similar countries, leaving the UK ranked 30 out of 39 Organization for Economic Cooperation and Development (OECD) countries.

Before the introduction of the Children Act 1989, a local authority could plead insufficient finance as a defence to the charge that it had failed to meet the claimant's statutory entitlement to support services, and the court could determine that this was an inadequate justification and direct the authority to provide the necessary services.[56] After the introduction of the Act, the Court of Appeal acknowledged that it was not empowered to review the basis upon which a local authority elected to use its resources[57] nor could it direct a local authority to recognise a child as being in need for the purposes of ensuring a service entitlement.[58] Not until the introduction of the Children and Social Work Act 2017 and the Care Act 2014 did this situation change. Nonetheless, the CRC remained concerned that, in this jurisdiction, 'parents have not been provided with adequate family support' and that 'children have reportedly been removed from their biological families owing to the family's economic situation or because a foster family may provide a more beneficial environment for the child'.[59] In sharp contrast, the poverty rate in Ireland fell from 4.9% in 2022 to 3.8% in 2023.[60] A 2021 report revealed a total of 630,000 people living in poverty of whom 190,000 – or one in four – were children.[61]

In the U.S., child poverty peaked at 23% in 2012 but by 2023 had fallen to 16% or 11.6 million children. The fall may be a consequence of federal initiatives such as the Family First legislation which, in a significant shift of emphasis, gave legal recognition to both the importance of parental care and to an accompanying parental entitlement for the state support necessary to maintain it. The Family First Prevention Services Act 2018 enables states to use federal funds to provide enhanced support for children and families, thereby preventing the need to take children into the public care system. The 2018 Act was reinforced by the Family First Transition Act 2019 and subsequently by the Further Consolidated Appropriations Act 2020 which provides financial relief for states to develop the prevention-focussed infrastructure for their child welfare systems. In Canada, according to an UNICEF

55 See, www.local.gov.uk/sites/default/files/documents/child-poverty-fact-sheet-221.pdf

56 See, *AG (ex rel Tiley) v. London Borough of Wandsworth* [1981] 1 WLR 854.

57 See, *R v. Cambridge District Health Authority ex parte B (No. 2)* [1995] 1 FLR 1055 and *Re C (Family Assistance Order)* [1996] 1 FLR 424.

58 See, *Re J (Specific Issue Order: Leave to Apply)* [1995] 1 FLR 699.

59 As noted in the UN Committee on the Rights of the Child, *Concluding Observations: United Kingdom of Great Britain and Northern Ireland*, United Nations, 2016, at para 52.

60 See, further, www.inou.ie/analysis/inou-view/2024/03/07/survey-of-income-and-living-conditions-2023/#:~:text=In%202023%20the%20at%2Drisk,over%20the%20year%20to%2013%25

61 See, Social Justice Ireland, *The Poverty Ireland 2021 Report*, www.socialjustice.ie/system/files/file-uploads/2021-09/2019-04-15-sjipovertyfocus2019final.pdf and the Borgen Project, *The State of Poverty in Ireland*, https://borgenproject.org/the-state-of-poverty-in-ireland/

survey, the child poverty rate is high: rising from 15.2% in 2020 to 17.8% in 2021. Although the Canada Child Benefit scheme, introduced in 2016, has lifted many children out of poverty, this country is nevertheless currently ranked 19th out of 39 comparable countries.[62]

A UNICEF survey of child poverty in Australia found that 17.1% of children – or one in six – lived in poverty in the period 2019–21. This represented a slight increase of 1.7% since 2012–14 and gave Australia a ranking of 18th out of 39 OECD countries.[63] The situation is slightly better in New Zealand where the Household Economic Survey found a child poverty rate of 12.5% – or one in eight children – in 2022–23.[64]

From the evidence provided by several recent reports, it is clear that France continues to have a serious, apparently systemic, problem of child poverty.[65] Of particular concern is the reference to 21% of French children – or one in five – living below the poverty line in 2022. Similar reports indicate that the situation is no better in Germany where, in 2021, one in five children were considered poor or 'at risk of poverty'[66] causing the CRC, in 2022, to reiterate its concern regarding 'the large number of children still living in poverty or at risk of poverty'.[67] As always, the burden of poverty falls heaviest on those already marginalised, and it would seem that in both countries it is the Roma community, other minority groups and migrants who are suffering most.

The latest UNICEF report *Child Poverty in the Midst of Wealth*,[68] which presents the most up-to-date picture of poverty affecting children in OECD and EU countries, found that some of the world's richest countries experienced sharp rises in child poverty between 2014 and 2021, a period during which they also experienced stable economic growth. It notes that five higher income countries – including the United Kingdom (+20%) and France (+10%) – saw the greatest increases in the number of children living in households experiencing financial hardship since 2014. In circumstances where rich countries are simultaneously increasing both their levels of wealth and of child poverty, it would seem reasonable to attribute such asymmetric growth to government policy – or lack of it – and the latter must be viewed as a price worth paying to achieve the former. As these leading developed democratic nations are unable or unwilling to guarantee their children a reasonable standard of living, they would seem to be in breach of Article 27. In so doing they are also demonstrating, clearly, that the role of the paramountcy

62 See, UNICEF Report Card 18: Canadian Companion, *Child Poverty in Canada: Let's Finish This*, Toronto, UNICEF Canada, 2023.

63 See, further, www.unicef.org.au/media-release/1-in-6-children-in-australia-stuck-in-plateau-of-poverty

64 See, further, www.stats.govt.nz/information-releases/child-poverty-statistics-year-ended-june-2023/

65 See, for example, Break Poverty, 2021, https://breakpoverty.com/en/an-intolerable-increase-in-early-childhood-poverty-as-a-result-of-the-health-crisis/

66 See, the Bertelsmann Foundation Report on Child and Youth Poverty in Germany, www.wsws.org/en/articles/2023/03/01/fd97-m01.html

67 CRC/C/DEU/CO/5-6, at para 34.

68 See, further, www.unicef.org/innocenti/

principle and the differential weighting of various functions in the law relating to the welfare interests and rights of children can be undermined when a government chooses to prioritise other aspects of public policy.

Jurisdictional differences and their significance: non-discrimination

Issues relating to equality and discrimination are currently generating an exponential expansion of human rights law, including in the law as it relates to children.

Child's rights: equality and freedom from discrimination

UN CROC, Article 2, directs that all Convention rights are to apply to children without exception and without discrimination of any kind. Article 2(2) requires that all appropriate measures must be taken to ensure that the child is protected against all forms of discrimination or punishment on the basis of specified grounds. The grounds are enlarged in the ECHR, Article 14, to include sex, race, colour, language, religion, political or other opinion, national or social origin, association with a national minority, property, birth[69] or other status. Article 14 is supported by Article 9 of the ECHR; Article 12 of Protocol 1; Article 21 of the EU Charter of Fundamental Rights;[70] Article 2 of UN CROC; and Protocol No.12; also by Convention on the Elimination of All Forms of Discrimination against Women, the International Covenant on Civil and Political Rights and ICESCR; and Article 2 of the Lanzarote Convention.

Historical legacy of state-sponsored discrimination

In the CANZUS nations the most striking example of discrimination lies in the state's historical, egregious treatment of Indigenous children. In all four nations the record of prolonged, state-mandated child abuse, specifically aimed against Indigenous children, has caused intergenerational trauma and testifies to the extent to which the state has been in breach of Articles 2 and 3 of UN CROC. However, historical state-driven discriminatory child abuse has not been exclusively concerned with direct state action against the Indigenous communities: the record of extensive clerical abuse is evidence of an indirect state role as it failed to protect children from discriminatory abuse in all CANZUS nations. In France and Germany the record of historical state-mandated child abuse against Jewish children and others from minority groups during the Nazi period, while clearly preceding UN CROC, nonetheless must constitute a particularly perverse breach of this fundamental principle.

69 See, *Ineze v. Austria* 10 EHRR 394. Also, see, *Marckx v. Belgium*, Op. cit.

70 Charter of Fundamental Rights, Title III (Equality), includes articles 20 (equality before the law), 21 (non-discrimination) and 23 (equality between men and women).

Arguably, the fact that the age of criminal responsibility is set at ten and 12 years of age in England and Ireland, respectively, also constitutes a breach of this principle – as it criminalises the behaviour of children below the CRC recommended age limit of 14 years – and, to that extent, more so in England than in Ireland and also in Australia and some states in the U.S. where the age limit might be as low as seven years. Similarly with parental chastisement, the fact that physically chastising a child continues to be a legal parental prerogative in countries such as England, Northern Ireland, many states in the U.S. and in Australia is, arguably, discriminatory in relation to the children involved.

Cultural/religious discrimination

In England and Wales, the regulatory body, Ofsted, has found the gender differentiation practices in Muslim faith–based schools to be culturally affirmative but discriminatory. On the other hand, an inverted form of discrimination probably also occurs, if not intentionally, in educational settings when Roma children – and others such as Muslims – are assimilated into generalised classroom learning programmes without regard for cultural sensitivities. As regards Ireland, the CRC was 'deeply concerned' about 'the structural discrimination against Traveller and Roma children, including as regards their access to education, health and an adequate standard of living'.[71] Related issues often come before the Irish courts as a consequence of state intervention in the way of life of the Traveller community, and there is also evidence that their culture is treated adversely, particularly in schools.

In the U.S., a considerable body of caselaw has accumulated which upholds the policy of insulating public schools from religious influence.[72] Essentially, the caselaw affirms the parental right to act as the representative of their child, in relation to what the parent perceives as being the latter's welfare interests. This was endorsed in *Wisconsin v. Yoder*,[73] when the USSC ruled that Amish parents could not be compelled to send their children to high school when they had "deep religious convictions" for not doing so.[74] The ruling established a legal precedent legitimating the home-schooling of children which, in the second decade of the 21st century is escalating as parents, dissatisfied with the religious or sexual orientation and gender identity (SOGI) awareness content of teaching in the public education system – 'too much, too soon' – now opt to teach some 3.5 million

71 UN Committee on the Rights of the Child, Concluding Observations of the Committee on the combined third and fourth periodic reports of Ireland, 2016, at para 69.

72 *Edwards v. Aguillard*, 482 U.S. 578 (1987) invalidating mandatory teaching of creationism; *Stone v. Graham*, 449 U.S. 39 (1980), invalidating mandatory display of the Ten Commandments; *Epperson v. Arkansas*, 393 U.S. 97 (1968), invalidating prohibition on teaching evolution; *McCollum v. Board of Education*, 333 U.S. 203 (1948), prohibiting in-class sectarian religious instruction; and *Bd of Educ. of Kiryas Joel Village School District v. Grumet*, 512 U.S. 687, 705 (1994).

73 *Wisconsin v. Yoder*, Op. cit.

74 Ibid.

children at home. Interestingly, in *Hearn and United States* v. *Muskogee Public School District*,[75] which concerned a Muslim girl suspended twice from school for wearing a hijab as required by her faith, the court ruled that she was entitled to do so: the school authorities, by singling her out because of her Islamic faith, had intentionally discriminated against her. The court quoted from the ruling in *Lukumi* that "at a minimum, the protections of the Free Exercise Clause pertain if the law at issue discriminates against some or all religious beliefs".[76] In Canada, the fact that state-funded denominational schooling is constitutionally protected has not prevented litigation alleging discrimination, has given rise to expressions of concern from the UN Human Rights Committee. In 2005, when it published its Concluding Observations regarding Canada's fifth periodic report, it noted that Canada had failed to "adopt steps in order to eliminate discrimination on the basis of religion in the funding of schools in Ontario". In July 2015 the Committee repeated its concern regarding the persistence of religiously discriminating grounds for funding and for accessing public schools.[77] As in the U.S., there have been a number of school prayer cases in which the mandatory recitation of Christian prayers was found to discriminate against non-Christian pupils. In *Zylberberg v. Sudbury Board of Education (Director)*[78] and *Russow v. BC (AG)*,[79] the judiciary established that the compulsory recitation of the Lord's Prayer – to the exclusion of prayers from any other religion – constitutes an impermissible infringement of religious freedom. School curriculum content has also been controversial.[80]

In Australia in particular, but also in the other CANZUS nations, there is overwhelming evidence that Indigenous children are grossly over-represented in the child welfare and juvenile justice systems: systems that appear to operate in a manner that systemically discriminates against such children. Indeed, some official reports claim that direct discrimination by agency staff may be contributing to that over-representation.[81]

The CRC has drawn attention to the continuation of discrimination: in France, directed towards Roma children, their families and communities,[82] and in Germany, against 'children in disadvantaged situations including asylum-seeking, refugee and migrant children, Sinti, Roma and other children of minority groups, children with disabilities, LGBTI children and socio-economically disadvantaged

75 020, No Civ 03 598-S (E.D. Ok., 2003).

76 *Church of Lukumi Babalu Aye, Inc. v. City of Hialeah*, 508 U.S. 520 (1993), at p 532.

77 See UN International Covenant on Civil and Political Rights, *Concluding Observations on the Sixth Periodic Report of Canada*, http://tbinternet.ohchr.org/_layouts/treatybodyexternal/SessionDetails1.aspx?SessionID=899&Lang=en#sthash.XzzyC1Bz.dpuf

78 1988 CanLII 189 (ON CA).

79 1989 BCSC 2688.

80 See, for example: *Chamberlain v. Surrey School Board District 36* (2002), 221 D.L.R. (4th) 156 (SCC), (refusal of School Board to approve three controversial books depicting same-sex parented families).

81 See, for example, O'Halloran, K., *Children, the Law and the Welfare Principle: Perspectives from Australia and New Zealand*, Routledge, 2023, at chapters 9 and 10.

82 CRC/C/FRA/CO/5, (2016), at para 23.

children'.[83] In a landmark ECtHR ruling[84] concerning Muslim parents living in Switzerland who, in accordance with their religious beliefs, would not permit their daughters to attend compulsory mixed-sex swimming lessons, the Court acknowledged that the human rights of the parents were being interfered with but denied that this amounted to a violation. In an important judgment of general application, the Court focussed instead on the children's welfare interests and observed that

> the children's interest in a full education, facilitating their successful social integration according to local customs and norms, took precedence over the parents' wish to have their daughters exempted from mixed swimming lessons and that the children's interest in attending swimming lessons was not just to learn to swim, but above all to take part in that activity with all the other pupils, with no exception on account of the children's origin or their parents' religious or philosophical convictions.

The ECtHR unanimously found that the Swiss authorities had the right to facilitate "successful social integration according to local customs and mores", had behaved legitimately by "seeking to protect foreign pupils from any form of social exclusion," and that this took precedence over parents' preferences. By implication, the ruling also infers that school policy took precedence over a foreign pupil's 'right' to maintain their cultural/religious practice, which is difficult to square with the importance the ECtHR generally places on that 'right'.

Disability discrimination

When children with a disability are required to receive state educational services in school settings that are set apart from the mainstream and the children are treated differently than others in their peer group, this may well constitute discrimination: affirmative state intervention, intended to offset social disadvantage but thereby preferencing one group over others, has long been challenged as a form of discriminatory practice.[85] So, in France, the practice of separating children with mental or physical impairments from others in educational settings has been condemned by the CRC as 'persistent discrimination against children with disabilities'. In particular, it urged France 'to take immediate measures to ensure that the rights of children with autism, especially their right to inclusive education, are respected.'[86] More recently, the CRC has been similarly critical of Germany, recommending that the

83 CRC/C/DEU/CO/5-6, at para 15(a).

84 *Osmanoglu and Kocabas v. Switzerland,* Application No. 29086/12, (2017).

85 See, for example, *Grutter v. Bollinger* 539 U.S. 306 (2003) and Laycock, D., *'The Broader Case for Affirmative Action: Desegregation, Academic Excellence, and Future Leadership',* 78 Tulane Law Review 1767 (2004).

86 CRC/C/FRA/CO/5, at para 57.

root causes of discrimination be addressed 'with a view to eliminating discrimination against . . . children with disabilities'.[87]

Disability discrimination in New Zealand is also an issue as evidenced by the findings of a 2008 Select Committee Inquiry, a 2013 Ministry of Health report and media investigations.

Core child-care needs: jurisdictional differences and related public service provision

As new areas of social need emerge (internet abuse, mass migration, etc.) and traditional areas such as health evolve to produce new problems (gender identity, genetic editing, etc.) so the public service response has to be more complex, flexible and joined-up. For present purposes, consideration focuses on the range of public services that more directly impact children (e.g. child protection) rather than those that do so indirectly (e.g. housing) and on services that affect the majority (e.g. education) rather than a minority (e.g. gender transitioning).

Jurisdictional differences and their significance: protection

The traditional legal function of 'protection' forms the bedrock of the law governing the rights and welfare interests of children in all jurisdictions while the modern concepts of equality and non-discrimination (and human rights in general) establish a contemporary operational context.

Child's rights: protection

UN CROC, Article 19, requires States Parties to take all appropriate measures

> to protect the child from all forms of physical or mental violence, injury or abuse, neglect or negligent treatment, maltreatment or exploitation, including sexual abuse, while in the care of parent(s), legal guardian(s) or any other person who has the care of the child.

In England and Wales, the authorities were found to have breached Articles 3 (prohibition of inhuman or degrading treatment) and 13 (right to an effective remedy) when – despite receiving reports of child abuse or of being in possession of information that should have alerted them to the risk of such abuse – they failed to promptly institute protective measures.[88] The consequent launching of the Adoption and Children Act 2002 introduced the paramountcy principle and marked a firmer policy towards the protection of children at risk of significant harm. Areas

87 CRC/C/DEU/CO/5-6, at para 15(a).

88 *Z and Others v. the United Kingdom*, Application No. 29392/95, (2001), *TP and KM v. UK* [2001] 2 FLR 549 and *E and Others v. the United Kingdom*, Application No. 33218/96, (2002). See, also, *O'Keeffe v. Ireland* [GC], Application No. 35810/09, (2014).

of weakness in this nation's child protection measures might include the lack of a mandatory public reporting requirement in respect of known or suspected instances of child abuse/neglect, the lack of a prohibition on parental chastisement in England and Northern Ireland and the absence of safe havens to provide protection for child victims of parental abandonment. In Ireland, following a damning series of official reports detailing historical child abuse suffered by many children in state care facilities, the child protection system was overhauled with a new nationwide agency – Tusla – established and constitutional amendments were initiated including one in 2012 that strengthened children's rights. Article 42A requires the best interests of a child to be the paramount consideration in all child protection proceedings including adoption, guardianship, custody and access. This was extended to child protection proceedings by an amendment to the Child Care Act 1991, s 24. The ECtHR in *O'Keefe v. Ireland*[89] found the Irish child protection threshold to be inadequate: the mere risk of abuse, rather than actual abuse, should trigger a duty to intervene; and not to do so violated Article 3 of the ECHR. The Irish judicial view now is that Article 42A has lowered the bar to permit,[90] and indeed to require, state intervention at an early stage.[91]

In the U.S., the Constitution as interpreted by the USSC, requires a state to show compelling reason for infringing rights of family privacy and for overriding parental autonomy[92] as these fundamental liberties are protected by the Fourteenth Amendment and its guarantee of due process.[93] As late as 1989, the USSC[94] was able to make a finding that the government was not obliged to protect its citizens against harm inflicted by private individuals, but by the turn of the century, in a significant change of policy, a separate focus on child protection took shape specifying grounds for coercive state intervention in family affairs.[95] The Keeping Children and Families Safe Act 2003 channelled the flow of federal funding towards designated aspects of child abuse and neglect, and the federal government sought to steer states into implementing a national strategy focusing on prioritising the protection of specified aspects of children's welfare interests. The Family First legislation placed an onus on HSS to increase intervention aimed at supporting failing parental care rather than at peremptorily rescuing children at risk. However, it continues to be the case that the rate of state intervention in families on child protection grounds is considerably higher in the U.S. than elsewhere (approximately 7.4 per 1,000 of children are in the public care system compared, for example, with 4.7 per 1,000 in England[96]). It is probable that the child protection threshold

89 Application No. 35810/09, (2014).

90 See, for example, *TR v. Child and Family Agency* [2017] IEHC 595.

91 See, *In the Matter of JJ* [2021] IESC 1.

92 *Santosky v. Kramer*, 455 U.S. 745 (1982).

93 *Meyer v. Nebraska*, 262 U.S. 390 (1923), *Stanley v. Illinois*, 405 U.S. 645 (1972) and *Wisconsin v. Yoder*, 406 U.S. 205 (1972).

94 *DeShaney v. Winnebago County Social Services*, 489 U.S. 189 (1989).

95 Including the Child Abuse, Domestic Violence, Adoption, and Family Services Act 1992.

96 See, further, data published by the Performance and Innovation Unit (UK), 2000.

in the U.S. is set quite low and that, as Vreeland alleges, parental poverty, rather than parental neglect or abuse, triggers coercive state intervention.[97] Curiously, at 8.2 per 1,000 , Canada has an even higher rate of admissions. In 2022, there were more than 63,000 Canadian children in foster care, representing a higher rate of care admissions than in most other developed nations. Moreover, the 2016 National Census revealed that although Indigenous children comprised only 7.7% of all Canadian children, they constituted 52% of the foster care population. Judging from the annual numbers of children admitted to the public care system, it would seem that Canadian thresholds are not only lower than in the U.S. but are lower than most other developed nations.

State intervention in family affairs on child protection grounds has a troubled history in Australia as explained in the report on the forcible removal of Indigenous children[98] from their families, communities and culture for adoption by white Caucasian strangers and the later report on the babies relinquished by their single mothers[99] as a consequence of unfair enducement or pressure, both involving the uprooting of hundreds of thousands of children. Moreover, in addition to the historical record of unwarranted state intervention in Indigenous families, the contemporary record shows that such intervention continues to disproportionately affect them: Indigenous[100] and Māori[101] children are grossly over-represented in their respective public care and justice systems; and most Indigenous and Māori children entering the public care system are admitted not because of harm wilfully inflicted but because of neglect due to environmental factors. In New Zealand, the rates of domestic violence, of child abuse and of teenage suicides – among the highest in the developed world – point to serious failure on the part of the state to adequately protect its children.

In France, the adequacy of state child protection was a matter of concern to the CRC in its 2023 report when it recommended that urgent measures must be taken in respect of abuse and neglect and sexual exploitation and abuse.[102] In its 2022 report on Germany, 'the high prevalence of violence against children, including sexual exploitation and online violence'[103] was a matter of 'serious concern'. It also recommended that 'the State Party take all measures to eliminate child marriage, including forced and religious marriages' and 'strengthen measures aimed at preventing

97 Vreeland, A.B. 'The Criminalization of Child Welfare in New York City: Sparing the Child or Spoiling the Family?', *Fordham Urban Law Journal*, Vol. 27, No. 3, pp 1053–1103, 2000.

98 See, the Australian Human Rights Commission, *Bringing Them Home Report*, 1997, https://humanrights.gov.au/our-work/bringing-them-home-report-1997

99 See, Senate Community Affairs References Committee, *Commonwealth Contribution to Former Forced Adoption Policies and Practices*, Canberra, Commonwealth of Australia, 2012.

100 See, further, www.aihw.gov.au/reports/child-protection/child-protection-australia-2020-21/contents/children-receiving-child-protection-services/aboriginal-and-torres-strait-islander-children-in-the-child-protection-system

101 See, further, www.rnz.co.nz/news/national/393208/oranga-tamariki-stats-increase-in-maori-children-taken

102 CRC/C/FRA/CO/6-7, at paras 26 and 28.

103 CRC/C/DEU/CO/5-6, at para 21.

female genital mutilation'.[104] It expressed concern about 'the increasing numbers of children living in alternative care and, in particular, in closed institutions'.[105]

The jurisdictional differences in state intervention in families on child protection grounds are quite striking. These sometimes vary within the same country: in Australia the number of children coming into state care in June 2021 was almost double the number in 2000–2011;[106] while in New Zealand during the period 2009–10 to 2018–19 the corresponding number decreased by 33.6%, despite the much higher than average national statistics indicating abnormal levels of child-related concerns. They may also vary between countries: for example, the rate of child incarceration in the U.S. is said to be more than nine times that in Germany (693 per 100,000 versus 76 per 100,000);[107] baby hatches are available in all states in the U.S., but not in the UK nor in New Zealand, despite the latter having one of the highest rates of domestic violence and child abuse in the world; while the Canadian province of Manitoba in 2011 had an admission to care rate ten times that of Western Australia.[108] They can also highlight singular jurisdictional characteristics such as the reliance on institutions rather than foster care in Germany.

Jurisdictional differences and their significance: health

Parents have a clear legal duty to ensure that their child's health is protected and are required to do so by availing of relevant public services when their child is in need of healthcare.

Child's rights: health

UN CROC, Article 24, provides for a child to have the right to enjoy the highest attainable standard of health and to be protected from violence and neglect. Article 24(2) specifically requires States Parties to address the issue of infant mortality. Articles 6, 18(3), 26, 27(1)-(3) and 33 are also relevant. The Convention is reinforced by the International Covenant on Economic, Social and Cultural Rights.

In England and Wales, as in Ireland, health services are proactive in protecting the health of children and promoting their welfare by, for example, the domiciliary visits of health visitors and district nurses in respect of very young children and by conducting regular opthalmic and dental monitoring and treatment programmes. Again, in both, the courts have consistently upheld the right and duty

104 Ibid, at para 24.
105 Ibid, at para 26.
106 See, Australian Institute of Health and Welfare, www.aihw.gov.au/child-protection/
107 See, The Crime Report, 2018, https://thecrimereport.org/2018/04/10/in-germany-its-hard-to-find-a-young-adult-in-prison/
108 See, Brownell, M.D. and Jutte, D.P., 'Administrative Data Linkage as a Tool for Child Maltreatment Research', *Child Abuse & Neglect*, Vol. 37, No. 2, 2013, at pp 120–124.

of authorities to intervene when parental refusal or neglect in relation to health and safety matters jeopardises the life of their child. It is possible that free access to treatment, through the NHS, incentivises parents in England and Wales to avail of non-stigmatising child welfare services to a greater extent than their Irish counterparts and probable that the opposite is the case in relation to availing of family planning services, access to which in Ireland may be subject to the religious beliefs of service providers.

In the U.S., a 2022 report warned that 'the U.S. child welfare system is falling short because of persistent child poverty'[109] and warns that there is a significant level of poor mental health among American children.[110] Another 2022 report[111] found that of all 38 countries surveyed in 2020, the U.S. had the highest infant mortality rate at 5.4 deaths per 1,000 live births, and the highest maternal mortality which was over three times the rate in most of the other high-income countries. The U.S. simultaneously spends most on healthcare and produces the worst results.[112] According to Children's Health Fund, at a minimum, 20.3 million children in the U.S. (28% of all children) faced barriers to accessing essential health care in 2016. Further, the findings of a 2022 report show that 'after the onset of the pandemic specifically, there were significant year-over-year increases in children's diagnosed behavioural or conduct problems, decreases in preventive medical care visits, increases in unmet health care needs'.[113] Given this evidence, it would seem fair comment that the healthcare of children in the U.S., like so much else, is very much left to market forces meaning that access to adequate healthcare for many children in the poorest families – who need it most – is unavailable.

In Canada child healthcare is, if to a lesser extent, also very dependent upon market forces. The fact that in 2020 an international body ranked Canada 30th out of 38 affluent countries for childhood well-being, would seem a troubling indictment of public health and social care provision for children. There would appear to be a strong health and wealth correlation in Canada; children in the poorer communities, especially the Indigenous, are the unhealthiest.[114] In Canada as in the U.S., both being governed by social determinants, the health and welfare interests of children are very much tied to parental socio-economic status.

109 See, further, https://theconversation.com/us-child-welfare-system-is-falling-short-because-of-persistent-child-poverty-180543

110 See, Lebrun-Harris, L.A., Ghandour, R.M. and Kogan, M.C., 'Five-Year Trends in US Children's Health and Well-Being, 2016–2020', *JAMA Pediatrics*, Vol. 176, No. 7, 2022, https://jamanetwork.com/journals/jamapediatrics/fullarticle/2789946

111 See, further, www.commonwealthfund.org/publications/issue-briefs/2023/jan/us-health-care-global-perspective-2022

112 See, further, at: https://www.ajmc.com/view/us-has-highest-infant-maternal-mortality-rates-despite-the-most-health-care-spending

113 See, Lebrun-Harris, L.A., Ghandour, R.M. and Kogan, M.C., Op. cit.

114 See, for example, Raphael D., 'The Health of Canada's Children. Part I: Canadian Children's Health in Comparative Perspective', *Pediatrics Child Health*, Vol. 15, No. 1, pp 23–29, 2010.

Research has shown that 'there are clear inequities in vulnerable children's health service utilisation in Australia'.[115] A 2012 report by the Australian Institute of Family Studies had shown that despite the high rate of childhood poverty, strategies to improve service accessibility for vulnerable families were inadequate.[116] This indeed had also been of concern to the CRC in 2012 when it then reiterated its previous recommendation[117]

> that the State party undertake all necessary measures to ensure that all children enjoy the same access to and quality of health services with special attention to children in vulnerable situations, especially Indigenous children and children living in remote areas. It further urges the State party to address socio-economic disadvantages, which constitute important root causes for the existing health deficits.[118]

More positively, the Children's Health Australia has led the development of charters for Australian and New Zealand children, tailored to the cultural needs of children in each country. In New Zealand, the infant mortality rate is higher than the OECD average,[119] and in 2018–19 an estimated 20% of children missed out on primary care services, while the highest hospitalisation rates in under-15-year-olds were observed for children living in areas with the highest deprivation scores. That correlation between high hospitalisation rates and areas of high deprivation was of concern to the Child Poverty Monitor which recommended state intervention to promote 'equitable distribution of resources within society and explicit commitment and action to achieve health equity for Māori'.[120]

While neither France nor Germany can be said to be wholly compliant with Article 24 – probably no country is – the rates of infant mortality have been high in France, though now much improved,[121] while Germany would seem to have a

115 See, Bull, C., et al., 'Inequities in Vulnerable Children's Access to Health Services in Australia', *BMJ Global Health*, Vol. 7, No. 3, 2022, www.ncbi.nlm.nih.gov/pmc/articles/PMC8961130/

116 See, Robinson, E., Scott, D. and Meredith, V., *Good and Innovative Practice in Service Delivery to Vulnerable and Disadvantaged Families and Children*, Canberra, Australian Institute of Family Studies, 2012.

117 Citing, CRC/C/15/Add.268, at para 48.

118 See, CRC/c/AUS/CO/4, Op. cit., at para 60.

119 See, OECD, *Infant Mortality Report 2020*, www.oecd.org/els/family/CO_1_1_Infant_mortality.pdf

120 See, The Child Poverty Monitor, p 4, https://ourarchive.otago.ac.nz/bitstream/handle/10523/10585/CPM_2020_TECHNICAL%20REPORT.pdf?sequence=6&isAllowed=y

121 See, Blondel, B. Durox, M. and Zeitlin, J., 'How Perinatal Health in France Compared With Other European Countries in 2015: Some Progress But Also Some Concerns About Newborn Health', *Journal of Gynecology Obstetrics and Human Reproduction,* Vol. 48, pp 437–439, 2019. According to the 2015 Euro-Peristat database, that includes 33 European countries, France was 14th for the rate of prematurity, 22nd for the stillbirth rate (3 per 1,000) and 22nd for the neonatal mortality considering live born children (2.4 per 1,000).

modern and efficient health system that caters adequately and appropriately for the healthcare needs of its children.[122] It is probable that neither country is fully achieving the requirement in Article 24(3) that they 'take all effective and appropriate measures with a view to abolishing traditional practices prejudicial to the health of children'. In particular, the practice of female genital mutilation is proving difficult to restrain in all developed nations.

Disability

UN CROC, Article 23, requires States Parties to ensure that a mentally or physically disabled child enjoys a full and decent life, in conditions which provide dignity, promote self-reliance and facilitate the child's active participation in the community. This is reinforced by the Convention on the Rights of Persons with Disabilities, Article 24, which affirms that State parties must ensure access to education to every child with a disability.[123]

In England and Wales a family with a child that has a disability is defined as a 'family in need' for the purposes of the 1989 Act. A local authority is then required to undertake a needs assessment in respect of family and child and is specifically required to provide appropriate social care support services. In Ireland, similar statutory duties to identify and assess rest on Tusla, though the delivery of services may well be carried out by voluntary organisations. The Ombudsman for Children's Office has expressed concern about the lack of adequate respite services available for children overall and more specifically for children in care with disabilities.[124]

In the U.S., the Individuals with Disabilities Education Act (IDEA) 2004 provides that all children with disabilities are entitled to a free appropriate public education to meet their unique needs and prepare them for further education, employment and independent living. In Canada, as has been pointed out: the service response to children and youth with disabilities is often not sufficient to meet their needs.[125]

In Australia, the final report of *The Royal Commission, into Violence, Abuse, Neglect and Exploitation of People with Disability* – established in 2019 – was published in 2023.[126] Among its 222 recommendations, those with relevance for children and which have since been championed by Children and Young People

122 See, Nolte, E., et al., 'Neonatal and Postneonatal Mortality in Germany Since Unification', *Journal of Epidemiology and Community Health*, Vol. 54, pp. 84–90, 2000 where it is reported that 'In both parts of Germany, infant mortality rates improved after unification'.

123 See, also, The EU Commission, *The Strategy on the Rights of Persons with Disabilities 2021–2030*, https://ec.europa.eu/social/main.jsp?catId=1484&langId=en

124 Ombudsman for Children's Office, *Molly Two Years On: Have Tusla and the HSE Delivered on Commitments to Children with a Disability in the Care of the State?* 2020, at p 5, www.oco.ie/app/uploads/2020/01/Molly-Two-Years-On.pdf

125 Gough, P., et al., 'An Overview of the Child Welfare Systems in Canada', *International Journal of Child Health and Human Development*, Vol. 2, No. 3, pp 357–372, at p 367, 2009.

126 See, further, https://disability.royalcommission.gov.au/publications/final-report

with Disability Australia[127] call for an end to segregated education and employment and the elimination of all restrictive practices against children and young people with disability. In New Zealand, disability policy has always been problematic, resting initially on eugenics and, until the early years of this century, on institutionalisation. Children with disabilities are much more exposed to this country's abnormally high incidence of domestic violence than other children.[128]

In France, while integration in mainstream schooling is legally facilitated, and the number of disabled pupils attending is said to have increased by 34% since 2017,[129] nonetheless it is reported that thousands of children with disabilities are unable to attend school due to a shortage of classroom support services.[130] This was a matter of concern to the CRC in its 2023 report.[131] A non-means-tested state benefit of almost 1,000 euros per month is payable to anyone with a disability. In Germany, the policy is to provide special educational support so as to enable children and young people with disabilities to exercise their right to a form of schooling, training and education tailored to their personal capabilities and needs. This form of support is not restricted to an educational context but extends to employment and to general participation in society in order to maximise the opportunity to live as independent a life as possible. Accessing services can be complicated in Germany, due to a heavy reliance on bureaucracy and to the relative independence of the *Länder.* In its 2022 report, the CRC recommended that Germany 'streamline all support for children with disabilities into one body, such as child and youth support services, with a view to ensuring that all children with disabilities have equal access to benefits'.[132] In response, the recently reformed Protection of Young Persons Act now includes further provisions that will end the practice of segregation by introducing a rule that children with and without disabilities are to be cared for together in child day care and other Youth Welfare facilities.

In respect of health matters overall, it is hard to escape the conclusion from the above data, that on this – the most basic indicator of child welfare – the wealthiest nations are failing the most children.

127 See, further, https://cyda.org.au

128 See, Simpson, K., Yeong, P. and Munford, R., 'Responses to Abuse, Neglect, and Trauma of Children with Intellectual Disability', *Aotearoa New Zealand Social Work,* Vol. 34, No. 1, pp 72–87, 2022.

129 See, speech given by French Minister Delegate for Persons with Disabilities, New York, June 13, 2023, https://onu.delegfrance.org/respecting-the-fundamental-rights-of-persons-with-disabilities-is-a-duty

130 See, further, https://easpd.eu/press-releases-detail/no-school-for-thousands-of-children-with-disabilities-in-france/

131 CRC/C/FRA/CO/6-7, at para 36.

132 CRC/C/DEU/CO/5-6, at para 29(a).

Jurisdictional differences and their significance: education

The responsibility to ensure that their child is educated to an appropriate standard is among the core parental duties: in most cases this is achieved through mandatory school attendance; in some instances home-schooling is permitted.

Child's rights: education

UN CROC, Articles 18(2), 28 and 29 require States Parties to ensure a child's right to access education. This is reinforced by the International Covenant on Economic, Social and Cultural Rights. The right is available to all children, including migrant minors.

In England and Wales, as in Ireland, the state education system imposes a strict statutory duty on parents to ensure that a child of compulsory school age – 5 to 16 years of age – attends an authorised school, unless parents have been granted permission to provide home-schooling. In Ireland, state education remains mainly faith based, very largely Catholic in nature and perpetuates a Catholic religious ethos aided by the fact that all teacher training colleges are denominational. Some 97% of primary schools and perhaps 50% of secondary schools are state funded but managed by religious organisations: 90% of all primary schools are controlled by the Catholic Church.[133] To that extent, it may be that the state education system could be said to be not wholly compliant with the welfare interests of children who need to be attuned to the broad social mores of contemporary society.

The relationship between parents, the state, and the welfare of children – in the context of education – generates contention in many countries and certainly does so in both Canada and the U.S. (as in all CANZUS nations and Ireland) where the legacy of residential schools stand as a reminder of how those relationships can become distorted by the state and adversely impact the welfare of children. In recent years that relationship has perhaps attracted most judicial attention in the U.S. – with more weight being given to parental interests – than in any other common law nation.[134] Currently, echoes of clashes generated by religious belief and the culture wars now reverberate throughout the classrooms of both countries[135] though, again, more so in the U.S. where a considerable body of caselaw has accumulated which upholds the policy of insulating public schools from religious influence.[136] Many parents, here as elsewhere, challenge the content of sex and health education programmes for young children, claiming that material dealing with

133 Op. cit.

134 See, for example, *Myer v. Nebraska*, 262 U.S. 390 (1923), at 399–400, *Pierce v. Society of Sisters*, 268 U.S. 510 (1925), at 534–535 and *Wisconsin v. Yoder*, U.S. 205, 214, 219 (1972).

135 See, for example, in the U.S., *Peloza v. Capistrano Unified School Dist.*, 37 F. 3d 517 (9th Cir. 1994) and in Canada, *SL v. Commission scolaire des Chênes* [2012] 1 SCR 235.

136 *Edwards v. Aguillard*, 482 U.S. 578 (1987) invalidating mandatory teaching of creationism; *Stone v. Graham*, 449 U.S. 39 (1980), invalidating mandatory display of the Ten Commandments; *Epperson v. Arkansas*, 393 U.S. 97 (1968), invalidating prohibition on teaching evolution; *McCollum v. Board of Education*, 333 U.S. 203 (1948), prohibiting in-class sectarian religious instruction; and *Bd of Educ. of Kiryas Joel Village School District v. Grumet*, 512 U.S. 687, 705 (1994).

SOGI and LGBT awareness, or with trans issues, exposes children to "too much, too soon" information and ideology, without effective opt-out opportunities.[137]

In Australia, in keeping with evidence pointing to investment in the early years educational programmes as a strategy that can do much to break the cycle of deprivation,[138] there has been some movement towards promoting such programmes at both state and Commonwealth levels.[139] However, while state-subsidised early intervention programs must boost access to education and increase the likelihood of positive outcomes, thereby generating better employment opportunities, even if they were embedded in all disadvantaged communities in Australia – which they are not – this would be insufficient in itself. Improving the welfare interests of children, particularly of Indigenous children and in the many other families stuck in systemic poverty, requires a stepladder of state intervention programs to ease access and provide support right through from 'breakfast clubs' to third-level education. In New Zealand non-school attendance would seem to be a significant issue, and this is concerning as it is a common factor in juvenile crime. It has been noted that 'almost 50% of young people in New Zealand who offend are not enrolled, are excluded, suspended or simply not attending school'.[140] In short, if under-achievement at school is a predictor of probable under-achievement in later life, then education is proving not to be a route out of poverty for many, among whom Māori – like the Indigenous children in Australia – are over-represented.

The CRC in its 2023 report on France[141] welcomed in particular the creation of the post of Secretary of State for Children but recommended that the state 'improve accessibility and the quality of education for children in disadvantaged and marginalised situations, including Roma children, migrant children, children living in precarious housing'.[142] In Germany, free but mandatory schooling is available for all children, from 6 to 14 years of age, including migrant minors. As might be expected, following the influx of migrants and more recently of refugees from Ukraine, the German social facilities – including schools – are stretched to capacity. Schooling has proven to be the most effective way of socialising children; it is a crucial means for promoting social inclusion and acts as a gateway to employment and social stability. It is also very often the juncture at which social tensions on community issues can become apparent. This has always been evident in relation to religion, more recently as regards LGBT and SOGI matters, and is currently

137 See, Morrar, S., 'Too Much, Too Soon: Families Rally at Capitol Against Sex Education and LGBT Curriculum', *The Sacramento Bee*, March 28, 2019, www.sacbee.com/news/local/education/article228532414.html (accessed April 24, 2019)

138 Ibid, at para 11.72.

139 Examples include the Victorian Government's *Best Start Strategy*, the *Families First Strategy* in New South Wales, Tasmania's *Together* strategy, Queensland's *Families: Future Directions* and the Commonwealth's *Stronger Families and Communities Strategy*.

140 See, Judge John Walker, Principal Youth Court Judge for New Zealand, *When the Vulnerable Offend – Whose Fault is It? Address to Northern Territory Council of Social Services Conference*, September 27, 2017, www.districtcourts.govt.nz/youth-court/publications/when-the-vulnerable-offend-whose-fault-is-it/

141 CRC/C/FRA/CO/6-7, https://juridique.defenseurdesdroits.fr/doc_num.php?explnum_id=21661

142 CRC/C/FRA/CO/6-7, at para 43.

noticeable in relation to asylum seekers/refugees/migrant minors. While schools in some nations – Ireland and the UK – have struggled to accommodate large numbers of children from disparate cultures, often on a transitory basis, it is remarkable that national education systems have on the whole responded so well to the challenge which must contribute significantly to securing the welfare interests of very many children.

Jurisdictional differences and their significance: employment

Children and employment may appear to be largely mutually exclusive, at least in the contemporary societies of the developed nations. In fact, though perceived as peripheral by children, stable employment is clearly often crucial if parents are to safeguard their child's welfare interests and may well also be of direct relevance to such a child should the child be employed part-time while at school or full time on leaving it at age 16 years.

Child's rights: employment

UN CROC, Article 32, addresses the conditions on which a child may be employed. These include factors such as their age, parental permission, hours of working, wages and safety of working environment. In 2021, when the UN declared the UN International Year for the Elimination of Child Labour, it might have seemed that such concerns were about to become redundant. This has not proven to be the case.

In England and Wales, as children are legally required to continue education until the age of 16 years, the terms and conditions of full time employment only become relevant at that age when they are legally restricted to 'light work'. In Ireland, the laws applying to mandatory education and the working conditions of 16- to 18-year-old children are much the same as in the UK, though the cultural context is different. A 2023 national referendum rejected the Irish government's proposal to replace Article 41.2 of the Constitution which declares that 'by her life within the home a woman gives to the State a support without which the common good cannot be achieved,' and guarantees to protect mothers from having to work outside the home 'to the neglect of her duties within the home'. This gender stereotyping – a cultural anomaly – which must act as a constraint on mothers who wish to pursue a career and is not in keeping with practice in other developed societies, is unlikely to promote the welfare interests of children but has been retained as a constitutional provision.

In the U.S., federal legislative benchmarks for the employment of children were first established by the Fair Labor Standards Act 1938 which continue in effect, setting out protective measures in respect of children aged 16 years or younger, to ensure that employment opportunities do not subvert their education, and to prohibit forms of employment that would jeopardise their health and safety. However, Human Rights Watch has expressed concern regarding the current health and safety conditions of child employment in the U.S. agricultural industry including that 'child farmworkers as young as 12 years old often work for hire for 10 or more hours a day, five to seven days a week . . . some start working part-time at age 6 or 7'.[143] In Canada, the federal Canada Labour Standards Regulations 2013, as amended and as largely replicated throughout the provinces, state that persons under 17 years of age may be employed provided that they are not required by provincial law to attend school; the work is not likely to endanger their health or safety; they are not required to work underground in a mine or in employment prohibited for young workers; and they are not required to work between 11 p.m. on one day and 6 a.m. on the following day. Again, however, Human Rights Watch has expressed concern: drawing attention to the fact that Canada has not taken action to eliminate the overseas practice of employing child labour – at exploitive rates of pay while working long hours in poor workplace conditions – to produce products that feed into the Canadian consumer chain.

In Australia, the employment of children under the age of 15 years is not unusual, though employers need a licence. The terms and conditions of employment vary according to the age of the child, the type of work and education commitments. Given that the highest proportion of those living below the poverty line are in households where the main income earner is unemployed, work opportunities for older children can be important. According to the ACOSS 2022 report,[144] although this country has experienced sustained economic growth for the past 30 years, poverty is also growing, facts which are difficult to reconcile in a modern democracy and which may place undue pressure on children to contribute to family income. In New Zealand, the 2015 report to the CRC noted that 'New Zealand's consistent approach to children's employment is that our existing policies and legislative framework provides effective age thresholds for entry to work in general, and for safe work'.[145] The socio-economic context is not unlike that of Australia in that as of 2022, although the rate of unemployment – 3.2% – was at an all-time low, nonetheless the Ministry of Social Development's Child Poverty Report for 2022 showed that one in ten children are growing up in material hardship[146] which, again, may put pressure on children to find employment: either outside compulsory school hours or to do so by leaving school at age 16 years.

In France, as in other EU countries, minors are allowed to work from 16 years of age with parental consent, working hours are strictly regulated by law, night work is prohibited and minors between 14 and 16 years of age are allowed to do "light work". The 2021 announcement to the ILO of France's intention to become a 'pioneer country' in the elimination of child forced labour proved to be over-ambitious. The constant flux of undocumented and transient migrant minors, in need of temporary employment in order to maintain a subsistence standard of

143 See, Human Rights Watch, *Fields of Peril: Child Labor in U.S. Agriculture and US: Child Farmworkers Dangerous Lives*, www.hrw.org/news/2010/05/05/us-child-farmworkers-dangerous-lives

144 See, Australian Council of Social Service, *One in Eight People in Australia are Living in Poverty*, www.acoss.org.au/media_release/one-in-eight-people-in-australia-are-living-in-poverty/

145 See, UN CRC, 5th Periodic Report, 2015, at para 228.

146 See, further, www.msd.govt.nz/documents/about-msd-and-our-work/publications-resources/research/child-poverty-in-nz/2022-child-poverty-report-overview-and-selected-findings.pdf

living but vulnerable to exploitation under threat of exposure to the authorities, is such as to make effective regulatory intervention virtually impossible. In Germany, children of compulsory school age (younger than 14 years of age) are prohibited from being employed, and the conditions of employment for those aged 15 to 18 years are tightly regulated. The sub-contracting of production to countries where child labour is utilised is a less tangible and more difficult problem to address. In January 2023 the federal government introduced the Supply Chain Act which sets minimum human rights standards in the supply chains of major companies, and while it should help protect many children it suffers from serious limitations. As Human Rights Watch points out: it is only applicable to large companies with 1,000 or more employees; and it is only binding on immediate suppliers, not those further down the supply chain, where the most serious child labour violations often occur.[147]

In all jurisdictions considered, the employment of children is subject to layers of international and domestic law, and yet in all there is cause for concern regarding the exploitation of children in an employment context. There are perhaps two main reasons for this. First, there is the level of poverty that subsists in these leading developed nations: despite their wealth, there would seem to be a lack of political will to generate the initiatives necessary to ensure that public services are sufficiently resourced to cope with families in need and protect the welfare interests of their children; so the latter are often in employment in order to supplement family income, and their needs may often be overlooked by one or both parents who, despite being in full time employment, are unable to cope with the upwardly spiralling cost of living. Second, the problems of child trafficking, modern slavery and exploitation have been greatly exacerbated by the current volume and transient nature of unaccompanied minor migrants seeking opportunities for a more secure life. The tens of thousands of children that constitute this phenomenon are preyed upon by organised gangs on both sides of the Atlantic and exploited for many purposes including cheap labour. For so long as the wealthy democracies are prepared to accommodate systemic poverty but are unprepared to fund the public services necessary to mitigate its effects, it is difficult to see how this situation can improve.

Jurisdictional differences and their significance: Indigenous

The most conspicuous and shared characteristic of the child welfare and juvenile justice systems of the CANZUS nations is the gross and consistent over-representation of Indigenous children compulsorily placed therein. Needless to say, this must be largely attributed to a common legacy of initial colonial

147 See, further, www.hrw.org/news/2021/06/08/germany-child-labor-rising-covid-19-supply-chain-law-even-more-urgent

abuse and cultural subjugation followed by generations of discrimination and marginalisation.

Child's rights: Indigenous

The UNDRIP and the UN CROC form the main axis of internationally recognised protective rights for the welfare/rights of their children, but other international laws are also relevant as are bodies such as the Inter-American Court of Human Rights. UN CROC, Articles 17, 29 and 30, expressly requires States Parties to respect the rights of Indigenous people – including children – so also does the International Covenant on Economic, Social and Cultural Rights, Article 12, as developed by the CRC in General comment No. 11 (2009) *Indigenous children and their rights under the Convention [on the Rights of the Child]*.[148]

Children in the Indigenous communities of the CANZUS nations are often chronically disadvantaged. In part this may be attributed to jurisdictional slippage between federal and regional governments in responsibility for funding the necessary services. In both the U.S. and Canada long-standing problems have obstructed tribal access to federal funding allowing the wealth disparity between high- and low-income families to reach a level of structural inequality, insufficiently offset by public service provision, which must exacerbate child welfare issues. A strong argument can be made that the over-representation of Indigenous children across all indices of social disadvantage – perhaps particularly in the child welfare and juvenile justice systems – is attributable in good part to their under-representation as recipients of government preventative services. Such over-representation provides a stark measure of failed preventative state intervention and evidence of a reliance instead on containing the effects of social dysfunction rather than on a willingness to promote the welfare of children.[149]

The Indigenous people of the CANZUS nations are still relatively distinct cultural communities which, to a varying degree, continue to be coherent entities founded on rules, traditions and beliefs that govern relations within and between families and apply to the functioning of their social system as a whole. They differ from the societies of their westernised hosts in many ways, not least in the respective sets of laws and customs that govern the family.

For the American Indians and Alaskan Native (AI/AN) of the U.S., the principle of tribal sovereignty has been of central importance and has featured in many

148 CRC/C/DEU1.CRC/C/GC/11 (February 12, 2009). Also, see: the International Convention on the Elimination of All Forms of Racial Discrimination, 1965; the International Covenant on Civil and Political Rights, 1966; the International Covenant on Economic, Social and Cultural Rights, 1966; and the International Labour Organization Convention No. 169 concerning Indigenous and Tribal Peoples in Independent Countries, 1989; and the UN Declaration on the Rights of Indigenous Peoples, 2007.

149 See, further, https://quintechildrenshomes.com/foster-care-statistics-in-canada/

treaties. So, for example, in *Worcester v. Georgia*,[150] Justice Marshall found that "Indian nations have always been recognized as distinct, independent, political communities" and are, as such, "qualified to exercise powers of self – government, not by virtue of any delegation of powers from the Federal Government, but by reason of their original tribal sovereignty".[151] In practice, however, sovereignty has proven to be largely illusionary, as demonstrated by the numbers of AI/AN children in the care and justice systems of the U.S., and matters are no better north of the border. In Canada, children of the First Nations – the Inuit, Métis and others – have been the subject of several official reports. In its 2015 report, the Truth and Reconciliation Commission set out a series of measures for reducing the over-representation of Indigenous children within child welfare systems, while in 2019 the Viens Commission concluded that systemic discrimination existed against First Nations and a youth protection system that placed Indigenous children with non-Indigenous foster families was inappropriate. That same year, the National Inquiry into Missing and Murdered Indigenous Women and Girls made several recommendations also aimed at placing the design and implementation of culturally appropriate child and family services in the hands of Indigenous peoples as part of the exercise of their right to self-determination. Whether the autonomy promised the First Nations will prove to be any more real than that promised the AI/AN remains to be seen.

In Australia, the concept of 'tribal sovereignty' is not mentioned in the Constitution nor are Indigenous people given any form of recognition in it, and its relevance was summarily dismissed by the High Court of Australia on the basis that Aboriginal claims to sovereignty were not "justiciable".[152] In contrast to the approach taken in the other CANZUS nations, in Australia there has been no real devolution of authority to tribal leaders and in the absence of any legal status conferred on the Indigenous people in the Constitution or by treaty, it would appear that as regards Indigenous children the welfare principle is severely constrained. It fails to have much effect on either the provision of sufficient, relevant and accessible supportive services, or on their consistently disproportionate admission to the public care and juvenile justice systems. The rate of infant mortality is alarmingly high – twice that of infants in the rest of the population – and their neglect is apparent across a range of social indicators – such as overcrowding, unemployment and in limited access to services.[153] The CRC, in recognition of this problem and its disproportionate impact on Indigenous communities, has expressed concern at what it viewed as 'the serious and widespread discrimination faced by Aboriginal and Torres Strait Islander children, including in terms of provision of and accessibility to basic services' and

150 31 U.S. 515.

151 Cited by Daes, E.-I. A., 'Indigenous Peoples Permanent Sovereignty Over Natural Resources', paper presented at the National Native Title Conference, Adelaide, June 3, 2004.

152 *Coe v. The Commonwealth* (1979), 53 ALJR 403 but see *Love/Thoms v. Commonwealth of Australia* [2020] HCA 3.

153 See, further, Scott, D., *Understanding Child Neglect*, 2014, https://aifs.gov.au/resources/policy-and-practice-papers/understanding-child-neglect

strongly recommended that the state 'take urgent measures to address disparities in access to services'.[154] Moreover, there is a significant over-representation of Aboriginal and Torres Strait Islander children in the child protection system with the rate of removal of such children from their families remaining almost 11 times higher than for others[155] and reported to be 14 times higher in Western Australia. This mirrors the situation in the justice system where almost half (49%) of all children being supervised by the Youth Justice Service on an average day in 2020–21 were Indigenous despite only 5.8% of young people aged 10 to 17 years nationally identifying as being from that ethnic group.[156]

In New Zealand, the Treaty of Waitangi – *te Tiriti o Waitangi* was signed by Māori chiefs and the British Crown on 6 February 1840. Thereafter, unlike the Indigenous people of Australia, the Māori were vested with a legal status enabling them to formally negotiate with the authorities on many matters including family affairs and the welfare of their children. However, the disruption caused to the coherence of Māori communities and their cultural identity – as also to that of the Indigenous people – by the earlier and wholly destructive state assimilationist strategy has made it necessary to pursue contemporary interventionist policies, such as child protection, very cautiously. Unlike Australia, which is largely reliant on the Family Law Act 1975 (Cth), New Zealand has a body of relatively modern legislation much of which is specific to children – with equal application to those of Māori descent – that establishes the paramountcy principle as the gold standard for dealing with their welfare interests. Governments in both countries, however, face the same problem of how to address the fact that most Indigenous and Māori children entering the public care system are admitted not because of harm wilfully inflicted but because of neglect due to environmental factors that are amenable to remedial intervention. This should prompt state authorities to direct intervention towards mitigating the prevailing adverse circumstances. The abnormally high infant mortality rates, together with the over-representation of Indigenous and Māori children in their child welfare and youth justice systems, are among the negative indicators that suggest this is not and has not been happening.

State intervention in the family life of Indigenous people, on child welfare grounds, has not fared well. The legacy of mistrust resulting from a long period of intergenerational trauma makes it very difficult to now establish a positive working relationship between government and the Indigenous communities such as would enable the children of the latter the rights enumerated in UN CROC to escape the current levels of poverty, over-representation in the criminal and welfare systems, and avail of the opportunities in education, training and sport – the

154 CRC/c/AUS/CO/4, *Concluding Observations: Australia*, 2012, at para 29.

155 Liddle, C., et al., *The Family Matters Report 2021: Measuring the Trends to Turn the Tide on the Over-Representation of Aboriginal and Torres Strait Islander Children in Out-of-Home Care in Australia*, 2021, www.familymatters.org.au/wp-content/uploads/2021/12/FamilyMatters Report2021.pdf

156 See, further, www.aihw.gov.au/reports/youth-justice/youth-justice-in-australia-2020-21/contents/summary

well-trodden pathways to socio-economic success – as their non-Indigenous fellow citizens have.

Conclusion

The relationship between social need and government service provision has probably always been asymmetrical: it is doubtful if any society at any time has achieved an equitable balance; most would not want to fearing that this might undermine the basis of meritocracy, nullify the aspirations of individuals and threaten social progress. However, these are all modern liberal democracies which are prosperous, some containing the highest concentration of billionaires in the world, and yet they would seem prepared to accommodate a growing proportion of their citizens living in poverty. Many of those citizens are children. Whether Indigenous or not, children are as entitled to the rights and protection of their interests as adults: not just to the rights enumerated in UN CROC but also to those in the ECHR and in many other treaties, conventions and protocols.

That being the case, it does seem a travesty that such democratic societies – as they grow wealthier – are willing to also allow the rates to grow of infant mortality and of children being admitted to public care and justice systems. There is little indication that the legal protection now legislatively afforded to children's rights and welfare interests is in practice leveraging any improvement in established indices of social disadvantage.

Part III

Coherence in family law

Balancing welfare interests and rights

8 Family law coherence

Welfare interests and rights

Introduction

Child trafficking, famine in Africa, war in Gaza, transgender issues, alarming child mortality rates and the many thousands of children missing in Europe or abducted into Russia are among the matters currently focusing concern on the welfare interests of children and questioning the reality of their rights.

This final chapter, in three sections, reflects on the themes that have emerged in this book and the series, examines their effect on the changing balance between children's welfare interests and their rights, and considers the implications for overall coherence in family law. The first section examines the 'family', 'family law' and 'family forms'; the second focuses on the welfare interests principle as pivotal to the reconfiguration of family law, its inclusion of hybrid proceedings and the role of the parent/child bond; and the final section concludes the book and the series with a brief review of changes in the parent/child/state relationship, considering the nature and significance of the growing number of hybrid family law proceedings.

Family and family law

Families have changed more in the past few decades than in as many preceding centuries: the marital family is not the ubiquitous norm; marriage has lost its 'for life' commitment; parental monogamy is not guaranteed; a parent or parents are no longer necessarily heterosexual nor necessarily limited to one or two; families may be composed of parents and children who are not genetically related; and families are not fixed entities, the composition of many will change over time. Structured social homogeneity has given way to a more fluid, multicultural society with permeable boundaries where family life is more impermanent and serial parenting and shared care arrangements increasingly common. The modern self-reliant, fairly mobile nuclear unit is less likely to be reinforced by an extended kinship network or by community links and has become more transient as families relocate in pursuit of employment and other opportunities. Moreover, these changes have been accompanied by improvements in family planning, in welfare benefits, housing and by the fading vestiges of stigma, which together have transformed the socio-economic circumstances of unmarried mothers.

DOI: 10.4324/9781003510383-12

Family law has been playing catch-up. It now deals with a range of relationships recognised as constituting a 'family' that have broadened in ways that previous generations would have found hard to imagine. The right to found a family, as guaranteed under Article 12 of the European Convention on Human Rights (ECHR), has in recent years validated new relationship frameworks, and 'family' is now better defined by the quality and functionality of relationships between its members, whether or not they are genetically linked and regardless of duration, rather than the form or legal status it happens to take (see, further, Chapter 3). As the European Court of Human Rights (ECtHR) explained in *I.S. v. Germany*[1] "biological kinship between a natural parent and a child alone, without any further legal or factual elements indicating the existence of a close personal relationship, might be insufficient to attract the protection of Article 8". Incrementally, as the law conferred legal status on same-sex civil unions, registered partnerships and ultimately on marriage, this process led to recognition being granted to same-sex families in the context of adoption and as regards issues such as succession rights relating to pensions and tenancies.[2] In *Oliari and Others v. Italy*,[3] the ECtHR found that there was an emerging consensus in Europe and elsewhere favouring granting legal recognition and protection to stable same-sex relationships while, in the meantime, the U.S. Supreme Court in *Obergefell v. Hodges*[4] had established such recognition across the U.S. Such a fundamental de-construction of 'family' clearly must have long-term ramifications for family law.

Not until 2016, however – in *Pajić v. Croatia*[5] – did the ECtHR explain that gender identification, sexual orientation and sexual life fell within the scope of 'private life' as understood by Article 8. Any room for continued prevarication was removed by a series of cases in which the courts affirmed, on equality grounds, a parity of legal status between family units led by heterosexual and same-sex couples[6] and established that under Article 8 of the ECHR, respect for family life must also consider developments in society and changes in the perception of issues, including the changing ways of forming a family and living a private life.[7] In the U.S. the constellation of liberties protected through the Fourteenth Amendment facilitated a similar development in respect of private family life as only a 'compelling reason' would justify infringing rights of family privacy.[8] As declared by Thomas J in *Troxel*: "parents have a fundamental constitutional right to rear their children, including the right to determine who shall educate and socialize them".[9]

1 Application No. 3102/08, (2014).
2 See, for example, *Kozak v. Poland*, Application No. 13102/02, (2010).
3 Application Nos. 18766/11 and 36030/11, (2015).
4 135 S. Ct. 2584 (2015).
5 Application No. 68453/13, (2016).
6 See, for example, *Kozak v. Poland*, Op. cit.
7 See, also, *Taddeucci and McCall v. Italy*, Application No. 51362/09, (2016).
8 See, *DeShaney v. Winnebago County Social Services*, 489 U.S. 189 (1989) when Rehnquist CJ, on behalf of the U.S. Supreme Court, expressed the view that non-intervention in a child protection matter was explicable and excusable as intervening officials are often charged with "improperly intruding into the parent-child relationship". See, also, *Santosky v. Kramer*, 455 U.S. 745 (1982).
9 *Troxel v. Granville*, 530 U.S. 57 (2000).

When the Family First legislation was introduced in 2019 that approach begin to change as a more assertive state intervention policy, on child protection grounds, emerged.[10] Further change was heralded by the *Dobbs* decision:[11] the rationale of which is grounded on the Fourteenth Amendment and may logically be extended to include state restrictions not just on access to abortion but also on access to contraceptives, surrogacy and other associated developments that have since helped to redefine 'the family'. Meanwhile, in Europe, quite the opposite policy was signalled when France, in 2024, become the first country to explicitly embed the right to abortion in its constitution, thereby upholding the right to private family life and rejecting state intrusion on such matters.

Against this background the welfare interests and indeed the rights of the child have steadily become more prominent and nuanced. This is partly a consequence of increased knowledge of child development: a product of research in the fields of child psychiatry and developmental psychology; and to the resulting theories of attachment, bonding and the 'psychological parent'; all of which have done much to bring more depth to the professional understanding of what, for any particular child, might constitute their 'welfare', thereby helping to correct the tendency towards reification.[12] It has also been due, throughout family law, to a process of general withdrawal from a defence of the status determined obligations of adults (e.g. marriage) to one of upholding the principle that the welfare interests of children must prevail. This, in turn, has led to the principle undermining the age-old binary divide between public and private family law, generating hybrid proceedings and opening the door to allow a more complex body of family law to evolve (see, Chapters 4–7 incl).

Family forms

Each of the eight jurisdictions being studied in this series now has a modernised body of matrimonial legislation catering for the marriage, divorce and separation of heterosexual and same-sex couples. All eight – or at least those of the common law tradition – have also repeatedly experienced court cases involving three or more adults competing for custody rights in respect of a child or children they had been jointly parenting in their collective family.[13] There is judicial recognition that – in surrogacy arrangements – a child may have up to five 'parents'.

The ECtHR, in keeping with prevailing jurisprudence in other modern developed nations, has long been clear that the definition of 'family' is not restricted to one based on marriage: it includes unmarried couples, single-parent families, non-marital children and lesbian or homosexual relationships.[14] The definition is

10 A policy change signalled by the introduction of the Adoption and Safe Families Act 1997 (ASFA) which had promoted adoption as a private resource for the care of children in the public care system.

11 *Dobbs v. Jackson Women's Health Organization*, 597 U.S. 215 (2022).

12 See, for example, Sutton, A., 'Science in Court', in King, M. (ed.), *Childhood, Welfare & Justice*, Billing & Son Ltd., 1981, at p 55.

13 Though possibly not Ireland.

14 *Keegan v. Ireland*, Application No. 16969/90 (1994) Series A No. 290, 18 EHRR 342, at para 44.

likely to be expanded by advances in reproductive medicine[15] which, together with the increase in the number of same-sex couples and changes in social norms, have already allowed other family forms to join the traditional model,[16] some being deferred by means of storing frozen eggs. Further advances, including in gene editing – with the wonders of CRISPR/Cas 9 and its potential to lead to 'designer babies' – will push the boundaries of family definition into territory that for now remains speculative.

Jurisdictional differences and their significance

It is no longer uncommon for same-sex parents to build families through co-parenting, conceiving children who then have two mothers and either one or two fathers. Multi-parent families can also be created where the parents are in a polyamorous relationship, and in all jurisdictions the proportion of one-parent birth families has greatly increased. The phenomenon of men giving birth is also becoming more common,[17] in fact trans parenting has become an established and growing variant of parenting in many Western countries.[18] As was recently stated by the President of the Family Division in England and Wales, for example:[19]

> It is now medically and legally possible for an individual, whose gender is recognised in law as male, to become pregnant and give birth to their child. Whilst that person's gender is 'male', their parental status, which derives from their biological role in giving birth, is that of 'mother'.

So much, then, for the rule of *pater est quem nuptiae demonstrant* (the father is the spouse of the mother), a common law maxim that was law for many generations and in many countries which, if it had not already become redundant, would certainly not have survived into the 21st century.

While new family forms are now not uncommon, it is also not uncommon for such families to collapse into parental competitions for custody, and it is then – when coping with custody claims in respect of children being parented by three or more

15 See, for example, the introduction of mitochondrial donation treatment which, if successful, necessarily results in a child with DNA from three different persons.

16 See, further, for example, Sturge, C., 'Current Issues in Relation to Gay and Non-Biological Parenting', paper presented at the 2007 Dartington Conferences published by Family Law under the title "Integrating Diversity" in 2008.

17 Thomas Beatie, a transgender man who preserved his female organs was billed as the world's first pregnant man in 2007.

18 In Australia, for example, 205 men are recorded to have given birth between 2013 and 2018 and 54 in 2023. See, further, http://medicarestatistics.humanservices.gov.au/statistics/do.jsp?_PROGRAM=/statistics/mbs_item_age_gender_report&VAR=services&STAT=count&PTYPE=finyear&START_DT=201307&END_DT=201806&RPT_FMT=by+time+period+and+state&GROUP=16519

19 See, *R (McConnell and YY) v. Registrar General for England and Wales* [2020] EWCA Civ 559, *per* the Right Honourable Sir MacFarlane, P.

adults – that family law has run into difficulties. As an ever-increasing volume of complex family law litigation comes before the courts, this is accompanied by evermore opportunities for judicial exploration of what, in law, now constitutes a 'family'.

In the UK, for example, the law will only extend legal recognition to two parents, though there is no limit on the number of individuals who may be awarded a parental responsibility order. The resulting complexities were illustrated in *A v. B and C*,[20] which concerned B who was in a same-sex relationship with C and had entered into a marriage of convenience in 2007 with the father A, neither spouse ever having any intention to live together. Instead, it was intended that their child would be living in the household of B and C from birth. Prior to the child's birth, the three adults discussed the level of involvement that the father would eventually have in the child's life, he hoping for overnight contact and a greater role than B and C were prepared to offer. The subsequent litigation concluded in the Court of Appeal which overruled the High Court decision to refuse the father overnight contact, adding that there could be no strict guidelines in these difficult and important cases – except that the needs of the child should predominate. The Court of Appeal, with wholly justified prescience, warned that the law was still evolving to meet the demands of new family structures. In Ireland, until the last decades of the 20th century, a deeply embedded Catholic morality, reinforced by the Constitution which nurtured a culture adverse to any interference with traditional religious values – centred on the marital family unit and on stereotyped gender roles – prevailed and constrained the development of any equivalent to the range of family forms to be found in the neighbouring UK jurisdictions and in those noted earlier. While much progress was made at the end of the 20th century and into the 21st century in modernising Irish family law and family forms, this progress suffered a considerable setback when the government's 2024 referendums on the 39th and 40th amendments to the Constitution were defeated. The fact that by a large majority the Irish population voted to retain provisions that constitutionally ensure a very conservative perspective on family life is at variance with the other jurisdictions studied – such as France – though may well be in keeping with predicted developments in the U.S.[21]

The law relating to competing parental rights in multi-parent families is far from certain in the U.S. where in some states, such as California, more than two individuals may be recognised as parents of a child if they can establish that "recognizing only two parents would be detrimental to the child". In the absence of federal legislation, each state is at liberty – within reasonable parameters – to develop its own jurisprudence which necessarily complicates an overall jurisdictional picture. The Inter-American Commission on Human Rights has noted that although

20 Ibid.

21 The retained constitutional provisions include: in Article 41.3.1, 'The State pledges itself to guard with special care the institution of Marriage, on which the Family is founded, and to protect it against attack'; and in Srticle 41.2.1, 'In particular, the State recognises that by her life within the home, woman gives to the State a support without which the common good cannot be achieved'.

the U.S. has ratified the Optional Protocols to the United Nations Convention on the Rights of the Child (UN CROC) on the Sale of Children, Child Prostitution and Child Pornography, and the Involvement of Children in Armed Conflict, its domestic laws do not adequately or consistently reflect the principle of the primacy of the best interests of the child.[22] This uncertainty was illustrated in the *Matter of Tomeka N.H. v. Jesus R*[23] which concerned the birth parents of a child and the mother's same-sex lover: the father told the mother, during the pregnancy, that he wanted nothing to do with the child; the mother began a relationship with Tomeka and both agreed, prior to the child's birth, that they would raise and parent the child together; thereafter, Tomeka acted in every capacity as a parent while the father remained uninvolved, even to the point of denying paternity. When the child was aged two years, Tomeka sought to formally adopt her but the application was contested by the father asserting paternity and producing a positive DNA test. He was legally established as the child's second parent (in addition to the biological mother), despite which Tomeka – not the father – continued to act as a parent for the next five years, with the consent and acquiescence of both biological parents. When the child was aged six years, Tomeka filed for custody, but her petition was dismissed by the court which held that she did not have standing as she was not a parent. On appeal to the Family Court, the attorney for the child reported that the child considered Tomeka a parent and wanted her to remain a constant presence in her life. However, shortly afterwards Tomeka and the biological mother ended their relationship, and Tomeka was no longer allowed to see the child.[24]

On further appeal, the Fourth Department, relying on the earlier decision in the Court of Appeals case *Brooke S.B. v. Allison A.C.C.*,[25] affirmed the Family Court's decision, holding that Tomeka could not possibly have standing as a parent as the wording of statute law "simply does not contemplate a court-ordered tri-custodial arrangement".[26] The Fourth Department upheld that ruling stating that because the child already had two biological parents, "there simply can be no more,"[27] Leave to appeal was refused. This decision is at odds with others issued by New York courts: the Suffolk County Supreme Court has held that "tri-custody is the logical evolution of the Court of Appeals' decision in *Brooke S.B.*",[28] while the New York County Family Court has held that "[t]he parent-child relationships fostered by children . . . who are being raised in a tri-parent arrangement, should be entitled to no less protection than children raised by two parties".[29] All

22 See, Inter-American Commission on Human Rights, *Children and Adolescents in the United States' Adult Criminal Justice System*, 2018, at p 134, www.oas.org/en/iachr/reports/pdfs/Children-USA.pdf

23 183 A.D. 3d 106, 122 N.Y.S. 3d 461 (4th Dep't 2020).

24 See, further, Williams, J.R., *Who's a Parent? The Appellate Division is Divided on the Answer*, https://nysba.org/whos-a-parent-the-appellate-division-is-divided-on-the-answer/#_edn13

25 28 N.Y. 3d 1 (2016).

26 Op. cit.

27 *Tomeka N.H.*, 183 A.D.3d at 111.

28 See, *Dawn M. v. Michael M.*, 55 Misc. 3d at 870.

29 See, *David S. v. Samantha G.*, 59 Misc. 3d at 966.

of this is legally confusing and muddles what might be the rights of a child in such circumstances.

In Canada, new family forms did not seem to generate as much contention or judicial equivocation as elsewhere. Fowler J noted in *C.C. (Re)*,[30] that "society is continuously changing and family structures are changing along with it. This must be recognised as a reality and not as a detriment to the best interests of the child". So when judicial notice was taken of the fact that a family could comprise three legal parents (two fathers and one mother), based on the throuple's sexual relationship, both men were declared fathers. The judge commented that "I can find nothing to disparage that relationship from the best interests of the child's point of view".[31]

In Australia, the case of *Wilson and Anor & Roberts and Anor (No.2)*[32] was not untypical of many other cases of less orthodox family forms in various jurisdictions. It concerned two same-sex couples – one female and one male – who collectively concluded a co-parenting agreement whereby the latter donated sperm to the former, resulting in the birth of a girl who was duly co-parented by all four adults until their relationship broke down and they went to court with competing claims for parental rights. Dessau J then found that the girl's primary attachment was to the women, and as she could not possibly be parented by all four adults – due to their acrimonious relationships – he awarded parental responsibility to the 'two mothers'. This decision, based upon the child's right to have her emotional attachments protected at such a formative stage in her life – whether or not the attachments are to a genetically related parent – is very representative of similar outcomes in such multi-parent family breakdowns. In New Zealand, family and gender fluidity – a feature of the neighbouring Samoan culture – has facilitated the contemporary acceptance of a variety of family forms, while the statutory application of the paramountcy principle across most critical areas of children's law ensures protection for their rights to parental care and contact.

French family life has existed in many different forms. In *Gas and Dubois v. France*[33] the ECtHR found that it existed in the relationship between two women who were living together and had entered into a civil partnership, with the child conceived by one of them – through means of assisted reproduction – being parented by both. In *Boughanemi v. France*[34] it was found that the relationship between two siblings constituted family life. In both *Mennesson v. France*[35] and *Labassée v. France*[36] the ECtHR found that the commissioning couples in surrogacy arrangements had acted as the parents of the children from the time of the latter's birth and

30 2018 NLSC 71. Following on from *A v. B*, 2007 ONCA 2, 83 OR (3d) 56 I when Ontario recognised a three-parent family.

31 Ibid, at para 34.

32 [2010] FamCA 734.

33 Application No. 2595/07, (2010).

34 Application No. 22070/93, Reports 1996-II, No. 8, p 593, 22 EHRR 228.

35 Application No. 65192/11, (2014).

36 Application No. 65941/11, (2014).

lived with them in a way that constituted family life. *C.E. & A.L. v. France*[37] concerned two women in a relationship during which one gave birth, following donor insemination, and both jointly parented until the child was aged six years when their relationship ended. For the next nine years the ex-partner enjoyed visitation and accommodation rights in respect of the child and also paid child support. In 2015, her adoption application – supported by the child's mother – was refused, as under French law, such an adoption would compromise the child's filiation and thus not be in their best interests.[38] In Germany, the traditional patriarchal model of the marital family (70% of all families) and the roles of those within it have endured rather longer, in fact and in family law, than elsewhere. However, the high incidence of family breakdown means that a growing proportion of German children in each generation are being exposed to a flux of care relationships in which their attachments and welfare interests may well be vulnerable.[39]

In short, it would seem clear that the dismantling and reconfiguration of the traditional model 'family' is well underway – even if for the majority of children their upbringing continues to find protection within that model – and in this unsettled period, family law is falling back to stabilise its core components.

The parent/child bond: intrinsic to welfare, generator of rights and now pivotal in family law

As family forms increase, but with decreasing sustainability, family law is retreating from its traditional concerns – structured around marital and non-marital relationships, associated legal status and property – to cohere instead around the parent/child relationship. As Kilkelly[40] has explained, the ECtHR has now established that such a relationship will constitute family life 'in all but very exceptional cases regardless of the parents' marital status,[41] the family's living arrangements,[42] or their apparent lack of commitment to their children'.[43] Moreover, that relationship has come to form a model of care which is transferable when the parental role

37 Application Nos. 29775/18 and 29693/19, (2022).

38 The *Cour de cassation* had previously ruled that the Civil Code "precludes two maternal or two paternal legal parent-child relationships from being established in respect of the same child".

39 Nonetheless, the Organization for Economic Cooperation and Development statistics indicate a greater level of family stability in Germany than in many of the 30 countries it surveyed. See, further, www.huffingtonpost.co.uk/2012/12/29/uk-family-breakdown-rate-_n_2379845.html?view=print

40 See, Kilkelly, U., 'Child and Family Law', in Kilkelly, U. (ed.), *ECHR and Irish Law*, Jordans, 2004, at p 112.

41 See, *Marckx v. Belgium*, Ibid, (unmarried mother and her child); *Johnston v. Ireland*, Application No. 9697/92, (1987) (unmarried parents and their child).

42 See, *Berrehab v. Netherlands*, Application No. 10730/84, (1988).

43 See, *C v. Belgium*, Application No. 21794/93, (1996) and *Ahmut v. Netherlands*, Application No. 21702/93, (1996). See, also, *Söderbäck v. Sweden*, Application No. 24484/94, (1998). However, purely genetic relationships – such as the relationship between a sperm donor and the child born as a result – are unlikely to constitute family life. See, *G v. Netherlands*, Application No. 16944/90, (1993).

has been assumed by others, though whether any such relationships are entitled to respect in the eyes of the law[44] will depend upon whether they constitute a family.[45] At the very least this requires a potential relationship between, for example, a child born[46] to unmarried parents and his or her birth father;[47] or the relationship that arises from a genuine marriage, even if family life has not yet been fully established;[48] or the relationship that arises from a lawful and genuine adoption.[49] The existence of 'family life' will depend upon factors such as whether the couple live together, the length of their relationship and whether they have demonstrated their commitment to each other by having children together or by other means.[50] Again, as Kilkelly has pointed out – the ECtHR has recognised[51] that "family life may exist between children and their grandparents,[52] between siblings,[53] between an uncle and his nephew,[54] and between parents and children born into second relationships".[55] The law has extended its recognition and protection to family life that takes the form of adopters and child,[56] foster parents and child,[57] migrant parents and child,[58] same-sex relationships and child[59] and surrogate arrangements and child.[60] In *Lebbink v. The Netherlands*,[61] as in the earlier *Hokkanen v. Finland*[62] (see, further, Chapter 3) the ECtHR accepted that cohabitation was not essential, other factors may serve to demonstrate the required constancy of relationships such as, in that instance, the father's position as auxiliary guardian and his established pattern of contact with the child.

The parent/child bond – whether actual or simulated – being an intrinsic and irreducible component of family life is also, and for that reason, crucial to the welfare principle. The bond has given rise to certain rights and is now, arguably,

44 See, *V.D. and Others v. Russia*, Application No. 72931/10, (2019).
45 See, *Marckx v. Belgium*, Op. cit.
46 An unborn child would not qualify: *Paton v. The United Kingdom*, Application No. 8416/78, (1981).
47 See, *Nylund v. Finland (dec.)*, Application No. 27110/95, (1999).
48 See, *Abdulaziz, Cabales and Balkandali v. the United Kingdom*, Application Nos. 9214/80, 9473/81 and 9474/81, (1985).
49 See, *Pini and Others v. Romania*, Application Nos. 78028/01 and 78030/01, (2004).
50 *X, Y and Z v. United Kingdom* [1997] 2 FLR 892.
51 See, Kilkelly, U., 'Child and Family Law', Op. cit., at p 113.
52 See, *Marckx v. Belgium*, Op. cit., at para 45.
53 See, *Olsson v. Sweden*, Application No.10465/83, Series A No. 130, 11 EHRR 259. See also *Boughanemi v. France*, Application No. 22070/93, Reports 1996-II, No. 8, p 593, 22 EHRR 228.
54 See, *Boyle v. UK*, Application No. 16580/90, Comm Rep, 9.2.93.
55 See, *Jolie & Lebrun v. Belgium*, Application No. 11418/85, Dec. 14.5.86, DR 47, p 243.
56 See, for example, *Zait v. Romania*, Application No. 44958/05, (2015).
57 See, for example, *Moretti and Benedetti v. Italy*, Application No. 16318/07, (2010) and *Kopf and Liberda v. Austria*, Application No. 1598/06, (2012).
58 See, for example, *Sen v. the Netherlands*, Application No. 31465/96, (2001).
59 See, for example, *X, Y & Z v. UK*, Application No. 21830/93, Reports 1997-II No. 35, p 619, 24 EHRR 143.
60 See, for example, *Mennesson v. France*, Application No. 65192/11, (2014).
61 Application No. 35582/99, (2004).
62 (1994) 19 EHRR 139.

the most fundamental element in contemporary domestic and international family law.

Intrinsic to welfare interests

Latterly, the traditional preoccupation with the physicality of welfare interests – care and protection, health and safety, etc. – has been supplemented by contributions from disciplines such as developmental psychology, cognitive science, evolutionary biology and others, which have fuelled a step change in professional and judicial understanding of what constitutes the 'welfare interests of the child'.[63] Beginning in the mid-1960s, judicial notice was increasingly taken of the work of leading British child psychiatrists and psychologists, together with that of their U.S. counterparts, and decisions became grounded as much on evidence of the child's emotional and psychological welfare as on their material well-being.[64]

Child psychiatry probably only gained traction as a mainstream discipline in the 1970s, largely due to the influential research and publications of psychiatrists such as Robin Skynner[65] and Michael Rutter.[66] By the end of the 20th century, child psychiatry clinics were to be found in regional healthcare settings – hospitals or healthcare surgeries – bringing considerable expertise and positive intervention to local public services engagement with troubled children and their families. Educational psychology did much to raise awareness of children's learning capacity at different stages of their development. Working alongside teachers, social workers and speech therapists to assist any child with learning difficulties, they constructively mediated on the behalf of children in institutional environments.

Attachment theory

John Bowlby,[67] a leading exponent of attachment theory, was a psychologist, psychiatrist and psychoanalyst who specialised in child development in the late 1960s and introduced child-care professionals and the judiciary to the importance of preserving the bonding relationship between mother and child. He continued the earlier work of Melanie Klein,[68] a British psychologist who had researched child anxiety, insecurity, their causes and the relevance of play therapy. Along with Mary Ainsworth, Bowlby researched and published on the consequences of maternal deprivation for a child's ability to thereafter form the secure emotional attachments

63 See, O'Halloran, K., *Children & the Law: Shaping the Modern Welfare Principle in the British Isles*, Routledge, 2022, at chapter 4.

64 See, evidence of such a trend beginning with the judgment in *Re C(L) (an infant)* [1965] 2 QB 449 and culminating in the HL judgment in *Re W (an infant)* [1971] AC 682.

65 Skynner, R., *Families and How to Survive Them*, Cedar Books, 1984.

66 Rutter, M., *Maternal Deprivation*, Wiley, 1972.

67 Bowlby, J., *Attachment and Loss*, Pimlico, New York, Basic Books, 1968.

68 Klein, M., *The Psycho-Analysis of Children* (first published in 1932), Vintage, 1997.

essential to the child's welfare interests.[69] He understood attachment as a lasting psychological connectedness between human beings which suggested that a child had an innate need to form an early emotional bond with a caregiver. Importantly, Bowlby took the view that the mother was the caregiver best placed to provide the nurture that fostered the bond, though he conceded that the relationship need not be exclusively maternal, other caregivers could share or replace the maternal role and achieve an equivalent bond. Subsequent research by the child psychiatrist Michael Rutter,[70] which focussed on maternal deprivation and the consequent effects of privation, raised a significant challenge to the Bowlby thesis, arguing that a child needed to develop multiple attachments rather than be dependent upon a single caregiver such as their mother.

The 'psychological bond'

It was only after dissemination of Bowlby's research that the judiciary and others begin to recognise the importance of preserving the 'psychological bond' (see, also, Chapter 1) which allows a child to develop and sustain a relationship with at least one nurturing adult; the younger the child, the more important is the bond and the more probable, at that stage, that this is best supplied by a mother or maternal figure. Distinct, but often in practice closely related, was the judicial significance attached to the 'blood-tie'. The preference shown for care arrangements which permit a child to have his or her home with a parent or member of their family of origin became evident, for example, in contests between first and third parties. It could also be seen playing a part in step-parent adoptions where the order made favoured the caring parent in a position to provide the child concerned with continuity of home environment.

Judicial recognition of the central importance of attachments and the 'psychological bond', to the interpretation of any and every child's welfare interests, has become instrumental to both generating hybrid public/private proceedings and providing the linkage that holds together this increasingly diffuse body of family law.

Jurisdictional differences and their significance

As an extension of the respect for the 'psychological bond', judicial reasoning now includes those reference points which can also be demonstrably important for a child's psychological development, such as contact with grandparents and other members of their nuclear and extended family, friends, school, neighbours and neighbourhood. This insight was one reflected in the broadening of the welfare

69 A theoretical approach which echoed that of Romilly MR a century earlier in *Austin v. Austin* (1865) 34 Beavan 257: The welfare of the child is so intimately connected with its being under the care of the mother that no extent of kindness on the part of any other person can supply that place.

70 See, for example, Rutter, M., *Maternal Deprivation Reassessed,* Penguin, 1972.

principle from traditional care and protection concerns to accommodate emotional and psychological needs and an awareness of the need to address a child's 'attachment issues'. However, this has been open to somewhat different jurisdictional interpretations.

In England and Wales, as in the U.S., attachment theory underpins the policy of adoption from public care: concurrent placements give effect to a strategy for facilitating the development of foster carer/child attachments which will in time become sufficiently integral to their welfare to justify a public to private transfer of care responsibility to the foster parents by way of adoption. In Ireland, and more generally in the other five jurisdictions, there has so far been less of a public policy push for such a transfer: the attachments between long-term foster parents and the children placed with them have been considered sufficient to provide for the development of a 'psychological bond'; but in recent years a shortage of foster parents has resulted in the bonding process being compromised by the necessity to shuttle children between foster placements in order to free places for urgent admissions. This problem is most acute in the CANZUS nations where the shortage of Indigenous foster parents can lead to cross-cultural placements and to much controversy should the resulting attachments prompt foster parent adoption applications. It is also a factor that goes some way towards explaining the relatively weak reliance on foster care in Germany and to a lesser extent in France.

Generating rights and promoting paramountcy

'The best interests of the child: a right, a principle and a rule of procedure.' So proclaimed the CRC in 2013.[71] However, while it is now well beyond doubt that the law relating to children must take into account, weigh and protect their differing welfare interests, there remains some uncertainty as to the circumstances in which it should also, or instead, respect and accommodate their rights. Indeed, the distinction itself has been questioned (see, further, Chapter 1), though the better view now would be that UN CROC has introduced a sharper distinction between welfare interests and rights which the ECtHR, the UN Committee on the Rights of the Child (CRC) and to a lesser extent the Court of Justice of the European Union (CJEU), have further developed. As noted earlier, from an initial focus restricted to safeguarding the child's physical integrity, research contributions in recent decades from child psychiatry, developmental psychology and other disciplines have greatly broadened the interpretation of welfare interests while simultaneously establishing certain basic rights.[72] The parent/child bond, amplified by a growing recognition of its psychological significance for welfare interests, has played an important role in that context. While many rights have a relevance for children – including those

71 See, Committee on the Rights of the Children, *General comment No. 14 (2013) on the Right of the Child to Have His or Her Best Interests Taken as a Primary Consideration*, www.refworld.org/legal/general/crc/2013/en/95780

72 See, further, *The Principle of the Welfare of the Child: A History*, 2022, Op. cit.

enumerated in the ECHR and UN CROC – the rights with a bearing on that bond, such as the following, have become judicially recognised as more important when determining issues relating to the welfare of a child and have very largely been legislatively entrenched in national child-care 'welfare checklists'. Other rights, such as those relating to justice, while also important have less of a direct bearing on the parent/child bond (see, further Chapter 2).

Personal rights

Unquestionably, for children the rights that matter most are those that structure and protect their relationships with the adults who have nurtured them and with whom, over time, they have formed attachments and developed their 'family life'. In most cases, but not always, this will mean their birth parents.

Right to respect for family life

Article 8, the right most heavily relied upon in proceedings affecting the welfare interests of the child, declares that 'everyone has the right to respect for his private and family life, his home and his correspondence' and that 'there shall be no interference by a public authority with the exercise of this right except such as is in accordance with the law and is necessary in a democratic society' (see, further, Chapter 3). This is not dissimilar to the corresponding interpretation given to private family life in the Fourteenth Amendment of the U.S. Constitution. On both sides of the Atlantic, it has been interpreted very broadly to include matters such as personal privacy and autonomy; personal identity (e.g. sexual orientation and gender affirmation), cultural identity (e.g. to belong to culture of birth) and the right to access the information necessary to preserve that identity. It has also been reinforced by the provisions of UN CROC.

Most importantly, in this context, Article 8 refers to a child's right to protection from interventions that may threaten links with their birth family and, if he or she is removed, it affirms their right to maintain contact and ultimately to be reunited with them. As the ECtHR stressed in its criticism of local authority practice in *YC v. the United Kingdom*:[73] "family ties may only be severed in very exceptional circumstances and that everything must be done to preserve personal relations and, where appropriate, to 'rebuild' the family".

Right to private life

The ECtHR has stated that "private life", in the Court's view, "includes a person's physical and psychological integrity and can sometimes embrace aspects of an

73 (2012) 55 EHRR 33.

individual's physical and social identity"[74] (see, further, Chapter 3). The reference to 'physical and psychological integrity' has prompted the ECtHR and the CRC to rule that the physical chastisement of a child – whether by parent, schoolteacher or others – would violate that child's right to respect for their private life. The ECtHR has found that birth and the circumstances of birth form part of a child's private life. "[I]nformation concerning highly personal aspects of [one's] childhood, development and history" can constitute a "principal source of information about [one's] past and formative years".[75]

Right to identity

The right to an identity is rooted in international law.[76] Both the ECtHR and the CJEU have ruled on aspects of the Article 8 right relating to identity and personal development: people have a "right to establish details of their identity as individual human beings".[77] Moreover, the non-recognition of a parent/child relationship constitutes a violation of the child's Article 8 rights. So, for example, denying the applicant's request for DNA tests to be performed on the body of a deceased man believed to be his biological father, prevented the applicant from establishing paternity and thereby stopped him from confirming a crucial aspect of his identity in violation of his Article 8 rights.[78]

The Article 8 right to information needed to authenticate personal identity finds support in Article 22(3) of the European Convention on the Adoption of Children 2008 which provides for the right of an adopted child to access information held by the authorities concerning his or her origins. The right probably appears before the courts most frequently in relation to applicants wishing to access origins information, whose birth circumstances are obscured by adoption,[79] surrogacy[80] or in vitro fertilisation.[81] Identity rights include cultural identity and gender identity. Nonetheless, there have been a number of cases where an adoptee has been unable to legally overcome the veto on disclosure of identifying information imposed by a mother who wished to remain anonymous. One such case was *Godelli v. Italy*[82] where the Court held that there had been a violation of Article 8, since the Italian legislation did not allow a child who had not been formally recognised at birth and was subsequently adopted to request either non-identifying information about his or her origins or the disclosure of the birth mother's identity with the latter's consent.

74 *Mikulić v. Croatia*, Application No. 53176/99, (2002), at para 53.
75 *Gaskin v. the United Kingdom*, Application No. 10454/83, (1989), at para 36.
76 See, for example: the UDHR, article 27; the EU Treaty, article 4; and the ECHR, articles 8, 9 and 11.
77 *Christine Goodwin v. the United Kingdom*, Application No. 28957/95, (2002), at para 90.
78 *Jäggi v. Switzerland*, Application No. 58757/00, (2006).
79 *Godelli v. Italy*, Application No. 33783/09, (2012).
80 See, *K. K. and Others v. Denmark*, Application No. 25212/21, (2022).
81 *Mikulić v. Croatia*, Application No. 53176/99, (2002) and *Mizzi v. Malta*, Application No. 26111/02, (2006).
82 Application No. 33783/09, (2012). Also, see, *Odièvre v. France*, Application No. 42326/98, (2003).

Right to cultural identity

Article 30 of UN CROC guarantees a child, belonging to a national minority or to an Indigenous community, the right 'to enjoy his or her own culture, to profess and practise his or her own religion, or to use his or her own language' which is replicated in the Convention on the Avoidance of Statelessness in relation to State Succession.[83] This right comes to the fore in such contexts as intercountry adoption, parental abduction of a child, adoption and foster care of Indigenous children by non-Indigenous persons[84] and in care arrangements for unaccompanied migrant minors.

Right to contact with both parents

Clearly, if the parent/child bond is to have any meaning then there must at the very least be contact between them. The right to do so is stated in several international instruments including Article 24(3) of the Charter: 'every child shall have the right to maintain on a regular basis a personal relationship and direct contact with both his or her parents, unless that is contrary to his or her interests'.

Johansen v. Norway,[85] for example, was one of nine Norwegian cases in which the domestic courts had directed that a child be taken into care, placed in a foster placement with a view to adoption, without any – or very restricted – contact between the child and their birth parent/s. The ECtHR viewed these measures as "particularly far reaching in that they totally deprived the applicant of her family life with the child and were inconsistent with the aim of reuniting them". Further, in *Pedersen*,[86] the ECtHR emphasised that post-adoption contact in itself is not enough: the child must be given an opportunity to develop a 'meaningful relationship' with their biological parents. The implication being that indirect contact – in the form of an exchange of letters or cards at a prescribed number of times every year – would be insufficient to keep alive the parent/child bond. These cases, particularly *Pedersen*, highlight just how much importance the ECtHR now places on the parent/child bond in recognition, seemingly, of its significance for the private life and welfare interests of the child concerned.

In *Suur v. Estonia*,[87] the ECtHR considered the applicant's complaint that, following the ending of joint parental custody of their son, with whom he then had no contact for several years, the authorities had wrongfully made future contact dependent on the child's mother having knowledge of it and giving consent. The Court referred to the general principles that: "the mutual enjoyment by parent and child of each other's company constitutes a fundamental element of family life even

83 Council of Europe, CETS No. 200, 2006.

84 The importance of cultural identity is conveyed in the expression by Australian Indigenous people that 'if you don't know your mob, you can't know yourself'.

85 (1996) 23 EHRR 33.

86 *Pedersen et al v. Norway*, Application No. 39710/15, (2020).

87 Application No. 41736/18, (2020).

when the relationship between the parents has broken down";[88] domestic measures hindering enjoyment of family life such as a decision granting custody of children to a parent constitutes an interference with the right to respect for family life[89] unless it is "in accordance with the law", pursues an aim or aims that are legitimate under Article 8(2) and can be regarded as "necessary in a democratic society".[90] The Court noted it had repeatedly held that Article 8 includes a right for parents to have measures taken with a view to their being reunited with their children, and an obligation rests on the national authorities to take such measures. It added that the key consideration is whether those authorities have taken all necessary steps to facilitate contact as can reasonably be demanded in the special circumstances of each case.[91] It reiterated that while its caselaw requires children's views to be taken into account, those views are not necessarily immutable and their objections, which must be given due weight, are not necessarily sufficient to override the parents' interests, especially in having regular contact with their child: the child's interests but not necessarily their wishes would have primacy; and the interests were for the court to determine. In the circumstances, the Court concluded that the domestic authorities had sufficient evidence to decide that to force the child to have meetings with his father would be against his best interests. More recently an ECtHR ruling emphasised the right of a child to contact with their parents.[92]

Jurisdictional differences and their significance

In public family law, non-consensual adoption from the public care system has the greatest potential to contravene the personal rights of a child than any other form of state intervention on child welfare grounds. While the benefits to the children concerned will very often wholly outweigh the deficits, there will be few children without unresolved attachment concerns and many who feel that their identity – personal and cultural – has been compromised. The authorities' management of birth parent/child contact arrangements prior to adoption can be deliberately attenuated to permit the fading of that relationship and its replacement by the adopter/child relationship. Of the jurisdictions studied, only the UK, the U.S. and some parts of Australia currently pursue this strategy as a firm public policy in respect of children in public care.

The same problem, though to a much lesser degree, exists in relation to foster care. This has been the state placement of choice in all the jurisdictions considered – except Germany – for many years but has recently attracted fairly consistent criticism, particularly in the U.S., because it is expensive and seen as not conducive to rehabilitating a child with their birth family. Instead, foster care is

88 Citing, *Keegan v. Ireland*, Application No. 16969/90, (1994).

89 Citing, *Diamante and Pelliccioni v. San Marino*, Application No. 32250/08, (2011).

90 *Elsholz v. Germany* [GC], Application No. 25735/94, § 45, ECHR 2000-VIII.

91 Citing, *A.V. v. Slovenia*, Application No. 878/13, (2019).

92 *Deltuva v. Lithuania*, Application No. 38144/20, (2023).

being steadily displaced by kinship placements which, by keeping the child within the extended family circle and enabling supervised contact with the birth family, is less likely to be disrupted and greatly reduces the likelihood of future identity and cultural issues.

In private family law, state retreat from intervention continues to be the most characteristic aspect of policy in all jurisdictions, though to a lesser extent in Ireland, as the volume of family breakdowns increases, the state would seem to have pragmatically concluded that the welfare of the children concerned is essentially a private matter for the parents, unless the latter decide otherwise and disclose issues for the court to determine (i.e. the onus to initiate state intervention is private rather than public). In addition, most jurisdictions have now also introduced legislation to divert step-parents away from adoption. While the right to private life is strongly affirmed both in the U.S. under the Fourteenth Amendment and in Europe under Article 8, there are interesting jurisdictional differences and commonalities in how this is interpreted. The rights to private adoption and commercial surrogacy, for example, as practised in the U.S – often involving for-profit agencies – has no equivalent on the other side of the Atlantic. On the other hand, the maternal right to attach a veto preventing disclosure of identifying information when relinquishing her child for adoption, persists on both sides: the 'sealed adoption files' in the U.S. continue to be a contentious issue in many states; while in France the continuance of the '*accouchement sous X*' practice is equally contentious. Both are clearly non-compliant with the welfare principle and the right of a child to a personal/cultural identity.

The right for a child 'to enjoy his or her own culture' is proving difficult for states to respect in a context where so many unaccompanied migrant children are arriving in Europe from a wide range of countries in the 'global south'. In addition, all CANZUS (Canada, Australia, New Zealand, United States) nations have experienced difficulties in managing the shortfall between the many Indigenous children requiring foster care and the few Indigenous foster parents available, a problem that strengthens the argument for kinship care which incorporates the added advantage of facilitating the parent/child bond.

Protection rights

Children have certain protection rights specific to them in recognition of their unique status as such with innate dependency needs, particular vulnerabilities and limited self-help skills. The sustained willingness and competence of the adults undertaking the protective role provide the foundation for a developing parent/child bond.

Right to life

This, the most fundamental right of the child – as declared in Article 6 of UN CROC and in Article 2 of both the ECHR and the Charter of Fundamental Rights of the European Union – is inevitably often bound up with parental socio-economic status and their access to health services and welfare benefits. Entanglement with reproductive rights, particularly abortion, is also possible. In an initiative to provide a socio-economic safety net, the Council of Europe in 2021 adopted the European Child Guarantee with a view to ensuring that every child in Europe at risk of poverty or social exclusion has access to the most basic of rights such as healthcare.

The right is often violated in domestic disputes. So, for example, in *Kontrová v. Slovakia*,[93] where despite advance notice the husband shot dead himself and his two children, the ECtHR found the Slovak authorities to have breached Article 2. When a child is in the public care system a particularly heavy onus rests on the authorities to ensure adequate protection. The relevant domestic authorities were found to have violated Article 2 when, due to a lack of preventative measures, a newborn baby contracted HIV virus during blood transfusions at a state hospital[94] and when a HIV-positive Roma teenager, who had had been in state care throughout his life, died at the age of 18 years from tuberculosis, pneumonia and hepatitis.[95]

For children, the right to life is at its most precarious in the context of war. Since October 2023, the war in Gaza – "a war on children"[96] – had, by summer 2024, claimed the lives of at least 13,000 children with many more missing, feared dead. UNICEF points out that whereas usually up to 20% of casualties in war are children, in Gaza it is close to 40%.[97] More have died in Gaza in recent months than in four years of conflict worldwide,[98] a harrowing counterpoint to the niceties involved in the debate regarding the differences between the weighting of primary consideration and paramountcy in relation to a child's welfare interests and a salutary reminder of the vulnerability of children when exposed to gratuitous violence.

Right to care and protection

This, a derivation from the right to life, is now free-standing and has long been recognised by the ECtHR while Article 24 of the European Charter of Fundamental Rights declares that children 'have the right to such protection and care as is necessary for their well-being' and that their best interests must be a primary consideration in 'all actions relating to children, whether taken by public authorities or private institutions'.

Child abuse is increasing in all jurisdictions studied, but it cannot be said that the ability of the state to provide care and protect children is increasing proportionately.

93 Application No. 7510/04, (2007).

94 *Oyal v. Turkey*, Application No. 4864/05, (2010).

95 *Centre for Legal Resources on behalf of Valentin Câmpeanu v. Romania*, Application No. 47848/08, (2014).

96 See, further, UN Relief and Works Agency Commissioner-General Philippe Lazzarini: "This is a war on children. It is a war on their childhood and their future".

97 See, further, UNICEF (March 21, 2024).

98 See, further, UNRWA Commissioner-General Philippe Lazzarini, https://turkiye.un.org/en/263401-gaza-number-children-killed-higher-four-years-world-conflict

In theory, state consensual intervention to provide statutorily authorised family support services should do much to alleviate the problem, protect children and strengthen the parent/child bond, but in practice cash-strapped authorities in all jurisdictions are probably equally guilty of channelling resources from preventative to protective services. Nowhere is this more obvious and more detrimental to children than in relation to the Indigenous communities of the CANZUS nations.

Right to freedom from discrimination

Discriminatory treatment of a child, for whatever reason, is especially invidious as they lack the understanding to know why they are being singled out, what it is that they represent to others and why it should make such a difference. Whatever it is, they cannot help it.

Article 14 of the ECHR provides that the rights enumerated in the Convention shall be assured without discrimination on grounds such as sex, race, colour, language, religion, political or other opinion, national or social origin, association with a national minority, property, birth[99] or other status. It has no independent validity but operates to complement other substantive rights enumerated in the Convention. It is supported by Article 9 of the ECHR, Article 1 of the First Protocol, Article 21 of the EU Charter of Fundamental Rights, Article 2 of UN CROC and Protocol No.12; also more generally by Convention on the Elimination of All Forms of Discrimination against Women, International Convention on the Elimination of all forms of Racial Discrimination, International Covenant on Civil and Political Rights and Article 2 of the Lanzarote Convention.

Children can be discriminated against on multiple grounds – age, race, gender, class, disability, language and sexual orientation – and, like any other threat against a child, it will prompt a reflexive protective response from parents and strengthen the parent/child bond. Mostly, children encounter it in a school setting where it is likely to be grounded on religion, race or disability.

Religious discrimination was the issue in *Grzelak v. Poland*[100] when, in conformity with the wishes of his agnostic parents, a pupil did not attend religious instruction. His parents systematically requested the school authorities to organise an alternative class in ethics for him, but no such class was provided throughout his entire schooling at primary and secondary level because there were not enough pupils to justify it. Consequently, his school reports and certificates contained a straight line instead of a mark for 'religion/ethics'. The ECtHR found that the absence of a mark for "religion/ethics" on his school certificates throughout the entire period of his schooling had amounted to his unwarranted stigmatisation, in breach of his right not to manifest his religion or convictions. *D.H. and Others v.*

99 A marital child cannot be accorded prior legal rights over a non-marital child. See, *Ineze v. Austria*, 10 EHRR 394. Also, see, *Marckx v. Belgium*, Op. cit.

100 Application No. 7710/02, (2010). See, also, *Perovy v. Russia*, Application No. 47429/09, (2020).

the Czech Republic[101] was one of many cases dealing with discrimination against the Roma community, contrary to the EU Racial Equality Directive. The ECtHR found that a disproportionate number of Roma children were placed in special schools for children with learning difficulties without justification, a practice which ensured they received an inferior education, stigmatised them and compromised their subsequent personal development. As regards disability, any associated discrimination is prohibited under international law (e.g. Article 21 of the Charter of Fundamental Rights; Article 14 of the ECHR; the UN Convention on the Rights of Persons with Disabilities 2006; and Article 1 of Protocol No. 12). The UN Convention requires member states to ensure that the rights and welfare interests of children with disabilities are protected on the same basis as other children. However, this may not necessarily mean that children with disabilities will be mainstreamed into the education system.[102] Nor would it guarantee extra care for their special vulnerabilities as was demostrated in *Nencheva and Others v. Bulgaria,*[103] which concerned a home for the physically and mentally disabled where 15 children and young adults died of neglect and where, as in other cases, the ECtHR found that the state failed to take the necessary measures to protect a number of children with disabilities.[104]

Jurisdictional differences and their significance

The child's right to life – as declared in Article 6 of UN CROC to which all eight jurisdictions currently being studied are signatories (though not ratified by the U.S.) – is reinforced in Europe by the ECHR and other instruments, and in the U.S. by the Equal Protection Clause of the Fourteenth Amendment, if to an uncertain degree. However, the extent of state protection afforded to children in the U.S. differs considerably from their European counterparts. For example, infant mortality rates are relatively high in the UK and in France[105] (3.9 and 3.3 per 1,000 births, respectively)[106] but are much worse in the U.S. where, in 2023, rates reached 5.48 per 1,000 live births (the first rise in 20 years).[107] Broad thresholds for the welfare interests of children can seem less rigorously policed by the state than elsewhere. As Human Rights Watch recently pointed out: 'children in the U.S. can be legally married in 41 states, physically punished by school administrators in 47 states,

101 Application No. 57325/00, (2007). See, also, *Oršuš and Others v. Croatia*, Application No. 15766/03, (2007).

102 See, *Dupin v. France,* Application No. 2282/18, (2019).

103 Application No. 48609/06, (2013).

104 See, for example, *Çam v. Turkey*, Application No. 51500/08, (2016), *Dupin v. France*, Op. cit., and *G.L. v. Italy*, Application No. 59751/15, (2020).

105 The CRC has expressed alarm at the persistent excessively high level of infant mortality in France. See, further, CRC/C/FRA/CO/5, (2016).

106 Compared, for example, with 2 deaths per 1,000 births in Finland and Luxembourg. See, further, https://data.worldbank.org/indicator/SP.DYN.IMRT.IN

107 See, further, the BMJ, www.bmj.com/content/383/bmj.p2569

sentenced to life without parole in 22 states, and work in hazardous agriculture conditions in all 50 states'.[108]

A child's need for care and protection most often arises from disputes in the family home. Parental action or inaction may breach their child's right to protection: parental chastisement of a child for unacceptable behaviour, by administering corporal punishment,[109] constitutes a violation in most of the jurisdictions studied (Ireland, New Zealand, France and Germany), but not in England, Canada and many states in the U.S., if the force used is reasonable; long-term neglect by parents[110] similarly causes a violation; as does exposure to domestic violence which may well result in emotional harm to the children concerned. If not originating in the family home and from a family member, the violation may well be perpetrated by a familiar and trusted person such as the teacher in an Irish school who repeatedly sexually abused a pupil.[111] In this context, it might be noted that in New Zealand, the particularly high rates of domestic violence and teenage suicide may be linked to the low rates of admissions of children to state care.

The prohibition against discrimination in England and Wales is largely to be found in the Equality Act 2010 which offers protection to children with a disability (e.g. deafness, autism or special needs) particularly in a school context. In a fairly recent case, the Upper Tribunal considered a decision to exclude a boy with autism from school because of his aggressive behaviour. The court concluded that the regulations authorising exclusion[112] violated the pupil's right not to be discriminated against under Article 14 ECHR when read in conjunction with Article 2 of the First Protocol.[113] Discrimination in Ireland was referenced in the 2016 CRC report in which concern was expressed regarding 'the structural discrimination against Traveller and Roma children and their families'.[114] In the U.S. this matter has generated many cases, usually pursued under the Equal Opportunity Clause and most often dealing with racial segregation or racial discrimination.[115] In 2023, the U.S. Supreme Court ruled in favour of Miguel Luna Perez.[116] For 12 years,

108 Human Rights Watch Report, *How Do US States Measure Up on Child Rights?* 2023, www.hrw.org/feature/2022/09/13/how-do-states-measure-up-child-rights

109 *Tyrer v. the United Kingdom*, Application No. 5856/72, (1978); *M.C. v. Bulgaria*, Application No. 39272/98, (2003), at para 150; *O'Keeffe v. Ireland* [GC], Op. cit., at para 146.

110 *Z and Others v. the United Kingdom* [GC], Application No. 29392/95, (2001).

111 *O'Keeffe v. Ireland* [GC], Application No. 35810/09, (2014).

112 The Equality Act 2010 (Disability) Regulations 2010, Reg 4(1)(c).

113 See, further, *C & C v. The Governing Body of a School, The Secretary of State for Education (First Interested Party) and The National Autistic Society (Second Interested Party) (SEN) (Disability discrimination in schools)* [2018] UKUT 269 (AAC).

114 UN Committee on the Rights of the Child, Concluding Observations of the Committee on the combined third and fourth periodic reports of Ireland, 2016, at para 27.

115 See, for example, *Brown v. Board of Education*, 347 U.S. 483 (1954), *Swann v. Charlotte-Mecklenburg Board of Education*, 402 U.S. 1 (1970), *San Antonio Independent School District v. Rodriguez*, 411 U.S. 1, (TX, 1973), *Milliken v. Bradley*, 433 U.S. 267 (1974) and *Missouri v. Jenkins*, 495 U.S. 33 (1995).

116 See, *Perez v. Sturgis Public Schools*, 598 U.S. 142.

Miguel – who is deaf – was denied reasonable classroom support services and consequently was unable to learn or communicate with others, dramatically limiting his employment prospects and earning capacity. The ruling will allow children with disabilities, formerly denied free and appropriate public-school education, to secure support services under federal anti-discrimination law. In Canada the Charter has, since 1982, played a fundamental role in influencing the development of equality and non-discrimination laws and policies, as they relate to children across the country. So, for example, in the landmark ruling *Multani v. Commission scolaire Marguerite-Bourgeoys*,[117] the Supreme Court of Canada found that the prohibition preventing a Sikh schoolboy from wearing a kirpan (a sheathed knife and religious symbol for Sikhs) to school infringed his freedom of religion. This decision highlighted the need to remove obstacles that constituted indirect discrimination. Upholding his right to wear the kirpan was an important benchmark in the evolving relationship between religious freedom, multiculturalism and public education in Canada.

The socio-political history of Australia is one in which racial discrimination has had a prominent role[118] and to some it seemed that *Noble v. Australia*[119] represented its continuation. This concerned an intellectually impaired Indigenous teenager facing criminal charges who was unfit to plead and was imprisoned without trial for ten years, after which he was released but subject to severe constraints on his liberty. The Committee on the Rights of Persons with Disabilities found Mr Noble had been denied a fair trial, equal protection under the law, and the support he required to exercise his legal capacity. The Committee found his disability was the 'core cause' of his deprivation of liberty and breached Article 14(1)(b) of the Convention: 'one of the most serious and pervasive forms of violations of the rights of persons with disability'. His treatment constituted violations of the Convention on the Rights of Persons with Disabilities, Articles 5(1) and 5(2), concerning equality and non-discrimination. This case triggered calls for ending the imprisonment of unconvicted people with a disability and ensuring support and accommodation for people with disability in the criminal justice system. The UN CRC has expressed concern at what it viewed as 'the serious and widespread discrimination faced by Aboriginal and Torres Strait Islander children' including 'their overrepresentation in the criminal justice system'.[120] In New Zealand also, the treatment of children with intellectual disabilities has been found to be discriminatory.[121] In addition, it might be noted that the Convention on the Elimination of All Forms of Discrimination against Women Committee has repeated its recommendation that the government establish a royal commission of inquiry into the family court to ascertain 'the

117 [2006] 1 SCR 256.

118 See, further, O'Halloran, K., *Children, the Law and the Welfare Principle: Perspectives from Australia and New Zealand*, Routledge, 2023, at chapter 9.

119 UN Convention on the Rights of Persons with Disabilities, 2016.

120 CRC/c/AUS/CO/4, *Concluding Observations: Australia*, 2012, at para 29.

121 See, *Ministry of Health v. Atkinson* [2012] NZCA 184.

legislative and structural changes necessary to make the family courts safe and just for women and children, in particular in situations of domestic violence'.[122]

There is a considerable amount of French discrimination caselaw – some involving children – and some of those with a bearing on the parent/child bond. One such case was *Dupin v. France*[123] which concerned an autistic child and the perennial issue of whether the child's education should conform with parental choice (local mainstream school) or with authority's requirements (specialised unit providing care for intellectually challenged children). On being refused their option of choice, the parents took their complaint to the ECtHR which concluded that the authorities had been justified and that there had been no interference with the child's right to education under Article 2 of Protocol 1. The Court made no reference to the UN Convention on the Rights of Persons with Disabilities which prioritises inclusiveness as the way to realise equal access to education – an objective which had been endorsed by the Court in previous cases[124] – relying instead on the principle of subsidiarity and the competence of the responsible authorities. Interestingly, the possible bearing of Article 14 was evidently not considered, but the Court may have been influenced by the fact that by the time of the hearing the parents had separated and the child was living with the father who approved of the specialised unit option. The Court reached a similar decision in *C.E. and Others v. France*[125] when it ruled that the French authorities' refusal to allow the establishment of a legal parent/child relationship between a child and a woman who was the former partner of their biological mother – also the child's legal parent – did not violate Article 8.[126] The case, as mentioned earlier, concerned two joined applications from the former partners in same-sex relationships each seeking a legal status for their continuing relationship with the child they had jointly parented before their respective family breakdowns, which had been refused by the domestic courts. Both applicants claimed that a legal parent/child bond had been established over many years and that this bond required a legal status as it constituted an element intrinsically linked to the identity of the person and shapes it. The refusal of the French authorities placed the child in legal uncertainty: "his or her *de facto* family situation did not correspond to his/her legal situation". Moreover, the domestic courts decisions were not in the best interests of the children as they deprived the children of inheritance rights, etc.[127] They also complained of discrimination, arguing that such a refusal would not have been made in a heterosexual parenthood context. The ECtHR dismissed the latter discrimination claim and held that the French authorities' refusal to allow

122 CEDAW/C/NZL/CO/8, at para 48.

123 Application No. 2282/17, (2018).

124 *Enver Şahin c. Turquie*, Application No. 23065/12, (2018).

125 Application No. 29775/18.

126 For a thorough analysis of this interesting case, see Derave, C. and Ouhnaoul, H., *Strasbourg Observers*, https://strasbourgobservers.com/2022/10/07/c-e-al-v-france-legal-recognition-of-intended-parenthood-from-previous-same-sex-relationships-between-women/

127 As in *Fabris v. France*, Application No. 16574/08, (2013).

the establishment of a legal parent/child relationship did not violate Article 8 of the Convention (see, also, Chapter 3).

Sommerfield v. Germany[128] concerned the applicant's complaint that the German court decisions dismissing his request for access to his daughter, born out of wedlock, amounted to a breach of his right to respect for his family life and that he was a victim of discriminatory treatment in that respect. He and the child's mother had lived together for five years after their child's birth, but following their separation she prohibited any contact between the applicant and their child. The ECtHR found that natural fathers had no right of access to their children and the mother's refusal of access could only be overridden by a court when access was 'in the interest of the child'. The Court found that weighty reasons need to be put forward before a difference in treatment on the ground of birth, out of or within wedlock, can be regarded as compatible with the Convention.[129] The Court discerned no such reason in this case and ruled in favour of the applicant, holding that his rights under Articles 8 and 14 had been violated. On similar facts, in *Sahin v. Germany*,[130] the ECtHR reached a similar conclusion. Noting that the approach taken by the German courts reflected the underlying legislation, which put fathers of children born out of wedlock in a different, less favourable position than divorced fathers, the ECtHR found the crucial point to be that the courts had not regarded contact between a child and the natural father *prima facie* as in the child's interests but had attached decisive weight to the mother's negative attitude. It concluded that there had been a breach of Article 14 of the Convention taken in conjunction with Article 8. The Court's decisions in both *Sommerfield* and *Sahin*, while clearly important in rectifying an overtly discriminatory policy in the treatment of unmarried relative to divorced fathers in Germany, would also seem to constitute a firm gender-neutral stand against the use of a veto to break the parent/child bond. (The father in *Sommerfield* had jointly parented his child for the first five years of her life.)

There is little to no hard evidence that assigning the welfare principle a paramountcy weighting has resulted in a corresponding increase in state capacity to protect its children and none that legislative provisions upholding their welfare interests or rights has protected them from domestic or state-inflicted violence. For example, state intervention in families on child protection grounds would seem to be considerably higher in the U.S. – where the paramountcy principle has no federal application (approximately 74 per 10,000 of children are in the public care system) than in England where it does (the comparable figure is 47 per 10,000).[131] In Canada, the paramountcy principle is broadly excluded from statutes governing decision-making in relation to a child in need of protection, but its child-care

128 Application No. 31871/96, (2003).

129 Citing see *Mazurek v. France*, Application No. 34406/97, at para 49, ECHR 2000-II, and *Camp and Bourimi v. the Netherlands*, Application No. 28369/95, at paras 37–38.

130 Application No. 30943/96, (2003).

131 See, further, data published by the Performance and Innovation Unit (U.K.), 2000.

population is relatively large[132] causing the CRC to be 'deeply concerned'.[133] In Australia, where the paramountcy principle is firmly embedded in the Family Law Act 1975, s 60CA, the number of care orders issued in 2021 was double the number issued a decade earlier. In New Zealand, the *Oranga Tamariki* Act 1989, s 4A, states that 'the well-being and best interests of the child or young person are the first and paramount consideration' and yet the *Oranga Tamariki* agency reports that the number of recorded child welfare concerns has been steadily falling: from nearly 82,000 in 2017, to under 78,000 in 2021;[134] while UNICEF states that this country has one of the worst rates of child abuse in the developed world and the world's highest rate of teenage suicides.[135] In France, where the paramountcy principle is directly applicable in child protection issues,[136] the French child-care population in 2015 was 295,357,[137] an increase from 273,000 in 2010 and a dramatic increase from 112,800 in 1990. Finally, in Germany, where there is no unequivocal statement in the Constitution nor in the Civil Code regarding the application of the principle to child protection matters, approximately 47,500 children were taken into care in 2021 on grounds of protection, an increase of 5% from the previous year. The correlation, if there is one, between the numbers coming into public care and the existence of a statutory duty to treat welfare interests as a matter of paramount importance in a child protection context, would seem to lead to contradictory results: in the U.S. and Canada there is no such federal principle but a high child protection intake; in New Zealand the presence of the principle is matched both by a falling intake and the globally highest rate of child abuse. Furthermore, in Ireland there has been judicial advice that Article 42A (incorporating paramountcy) has significantly lowered the bar for state intervention in circumstances where parental failure endangers a child's safety and welfare.[138]

Pivotal in family law

While generalisations are always risky, it does seem that the social status of the marital family unit is steadily fading in importance, along with a corresponding

132 In 2001, 1.1% of Canadian children were in care, compared with 0.07% in Germany (in 2004); 0.17% in Japan (in 2005); 0.55% in England (in 2005); 0.66% in the U.S. (in 2005), and 1.2% in France (in 2003). See, further, Thoburn, J., 'Globalisation and Child Welfare: Some Lessons from a Cross-National Study of Children in Out-of-Home Care', in *School of Social Work and Psychosocial Studies* (Vol. 228), University of East Anglia, 2007.

133 See, the UN Committee on the Rights of the Child, 61st session, C/CAN/CO/3-4, October 2012, at para 55.

134 See, further, www.orangatamariki.govt.nz/support-for-families/how-we-support-whanau/the-statistics/

135 See further, for example, www.theguardian.com/world/2018/mar/08/study-one-in-four-new-zealand-children-reported-welfare-agencies

136 See, *Maumousseau and Washington v. France,* Application No. 41615/07, (2011) where it was stated that "the Court notes that since the adoption of the [CRC], 'the best interests of the child' in all matters concerning it ... have been paramount in child protection issues".

137 See, further, https://onpe.gouv.fr/chiffres-cles-en-protection-lenfance

138 See, *In the Matter of JJ* [2021] IESC 1, *per* McKechnie J.

fading of state investment in protecting it as a valuable social institution. That investment was always more defensive than affirmative: mainly evident in policing the thresholds for both entering and exiting the institution and of acceptable behaviour between family members in the intervening period; but less noticeable in the provision of family support resources, a role most often left to voluntary and charitable organisations. As a consequence of growing family instability, the state like the church virtually abandoned its protective role as incentives for choosing marriage rather than cohabitation largely fell away[139] in the face of human rights and non-discrimination laws, while grounds justifying divorce were reduced from adultery, to unreasonable behaviour and then to simple incompatibility.

Emerging from the slow dissolution of this social institution, there would appear to be one or two indicators of how family law is being reconfigured to give effect to a future parent/child/state relationship.

Parental responsibility

The concept and legal construct of 'parental responsibilty' has taken hold in a number of leading developed nations. This would seem to signify both a clear rejection of 'rights' as a basis for modern parenting and its replacement by a resolute state reminder that future parenting would have to comply with standards, for any breach of which the parents would be held accountable. In so doing the state is establishing itself as invigilator of what does not constitute 'good enough' parenting, imposing parameters on private family life and indicating the ongoing nature of a parent's obligations in respect of their child: the parent may move on and leave their family life behind, but he or she would take their parental responsibilities with them.

Reciprocal child rights

Family life and family breakdown, in whatever form these might take, will protect – as the intrinsic and irreducible component of the welfare principle – the child's right to maintain the parent/child bond: a bond which is based on emotional attachment; and which, in practice, may be one that ties someone other than a birth parent – perhaps an older sibling, grandfather or non-relative – in an established, safe and nurturing relationship to the child. The right must be given effect through arrangements which secure, for the child, sufficient direct contact opportunities to at least maintain a meaningful personal relationship and, where appropriate, accommodate a cultural connectedness.

139 Though not entirely: for example, the rules governing distribution of assets on family breakdown differ in accordance with marital status.

It would seem that while the state will surrender ground in relation to defending the traditional status of the marital family, it will stand firm on the welfare interests of the child and the residual core element of family life, the parent/child bond.

Centrality of the welfare principle

From divorce to parental child abduction, welfare benefits to surrogacy, juvenile justice to illegal migrants, the welfare principle now cross-cuts family law: transecting public, private and hybrid child-related domestic proceedings; and linking domestic to international law. It determines how other principles are applied, shapes court procedures and has prompted the introduction of specialist courts, judiciary and lawyers, often supplemented by child support staff, while court orders – that have come to increasingly bind the different sectors of family law – reflect a policy which recognises the instability of modern families and has refocussed on the common strand of securing the future welfare of children placed at risk by parental choice, fault or default. It would seem that the contemporary functions of the principle are set to continue its traditional role as 'the golden thread'[140] running through and joining up all child-related aspects of family law, including the new hybrid forms.

Structural

By the turn of the century, the traditional civil and common law court hierarchies had made room for new child-specific forums and institutions such as the Children's Ombudsman, Children's Commissions, Special Rapporteurs, etc. In tandem with these structural innovations, new government posts – such as Minister for Children – were introduced for the similar purpose of monitoring the application of children's welfare interests and rights and ensuring their prioritisation at all levels. These were established in the UK and Ireland, across most of Europe, in Australia and New Zealand and, if to a lesser extent, in the U.S. and Canada.

From a user perspective, perhaps the most meaningful structural changes were those that made the courts more child friendly. To take the UK as an example: Cafcass, established in 2001, amalgamated all court services relating to children into one body; the Family Court, introduced in 2014, restructured and streamlined relevant judicial services; and specialised training programmes were instituted for all staff, including the judiciary, who worked with children. Overall coherence has been greatly assisted by this restructuring of the court system around the Family Court and Cafcass. It has provided an opportunity to build expertise and teamwork focussed on children. The modernised infrastructure issued a new and more functional set of orders, substituting the 'parental responsibility order' and 'child

140 The origins of this expression most probably lie in the case of *Woolmington v. DPP* [1935] AC 462, *per* Viscount Starkey LC, at 481.

arrangements order' for the traditional and more patriarchal 'parental rights' and 'custody' and 'access' orders, many of which were now equally applicable in public, private and hybrid family law proceedings, thereby serving to bind – or perhaps stratify – the law into a more coherent body unified around the consistency of welfare/rights related judicial rulings. Further, to reduce the strain on the court system, there is now in place a policy of referring private family law disputes for arbitration, before or instead of adjudication, and this may become mandatory.[141] While it cannot be said that all eight jurisdictions being studied adopted the same changes, mostly they did – the U.S. being a conspicuous outlier – while Ireland is currently launching a family courts review process.[142] France continued with its own singular model but all other jurisdictions – if they had not already done so – structurally divided their courts, staff and proceedings into civil and criminal blocks, in the latter of which the welfare principle was naturally assigned a lesser role. While the welfare of the child provided a unifying principle in respect of children's needs (in the contexts of care and protection and family breakdown), it also served to distance that nexus from the law relating to children's deeds: in that respect, the gap between the civil and criminal jurisdictions would seem to have widened (see, also, Chapter 2).

Interestingly, the Indigenous communities in the CANZUS nations would appear to be engaged in much the same process. In all four nations there is a move to vest more responsibility in the tribal authorities, enabling them to implement culturally appropriate preventative programmes; police a range of antisocial and criminal behaviour; adjudicate on breaches of the law in newly established tribal courts; and impose non-custodial penalties. The welfare/rights of the child – as articulated in the 'placement principle' – will be central to that parallel legal system.

Content

One aspect of a more user-friendly court is provision for effective participation, and this is given effect through the child's right to be heard. While in France and Germany a child has an established legal right to be heard by the court on a matter affecting their welfare interests, this right is not uniformly applicable in all common law countries, and the CRC have drawn attention to the need for greater use to be made of it.[143] Also, there has yet to be any initiative to ensure that independent representation for children is universally available across all family law proceedings.

Another aspect of the modernisation of the court system has been the introduction of greater transparency. As part of the normalising of family and child-care

141 See, *Churchill v. Merthyr Tydfil CBC* [2023] EWCA Civ 1416.

142 See, further, www.lawsociety.ie/news/news/Stories/family-court-reform

143 United Nations, Committee on the Rights of the Child (CRC), *General Comment No. 12 (2009) on the Right of the Child to be Heard*, CRC/C/GC/12, July 1, 2009.

proceedings – removing the veil of privacy and anonymity – they will no longer be held 'in camera', instead media will have access to proceedings, unless this would be contrary to the welfare interests of the child concerned. Moreover, the role of certain other cross-cutting principles – particularly 'parental responsibility' – and the UN CROC rights together with the welfare 'checklists', have contributed greatly to promoting judicial consistency in decisions relating to child welfare interests and to the overall coherence of family law.

Interpretation

It would be hard to overstate the importance of layers of international legislation, the supranational courts – ECtHR, the CJEU and the CRC – together with such institutions as the Council of Europe and the UN, in introducing a common interpretation of the law governing the welfare/rights of a child, benchmarking certain standards and shaping a more consistent national application of the welfare principle to the same agenda of issues. The interpretive function is also important in relation to the role of the principle as a tool to screen legislation and test for welfare compatibility. This 'welfare proofing' can result in legislative provisions being struck down for not being welfare compliant.[144]

Overall, the principle of the welfare of the child – as examined in this and other books in the series – can be fairly said to have transformed all aspects of family law, nationally and internationally.

Conclusion

Because of their innate dependency, children have always had their welfare interests defined and determined by others. Family law identifies the welfare-related areas in which decisions may need to be taken, sets the parameters and processes for decision-making and identifies or authorises those who may make the decisions. UN CROC, the ECHR and various other instruments, as interpreted and applied by the ECtHR and other bodies, are steadily broadening the grounds for placing decision-making authority on welfare-related matters into the hands of the child, as mediated – where necessary – by their legal representative. At much the same time, the traditional neat compartmentalisation of public and private family law proceedings is slowly being eroded and making room for hybrid variants. Throughout this change process, the one certain and transcending principle has that of the welfare interests of the child.

144 See, *Family Reunification Directive European Parliament v. Council (family reunification)* [2006] ECR I-5769.

Book conclusion

For centuries the centrifugal forces of family law revolved around the axis of the marital relationship, now they do so around the welfare interests/rights of the child. This is due not so much to the impact of child psychology resulting in those interests/rights being viewed as more important than formerly – though certainly a significant factor – nor to the increasing range of family forms, but to the short and serial nature of many contemporary marital and non-marital relationships: a higher proportion of families than ever before would seem to be in a state of flux and reconfiguration.[1] The children concerned usually go on to be absorbed into other families. Given the short shelf-life of so many adult relationships and the volume of litigation on custody and access issues generated by serial parenting, it is unsurprising that the focus in family law has switched from adjudicating on the rights of parents to safeguarding the welfare interests/rights of their children. But there is some way to go before their welfare interests are transformed into actionable rights. The capacity of the law itself to ensure effective implementation of its provisions and change social realities is very limited. The grim reality of international politics and the exigencies of domestic governments trying to juggle the falling tax revenues and rising dependency needs of its citizens, against a background of adverse population trends and the known and unknown implications of climate change, will continue to hold in check the promises of the United Nations Convention on the Rights of the Child (UN CROC). This should not distract from a recognition that there has been significant progress along what will be a long route from welfare interests to eventual legal rights.

The past iteration of the welfare principle was demonstrated in such charitable initiatives as shipping tens of thousands of children from Britain to the colonies, the

1 For example, in the UK, children born to cohabiting parents are 94% more likely to see their parents break up before age 12 years, compared to children born to married parents. Even among married couples, the UK has some of the highest rates of family breakdown in Europe. A third (32%) of British 12-year-olds whose parents were married when they were born have experienced family breakdown. See, further, Social Trends Institute, *The Co-Habitation-Go-Round: Co-Habitation and Family Instability across the Globe*, http://worldfamilymap.ifstudies.org/2017/files/WFM-2017-FullReport.pdf

DOI: 10.4324/9781003510383-13

U.S. 'Orphan Train' movement[2] and the Church-facilitated adoption of Indigenous children by white Caucasians. Subsequently, the child rescue initiatives of western charities, churches and individuals have saved many children orphaned by war and disease in the under-developed nations of the 'global south' and given them a safe future, if one estranged from their roots. More recently – from the cultural context of Rotherham[3] to that of the Ceauşescu regime in Romania and the Inuit villages of Nunavut[4] – the welfare of the child has attracted state intervention and legal action. Currently, the principle can be seen playing a determinative role in many and varied circumstances – from child protection to migration, child abduction to juvenile justice, secure accommodation to baby hatches and from adoption to gene editing and trafficking – across the breadth of contemporary family law.

The UN Committee on the Rights of the Child and the welfare principle

More than a decade has now passed since the UN Committee on the Rights of the Child (CRC) issued its General Comment No 14, *On the Right of the Child to Have His or Her Best Interests Taken as a Primary Consideration*,[5] but it remains relevant for present purposes as it usefully deconstructs the terminology used Article 3(1):[6]

> In all actions concerning children, whether undertaken by public or private social welfare institutions, courts of law, administrative authorities or legislative bodies, the best interests of the child shall be a primary consideration.

In an instructive analysis it identifies both the wide range of public and private institutions and facilities that should be giving effect to the child's best interests and also the equally wide range of different methods for embedding the principle.

Domestic law: permeation and pervasiveness

The CRC interpretation of the principle and the manner of its implementation[7] was reiterated a decade later when the Committee repeated its message that the

2 From 1854 to 1929, as many as 200,000 children were transported by charities such as the Children's Aid Society, from the eastern cities of the U.S. to rural parts of the Midwest, where they were fostered or adopted, often to provide farm labour.

3 The prolonged scandal of organised child sexual abuse – very largely of white Caucasian girls in state care by Muslim men – occurred in the town of Rotherham, South Yorkshire, Northern England, without effective intervention by police or local authorities from the late 1980s until 2013 and involved at least 1,400 girls.

4 The risks in customary adoption among the Inuit in Canada, see further, www.cbc.ca/news/canada/north/inuit-custom-adoption-puts-children-at-risk-in-today-s-world-says-nunavut-mla-1.4700303

5 See, Committee on the Rights of the Child, *General Comment No. 14: On the Right of the Child to Have His or Her Best Interests Taken as a Primary Consideration*, article 3(6).

6 Convention on the Rights of the Child 1989, article 3(1).

7 See, further, the *CRC General Comment No. 5 (2003) on the General Measures of Implementation of the Convention on the Rights of the Child*, at para 12; and the *CRC General Comment No. 12 (2009) on the Right of the Child to be Heard*, at para 2.

state obligation to consider the child's best interests is a comprehensive obligation 'encompassing all public and private social welfare institutions, courts of law, administrative authorities and legislative bodies' involving or concerning children.[8] This consistent and sustained CRC approach lends great weight to the proposition that the welfare principle must now be seen as of central and primary importance in all child-related law because of its permeation and pervasiveness.

Functionality

The right of the child to have his or her best interests taken as a primary consideration is guaranteed in all decisions and actions – including all acts, conduct, proposals, services, procedures and other measures – concerning children. This means that every action relating to a child or children – whether in civil or criminal proceedings and across both public and private family law – has to take into account their best interests as a primary consideration. Inaction or failure to take action and omissions are also "actions", for example, when social welfare authorities fail to take action to protect children from neglect or abuse. The CRC reiterates[9] that such actions include those aimed at children (e.g. related to health, care or education), as well as actions which include children and other population groups (e.g. related to the environment, housing or transport).[10]

The Committee[11] underlines that the concept of the child's best interests is conceived both as a collective and individual right, and specifically stresses that its application to Indigenous children as a group requires consideration of how the right relates to collective cultural rights. The concept is viewed as complex, flexible and adaptable, to be adjusted and defined on an individual basis, according to the specific situation of the child or children concerned, taking into consideration their personal context, situation and needs. It must be assessed and determined: for individual decisions, in light of the specific circumstances of the particular child; for collective decisions – such as by a legislator – in light of the circumstances of the particular group and/or children in general.

Public/private family law

General Comment No 14 begins with the CRC drawing attention to the fact that the Convention explicitly refers to the child's best interests in other Articles. In private family law proceedings, it notes that the role of the principle is recognised in Article 9, separation from parents; Article 10, family reunification; Article 18, parental responsibilities; Article 20, deprivation of family environment and alternative care; and in Article 21, adoption. In public family law the Convention

8 CRC/C/GBR/CO/6-7 (2023), at para 25.

9 As previously stated in *CRC General Comment No. 7 (2005)*.

10 CRC/C/GBR/CO/6-7 (2023), at para 13(b).

11 See, *General Comment No. 11 (2009) on Indigenous Children and Their Rights under the Convention*, at para 30.

similarly recognises the role of the principle in Article 37(c), separation from adults in detention; and Article 40, 2(b)(iii), procedural guarantees, including presence of parents at court hearings for penal matters involving children in conflict with the law. It draws attention to the links between the welfare principle and other Convention principles such as the child's rights to non-discrimination, to be heard and to life.[12] In hybrid private/public proceedings – as noted in this and the previous book – the role of the principle together with associated Convention protective measures have been examined by the ECtHR in relation to hybrid matters such as surrogacy, parental abduction and adoption from state care. The CRC also notes that the scope of the principle was subsequently extended by the Optional Protocol to the Convention on the sale of children, child prostitution and child pornography (preamble and Article 8) and in the Optional Protocol to the Convention on a communications procedure (preamble and Articles 2 and 3).

This network of linkages across so many aspects of the law as it relates to children would seem to confirm that the contemporary functions of the principle continue its traditional role as 'the golden thread' running through family law.[13]

Social welfare institutions

As regards 'public or private social welfare institutions', the CRC advises that this composite term should be understood as referring to all institutions whose work and decisions impact on children and the realisation of their rights. These would include not only those related to economic, social and cultural rights (e.g. care, health, environment, education, business, leisure and play, etc.) but also institutions dealing with civil rights and freedoms (e.g. birth registration, protection against violence in all settings, etc.). It would include any private sector organisations – either for-profit or non-profit – which play a role in the provision of services for children, with or on behalf of government bodies. In relation to the term 'courts of law', the Committee explains that this refers to all such forums and their staff, whether judicial or laypersons. Switching from forums to processes, the Committee adds that similarly all relevant procedures concerning children – including conciliation, mediation and arbitration – must also give priority to this principle. It stresses that protecting the child's best interests means that the traditional objectives of criminal justice, such as repression or retribution, must give way to rehabilitation and restorative justice objectives when dealing with child offenders. While in civil cases, the child may be either directly involved in defence of his or her interests perhaps aided by a legal representative (e.g. in cases of paternity, child abuse or neglect, family reunification, accommodation, etc.) or may be indirectly involved (e.g. in cases of parental separation or divorce) but in either circumstance the courts must provide for the best interests of the child to be considered and must demonstrate that they have effectively done so.[14]

12 Op. cit., n 39, at paras 41–45 incl.

13 The origins of this expression most probably lie in the case of *Woolmington v. DPP* [1935] AC 462, *per* Viscount Starkey LC, at 481.

14 See, further, CRC, *General Comment No. 10 (2007) on Children's Rights in Juvenile Justice*.

Administrative authorities

The Committee considers that the term 'administrative authorities' accommodates a great many decision-making forums with relevance for the best interests of children. It emphasises that the scope of decisions made by administrative authorities at all levels is very broad, covering decisions concerning education, care, health, the environment, living conditions, protection, asylum, immigration, access to nationality, among others. It advises that all individual decisions taken by administrative authorities in these areas must be assessed and guided by the best interests of the child. Finally, the Committee notes that the reference to 'legislative bodies' clearly shows that Article 3(1) is intended to relate to children in general, not only to children as individuals. The inference is that the adoption of any law or regulation as well as collective agreements – such as bilateral or multilateral trade or peace treaties which affect children – should be governed by the best interests of the child. The right of the child to have his or her best interests assessed and taken as a primary consideration should be explicitly included in all relevant legislation, not only in laws that specifically concern children. The Committee adds that 'the obligation extends also to the approval of budgets, the preparation and development of which require the adoption of a best-interests-of-the-child perspective for it to be child-rights sensitive'. Considering that so much of the decision-making in respect of the welfare interests of children lies within the remit of administrative agencies, the infusion of the principle into the machinery of such agencies gives it a broad based, all-encompassing functionality.

International law: intersecting and interlocking

The ever-growing, and evermore complex, platform of international law includes many provisions which impact upon children. Some do so directly: most importantly, UN CROC and the European Convention on Human Rights (ECHR), as supplemented by such others as Hague Convention on the Civil Aspects of International Child Abduction 1980, European Convention on the Exercise of Children's Rights 1996, United Nations Guidelines for the Alternative Care of Children 2009 and the three Optional Protocols.[15] Some are more indirect: such as the International Covenant on Civil and Political Rights 1966, International Covenant on Economic, Social and Cultural Rights 1966, International Convention on the Elimination of all forms of Racial Discrimination 1965, Convention on the Elimination of all Forms of Discrimination against Women 1979; and the European Social Charter 1966 (revised in 1996).

The caselaw generated by this body of international law has woven such an intricate 'cats cradle' of cross-referenced interpretations that no one instrument can

15 Optional Protocol to the Convention on the Rights of the Child on the involvement of children in armed conflict, 2000; Optional Protocol to the Convention on the Rights of the Child on the sale of children, child prostitution and child pornography, 2000; and Optional Protocol to the Convention on the Rights of the Child on a communications procedure, 2011.

really be considered in isolation, in particular UN CROC and the ECHR must now be read – to a large degree – as being mutually interdependent. The overall effect is to gradually and comprehensively impose unity and congruity on national and international – public, private and hybrid – family law.

The United Nations Convention on the Rights of the Child 1989

The Convention, supported by 196 signatory states, has been ratified by all but one (the U.S.) of those currently being considered, many of which have fully incorporated its provisions into domestic legislation. This has clearly done much to disseminate a common interpretation of welfare interests and of their importance relative to all other family matters. It demonstrates 'the global nature and reach of the Convention'[16] aided by the requirement that the principle be 'taken into account to resolve any possible conflicts among the rights enshrined in the Convention or other human rights treaties'.[17] Article 3 of the Convention has been reinforced by Article 24(2) of the Charter of Fundamental Rights of the European Union 2010 in similar wording.

Dissemination has been assisted by occasional CRC rulings on domestic issues and by its rolling 'periodic review process', requiring each government to submit a report every four or five years on progress made in protecting children's rights, to which the Committee responds by publishing its 'concluding observations', essentially setting out the Committee's concerns and making recommendations for improvements that will be checked at the next review. Although not intended as a 'name and shame' procedure, the fact that the Committee's findings are published, with deficiencies in compliance clearly identified, must serve to reinforce a common understanding of the role of the welfare principle, in addition to nudging governments towards more effective implementation of UN CROC provisions.

Unfortunately, in the absence of any enforcement capacity, the CRC is restricted to making recommendations which governments are free to ignore. For example, the recently concluded UK review process (the previous one being in 2016) listed some 200 recommendations, prefaced by the warning that[18]

> What is highly concerning is where the same concerns continue to be raised, and recommendations continue to be made, but nothing changes – or where there has even been regression on some issues. Equally worrying is where new violations or children's rights issues of concern – that have never previously been reported on – have emerged in this reporting cycle, adding to a growing list of children's rights issues. The Committee identified serious concerns regarding persistent discrimination, levels of protection from abuse,

16 CRC/C/GC/14 (2013), at para 16(c).

17 Ibid, at para 33.

18 CRC/C/GBR/CO/6-7, 2023, https://childrenslegalcentre.wales/un-committee-on-rights-of-child-uk-concluding-observations-2023/#

the care system, child mental health, child poverty, asylum-seeking, refugee and migrant children and the child justice system.

Nonetheless, by continuously benchmarking the performance and progress of almost 200 countries against the standards required by UN CROC, and customising its recommendations to remedy deficits and guide each nation into closer compliance with those standards, the CRC is contributing greatly to raising the salience of children's welfare interests/rights and to shaping international values in respect of children.

The European Court of Human Rights

The same point applies to the influence of the ECtHR. Decades of rulings by the Court on the nature and extent of domestic breaches of international standards – as represented by the provisions of the ECHR and assimilated UN CROC requirements – have naturally done much to imprint on the countries concerned an awareness of the fundamental importance of the rights and welfare interests of the child. This has been greatly facilitated by the requirement that all domestic 'public or private social welfare institutions, courts of law, administrative authorities or legislative bodies'[19] incorporate and apply ECtHR rulings in respect of welfare interests which, aided by the principle of subsidiarity, has the effect of domestic courts resolving issues by following precedents established by the ECtHR. This can be seen, for example, in the ECtHR rulings that emphasise the duty of the state to protect the welfare interests of the child[20] (see, also, Chapter 1).

***The principle of the welfare interests of the child as a* grundnorm**

Hans Kelsen, in his *Pure Theory of Law*,[21] introduced the concept of a *grundnorm* – an underpinning basic norm, principle or proposition that is the foundation for a system – as a construct for understanding the structure of law in terms of a hierarchy of norms. His theory provides a useful explanation of how authority is organised in a legal system: the way in which norms relate to each other; how they exist in a hierarchy; the validation of lesser norms by a *grundnorm*; which affirms the legitimacy of the system and permits its recognition as such by external authorities.[22] According to Kelsen's theory, a legal system can be so defined because all its norms are inter-related, and it is logically necessary that in every legal system there must exist one basic norm or proposition – a *grundnorm* – on which the system is grounded.

19 Ibid, at para 25.

20 See, for example, *Wallová and Walla v. the Czech Republic*, Application No. 23848/04, (2006), *K.A. v. Finland*, Application No. 27751/95, (2003) and *Pini and Others v. Romania*, Application Nos. 78028/01 and 78030/01, (2004).

21 Kelsen, H., *Pure Theory of Law (Reine Rechtslehre, 1934)*, NJ, US, The Lawbook Exchange, Ltd., 2009.

22 See, for example, Raz, J., *The Concept of a Legal System*, New York, US, Oxford University Press, 1980.

It may not be too much of a stretch to suggest that the principle of the welfare interests of the child are now becoming the *grundnorm* in contemporary family law. The principle has clearly gained access to all areas of relevance to the child, and it is the child rather than parents or any other entity that is now of central importance to family law: beginning with the 'psychological bond' it underpins all aspects of family law. On a domestic level, it is pervasively spread across the wide range of relevant public and private institutions and facilities; it has penetrated an equally wide range of mediums and methods – legislative and other – for dissemination; and all other family law principles or norms have become subordinate to it. Internationally, whereas the principle was initially largely confined to the ECHR and UN CRC, it is now referenced – if with a variable weighting – in a whole host of international instruments, while judicial scrutiny and rulings by the ECtHR, the CJEU and the CRC are constantly weighing, balancing and calibrating the principle against all other considerations.

As the various pillars that traditionally supported this body of law – marriage, parental rights, etc. – fall away, and the institutionalised demarcation between public and private is eroded, it would seem that this principle is filling the gaps and growing in importance as the central reference point for family law matters. In a consistent and systematised fashion, the role of the principle in a network of domestic family law proceedings – from custody and access to juvenile justice – has essentially been replicated, or at least finds broad support, in a not dissimilar network of international provisions.

Selected bibliography

Books & articles

B

Bala, N. and Ashbourne, C., 'The Widening Concept of Parent in Canada: Step-Parents, Same-Sex Partners, & Parents by ART', *American University Journal of Gender Social Policy and Law*, Vol. 3, 2012.
Bean, P. and Melville, J., *Lost Children of the Empire*, London, Unwin Hyman Ltd., 1989.
Berger, M., *The Failure of Child Protection Services*, Paris, Dunod, 2003.
Bettelheim, B., *Love is Not Enough*, Free Press, 1950.
Bowlby, J., *Attachment and Loss*, London, Hogarth Press, 1973.
Bull, C., et al., 'Inequities in Vulnerable Children's Access to Health Services in Australia', *BMJ Glob Health*, Vol. 7, No. 3, 2022, www.ncbi.nlm.nih.gov/pmc/articles/PMC8961130/

C

Cass Final Report, 2024, https://cass.independent-review.uk/home/publications/final-report/; www.ncbi.nlm.nih.gov/pmc/articles/PMC9319150/
Chou, S. and Browne, K., 'The Relationship Between Institutional Care and the International Adoption of Children in Europe', *Adoption & Fostering*, Vol. 32, No. 1, pp 40–48, 2008.
Choudhry, S. and Fenwick, H., 'Taking the Rights of Parents and Children Seriously: Confronting the Welfare Principle under the Human Rights Act', *Oxford Journal of Legal Studies*, Vol. 25, No. 3, pp 453–492, 2005.

D

DeRose, L., et al., *The Cohabitation Go-Round: Cohabitation and Family Instability Across the Globe*, New York, Social Trends Institute, 2017.
Dornan P. and Woodhead M., *How Inequalities Develop through Childhood*, UNICEF, 2015, www.younglives.org.uk/sites/default/files/how-inequalities-develop-through-childhood.pdf
Douglas, G. and Sebba, L. (eds.), *Children's Rights and Traditional Values*, Aldershot, Ashgate, 1998.

E

Eekelaar, J., 'The Role of the Best Interests Principle in Decisions Affecting Children and Decisions About Children', *International Journal of Children's Rights*, Vol. 23, No. 1, pp 3–26, 2015.

Eglin, M., *Judicial Child Protection in France and England: A Comparative Approach*, June 2001, www.afmif.fr/Judicial-child-protection-in.html

F

Fallon, B., et al., *Denouncing the Continued Overrepresentation of First Nations Children in Canadian Child Welfare*: Findings From The First Nations/Canadian Incidence Study Of Reported Child Abuse And Neglect-2019, 1(2), at: https://cwrp.ca/sites/default/files/publications/FNCIS-2019%20-%20Denouncing%20the%20Continued%20Overrepresentation%20of%20First%20Nations%20Children%20in%20Canadian%20Child%20Welfare%20-%20Final_1%20%282%29.pdf

G

Gibbons, J. and Rotabi, K. (eds.), *Intercountry Adoption: Policies, Practices, and Outcomes*, Farnham, Ashgate, 2012.

Gilbert, R., et al., 'Child Maltreatment: Variation in Trends and Policies in Six Developed Countries', *Lancet*, 2011, https://scholar.google.com/scholar_lookup?hl=en&publication_year=2011&author=R+Gilbert&author=J+Fluke&author= M+O%27Donnell&author=A+Gonzalez-

Ginsburg, R. B., 'Some Thoughts on Autonomy and Equality in Relation to Roe v. Wade', *North Carolina Law Review*, Vol. 63, pp 375–386, 1985.

Goldstein, J., Freud, A. and Solnit, A., *Beyond the Best Interests of the Child*, Free Press, 1973.

H

Herring, J., 'The Human Rights Act and the Welfare Principle in Family Law: Conflicting or Complementary?', *Child and Family Law Quarterly*, Vol. 11, No. 3, pp 223–237, 1999.

Horgan, J., 'The United Nations Convention on the Rights of the Child and Irish Family Law', *ILT*, Vol. 9, p 162, 1991.

Hubinette, T., 'Adopted Koreans and the Development of Identity in the Third Space', *Adoption & Fostering, London, BAAF*, Vol. 28, No. 1, pp 16–24, 2004.

Humphreys, M., *Empty Cradles*, Random House, 2009.

J

Jorgensen, S., 'Transition Regret and Detransition: Meanings and Uncertainties', *Archives of Sexual Behavior*, Vol. 52, No. 5, pp 2173–2184, 2023.

K

Katz, S., Eekelaar, J. and Maclean, M. (eds.), *Cross Currents: Family Law and Policy in the United States and England*, Oxford, Oxford University Press, 2000.

Kilkelly, U., *Children's Rights in Ireland: Law, Policy and Practice*, Tottel, 2008.

L

Latham, A., 'Puberty Blockers for Children: Can They Consent?', *The New Bioethics*, Vol. 28, No. 3, pp 268–291.

Luo, D., 'The Overrepresentation of Indigenous Youth in the Criminal Justice System; Exposing a Problematic Reality of Imprisoned Marginalized Groups in Canada', *The*

Society: Sociology & Criminology Undergraduate Review, pp 69–74, https://jps.library.utoronto.ca

M

Mandelbaum, R., 'Why Does the Federal Government Get a Pass? Applying Child Welfare Principles to the Circumstances of Migrant Children and Families', *American University Law Review*, Vol. 71, No. 5, 2022, SSRN, https://ssrn.com/abstract=3926325

Milotte, M., *Banished Babies: The Secret History of Ireland's Baby Export Business*, New Island Books, 1997.

Moore, K., et al., *Children in Poverty: Trends, Consequences, and Policy Options, Child Trends*. Washington, DC, 2009, https://cms.childtrends.org/wp-content/uploads/2013/11/2009-11ChildreninPoverty.pdf

Morris, A. and Giller, H., *Understanding Juvenile Justice*, London, Croom Helm, 1987.

N

National Coalition Germany, *Interim Report on the Child Rights Situation in Germany*, p 40, 2023, https://eurochild.org/uploads/2024/04/NC_ZwischenBericht-24-EN-RZ__web.pdf

O

O'Connor, D., 'Children's Rights and Youth Justice in the USA', *International Family Law Journal*, 2006.

P

Parker, R., *Uprooted: The Shipment of Poor Children to Canada, 1867–1919*, Bristol, The Policy Press, 2008.

Piaget, J., *The Psychology of the Child*, New York, Basic Books, 1972.

R

Ramirez, D., 'Comparative Immigration Policies for Unaccompanied Minors: A Shared Challenge', *Loyola University Chicago International Law Review*, Vol. 19, No. 2, pp 157–185, 2023.

Raz, J., *The Concept of a Legal System*, New York, US, Oxford University Press, 1980.

Robbins, J., *The Lost Children: A Study of Charity Children in Ireland 1700–1900*, Dublin, Institute of Public Administration, 1980.

S

Scott, D., *Understanding Child Neglect*, 2014, https://aifs.gov.au/resources/policy-and-practice-papers/understanding-child-neglect; https://assets.hcch.net/docs/3bead31e-6234-44ae-9f4e-2352b190ca21.pdf

Selman, P., 'The Rise and Fall of Intercountry Adoption in the 21st Century: Global Trends from 2001 to 2010', in Gibbons, J.L. & Smith Rotabi, K. (eds.), *Intercountry Adoption: Policies, Practices, and Outcomes*, Ashgate Publishing Co, 2012, pp 7–27.

Sethi, A., 'Domestic Sex Trafficking of Aboriginal Girls in Canada: Issues and Implications', *First Peoples Child & Family Review*, Vol. 3, No. 3, pp 57–71, 2007.

Siegel, R. and Greenhouse, L., 'The Unfinished Story of Roe V. Wade', in Murray, M., Shaw, K. and Siegel, R. (eds.), *Reproductive Rights and Justice Stories*, St. Paul, Foundation Press, 2018.
Simpson, K., Yeong, P. and Munford, R., 'Responses to Abuse, Neglect, and Trauma of Children with Intellectual Disability', *Aotearoa New Zealand Social Work*, Vol. 34, No. 1, pp 72–87, 2022.

T

Takács, N., 'The Threefold Concept of the Best Interests of the Child in the Immigration Case Law of the ECtHR', *Hungarian Journal of Legal Studies*, Vol. 62, No. 1, pp 96–114, 2022.
Titmus, R., *The Gift Relationship: From Human Blood to Social Policy*, The New Press, 1997.

U

UNICEF, Report Card, 2021, www.unicef.org.nz/stories/new-report-card-shows-that-new-zealand-is-failing-its-children

W

Walker, J., *When the Vulnerable Offend – Whose Fault is It? Address to Northern Territory Council of Social Services Conference*, September 27, 2017, www.districtcourts.govt.nz/youth-court/publications/when-the-vulnerable-offend-whose-fault-is-it/
Winnicott, D., *The Child, the Family, and the Outside World*, Penguin, 1973.

V

Vreeland, A.B., 'The Criminalization of Child Welfare in New York City: Sparing the Child or Spoiling the Family?', *Fordham Urban Law Journal*, Vol. 27, No. 3, pp 1053–1103, 2000.

Y

Young, L., 'Mature Minors and Parenting Disputes in Australia: Engaging with the Debate on Best Interests v. Autonomy', *UNSW Law Journal*, Vol. 42, No. 4, 2019.

Reports

A

AFCARS Report FY, 2019, www.acf.hhs.gov/sites/default/files/documents/cb/afcarsreport28.pdf
Australian Bureau of Statistics, *Recorded Crime – Offenders, 2019–2022; for New Zealand, Ministry of Social Development, Child and Youth Offending Patterns – Research Reports*, www.msd.govt.nz/about-msd-and-our-work/publications-resources/research/child-and-youth-offending-patterns/index.html
Australian Human Rights Commission, *Bringing Them Home Report*, 1997, https://humanrights.gov.au/our-work/bringing-them-home-report-1997
Australian Institute of Health and Welfare, *Youth Justice in Australia 2020–21*, www.aihw.gov.au/reports/youth-justice/youth-justice-in-australia-2020-21/contents/summary for New Zealand, www.1news.co.nz/2022/08/24/startling-link-revealed-between-state-care-and-prison/

B

Break Poverty, 2021, https://breakpoverty.com/en/an-intolerable-increase-in-early-childhood-poverty-as-a-result-of-the-health-crisis/

C

Canadian Bar Association (Child and Youth Law Section), *Alternative Report to the UN Committee on the Rights of the Child*, 2020, https://www.cba.org/CMSPages/GetFile.aspx?guid=fdb96dc7-35e0-4b6d-8918-40ba6607582a

Child Poverty Monitor 2020: Technical Report, Child Poverty Monitor Series, New Zealand Child and Youth Epidemiology Service; University of Otago, 12/2020, p 4, https://ourarchive.otago.ac.nz/bitstream/handle/10523/10585/CPM_2020_TECHNICAL%20REPORT.pdf?sequence=6&isAllowed=y

Council of Europe, Convention on the Protection of Children against Sexual Exploitation and Sexual Abuse, 2007, https://rm.coe.int/1680084822

Council of Europe, *Guidelines on Child Friendly Justice*, 2010, https://rm.coe.int/16804b2cf3

Council of Europe, *Strategy for the Rights of the Child*, 2012, https://rm.coe.int/16805a920a

Crime Report, 2018, https://thecrimereport.org/2018/04/10/in-germany-its-hard-to-find-a-young-adult-in-prison/

D

Directive 2003/86/EC of 22 September 2003 on the Right to Family Reunification [2003] OJL 251.

E

Eglin, M., *Judicial Child Protection in France and England: A Comparative Approach*, June 2001, www.afmjf.fr/Judicial-child-protection-in.html

EU Directive 2003/86/EC of 22 September 2003 on the Right to Family Reunification [2003] OJL 251.

EU Framework of Law for Children's Rights, 2012.

European Convention on the Exercise of Children's Rights, 1996.

European Parliament's Committee on Civil Liberties, Justice and Home Affairs, *EU Framework of Law for Children's Rights*, 2012, https://www.europarl.europa.eu/RegData/etudes/note/join/2012/462445/IPOL-LIBE_NT(2012)462445_EN.pdf

Eurostat, *Asylum Applicants Considered to be Unaccompanied Minors by Citizenship, Age and Sex – Annual Data*, https://ec.europa.eu/eurostat/databrowser/view/migr_asyunaa/default/table?lang=en

F

Family Justice Council, *Guidelines for Judges Meeting Children Who are Subject to Family Proceedings*, April 2010 [2010] 2 FLR 1872.

G

Global Surrogacy Market Grows at a Staggering CAGR of 6.25%, https://straitsresearch.com/press-release/global-surrogacy-market-size

H

Human Rights Watch, *Fields of Peril: Child Labor in U.S. Agriculture and US: Child Farmworkers Dangerous Lives*, www.hrw.org/news/2010/05/05/us-child-farmworkers-dangerous-lives

I

ILO, *Child Trafficking – Essentials*, Geneva, ILO-IPEC, 2010.

Inter-American Commission on Human Rights, *Children and Adolescents in the United States Adult Criminal Justice System*, p 9, 2018, www.oas.org/en/iachr/reports/pdfs/Children-USA.pdf

International Bureau for Children's Rights, *Child Trafficking in Canada*, www.ibcr.org/en/projets/la-traite-des-enfants-au-canada-2/

K

Kaltiala, R., *Helsingin Sanomat*, https://nypost.com/2023/02/22/four-out-of-five-kids-who-question-their-gender-grow-out-of-it-trans-expert/

L

The Lancet (editorial), 'Britain is Broken: Poor Child Health Proves It', *The Lancet*, Vol. 393, No. 10170, 2019, www.thelancet.com/journals/lancet/article/PIIS0140-6736(19)30162-X/fulltext

Lost in Europe Report, https://lostineurope.eu

N

National Academy of Medicine Report, *Medicine and Gender Trans Identity in Children and Adolescents*, 2022, www.academie-medecine.fr/la-medecine-face-a-la-transidentite-de-genre-chez-les-enfants-et-les-adolescents/?lang=en

Native Women's Association of Canada, *Trafficking of Indigenous Women and Girls in Canada*, 2018, www.ourcommons.ca/Content/Committee/421/JUST/Brief/BR10002955/br-external/NativeWomensAssociationOfCanada-e.pdf

O

OECD, *Infant Mortality Report*, 2020, www.oecd.org/els/family/CO_1_1_Infant_mortality.pdf

P

Pew Charitable Trust Report, *Time for Reform: A Matter of Justice for American Indian and Alaskan Native Children*, 2007, https://www.pewtrusts.org/-/media/legacy/uploadedfiles/wwwpewtrustsorg/reports/foster_care_reform/nicwareportpdf.pdf

R

Refugee Council Report, www.refugeecouncil.org.uk/latest/news/new-figures-reveal-scale-of-asylum-backlog-crisis/

S

Social Justice Ireland, *Poverty Ireland 2021 Report*, www.socialjustice.ie/system/files/file-uploads/2021-09/2019-04-15-sjipovertyfocus2019final.pdf and the Borgen Project, *The State of Poverty in Ireland*, https://borgenproject.org/the-state-of-poverty-in-ireland/
Special Rapporteur on Child Protection (Ireland), *Annual Report*, 2020, https://better-carenetwork.org/library/social-welfare-systems/child-care-and-protection-policies/annual-report-of-the-special-rapporteur-on-child-protection-2020
State Watch, www.statewatch.org/news/2023/may/detention-of-children-european-court-of-human-rights-rules-against-france-11-times/#:~:text=Since%202012%2C%20the%20ECHR%20has,%22flagrant%20lack%20of%20humanity%22

T

The Hague Conference on Private International Law, 'Transfrontier Contact Concerning Children', *Family Law*, 2008, https://assets.hcch.net/docs/aabaa1c1-4fb5-4c24-92bd-75a8b161e29a.pdf
UN Committee on the Rights of the Child, *General Comment No. 5*.
UN Committee on the Rights of the Children, *General Comment No. 14 (2013)*.
UN CRC, *General Comment No. 10 (2007) on Children's Rights in Juvenile Justice*.
UN CRC, *General Comment No. 11 (2009) Indigenous Children and Their Rights under the Convention [On the Rights of the Child]*.
UN CRC/C/GBR/CO/6-7, 2023, https://childrenslegalcentre.wales/un-committee-on-rights-of-child-uk-concluding-observations-2023/#
UNICEF, *Child Poverty in the Midst of Wealth*, www.unicef.org/innocenti/
UNICEF Innocenti Report Card, 2020, www.newstalkzb.co.nz/on-air/kerre-woodham-mornings/audio/nathan-wallis-new-zealand-ranks-bottom-of-developed-countries-on-youth-mortality-rates
UNICEF Report Card 18: Canadian Companion, *Child Poverty in Canada: Let's Finish This*, Toronto, UNICEF Canada, 2023.
United Nations, *Guidelines for the Alternative Care of Children*, UN Doc. A/HRC/11/L.13, 2009.
United Nations, Committee on the Rights of the Child (CRC), *General Comment No. 12 (2009) on the Right of the Child to be Heard*, CRC/C/GC/12, July 1, 2009.
United Nations, Committee on the Rights of the Child (CRC), *General Comment No. 24 (2019) on Children's Rights in the Child Justice System*, CRC/C/GC/24, 2019.
UNODC, *2020 Report Trafficking in Persons*, p 91, www.unodc.org/documents/data-and-analysis/tip/2021/GLOTiP_2020_15jan_web.pdf; www.ohchr.org/en/instruments-mechanisms/instruments/united-nations-standard-minimum-rules-administration-juvenile

Index